The Fledgling Province

*The Institute of Early American History and Culture
is sponsored jointly by The College of William and Mary in Virginia
and The Colonial Williamsburg Foundation.*

The Fledgling Province

SOCIAL AND CULTURAL LIFE IN COLONIAL GEORGIA
1733–1776

by Harold E. Davis

Published for the
Institute of Early American History and Culture
Williamsburg, Virginia
by The University of North Carolina Press
Chapel Hill

Library of Congress Cataloging in Publication Data

Davis, Harold E 1927–
  The fledgling province.

  Bibliography: p.
  Includes index.
    1. Georgia—Social life and customs—Colonial period,
ca. 1600–1775.   2.   Slavery in the United States—Georgia.
I.   Institute of Early American History and Culture,
Williamsburg, Va.   II.   Title.
F289.D24   975.8'02   76-2570
ISBN 0-8078-1267-6

*To Priscilla Arnold Davis,
my wife of twenty-one years*

Acknowledgments

This work owes much to the kindness of my family, friends, and colleagues. My wife, Priscilla, and our four children have stood patiently with me during the five years that *The Fledgling Province* has been in progress. My mother, Mrs. Florine S. Davis, has also taken a lively interest in the book as it developed, as have two special friends, the Reverend and Mrs. Wayne Eugene Britton.

From the academic community I have been the recipient of much assistance. James Z. Rabun of Emory University lent his considerable learning and skills to improving the manuscript. It has also been read and criticized for me by Harvey Young and John Juricek of Emory, Kenneth Coleman of the University of Georgia, Lilla M. Hawes of the Georgia Historical Society, William W. Abbot of the University of Virginia, and Norman S. Fiering, J. Frederick Fausz, and Joy Dickinson Barnes of the Institute of Early American History and Culture. Milton Ready of The University of North Carolina at Asheville has criticized the concluding section for me. In addition I would be remiss not to acknowledge my indebtedness to Noah Langdale, Jr., William M. Suttles, Glenn G. Thomas, Joseph O. Baylen, and Kenneth England, all of Georgia State University.

Archivists and librarians at the depositories cited in the bibliography have been supportive, and appreciation is hereby expressed to them all—most especially to Mrs. Hawes, John Wyatt Bonner, Jr., and Susan Tate of the University of Georgia; to Carroll Hart, Ruth Corry, and Ann Pederson of the Georgia Department of Archives and History; and to Pat Bryant, deputy surveyor general of Georgia. As this book neared completion, Ann Pederson and her associates quite independently were preparing a collection of Georgia colonial documents suitable for reproduction. Several illustrations for this book have come from her assemblage, some of which has also been printed by the Georgia Commission for the National Bicentennial Celebration.

Readers will quickly notice that the bulk of my citations are to original sources. This would be embarrassing if it were interpreted to mean that secondary works have left no deposit in this book. Like most other writers, I am indebted to the work of other scholars, and even if they are not cited repeatedly, I gratefully acknowledge their important contributions. In particular, I appreciate the scholarship of the following authors and editors who have done specialized work on colonial Georgia: William W. Abbot, Daniel Boorstin, Allen D. Candler, Kenneth Coleman, E. Merton Coulter, Louis De Vorsey, Jr., Adelaide L. Fries, Jack P. Greene, Lilla M. Hawes, Milton Sydney Heath, Charles Colcock Jones, Jr., George Fenwick Jones, Lucian Lamar Knight, James Ross McCain, Robert G. McPherson, Trevor Richard Reese, Albert B. Saye, Billups Phinizy Spalding, William Bacon Stevens, Reba Carolyn Strickland, Paul S. Taylor, and Clarence L. Ver Steeg. This work owes a special debt to the insights of Daniel Boorstin. Also, to E. Merton Coulter, my major professor while I was a master's student at the University of Georgia, I am especially grateful.

To Margo Atkinson and Waldtraut Seifert Lavroff goes my appreciation for assistance in translating some of the German sources, and to Cathy Connell, Pat Cera, Wayne Gilliam, Adelia Barnwell, Julia Iverson McPhail, and Marsha Jones, I express my thanks for help in preparing and checking the manuscript. Two of the three maps in the book were prepared by Gerald L. Holder of Sam Houston State University, Huntsville, Texas, and the cartography for all three maps was done by Patricia Jetmore of Georgia State University. My wife prepared the index.

In writing acknowledgments, authors are expected to reassure readers that any potential errors of fact and interpretation are the responsibility of the one whose name is on the title page. I do this by necessity as well as instinct, wishing to spare my family, friends, and colleagues an unwelcome and undeserved responsibility; at the same time, I wish to emphasize their indispensable contribution to whatever has been accomplished in the pages that follow.

Atlanta, Georgia

Contents

Illustrations

The Fledgling Province

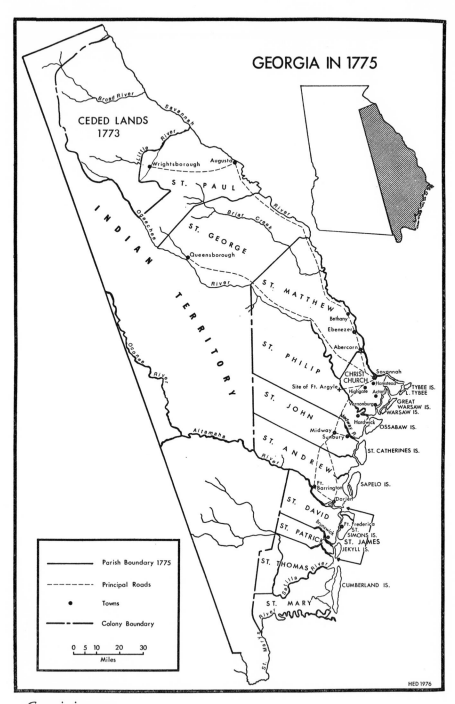

Georgia in 1775

(*Researched and developed by Gerald L. Holder; cartography by Patricia Jetmore.*)

Introduction

It has been said that Georgia was the youngest, the poorest, and the most sparsely populated of the thirteen colonies. These observations are correct, but they do not describe what was by 1776 a rapidly developing province. The colony's youth was beyond dispute even as the Revolution began: anyone older than forty-three was older than Georgia was. Still, by the time shots were fired at Lexington and Concord, this fledgling province was squarely in the mainstream of contemporary American experience, although it had not always been.

Although Georgia was different from Massachusetts, Rhode Island, and the other colonies in some ways, it resembled them, too. Except in the German community along the Savannah River, most Georgians either spoke English as a native tongue or used it increasingly as the era progressed. They had many of the same aspirations and dreams as the people in other colonies. As men and women living on the borders of Indian lands and foreign territory (before 1763), they faced the same kinds of challenges as frontiersmen to the north. The European cultural backgrounds from which they sprang, either directly or at some remove in time, were similar. Thus, in studying the surviving records of the colony to see what life was like there, it is not surprising to discover how much Georgia resembled the other colonies. The ways in which it differed from them are often subtle and more difficult to spot. They will become apparent as the book unfolds.

Georgia's colonial history divides naturally into two parts. The trustees, or proprietors, upon whom George II in 1732 conferred a charter for settling the province, directed its affairs until 1752, when they turned it back to the king. Georgia then became a royal province ruled by the king's deputies until the end of colonial times. In the earliest years of its planning and founding under trustee control, Georgia had created a good bit of excitement in Great Britain. There the second quarter of the eighteenth century was basically a down-to-earth age in which the trustees were among the few men who reached for grand and selfless designs. They sought no personal profit; instead their plan for settling Georgia shone with the double grandeur of noble conception and conspicuous altruism, even while it dealt with ordinary problems attendant upon relocating hundreds of persons, often poor and unemployed, in a new "utopia" across the sea. This undertaking, cast in an attractive mold, stirred idealism to life in Great Britain, and the trustees found themselves the happy recipients of gifts and benefactions from numerous well-wishers and, most important of all, from Parliament.

Although the trustees were not in the foremost ranks of British leadership, they were all prominent men, active in philanthropic projects. All of the original trustees had been connected with the Associates of Dr. Bray, an organization that aimed at converting blacks in the colonies to Christianity and at supplying parochial libraries in distant and sometimes destitute places. Some of the proprietors of Georgia had also supported the distinguished missionary organizations of the day. The two proprietors who exercised the largest influence in the settling of Georgia, and who most closely oversaw the nursing care lavished upon it by the trustees, were John Viscount Percival, later the earl of Egmont, and James Edward Oglethorpe, a member of the House of Commons. That the policies of these well-intentioned midwives and their compatriots very nearly killed the offspring was the result not of a lack of attention but of impractical and inflexible planning, even an excess of attention. In 1752 the proprietors abandoned their experiment, having made a hash of their dreams for the province.

The succeeding years of royal administration were a time of increasing hope and prosperity. Under the chief executives sent over by the king—John Reynolds (1754–1757), Henry Ellis (1757–1760), and James Wright (1760–1776, 1779–1782)—the province made great strides. Governor Wright (after 1772, Sir James Wright, Bart.), the best-remembered royal governor, was one of the most able men to have governed Georgia in any era. Wright's father had been royal chief justice of South Carolina, and he himself had been attorney general there. He was educated in England and was a barrister of

Gray's Inn. When he arrived in Georgia, he was well prepared for important public duties.

This book, in treating Georgia's experiences under both trustee and royal control, necessarily retraces some trails well blazed by others, particularly regarding the colony's founding, the goals and deficiencies of the trustees' plan, the efforts to secure a population, and Indian-white relations. But principally this work deals with the cultural and social factors that shaped the quality of life in eighteenth-century Georgia.

Many of the questions we must ask are elementary. What kinds of buildings did these Georgians live in? How did they accommodate their everyday wants? How did they solve the problem of transportation? We must also investigate such matters as the tasks they accepted as community responsibilities, their efforts to control crime and criminals, and their methods of resolving personal differences. We shall inquire about vocations in a province that, although primarily agricultural, offered a variety of other ways of earning a living.

Like other eighteenth-century peoples, Georgians lived in a socially differentiated society. Using documentary evidence, we shall be examining the factors that influenced social rank and moved white citizens up or down on the scale. We shall also look at women and the family to see if they performed as society expected. And naturally we shall examine the institution of slavery, which after 1750 provided the legal if unhappy base to society.

We must also investigate cultural, religious, and educational matters. What part did books, libraries, music, and art play in the lives of the people? What did colonial Georgians do for entertainment, and what function did official celebrations, clubs, and private societies serve? Turning to religion, we shall speculate on why this youthful province, in the absence of external pressures, decided in 1758 to establish the Anglican faith—a remarkable decision because it took place so late in the era and because large numbers of dissenters did not actively oppose it. All Christian sects except Roman Catholics were welcome in Georgia, and Jews were tolerated. Other questions, narrow and broad, must be asked about religion: Were Georgians devout in their beliefs? Did religion make a difference in the history of the colony and the lives of its people? Finally, we shall be examining the role of education and the nature of Georgia's schools in the light of society's needs and expectations.

These questions are the obvious ones, even if the answers are not. And to a large extent they parallel the concerns of those very human Georgians who before 1776 populated the fields and markets, the forges and shops, the roadways and waterways of the colony. But another matter is of more particular interest to the modern scholar. Many generations had come and gone in Massachusetts and Virginia by the time Georgia was founded in 1733, and the older provinces had advanced with more than a little struggle through a considerable pattern of development. How then did Georgia enter the onrushing stream of the American experience? Did it go back and repeat the earlier stages worked through with such travail by its older sisters, or did it benefit from their histories and mature more quickly?

Not all of these questions can be answered definitively, for pertinent records are sometimes missing. Still, the chapters that follow will examine the documentary evidence that has survived for more than two centuries and will attempt to provide such answers as can be definitely supported, or that seem positively indicated, without resorting to quantitative methods. It may be that other historians, using new techniques, will one day reveal aspects of Georgia's story that today remain hidden. It is hoped that this work, with its descriptive and narrative detail, will complement theirs.

*1. Sir James Wright, Bart. Lieutenant Governor of Georgia, 1760–1762;
Governor of Georgia, 1762–1776, 1779–1782.*

(From a portrait in a private collection.)

Chapter 1

The Settlement of Georgia

The men who ruled Georgia in both trustee and royal times knew that many prospective settlers would need assistance and encouragement from the government to make the journey to the new land. Under the trustees, or proprietors, and under the king, settlers were solicited and valued. The last royal governor, Sir James Wright, saw the population triple during his long service, in part because of the exertions of his administration to bring in people and to help them become established. He had much to gain personally if Georgia prospered, for he was one of its largest landowners and planters. Wright's knowledge of Georgia's needs after 1760 was as explicit as that of the trustees had been inexplicit thirty years earlier. Substituting good intentions for workable policy, the trustees secured settlers through a wise policy of aided immigration but lost them in large numbers through the effects of unpopular laws and regulations composed in London and sent to Georgia for implementation. The province was about twenty years old and the royal era was begun before it was indisputable that people were coming to Georgia faster than they were leaving it.

The trustees as individuals brought support to the enterprise in three ways. Some had already shown interest in charitable work and thus provided experience; others were able to give or to solicit financial assistance for the province; and some were members of the House of Commons. Since Parliament supplied much of the money to settle and maintain Georgia, the Commons was important. The twenty-one persons who in 1732 comprised the original board included ten members of Commons, two members of the House of Lords, five ministers of the Church of England, a philanthropist, a country gentleman, a tax commissioner, and a clerk in the South Sea House. The trust was open-ended, which meant that its membership could be expanded, and during the twenty years that the corporation was active, fifty additional persons were added. Of this entire group, however, only a few applied themselves to the business of Georgia on a day-to-day basis. The colony was usually a secondary concern to a majority of the men most responsible for it. Trustees could receive no monetary reward for their efforts; they could not even hold land in the province. And since their policies in a short time produced unhappiness in Georgia and criticism in Great Britain, the trustees, after the promising early years, received scant praise for their exertions and underwent no small amount of unpleasant interrogation. They had underestimated the cost of founding and supporting the colony, and their corporation was often in financial straits.

In sponsoring a "utopian" society on a distant shore, the trustees had three practical motives. First, and central to their philanthropic vision, they wished to relieve the worthy poor in Great Britain. To them this meant removing destitute but deserving persons from the streets and alleys of London and other British cities, where they were a burden and an offense to society, and sending them to Georgia, where they could earn a living. The trustees hoped to make the poor happy by providing a locale in which they could be productive.

This consideration was related to the second motive for establishing Georgia. The corporation wished the province to play a role in Great Britain's trade policy. It was widely believed at home that Georgia could produce silk and wine, which Englishmen at the time were compelled to buy from other nations at great expense. In the process of producing these useful commodities, the settlers would not only earn their own livelihoods but also have money left over to import a variety of British manufactures. Some influential Britons euphorically believed that silk culture alone could employ twenty thousand persons in Georgia.

The third motive for establishing Georgia was military. The new province would be a buffer for South Carolina, which was always threatened and had in the past been attacked by the Spaniards in Florida. The Spaniards' interest in the area was understandable since they had a legal claim to Georgia that was as good as Great Britain's and possibly better. Indeed, Spain could argue that South Carolina was hers as far north as Port Royal. But because possession of the territory carried weight and because South Carolina clearly needed a southern line of defense, it was believed that a colony south of the Savannah River would be useful. Needless to say, Carolinians supported the founding of Georgia. Councillor William Bull, a man of power in South Carolina and later lieutenant governor there, wished to lend encouragement with his advice and presence, and in 1733 he visited the Georgians at the Savannah River on the tall bluff that was to become the site of Savannah.

The trustees knew precisely the kind of colony they wished to establish; their plan was unified and not in the least ambiguous. First and foremost, Georgia was to be a colony of and for small farmers. Everyone except indentured servants was to have fifty acres of land, with no one receiving more than five hundred. All settlers were expected to work, there being an insufficient number of white servants and no black slaves. Great plantations such as those flourishing in colonies to Georgia's north were to have no place, resting as they did upon massive landholding and the institution of slavery. The trustees believed that competition from slave labor would undermine the small farmers who were at the base of their plan.[1]

The trustees' scheme for securing immigrants was an excellent one, and it bore first fruit when the *Anne* transported a carefully selected

1. Information about the trustees is taken in part from a standard work, James Ross McCain's *Georgia as a Proprietary Province: The Execution of a Trust* (Boston, 1917), 17–21, 28–56. For a discussion of the philanthropic side of Georgia's settlement, see Daniel J. Boorstin, *The Americans: The Colonial Experience* (New York, 1958), 71–96. For an appraisal of official policies of the trust, see Milton Sydney Heath's *Constructive Liberalism: The Role of the State in Economic Development in Georgia to 1860* (Cambridge, Mass., 1954), chaps. 1–3. Most authors consider trust policies to have been idealistic and well motivated but unworkable. However, Paul S. Taylor, in *Georgia Plan: 1732–1752* (Berkeley and Los Angeles, 1972), is not convinced that the collapse of the plan was inevitable. He argues that some of the small farmers saw the introduction of slavery as a threat to them and supported the trustees. The trust was undermined, he contends, by private adventurers with money to invest. They were more vocal than the small farmers and employed a lobbyist to work against the trust in London. The result, argues Taylor, was a drying up of funds for Georgia from parliamentary and private sources, a situation fatal to the model devised by the trustees. Taylor questions whether the plan's collapse has not unduly supported the proposition that the collapse was inevitable.

shipload of settlers in 1733. Among those first arrivals were poor persons assisted by the charity of the trustees, but some settlers in the group were not destitute. The trustees always held the gates open for men and women who could immigrate at their own expense. For both kinds of settlers, free land was the lure. To ease the transition to a new land, the trustees operated storehouses from which most colonists were supplied while they arranged for their own sustenance.

An old legend, now demolished, held that Georgia was a refuge for debtors from English prisons. It is true that several of the trustees, as members of the House of Commons, in 1729 had served on a committee to investigate the condition of British jails and that a concern had been expressed for imprisoned debtors. However, probably not more than a dozen of those unfortunates ever went to the province directly from prison, and these were not chosen simply because they were debtors.[2] The trustees were seeking qualifications other than need. For the embarkation that left England aboard the *Anne*, they scrutinized and sometimes interviewed the prospective settlers to differentiate between the worthy poor and those who seemed to deserve the low estate they occupied. Never again was a group so meticulously selected, although reasonable care was employed as long as the trustees continued to sponsor emigrating parties. Between 1732 and 1741 the trustees sent 1,810 persons at corporation expense, or "on the charity," as the contemporary expression termed it. This number included many Englishmen, more than 800 foreign Protestants, mostly of German, Swiss, or Austrian extraction, some Scots, and two Italians. During the same period 1,021 persons emigrated at their own expense.[3]

It was inconceivable that the trustees, who had picked their colonists with such care, would allow them unfettered free rein once they reached Georgia. Through their policies and laws, the trustees sought to direct the immigrants toward the happiness they were sure lay within the grasp of every diligent settler. They laid down laws and regulations to carry out their plan, provisions that made perfect sense upon the banks of the Thames but that bred discontent on the Savannah. By the time the trustees returned their charter to the king in 1752,

2. Albert Berry Saye, "Was Georgia a Debtor Colony?" *Georgia Historical Quarterly*, XXIV (1940), 323–341.
3. E. Merton Coulter and Albert B. Saye, eds., *A List of the Early Settlers of Georgia* (Athens, Ga., 1949), x.

only a reduced portion remained of the population they had assembled at great cost.

Three principal regulations led to immigrants' complaints: prohibitions about landholding, slaveholding, and hard liquor. Land policy was an especially important source of grievances. By encouraging small farmers to populate Georgia, the trustees expected to resurrect, thousands of miles across the sea, those agrarian virtues that had proved elusive at home. No man who went "on the charity" could get more than fifty acres of land, which would be separated into a small lot in town, upon which a dwelling would stand; a garden plot of about five acres near the edge of town; and, the largest part of the allotment, a farm in the countryside. The fifty acres thus subdivided in three plots would give each man enough land for his family's support but not more than the family could cultivate. Persons who arrived at their own expense might get larger tracts, but no one could legally have more than five hundred acres. With landholding thus controlled, huge plantations were proscribed.

The trustees sold no land—they gave it away—and their policy seemed generous and sensible in London. Yet it temporarily crippled the colony and was not abandoned until untold damage had been done. As every farmer was also potentially a soldier, farms were grouped around the towns so that settlers would be concentrated for defense in case of attack. As a result, land was assigned almost arbitrarily, with little regard for the fertility of the soil. Much of coastal Georgia was pine barrens—that is, level sandy land lightly covered with pine trees, not suitable for farming. With farms laid out to promote the needs of defense, it was inevitable that many settlers would find their fields were pine barrens.

Even more strenuously protested than the method of assigning land was the legal restriction under which the trustees made their grants. The farmer's allotment was not wholly his property to do with as he pleased. He could not sell it; he held it for his lifetime with a provision that he might will it to his male heirs only. No daughter or other female descendant could inherit land. Once more the regulation made sense in London, for it would prevent the lumping together of plots such as might occur if a daughter inherited property from her father and then married a man who also held land. Unskilled farmers would also be kept from concentrating relatively large tracts that could be developed better by others. The policy was also intended to retain a male on each farm, thus strengthening the defenses of the province. Restricting inheritance of land to male heirs was a carry-over from medieval times known legally as tail-male. Its application in the earliest years of the province disaffected large numbers of inhabitants who desired that their property be truly theirs. All of this effectively killed trade in land, the one resource of value that Georgia possessed in abundance. Protests against it failed to move the trustees, who saw their land policy as a necessary part of their plan.

For the first eight years of the colony's life, the granting of land was done mostly in London, but after 1741 the trustees transferred the controversial task across the Atlantic and charged the president of the colony and his assistants with the duty of apportioning property. These officials mitigated the trustees' policy as best they could; indeed, by then many exceptions to the narrow rule already existed. The president and his assistants gradually allowed larger grants and issued them in fee simple title.[4] Although the original policy was being weakened in practice, it was not officially abolished until only two years before the trustees surrendered their charter. On March 19, 1750, when Georgia was seventeen years old, the common council of the trustees surrendered on the question of land titles.[5] Thereafter land could be bought, sold, or inherited like any other commodity.

Another important prohibition was the barring of black slaves from Georgia. A later century would applaud the proprietors' efforts to debar slavery as a noble ideal ahead of its time, but to many Georgians in the 1730s and 1740s, the prohibition seemed to guarantee their perpetual poverty. A Georgian with a little capital to invest, or the prospect of acquiring some, needed only to look across the river toward South Carolina to become embittered. There seemed to be a correlation between that neighboring colony's relative prosperity and the institution of slavery. While the trustees later demonstrated a sensitivity to the needs of slaves, their ban on slavery was based not upon finer considerations of morality but upon beliefs that slaves would

4. Milton L. Ready, "An Economic History of Colonial Georgia, 1732–1754" (Ph.D. diss., University of Georgia, 1970), 237–240.

5. Allen D. Candler and Lucian Lamar Knight, comps., *The Colonial Records of the State of Georgia* (Atlanta, Ga., 1904–1916), II, 500. This series contains 25 published volumes. Vols. XX and XXVII–XXXIX are unpublished but are available for consultation at the Georgia Department of Archives and History, Atlanta; the Georgia Historical Society, Savannah; and the University of Georgia Library, Athens. Hereafter cited as *Col. Records of Ga.*

destroy the will to do hard work among the white inhabitants, that they were a threat to safety in time of war, and that they were not needed for the gentle arts of cultivating silk and wine with which Georgians were to occupy themselves. These considerations evoked a sympathetic response from some small farmers in Georgia, especially among the Germans and some of the Highland Scots. The Germans, contented to do their own work and isolated by the language barrier, were probably more satisfied than not with the trustees' plan. Other colonists, however, were stirred to active protest. Resenting both the land policy and the law against slavery, an articulate group called the Malcontents rallied itself in Savannah before the province was ten years old and led a movement out of the colony, many disaffected persons going to South Carolina. The officers of the trust government in Savannah were more relieved at their departure than concerned that Georgia was losing population. It was not until 1750 that the trust gave way on African slaves and allowed them in.

The third unpopular restriction forbade the importation or consumption of rum and other hard liquor while allowing wine and beer. The proprietors and many other persons considered strong drink to be injurious to the health; they knew it to be destructive to the Indians. Yet it was one thing to proscribe drink by law and another to prohibit it in fact, and the authorities in London and Savannah never stemmed the flow of rum into Georgia. Neither could they find juries to convict those who sold rum or those who drank it. The law was neither respected nor obeyed, being viewed as a ridiculous supererogation. Perhaps because this was the easiest major regulation to violate, it was the earliest to be set aside.

In theory the king supervised the proprietors in two main ways: first, his government retained authority to review the laws that the trustees devised for Georgia and, second, his government required many reports. The trustees never named a governor for Georgia, because the king would have had authority to instruct him. (James Edward Oglethorpe, the only trustee to set foot in Georgia, was sometimes called "governor," although he never had the title.) The proprietors ruled through petty officials and made regulations rather than laws, because regulations were not subject to review by the crown. In twenty years the proprietors secured passage of only three laws—acts regulating the Indian trade, outlawing rum, and prohibiting African slavery. Not until 1751, the year before they laid down their charge, did the trustees call Georgians together in an elected assembly to advise on local needs and concerns. Even then the colonists could merely advise and not legislate. This assembly, although limited in power, did offer an avenue for participation and consultation that had previously been lacking, so that complaints might be articulated and registered short of the ultimate protest so often practiced in the 1740s—that of departing the colony altogether. Still, the assembly came to little. Only when royal government took effective control in 1754 did the concept of a truly representative assembly with powers to legislate arrive with it. Georgians thereafter had much to say about their own affairs.

The philanthropic aims of the founders were so effectively communicated throughout the British Isles, and the credentials and connections of the proprietors were so impeccable, that a generous flow of private gifts and parliamentary grants came to the trustees from the beginning.[6] These benefactions kept the colony afloat, for they enabled the trustees to secure a population and to provide for it once it arrived in America. In 1733 the *Anne* had brought 114 persons. By the time the colony was about a year old, the white settlers in Georgia numbered 437, of whom 259 lived along Savannah's spacious streets and well-designed squares (see figure 1, in chapter 2). The 178 persons not in Savannah were living in villages or locations nearby—at Highgate, Hampstead, Abercorn, Thunderbolt, Ogeechee, Tybee, Hutchinson's Island, Cape Bluff, and Westbrook.[7] In picturing the migrations that populated Georgia, we should not envision hundreds of persons coming all at once. More correctly, we should think of dozens or perhaps a few score people entered at a time, while other individuals and families arrived in a continuing trickle.

Georgians were not a homogeneous people. By 1736, to function well in all parts of the colony, a person ideally needed what probably no one in Georgia had—fluency in English, French, German, and Gaelic. A knowledge of Spanish would also have been helpful. English was the language of record, but many Georgians did not speak it at all. Much writing of the provincial era survives only in German, and a smattering survives in French.

6. Verner W. Crane, "The Promotion Literature of Georgia," in *Bibliographical Essays: A Tribute to Wilberforce Eames* (Freeport, N.Y., 1967), 281–298.

7. Robert G. McPherson, ed., *The Journal of the Earl of Egmont: Abstract of the Trustees Proceedings for Establishing the Colony of Georgia, 1732–1738* (Athens, Ga., 1962), 39.

The Spanish spoken in Georgia was used by Jews. Of the 259 persons in Savannah when the town was a year old, almost one-sixth were Jewish. They had come uninvited, unexpected, unwanted, and at the expense of friends. Forty-two Jews arrived together in one ship on July 11, 1733, and although their presence aroused consternation in both Savannah and London, many of them remained and shamed the Christians by the exemplary quality of their lives.[8] Some were Ashkenazim (German Jews), but more than half were Sephardim (Spanish or Portuguese Jews), who for a time retained Spanish as their workaday tongue; the Anglican pastor in Savannah in 1737 set himself to learning it in order to speak to them.[9] When the first migration of Protestant immigrants from Salzburg arrived in Savannah in 1734, the Ashkenazim greeted them in their native German and served them a good rice soup.[10]

The Salzburgers, through their industry and common sense, were to distinguish themselves as the community of settlers who came closest to fulfilling what the trustees desired of all immigrants. Devout and hard-working small farmers who earned their bread by the sweat of their brows, they opposed slavery and were content not to stupefy themselves with rum.

These Germans had originally come from the Archbishopric of Salzburg, poised between Bavaria and Austria and embracing not only the ancient city of Salzburg but the beautiful countryside around it. There the seeds of Lutheranism had been planted early, soon after Martin Luther posted his Ninety-five Theses in 1517. From time to time the Lutherans of the archbishopric were repressed by the Roman Catholic authorities, who, finding themselves unable to stop the spread of the new doctrine in northern Germany, sometimes acted against it with vigor in the south. In 1727 a new archbishop, Leopold von Firmian, assumed the archepiscopal throne. A product of Italian Jesuit training, Firmian was alive with the spirit of the Counter-Reformation

8. Sheftall Diary, 1–2, Benjamin Sheftall Papers, Keith Read Collection, University of Georgia Library, Athens; Malcolm H. Stern, "New Light on the Jewish Settlement of Savannah," *American Jewish Historical Quarterly*, LII (1963), 175–177.

9. The Rev. Luke Tyerman, *The Life and Times of the Rev. John Wesley, M.A., Founder of the Methodists*, I (New York, 1875), 139.

10. George Fenwick Jones *et al.*, trans. and eds., *Detailed Reports on the Salzburger Emigrants Who Settled in America...Edited by Samuel Urlsperger* (Athens, Ga., 1968–   ), I, 60.

and obsessed with the notion that religious unity was necessary for the well-being of his temporal state; since he could not convert his Lutheran subjects, in November 1731 he posted a patent dictating their expulsion. Enthusiastic Protestant historians have sometimes claimed that thirty thousand Lutherans left Salzburg—one-seventh of the population—but that estimate is probably too high. Between 1731 and 1733 more than two dozen organized parties did depart, however, one of them consisting of about a thousand persons. Although most of these Lutherans took refuge in the realms of the sympathetic Protestant rulers in Germany, a few hundred found their way to Georgia. Two Germans, the Reverend Samuel Urlsperger and Chretien von Munch, a banker, corresponded with the trustees in England and became the instruments through which interested refugees arranged their passage to Georgia. The two were later designated corresponding members of the trust.

The Salzburgers who disembarked in Savannah on March 10, 1734, numbered 46 and were led by two Lutheran pastors. They first established the short-lived community of Old Ebenezer some twenty-five miles above Savannah. About nine months later, on December 27, 1734, another transport with 65 colonists arrived, followed by a third in February 1736 carrying 63. A fourth ship arrived in Savannah in December 1741. Additional organized groups of German-speaking settlers crossed the Atlantic in 1750, 1751, and 1752, coming principally from Württemberg. In 1751 John G. William DeBrahm brought 156 German-speaking persons who settled at Bethany near Ebenezer. DeBrahm, who made a considerable impact on the colony during his long career, was a distinguished engineer and the official surveyor general of the Southern Provinces of North America.

Augmented by other Germans, the center of the German culture in Georgia was always at Ebenezer. The original settlement of Old Ebenezer lay on an unnavigable creek. After two years the town was moved six miles to the banks of the Savannah River in order to secure better lands, a more healthful location, and reliable water transportation. Old Ebenezer was abandoned to nature and wild animals, with only a cow pen left behind. By 1742 New Ebenezer was populated by "77 men, 70 women, 60 girls, 42 boys, and 7 maidservants; in all 256" persons.[11] Although it was the center, it did not contain all the Germans living in Georgia, for others were at Savannah, Darien, White

11. *Col. Records of Ga.*, V, 674.

Bluff on the Vernon River, on St. Simons Island, at Hampstead, and in tiny German hamlets near Ebenezer: Zion, Goshen, and, after 1751, Bethany.

The Lutheran pastors who led the Salzburgers, the Reverend John Martin Bolzius and the Reverend Israel Christian Gronau, were among the best and most successful leaders in colonial Georgia.[12] Bolzius had been an inspector of an orphan house in a little hamlet near Halle, Germany; Gronau had been a tutor in the same orphan school. The trustees erected no form of civil government for Ebenezer but left the management of affairs to these pastors, of whom Bolzius was the senior, and they oversaw the frequently communal efforts by which Ebenezer was built. The Germans took all their problems to their ministers for resolution, including such minor matters as a husband's complaints about his wife's housework.[13] Bolzius saw his flock as especially blessed by God: "Every year God gives them what they need. And since they have been able to earn something apart from agriculture, through the mills which have been built and in many other ways, they have managed rather well with God's blessing, and have led a calm and quiet life of blessedness and honesty. They love the calmness, the church, and the school, do not begrudge others the glory of good and extensive plantations. . . . They fear debts like the plague and, therefore, enjoy such good credit with the merchants that they are glad to lend to them. . . . I do not wish to live and to die anywhere except among and with them at Ebenezer."[14]

By the 1770s the Georgia Germans probably numbered more than twelve hundred souls. United in language and religion, they had a sense of community that outlasted the colonial era, survived into America's national period, and disappeared in the first quarter of the nineteenth century only when the language was finally lost for everyday use.

Between 1735 and 1740 Georgia had one other distinctive group of German-speaking settlers. The Moravians in Germany were ex-

---

12. The name was often spelled Boltzius. Gronau died in 1745 and was succeeded by Hermann Henry Lemke. Bolzius led at Ebenezer until his own death in 1765.

13. Samuel Urlsperger, ed., *Der ausführlichen Nachrichten von der Königlich-Gross-Britannischen Colonie Saltzburgischer Emigranten in America* (Halle, 1735–1752), III, 538, hereafter cited as Urlsperger, ed., *Ausführliche Nachrichten*.

14. Klaus G. Loewald, Beverly Starika, and Paul S. Taylor, trans. and eds., "John Martin Bolzius Answers a Questionnaire on Carolina and Georgia," Pt. ii, *William and Mary Quarterly*, 3d Ser., XV (1958), 251–252.

periencing a revival of their ancient faith and were encountering misunderstanding and persecution. Count Nikolaus Ludwig von Zinzendorf, their leader, inquired of the trustees whether a party of Moravians might settle in Georgia. Receiving encouragement, a first small contingent arrived in Savannah in 1735. There were never more than forty-seven in the colony, and their stay spanned only five years, ending unhappily.[15] Their brief residence is significant, however, for it coincided with the service in the colony of the Reverend John Wesley, the Anglican minister who founded Methodism. Wesley's thought and later career were influenced, many think greatly, by the impression that the pious Moravians made on him. Wesley's debt to them was one that he cheerfully acknowledged.

The Moravians spoke almost no English, and Wesley learned German to converse with them. They were never integrated into the life of the colony but, even so, were for a short time among Georgia's most industrious citizens, making the most systematic effort in early Georgia to convert and educate the Indians. Charles Wesley, John's brother who was also briefly in Georgia, described the Moravians as "the most laborious, cheapest workers and best Subjects in the whole Province."[16] Their departure grew from a misunderstanding: they thought that everyone knew that their religion forbade the bearing of arms. But when the Spanish threat became intense in the late 1730s, culminating in actual invasion in 1742, Thomas Causton, chief magistrate of Savannah, sought to muster every male for defense, to the great dismay of the Moravians. Zinzendorf in 1737 wrote a protesting letter on their behalf. "I know that our brothers will never consent, either of their own will or by force, to go out to shoot at people in countries where they are seeking only the salvation of souls." The count explained that if the government insisted, the Moravians would leave. The trustees sought a compromise. Only two of the Moravians were freeholders (the remainder being servants of the count); so it was proposed that two men not of their faith be secured to serve in their place. The attempt came to nothing, and the Moravians, true to their threat, began a departure in 1737 that was complete by 1740.[17] The larger contingent removed to Bethlehem, Pennsylvania.

15. Adelaide L. Fries, *The Moravians in Georgia, 1735–1740* (Raleigh, N.C., 1905), 242.

16. McPherson, ed., *Journal of Egmont*, 215.

17. *Col. Records of Ga.*, XXI, 502, 504, XXIX, 406–407; Fries, *Moravians*

In the various transportations arranged by the trustees, Georgia acquired a French-speaking population substantial in size. Many of them had originally lived in Switzerland, and all were Protestant. They were assimilated more quickly than the Germans, but as late as 1746, when John Terry, the recorder at Frederica, was called before a Savannah court on a rape charge, five of the eighteen men on his jury spoke French, apparently as their native tongue.[18] Protestant church services for Savannah's French-speaking citizens were conducted in the 1730s and 1740s by the Reverend Henri Chiffelle, a pastor who journeyed twenty-four miles downstream from the South Carolina town of Purrysburg. Chiffelle also preached in German while in Savannah.[19] In 1745, when the trustees were searching for a pastor to fill the Anglican pulpit in Savannah, rare good fortune sent them an excellently qualified man who spoke three languages as well. The clergyman awarded the pastorate was the Reverend Bartholomew Zouberbuhler, who preached with distinction in English, French, and German for twenty years.[20]

Georgians were sometimes thought to be flexible about languages. On the eve of the Revolution, the publisher of the popular *Tobler's Almanack* was disappointed when his printer failed to have an English edition ready on time. However, he assured his English-speaking customers that they would find his German version to be a serviceable substitute, since the figures for the days of the week and month, for the hours of sunrise and sunset, for the moon's risings and phases, were the same in both books and transcended language.[21]

The principal servants of the trustees were especially well regarded if they were multilingual. Francis Harris and William Russell, both of whom later had important business careers in the province, spoke German, and Nicholas Rigby, another important servant of the trust,

in Georgia, 184, 187, 216. Just before the Revolution, two Moravians came to Georgia to teach at William Knox's plantation at Knoxborough.

18. *Col. Records of Ga.*, XXV, 111. After 1754 Georgia temporarily acquired a French-speaking Roman Catholic population. British policy required that some 6,000 Acadians be removed from Nova Scotia and deposited in colonies to the south. Georgia received perhaps 400 Acadians, and the assembly passed a measure regulating them. *Ibid.*, XVIII, 188–191. They were unwelcome in Georgia, and by Jan. 1764 the last of them had departed. *Georgia Gazette* (Savannah), Jan. 12, 1764.

19. *Col. Records of Ga.*, XXIV, 32–36.

20. *Ibid.*, I, 478.

21. Advertisement for *Tobler's Almanack, Ga. Gaz.*, Feb. 7, 1776.

was fluent in French. One day in 1744 Rigby was with William Stephens, who for about thirteen years after 1737 was the trustees' principal representative in Georgia, when Mrs. Lewis Camuse, a difficult woman who supervised the silk industry, entered the room in a rage. Rigby began to soothe Mrs. Camuse in French, the language she customarily spoke, but the woman, determined to have no part of assuagement, switched into Italian and for a half hour declaimed at Stephens and Rigby in a language neither of them understood. Finally, said Stephens, "She threw her self out of doors, leaving me not one Jot more knowing what she meant, than when she began."[22]

Yet another language flourished on the Altamaha River in the southernmost part of the colony. The trustees became concerned that the Spaniards were about to move against Georgia, and they commissioned two energetic and well-connected men to recruit tough fighters from the Scottish Highlands for resettlement in the colony. In Scotland, Lieutenant Hugh Mackay gathered settlers and fighters north of Inverness, while George Dunbar, a ship captain, gathered them to the south. These recruits, who spoke Highland Gaelic, left Inverness in 1735, with the trustees paying passage for 146 persons, and arrived in Savannah on January 10, 1736. The trustees proposed to place them as close to the Spaniards as they could without having them leave the colony; so plans were made to settle them at Barnwell's Bluff on the Altamaha River. Meanwhile, in Savannah a servant unwisely sought to alarm the Highlanders by telling them they would be so close to the Spaniards that if they looked out of doors they would be shot. The servant was quickly thrown into jail, but the Highland men, unfrightened, determined to go on to Barnwell's Bluff, drive the Spaniards away if they were there, build cover, and then send for their wives and children.[23]

The outpost on the Altamaha was named Darien for an unsuccessful attempt made by Scots in the seventeenth century to establish a settlement on the Isthmus of Panama and was usually referred to by that name, although it was sometimes called New Inverness. The Scots had their own minister, the Reverend John MacLeod of the Isle of Skye,

---

22. E. Merton Coulter, ed., *The Journal of William Stephens, 1741–1745* (Athens, Ga., 1958–1959), II, 83.

23. *Col. Records of Ga.*, XXI, 71–72. In 1684 a similar Scottish settlement was started in South Carolina below Charleston at Port Royal Sound. This settlement, called Stuart's Town, was attacked and burned by the Spaniards in Aug. 1686.

who served them quietly and well for five years before departing the colony, disappointed with the policies of the trustees. The servants of the trust at Darien spoke only Gaelic and could not work under anyone who could not direct them in their own tongue.[24] Oglethorpe, thinking to conform himself to custom, scheduled a visit to the settlement in 1736 and arrived in Highland dress, complete with bonnet, target, plaid, broadsword, and pistols. The Scots had heard he was coming, but he had so attired himself that, once he arrived, they demanded to know the whereabouts of Oglethorpe, not believing at once that it was he.[25]

The Highland Scots soon established themselves as industrious settlers.[26] Besides them, Georgia was also settled by a group of Lowland Scots, who colonized the village of Josephs Town upstream from Savannah. The Lowland Scots readily discovered that life on their farms was hard and laborious without slaves. Some of them deserted their lands and moved to Savannah, where they became the trustees' most articulate critics, the Malcontents. They assailed the trustees, denouncing the prohibition against slavery and the policy of land grants in tail-male, but completely failed to sway the proprietors' position. By 1740 they had determined that their future lay elsewhere.

In trustee Georgia most people resided in towns and villages rather than in the countryside. More colonial communities ultimately died than lived. Savannah, Augusta, Darien, and Brunswick survive to the present, but Old and New Ebenezer, Frederica, Sunbury, and Hardwick, which were once thriving establishments, are today locations of historical interest only. Gone, too, are the villages of Highgate, Hampstead, Josephs Town, Fort Argyle, Abercorn, Acton, Goshen, Bethany, Wrightsborough, and Queensborough. These villages and towns were abandoned for varying reasons, some quite individual and having nothing to do with poor location.

Several of the now vanished localities were related to important migrations; Sunbury, Wrightsborough, and Queensborough were each founded by immigrations of homogeneous groups. In 1752 a group of Congregationalists living in and around Dorchester, South Carolina, began to move into the Midway district south of Savannah, connected

24. Georgia Historical Society, *Collections* (Savannah, Ga., 1840–), III, 90, hereafter cited as Ga. Hist. Soc., *Colls.*
25. *South-Carolina Gazette* (Charleston), Mar. 13–20, 1736.
26. McPherson, ed., *Journal of Egmont*, 215.

to the city by an old military road. Georgia was then between governments. The trustees were surrendering their authority, and royal government had not yet arrived. Nevertheless, the Congregationalists, having originally arrived in New England in 1630 and moved to South Carolina in 1695, took encouragement from carry-over officials in Savannah and began to occupy huge tracts of Georgia land allotted for their use. The move into Georgia, which continued until 1771, was their final migration. It gave the province a sturdy people to develop St. John Parish, as it was called after 1758. The Congregationalists attempted first to use the old road to Savannah to serve their commercial purposes, but they soon found that land transportation alone was inadequate. In 1758 the town of Sunbury, destined to be an important port, was laid out on the Medway River. Although Sunbury was the only town of size in the parish, it was never the spiritual center; Midway Congregational Church, located nine or ten miles inland on the old road, held that distinction. Although the church was unquestionably the real heart of the parish, Sunbury was the commercial center. By 1762 its value was proved, and it was declared a port of entry.

The Congregational migration was modest in size; in 1771 the population of the Congregational community numbered probably 350 white persons and 1,500 slaves.[27] The people were industrious, were prosperous by the standards of the day, and were served by a pious ministry. At the outbreak of the Revolutionary War, the St. John parishioners owned nearly one-third of the wealth of the colony.[28]

The Congregationalists had departed South Carolina because their land there was depleted, and they came to Georgia because fertile tracts had been reserved for them. The lure of free land drew two more significant migrations during the royal period, both of them during the administration of Governor Wright. When Wright took office in 1760, the trustees' policy of sending worthy poor people at government expense was as dead as the trust government itself. Georgia needed a new policy to assist immigrants. Such plans were fairly common in the southern colonies; Virginia, for example, allotted land to settlers under the headright system until the Revolution began. Wright and the Georgia assembly saw merit in a township plan then in use

27. Charles C. Jones, Jr., *The History of Georgia* (Boston, 1883), I, 493.
28. The Rev. William Bacon Stevens, *A History of Georgia, from Its First Discovery by Europeans to the Adoption of the Present Constitution in MDCCXCVIII*, II (Philadelphia, 1859), 92.

in South Carolina and fashioned a similar one for Georgia. The general idea was to reserve land for a number of years for any desirable group wishing to move into the colony. In 1764 the assembly declared its willingness to create a township for any group of forty or more Protestant families arriving within three years. The settlers were to enjoy several advantages, including exemption from taxation (except upon slaves), and they were to have their lands surveyed without cost. The colonial government was also to provide £1,815 in direct assistance to them.

Although Wright approved the act, its transmission to Great Britain for review was held up until 1766.[29] The delay produced embarrassing results. In the interim three Georgia men had petitioned for fifty thousand acres to be laid out for Protestant settlers from Ireland, settlers who would come mostly from northern Ireland. The petitioners were John Rae, George Galphin, and Lachlan McGillivray, wealthy and vigorous Indian traders who had a thriving business in or near Augusta. Rae and Galphin had themselves come from Ireland. They proposed to create a township for Scotch-Irish settlers on the Great Ogeechee River in the backcountry of St. George Parish. Advertisements for settlers were placed in Ireland in the *Belfast News-Letter*, and the paper published a long letter from John Rae to his brother Matthew, who lived not far from Belfast, describing the advantages that lay in Georgia:

The land which I have pitched upon lies on a fine River called Ogichey, near to which I have my large Cow-pens of cattle settled, which will be very convenient for newcomers in to be supplied with milk cows; I can also furnish them with Horses and Mares, any number they may want. I am likewise in hopes of obtaining a Bounty at their arrival; but as this is a young Colony, and of course not rich, they cannot expect so much as Carolina gave to the People who came over with my servants, who are well and hearty. . . . Now, Brother, if you think a number of good industrious families will come over here I will do everything in my power to assist them; for nothing will give me more satisfaction than to be the means of bringing my friends to this country of Freedom; there are no rents, no

29. *Col. Records of Ga.*, XVIII, 743–748. The South Carolina township plan, the success of which doubtless influenced the Georgia scheme, was sponsored by Gov. Robert Johnson in the 1720s. The South Carolinians wished to attract white settlers to their colony largely to support their military defense. See Richard P. Sherman, *Robert Johnson, Proprietary and Royal Governor of South Carolina* (Columbia, S.C., 1966), 107–117.

tithes here, only the King's Quit Rent, which is only two shillings sterl. per hundred acres: who would define a cheaper rent? We have settled a firm peace with the Indians around us, and have agreed on boundary lines betwixt us and them, so that all is settled with them. . . . The people that I would advise to come to this country are those that have large families growing up, that they may get land to assist each other. Likewise tradesmen of all sorts, for that will draw a trade amongst them from other settlements, by which they will get money. I would have them bring a clergyman with them, and a schoolmaster that may be clerk, for they are scarce here, and they will have land given them, and what the people can afford with my mite, may procure him a living.

Dear Brother, I do not expect to have the pleasure of seeing you in this country, nor would I advise any person to come here that lives well in Ireland, because there is not the pleasure of society that there is there, and the comfort of the gospel preached, no fairs nor markets to go to, but we have greater plenty of good eating and drinking: for I bless God for it I keep as plentiful a table as most gentlemen in Ireland, with good punch, wine, and beer. If any person that comes here can bring money to purchase a slave or two, they may live very easy and well. A good slave will cost about fifty pounds sterling.[30]

Beset by economic difficulties in the 1760s, many Scotch-Irish read Rae's letter and subsequent items that appeared in the *Belfast News-Letter* and decided to start over in a new land. A contingent of emigrants was assembled and prepared for embarkation. A serious error had been made, though, for when the township act arrived in London, it was disallowed by the king upon advice of his ministers. The home government was apprehensive that the British Isles would lose valuable artisans if emigration to America became too attractive. The government was seldom happy to see mass removals. Not even the efforts of the trustees to resettle the poor in an earlier decade had met with unanimous acclaim, and in the 1760s the government decreed that for Georgia to assist settlers financially was inadmissible. The royal disallowance was dated August 26, 1767, but word of it did not reach Georgia until March 1768. Notice arrived too late to stop the sailing of the first vessel from Belfast, and the ship, with 107 men, women, and children aboard, put into Savannah late the same year. Wright, entrapped in a dilemma, wrote to the Board of Trade in London assert-

30. *Belfast News-Letter*, Sept. 3–Oct. 22, 1765. Quoted in E. R. R. Green, "Queensborough Township: Scotch-Irish Emigration and the Expansion of Georgia, 1763–1776," *WMQ*, 3d Ser., XVII (1960), 186–187.

ing the urgent necessity of helping new settlers. Meanwhile, the Georgia assembly voted £560 to assist an Irish township, which was named Queensborough.[31]

Wright and his Savannah associates were so determined to attract settlers that, under the guise of necessity, they continued to provide as much encouragement as they dared. At least six shiploads of Irish settlers arrived in Georgia—the *Prince George* in late 1768, the *Hopewell* in late 1769 and again in late 1770, the *Britannia* in early 1772, the *Elizabeth* in 1773, and the *Waddell* in 1774. The first five brought some 680 persons, and the *Waddell*, the last of them, brought an additional but undeterminable number.[32] Not all of the Irishmen took up residence at Queensborough. The township itself was only a modest success. As the Revolution approached, the town was inhabited by only about seventy families; the countryside nearby had an additional two hundred-odd families.[33] But as a catalyst to attract new population, the Queensborough settlement, as well as the activities of Rae, Galphin, and McGillivray, was significant.

The province erected another township to receive a migration of Quakers. Named Wrightsborough in honor of Governor Wright, it, like Queensborough, eventually died. In 1767 the Quakers, originally from Pennsylvania but then living in Orange County, North Carolina, petitioned for land.[34] They soon established their township in St. Paul Parish on a tributary of the Little River, about thirty miles from Augusta. Wrightsborough was located at a spot where an earlier Quaker settlement had failed in the 1750s. The Quakers there were led by their patriarch, Joseph Maddock.[35] They minded their own business and remained insular throughout colonial times, although they

31. *Col. Records of Ga.*, X, 460, XXVIII, Pt. ii b, 693–694.

32. Green, "Queensborough Township," *WMQ*, 3d Ser., XVII (1960), 189–196, 198. Other Irishmen went to Georgia in addition to those who went in the six embarkations mentioned here. Between Feb. 16 and 23, 1774, 150 passengers arrived in Savannah from northern Ireland. They were not aboard the *Waddell*, for on Feb. 23 that vessel was merely reported and had not yet landed. *Ga. Gaz.*, Feb. 23, 1774.

33. John Gerar William DeBrahm, *History of the Province of Georgia: With Maps of Original Surveys* (Wormsloe, Ga., 1849), 25. DeBrahm's *History* has been reprinted in Louis De Vorsey, Jr., ed., *DeBrahm's Report of the General Survey in the Southern District of North America* (Columbia, S.C., 1971), 139–166.

34. *Col. Records of Ga.*, X, 303–304.

35. William Bartram, *Travels Through North and South Carolina, Georgia, East and West Florida . . .* (Philadelphia, 1791), 36.

were joined by additional arrivals until the eve of the American Revolution. In December 1775, for example, a migration of Quakers arrived at Savannah. Between forty and fifty of them were led to Wrightsborough by one of their leaders, Thomas Taylor, who reported to an old friend in England:

The Distance hither is about 160 miles. We were eight Nights upon the Road, five of which we encamp'd out part of the Time in Rain, Frost, and Snow. The Country for the first hundred Miles is a mere sandy Plain with frequent Swamps all coverd with the long leav'd Pine. As you approach this Settlement the Land is much richer and diversified with Hills and Dales. The Country too is more populous, most of the Settlers having arriv'd within this eight years from the back Parts of Pennsylvania and Virginia. The Land here bears pretty good Wheat, Rye, Oats, Pease, Indian Corn, Indigo, Cotton etc. Peaches are pretty plentifull but no other Sort of Fruit, merely (I believe) for want of Culture.[36]

Wrightsborough was connected with Augusta by road, and although the little town itself encompassed only a bit more than a thousand acres, the township proper was immense and was populated by industrious settlers. In 1775 Wrightsborough was probably at the height of its growth. At that date 124 male Quakers can be identified as holding grants to more than thirty-thousand acres of land there. Eighty-two owned lots in the town itself.[37] Since most of the male Quakers probably had families, the township must have had a population of 600 or more by the eve of the Revolution.

Although migrations brought hundreds of new settlers into Georgia, they would have proved insufficient in populating the province if they had not been supplemented by large numbers of individuals and their families who came on their own.[38] After the establishment of royal government, ships and wagons brought men, women, and their families either at their own expense or as indentured servants. From South Carolina in particular, but also from Great Britain, the West Indies, and from colonies in the north, came some of the families whose members made significant marks in Georgia. The Bullochs,

36. Thomas Taylor to the Rev. Dr. Percy, Jan. 13, 1776, Miscellaneous Collection, William L. Clements Library, University of Michigan, Ann Arbor.

37. Alex M. Hitz, "The Wrightsborough Quaker Town and Township in Georgia," *Bulletin of Friends Historical Association*, XLVI (1957), 16.

38. The assembly sometimes assisted individuals who wished to settle. See *Col. Records of Ga.*, XIV, 181.

Tattnalls, Mullrynes, Arthurs, Bryans, Farleys, Elliotts, and some of the Gibbons family came from South Carolina. Lewis Johnson, Clement Martin, Sr., Richard Cunningham Crooke, and Edmund Tannatt came from the West Indies. From Great Britain came Alexander Wylly and John Simpson. Audley Maxwell was from Pennsylvania.

These men, and many others who enjoyed less success in the province, were attracted by land, the commodity in which Georgia was indisputably wealthy. On the first Tuesday of each month—called "Land Day" or "Land Tuesday"—the governor sat with his council giving acreages away. The system changed a bit toward the end of royal times. After a huge acquisition of Indian land in 1773—called the "Ceded Lands"—the colony began selling parcels to defray costs of the acquisition (see the maps on p. 2 and p. 30). But for about two decades previous, a petitioner might have had a hundred acres for himself and an additional fifty for each member of his family with little procedural difficulty and for nominal fees. (Slaves counted as family.) If a man could cultivate more land than this arrangement would allow him, the governor could sell him up to a thousand additional acres at one shilling for each ten. The surveyor general of the province or his deputies surveyed all plots.

Since land was the key to the colony's settlement, the government by necessity had to consider the Indians, for they claimed all lands upon which the white population proposed to settle. Indian relations lay beyond the scope of the average Georgian to influence, but the provincial government under both trustees and king was expected to enforce established policies. Georgia needed to consider most seriously the Creeks and the Cherokees, nations of such strength and propinquity that they could not be ignored. Other tribes had to be dealt with on occasion, too. To complicate matters, South Carolina had made a treaty with the Yamasees in 1715, in which that colony promised that the English would not settle south of the Savannah River. Under such circumstances colonial policy had to accommodate four considerations: (1) the authorities had to negotiate an arrangement with the Indians that would secure to Georgia settlers immediate and undisputed use of land granted by the king; (2) the overall policy of the British government needed also to be served in preventing an Indian alliance with the French and Spaniards; (3) the Indians had to be impressed by white strength so as to discourage attacks; and (4) the profitable Indian trade, competed for by South Carolinians and Georgians, had to be regulated. The tact and diplomacy of Oglethorpe secured for Georgia an early and favorable arrangement with the Indians near Savannah, giving white settlers free use of a strip of land about thirty miles wide between the Savannah and Altamaha rivers.

A pattern of fairly peaceful coexistence was also established. The colonial militia and the watch, as well as the regular troops stationed in the colony, were mustered as a matter of policy, and the conspicuous presence of a military force had its effect upon the Indians. Native warriors who came to Savannah upon official business were often processed through the ranks of military men standing at attention. Oglethorpe, shrewd as he was, used occasions of even the utmost sentimentality to impress upon the Indians the military self-sufficiency of Georgia, a self-sufficiency all the more necessary to demonstrate because it was in large part illusory. Oglethorpe in 1739 arranged the closest thing that Georgia could provide in the way of a state funeral for Tomochichi, the Indian chief who had greeted the first settlers at their arrival and who had assisted them with a treaty ceding the strip of land upon which they settled. Tomochichi was head of a small tribe of the Creek nation that lived at Yamacraw. Upon his death Oglethorpe had the body brought to Savannah, where it was borne to the center of a city square. The pallbearers were Oglethorpe, Stephens, and four military officers. As the air reverberated with discharging minute guns and volleys of fire from small arms, Tomochichi's body was laid to rest. For the occasion every man under arms who "could instantly be found" was present and firing.[39] If the Indians long recalled the respect shown their fallen leader, they also remembered the noisy and martial nature of his funeral exercises.

The return of international peace in 1763 changed the nature of the relationship between the Georgia government and the Indians, for the natives were no longer pawns in the dispute between England, France, and Spain. After 1763 the British flag waved from Canada to the tip of Florida, and Georgia had no threatening adversary closer than New Orleans. It is not clear whether Georgians perceived how much the peace had altered their position with regard to the Indians, but it had done so radically. No longer need Georgians fear that international enemies would instigate frontier raids. The local government was now free to devote its energies to acquiring more and more Indian lands. Cessions were necessary if the backcountry were to be opened,

39. *Ibid.*, IV, 428.

and the future of the colony was believed to depend upon the development of the backcountry. Among the remarkable, if morally ambiguous, accomplishments in colonial Georgia was Governor Wright's success in persuading the Indians to surrender enormous acreages voluntarily. In 1763 he secured a cession lying above Augusta as far as the Little River and running southwest to the Ogeechee River on the west (see the map of Indian cessions, following). He also secured a strip about forty miles wide on the coast between the Altamaha and the St. Marys rivers. In Oglethorpe's time the Indians had given up 1,152,000 acres, but in 1763 alone Wright secured 3,407,200 acres— or more than twice the original amount.[40] In 1766 an additional 20,000 acres were acquired, and at an Indian conference at Augusta in 1773, Wright extracted yet another 2,116,298 acres. The latter acquisition extended the colony's boundaries further up the Savannah River into the rich lands above Augusta and added large acreages in the backcountry just west of previously ceded territories.[41] To accomplish the cession of 1773 Wright had journeyed to England and had argued Georgia's need in high councils. To compensate the Indians for the territory, the British government agreed to assume the large debts they owed to white traders. The magnitude of Wright's accomplishments becomes clearer if we consider that before he became governor, white Georgians held undisputed use of only about 1,500,000 acres but that after he had finished acquiring land, another 5,500,000 had been added. The ever necessary bestowal of Indian gifts, combined with Wright's skill with both the aboriginal inhabitants and the British government, had secured the results.

Did the Indians understand what the cessions of their lands meant? In the narrow sense, they usually did; but they probably did not realize that the eventual result would be the uprooting of their homes and culture. The time for armed resistance had largely passed them by,

40. Ga. Hist. Soc., *Colls.*, III, 160. Henry Ellis, the second royal governor, was skillful in Indian relations, although he secured no large cessions of land. The first royal governor, John Reynolds, was inept at Indian affairs, as at much else.

41. *Ibid.* During the proprietorship the boundary between the settlers and the Indians was not formally marked. After the cession of 1763, however, the line was drawn, although demarcation was not completed until 1768. The boundary of lands ceded in June 1773 was set following the Augusta Conference. Demarcation of the line between the Ogeechee and Altamaha rivers was finished by Nov. 1773. Louis De Vorsey, Jr., *The Indian Boundary in the Southern Colonies, 1763–1775* (Chapel Hill, N.C., 1961), 136–180.

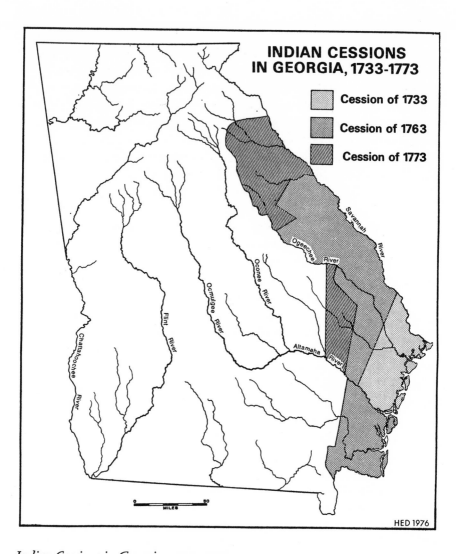

Indian Cessions in Georgia, 1733–1773.

(*Researched and developed by Gerald L. Holder; cartography by Patricia Jetmore.*)

however, at least along the seaboard. By the time Georgia was settled, the last of the great attacks launched on or near the Atlantic coastal plain was history. Virginia had not had a large assault since 1675. With the Tuscarora and Yamasee offensives, the major Indian wars had died out in South Carolina early in the eighteenth century. Still, there were instances where whites and Indians clashed savagely in colonial Georgia, particularly on the frontier and especially after 1773. Many of the Indians had not fully understood or agreed with the terms of the cession of that year, and some of them went on the warpath as a result. In the main, however, relations between the two races were reasonably peaceful, if anxiety ridden, during the years before 1773. The early tact of Oglethorpe, continued by those who came afterward, had placed matters on a workable footing. Through negotiation the provincial government secured the thing it most desired from the Indians—land.[42]

As the American Revolution drew near, Georgia enjoyed a relative prosperity based largely upon land and agriculture. It is difficult to measure the province's growth in population, for we cannot say with certainty just how much the Spanish invasion and dissatisfaction with trustee policies had reduced it in the 1740s. We do know that 2,831 white persons migrated to Georgia between 1732 and 1741, either at their own expense or at the expense of the trust. The trustees guessed that perhaps 1,400 persons remained in 1741, while their critics said that the number was no more than 500, plus 57 additional persons in Augusta.[43] Since both estimates derive from sources with self-serving arguments to advance, it is likely that the first figure is too high and the second too low. But a decade later, in 1751, the year before the trustees surrendered the charter and the year after the last of their most controversial policies had been suspended, the population may reliably

42. We should not underestimate the apprehensions that many settlers felt concerning the Indians. Queensborough and Wrightsborough, both near the frontier, were sometimes scenes of brutal encounters, and Indian relations became more strained in the years just before the Revolution. Settlers sometimes fled Queensborough and Wrightsborough in fear, but these instances of terror and loss, although deeply affecting individual lives, did not significantly affect either the history or the development of the province. *Col. Records of Ga.*, XII, 189; proceedings of the Commons House, *Ga. Gaz.*, Mar. 2, 1774.

43. Clarence L. Ver Steeg, ed., *A True and Historical Narrative of the Colony of Georgia by Pat. Tailfer and Others with Comments by the Earl of Egmont* (Athens, Ga., 1960), 135–136; affidavit 10, Ga. Hist. Soc., *Colls.*, II, 124.

be numbered at 1,900 white settlers and 400 blacks.[44] From this un-impressive level of 2,300 persons, the population increased during the next twenty-two years to 33,000. The increase was especially rapid after 1763, when the French and Indian War ended. There was no official census, but the population was about as follows:[45]

Date	Whites	Blacks	Total
1751	1,900	400	2,300
1753	2,381	1,066	3,447
1760	6,000	3,578	9,578
1766	9,900	7,800	17,700
1773	18,000	15,000	33,000

As the Revolution neared, Georgia had acquired the population of stable settlers it needed in order to prosper. The province in 1757 was very poor, and it could not yet boast ten men worth £500 each.[46] But by the end of the era, it had more than a few citizens wealthy enough to afford all the necessities and many of the comforts characteristic of a good life in the eighteenth century.

44. Extract of the "Journal of Mr. Habersham Mercht: at Savannah, in Georgia . . ." (June 11, 1751), 5, Habersham Family Papers, Perkins Library, Duke University, Durham, N.C.

45. The tabulation is compiled from *ibid.*; *Col. Records of Ga.*, XXVI, 415–416, XXXVII, 141; and Ga. Hist. Soc., *Colls.*, III, 167.

46. *Col. Records of Ga.*, XXVIII, Pt. i a, 58.

Chapter 2

Everyday Life: Part I

Nothing so characterized the buildings of trustee Georgia as their simplicity and their continual dilapidation. On March 1, 1733, Oglethorpe, who himself lived in a tent until it was in tatters, drove the first pin in the first house to be raised in Savannah.[1] The house was not beautiful, for most structures of the trustee era were designed for utility alone. In the earliest days of the colony, European culture did not extend much beyond the streets and regular squares of Savannah, and buildings were of frame construction and modest dimension. Georgians used precise terminology to describe their structures. In the first two decades, a "house" meant a frame building twenty-four feet long and sixteen feet wide; by 1737 most dwellings in Savannah were of these dimensions.[2] A "small tenement" was a frame building of less than those proportions, and a "large house" exceeded those dimensions. "Huts"—small structures made of round poles and split boards without framing—were built in quantity. If any measure of long-term usefulness was contemplated for these dwellings, Georgians built unwisely. The buildings sat upon wooden piers or palisades sunk into the earth where termites worked rapid destruction. They lasted little more than a decade, the victims of inadequate foundations and infrequent repairs.[3]

1. E. Merton Coulter, ed., *The Journal of Peter Gordon, 1732–1735* (Athens, Ga., 1963), 42.
2. *Col. Records of Ga.*, XXI, 466.
3. For a recent study, see James Wesley Stembridge, "The Settlement of Geor-

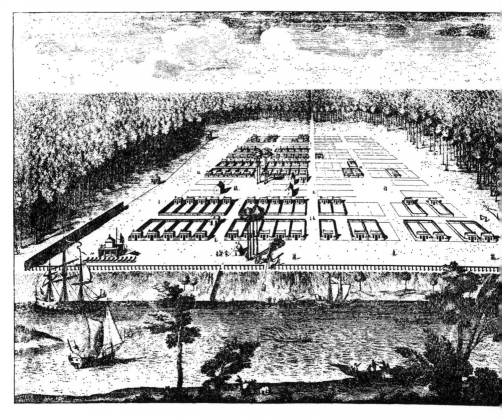

2. *A View of Savannah on March 29, 1734, by Peter Gordon.*

This early engraving showing the surveyed streets and squares of Savannah was made from a drawing done by Peter Gordon, a magistrate in the colony. A set of stairs leads up the steep bluff from the river to four trees under which Oglethorpe's tent stands.

(*Courtesy of the University of Georgia Library, Athens.*)

Some buildings not only were badly kept but were actually unsafe. A schoolmaster in Savannah moved into a little house so out of repair that toads found ready admission. He quickly vacated it after he saw two rattlesnakes coming through the door. By 1740 Savannah had 142 houses, huts, and public buildings, in addition to a jail, public store, house for receiving Indians, wharf, guardhouse, and courthouse that also served as a church.[4]

Outside Savannah, on plantations lying on or near the river, a few men of private means, including two of the trustees' principal officials, had built homes a bit better than the commonplace structures in town. Thomas Causton's house, Oxstead, and William Stephens's, Bewlie (a corruption of "Beaulieu"), were country estates that boasted construction above the town average, but it is doubtful if these dwellings were even remotely baronial.

In Savannah itself, only repeated repairs on public buildings saved them from collapse. The courthouse, built on logs like most of the town's buildings, began to sink in 1740, and immediate steps were required to save it. Further attention was necessary eighteen months later. When in 1754 John Reynolds, Georgia's first and worst royal governor, assembled his council in the old council house to discuss a site where they could meet in greater safety, the chimney at one end of the house collapsed as they conferred. Their escape was attributed to a merciful providence.[5]

South of Savannah, structures may have been better built and more carefully kept in the military town of Frederica, where relative prosperity, owing to a regimental payroll, made better construction possible. There a merchant built a large, three-story house, "which was looked on to be the best in Town, with Storehouses etc. for carrying on Trade."[6] Samuel Davison, a constable in Frederica, built a brick house in which he kept a tavern; excavations suggest that it was a substantial building.

But most Georgians in the trustee era found their personal pessimism confirmed by low property values. When DeBrahm, the sur-

gia: Town Planning and Architecture in the Colonial Period" (M.A. thesis, Georgia State University, 1971).

4. *Col. Records of Ga.*, XXVI, 59, XXXV, 304–305. The unsigned document referring to the snakes was doubtless written by schoolmaster Edward Holt.

5. *Ibid.*, XXII, Pt. ii, 470, VII, 21; Coulter, ed., *Journal of Stephens*, I, 87.

6. Coulter, ed., *Journal of Stephens*, II, 221.

veyor and engineer, arrived in Savannah as trustee influence was about to end, a house and lot sold for a few shillings. DeBrahm later reflected (with figurative if not literal truth) that for £20 sterling he might have bought nearly half of Savannah in 1751.[7] Had he done so, he would have been a rich man by the end of the colonial era, for the advent of royal rule ushered Georgians into a period when a man might prosper and where better times were reflected in increasing property values and expanding trade. Improved economic conditions, which can probably be dated from the 1750s but which had certainly arrived by the 1760s, allowed Georgians to build more substantially.

Most Georgians built in timber with some use of brick. Yellow pine, near at hand, made a lumber suitable for most buildings, while white spruce pine was preferred for floorings. The Germans at Ebenezer cut red pine and sold it in Savannah for the construction of Christ Church. So widespread was the use of lumber as opposed to brick that in 1758 it was observed that Savannah was built of lumber filled with resin.[8] Brick was locally made and was increasingly used as the era neared its end. The home of the Reverend John J. Zubly, pastor of the Independent Presbyterian Church in Savannah, was of brick, as was Jerusalem Lutheran Church at Ebenezer, but by 1762 there were still only three brick houses in Savannah. In that year Savannah was a gaily painted town of two hundred mostly wooden dwellings, some of which sported shades of blue and red. Where paint was not used, whitewash or stucco sometimes was; all helped to reflect the rays of the hot sun.[9] Georgians sometimes had the insides of their homes plastered. Wallpaper was easily bought, and men could be readily found to hang it.[10]

Since few of Georgia's earliest buildings survive, we must speak

7. DeBrahm, *History of Ga.*, 20–21.

8. *Ibid.*, 45; *Col. Records of Ga.*, XXV, 275–276; Joseph Ottolenghe to the Rev. Mr. Waring, July 12, 1758, Manuscripts of Dr. Bray's Associates, Pt. H (Library of Congress microfilm, reel 11, 355[film page]/211[orig. page]). All references are to the Library of Congress microfilm.

9. Papers Relating to the [Moravian] Lots in Savannah, Written by John Ettwein, Georgia Historical Society, Savannah (photographic copy; the original is in the Moravian Provincial Archives, Bethlehem, Pa.). Ettwein visited Savannah on Apr. 4 and 5, 1762. Jerusalem Church, begun in 1767 and completed in 1768, still stands in Effingham County, Ga., on the banks of the Savannah River and is still used for weekly Lutheran worship services (see fig. 7, in chap. 7).

10. Loewald, Starika, and Taylor, trans. and eds., "Bolzius Answers a Questionnaire," Pt. ii, *WMQ*, 3d Ser., XV (1958), 247–248; advertisement of James Bell, *Ga. Gaz.*, May 10, 1764; advertisement of Thomas Coleman, *ibid.*, Apr. 8, 1767.

cautiously concerning architecture. It is clear, however, that by 1765 the piazza, or long porch, had become commonplace in residential construction. Most Georgians built piazzas on one or more sides of their houses because of the climate; as a contemporary phrased it, the weather "must be extream hot indeed if one cant sit or walk very comfortably in these." Porches were the scene of "much conversation both sitting and walking." Henry Ellis, Georgia's first royal lieutenant governor (1757–1759) and second royal governor (1759–1760), sometimes sat on his piazza in Savannah to write his correspondence.[11]

Despite the scarcity of surviving buildings, it is possible to glimpse the insides and outsides of a few old homes. Governor Wright, a widower whose wife had drowned in 1763 while on a voyage to England, lived in Savannah's St. James's Square (see the map of Savannah on p. 71). His house was good by local standards but was probably no better than those occupied by other well-to-do Savannahians, for it seems to have been bought rather than built for him. Wright's dining room had one picture or portrait—that of King George II, who had initially sent him to Georgia—and was furnished with a sideboard, a cistern (probably for punch), two dining tables, a breakfast table, two mahogany trays, two looking glasses, and eleven chairs made and ornamented with brass nails. The fireplace had a screen and the usual utensils: dogs, shovel, tongs, fender, hearth brush, and bellows. In the governor's study was a piano, two mahogany desks (one small), two tables, three chairs, five cases of knives and forks, and a box of glasses and tea china. Despite its name, the governor's bedroom parlor contained no bed. There he took his tea and had his card games, for the room boasted a tea table, two mahogany card tables, and two gilt-frame mirrors. Governor Wright could seat seventeen guests in the parlor, and all might be warmed by a fire on winter days and nights. The governor slept in a bedroom with a fireplace, bed, oval dressing table and glass, mahogany desk, square table, and six chairs, three of them with red bottoms. Two other bed chambers were styled the "low bedroom" and the "lady's room," and yet another bed was set up in a large closet, where the governor shelved his library. The low bedroom was prob-

11. John Bartram, "Diary of a Journey Through the Carolinas, Georgia, and Florida from July 1, 1765, to April 10, 1766," ed. Francis Harper, American Philosophical Society, *Transactions*, N.S., XXXIII, Pt. i (1942), 30; *The London Magazine: Or, Gentleman's Monthly Intelligencer*, XXVIII (1759), 371. Frederick Doveton Nichols, in *The Early Architecture of Georgia* (Chapel Hill, N.C., 1957), has brought together surviving evidence on Georgia's colonial structures.

ably the principal guest chamber; it was the most splendidly furnished. Besides fireplace equipment, it had a feather bed and mattress, clothespress (cupboard), night chair and washstand of mahogany, dressing table and glass, seven chairs with brass nails, and five carpets—one Turkish, two Wiltons, and two that were probably throw rugs for the bedside. The pantry was ample, and the governor kept a sufficient kitchen and cellar; all were the demesne of the English butler.[12]

For another dwelling, we should look at the combination home and shop of Abraham Minis. Minis was a Savannah merchant and a member of the colony's Jewish community. He had arrived in Georgia in 1733 with a wife and two children and at his death in 1757 left a wife and seven living children. In 1736 he had set up a shop and tavern on one of Savannah's main streets, and twenty-one years later his dwelling and business house had five rooms, a garret, and a kitchen. One of the rooms was his countinghouse, another was his shop. Much of the establishment was given over to tavern use, and beds were placed throughout the house. In eighteenth-century taverns a guest usually rented a bed or a part of a bed rather than an entire room. One of the rooms Minis called the "new room," suggesting that the house might earlier have been smaller than it was in 1757. Every room, including the garret and kitchen, was cluttered. The new room contained two tables, a bed, a bedstead with white curtains, two pillows, a blanket and quilt, a clothespress and looking glass, and a pair of iron dogs for the fireplace. The middle room had a looking glass, two tables, and a pair of fire dogs. In a small area joining the middle room was a bed with bolster, pillow, blanket, quilt, and table. The garret held a desk, couch, two small beds, and a box bedstead. Minis set up additional beds in both his shop and countinghouse. The shop had a bed with bolster, blanket, quilt, two pillows, two tables, and a looking glass; the countinghouse held a bed with bolster, blanket, quilt, two pillows, a small looking glass, and a table, which was probably long, as there were thirteen chairs in the room.

The inventory of kitchen utensils suggests much about colonial cooking, even though the Minis kitchen, often obliged to provide food

---

12. Miscellaneous Bonds Book Y–2, 502–504, Department of Archives and History, Atlanta, Ga. From 1772 to 1776 Wright's English butler was John Martindale. Statement of Sir James Wright on behalf of John Martindale, Sept. 14, 1776, Georgia Loyalist Claims, A.O. 13/36, Public Record Office (microfilm at Dept. of Archives and Hist., Atlanta, Ga.).

for guests, was doubtless better equipped than most. There was a pair of dogs for the fire, a bellows, a tack (hanging shelf), four flatirons, a gridiron, an iron dripping pan, a split, tongs, frying pan, two iron skillets, two pothooks, three iron pots, two iron pans, two brass kettles, a tin fish kettle, two tea kettles, two coffeepots, a copper gallon pot, a brass mortar, two brass lamps, a warming pan, seven candlesticks, three pairs of iron candle snuffers, two trivets, a flour box, a case of bottles, five pewter candle makers, and a pewter cistern and basin. At the kitchen table, where presumably both family and guests ate, were two benches and four stools. There were six tablecloths. The kitchen could be set up with three cots and transformed into a bedroom.[13]

Georgia homes more often resembled the crowded residence-business establishment of the Minis family than the spacious home of Governor Wright. Beds were often put in the garret under the roof due to a shortage of bedroom space on the floors below. It may be that the popularity of porches lay not only in their coolness but in the escape they afforded from crowded interiors. In 1765 Dr. Lewis Johnson, apothecary, merchant, councillor, and later royal treasurer, offered a house for sale or lease near the Savannah riverfront that had served him as both family dwelling and business establishment. Several out-buildings went with the house, according to the advertisement: "The dwelling-house contains a large store well fitted for dry goods, four fire rooms, and three rooms without fire places, a large brick cellar for the use of the store, and a smaller one for the use of the family. Amongst the out-buildings there are two good lodging rooms with fire places, a kitchen, back-store, wash-house, stable, chair-house, pigeon-house, etc. etc. and a good well in the yard."[14] Outbuildings were commonly used in royal Georgia, for they segregated the fire hazards posed by kitchens and washhouses, as well as affording relief from crowding.

Georgians by the 1760s were a distance removed from the "huts," "houses," "large houses," and "small tenements" of trustee times. Even the word "tenement" no longer necessarily meant a small frame house. A tenement in royal Georgia could be a town dwelling suitable for a member of the council.[15] Private dwellings were becoming trim and

13. Estate of Abraham Minis, June 30, 1757, Inventory Book F, 49–51, Dept. of Archives and Hist., Atlanta, Ga.

14. Advertisement of Lewis Johnson, *Ga. Gaz.*, July 4, 1765.

15. Advertisement of Heriot Crooke, *ibid.*, Oct. 22, 1766.

handsome. James Habersham, who had come to the colony as a school-master in 1738 but who subsequently became temporal manager of Bethesda orphanage, secretary of the province, a pioneering merchant and planter, president of the council, and in the 1770s acting royal governor, set something of the style in town architecture. In 1765 he ceased living regularly at his plantation, named Silk Hope, and spent between £400 and £500 on a new home on Johnson Square that soon became a landmark.[16] The house was neat but not gaudy. In the years following, other Georgians built homes finer than Habersham's. The home of Captain William Lyford, the colony's navigational pilot who lived on Cockspur Island in the river just below Savannah, was burned by some of his slaves in 1774; the loss, including furniture and papers, was about £2,000.[17] Lieutenant Governor John Graham, a wealthy merchant-planter with extensive estates, was attempting to build a fine home at Mulberry Grove as the Revolution began. This residence, valued at £1,250, was subsequently taken from him and awarded to General Nathanael Greene as a reward for patriotic services. General Greene found the house completed, or nearly so, and pronounced the main structure magnificent, adding: "We have a coach-house and stables, a large out-kitchen, and a poultry-house nearly fifty feet long, and twenty wide, parted for different kinds of poultry, with a pigeon-house on the top, which will contain not less than a thousand pigeons. Besides these, there are several other buildings convenient for a family, and among the rest, a fine smoke-house. The garden is in ruins, but there are still a great variety of shrubs and flowers in it."[18]

In the last years of trustee control, Georgia was "still forests, and small plantations" had "been established only here and there."[19] Yet the movement to the countryside was about to begin and can be dated from about 1754. A settler at that time declared that the spirit of the colony had previously been "unsettled, and the People in it no way fixd either in their Determinations to settle in Town or Country."

16. Ga. Hist. Soc., *Colls.*, VI, 39; advertisement of Daniel Ocain, *Ga. Gaz.*, June 11, 1766.

17. *Ga. Gaz.*, Sept. 14, 1774.

18. Memorial of Anthony Stokes and James Robertson on behalf of John Graham, June 12, 1783, Ga. Loyalist Claims, A.O. 13/106; William Johnson, *Sketches of the Life and Correspondence of Nathanael Greene . . .*, II (Charleston, S.C., 1822), 418–419.

19. Loewald, Starika, and Taylor, trans. and eds., "Bolzius Answers a Question-naire," Pt. i, *WMQ*, 3d Ser., XIV (1957), 246.

But with the arrival of royal government, "many Families are withdrawn into the Country to their Plantations."[20] Georgians believed that prudence would help them master the forests and that after two or three years, a person could live economically on his country property. They knew how a man should proceed: "At first he ought to build his house as poorly as will barely preserve his health. Industrious people not only plant in the field, but after they have built and planted the minimum they show their Negroes and servants how to saw boards, staves, and shingles, also how to make hoops for barrels and household lumber, which is very lucrative.... He must not get involved in buying Negroes and extensive buildings but must always distinguish between the necessary and the useful, and choose the former."[21]

The opening of the backcountry required energy and self-reliance. The Reverend John Martin Bolzius of Ebenezer said that the Germans who came to Georgia from the cities of Europe fretted at first because they could not buy fresh meat, bread, and butter except at Savannah and Charleston; only on occasion were such items for sale at Ebenezer. Necessity usually forced them to satisfy their own needs. Even the most prosperous farmers patterned themselves after Abraham and the patriarchs, who, when they wanted meat, "slaughtered and also baked cake or a kind of bread for arriving friends, but normally were satisfied for their daily necessities with that which their household yielded." Planters slaughtered their own oxen and pigs in the fall and winter when the cold helped preserve the meat. They ate domesticated animals—chickens, geese, ducks, sheep, lambs, and calves—and wild game from the forest. These settlers baked on boards at the hearth. If they could not buy flour from a mill, they did without or baked cakes made from Indian corn or wheat. "Well-managed households ... have at least milk year in and year out, even if in winter they cannot often make fresh butter. In summer they salt away some of it, or make lard from it so as to eat it in winter."[22]

The cessions of Indian lands that Governor Wright arranged in 1763 and 1773, in combination with the colony's liberal land policy, guaranteed that a white settler could have his own farm if he were will-

20. Ottolenghe to Associates of Dr. Bray, Nov. 18, 1754, MSS of Dr. Bray's Associates, Pt. H (L.C. reel 11, 335/222).

21. Loewald, Starika, and Taylor, trans. and eds., "Bolzius Answers a Questionnaire," Pt. i, *WMQ*, 3d Ser., XIV (1957), 244–245.

22. *Ibid.*, 229.

ing to take it where lands were available. Some wealthy men acquired property in all parts of the province. Anthony Stokes, who arrived in Georgia in 1769 and served as chief justice until the end of colonial times, embarked upon a course of land acquisition and finally owned about 4,500 acres of land in four parishes. He had never seen some of his property, even though it lay within thirty miles of Savannah.[23] John Graham, who entered the province in 1753 from Scotland, and who later served as lieutenant governor after a long career of public service, made a substantial fortune as an importer and exporter and acquired 26,578¼ acres in several locations.[24] Governor Wright was in possession of eleven plantations as the Revolution began, three of them near Savannah.[25]

The spectacular acquisitions of the rich, however, should not overshadow the fact that a poor man could settle in the backcountry with little or no wealth. He could go as his own man if he had a bit of capital. If he had none, he could go out as an overseer for a plantation owner, as a worker or superintendent at one of many sawmills, or as a blacksmith, cooper, or carpenter in a backcountry settlement.[26] In 1774 a government official traveling downriver from Purrysburg, South Carolina, to Savannah, passed the homes of numerous farmers on the river banks. Some had located high up on bluffs, and others had built on low land, where their homes were surrounded by water when the river overflowed.[27] The following year a South Carolinian called at such a farm and found it enclosed by palisades. "On one side you have a rough and agreeable view of the river, and the lands of South Carolina; on the other you have a broken prospect of woods and fields. The building is tolerably good, and the people kind."[28] Still another visitor discovered modesty and kindness near Ebenezer in the small home of the Reverend Christian Rabenhorst, who during the 1770s

23. Advertisement of Anthony Stokes, *Ga. Gaz.*, Jan. 5, 1774.

24. Misc. Bonds Book KK–2, 286–297.

25. Misc. Bonds Book Y–2, 511–514.

26. See the advertisement for a blacksmith to bring his family to the Briar Creek area. *Ga. Gaz.*, Dec. 23, 1767.

27. Hugh Finlay, *Journal kept by Hugh Finlay, Surveyor of the Post Roads on the Continent of North America, during his Survey of the Post Offices between Falmouth and Casco Bay, in the Province of Massachusetts, and Savannah, in Georgia; begun the 13th Septr. 1773 and ended 26th June 1774* (Brooklyn, 1867), 54.

28. R. W. Gibbes, *Documentary History of the American Revolution: Consisting of Letters and Papers Relating to the Contest for Liberty, Chiefly in South Carolina...* (Columbia, S.C., 1853; New York, 1855–1857), I, 237.

was one of Georgia's two Lutheran ministers. "I had imagined from various descriptions of this preacher's plantation that I would find a large, costly residence or palace, but found instead a little house made of wood, set on four blocks several feet above the sandy ground, with a cramped sitting room and bedroom on the first floor, under which the geese, etc. have their abode. They very happily vacated their bedroom and went to sleep in the upper floor under the roof." The same visitor found no palaces at Ebenezer and feared that the buildings might fall in a vigorous windstorm.[29]

We have a rather complete description of a substantial place near Augusta, based on an advertisement for its sale in 1769. The owner of the property did not insist upon labeling it a plantation and sometimes called it a farm. The land measured about 500 acres, of which 250 were cleared and under fence, with the remainder in oak and hickory trees. A purchaser would find a home freshly painted, in which there were two chambers, a dining room and hall, four shed rooms, and three fireplaces. Nearby was a store thirty feet by twenty feet, and a kitchen of the same size. A smokehouse, meat house, and milk house were of featheredged boards underpinned by brick. The barn measured forty feet by twenty-four feet and was floored with two-inch planks. There was a poultry house, and another house under the same roof could hold a wagon, cart, and riding chair. The stable would accommodate six or eight horses. There were three corn houses and a house set apart for the overseer. Nearby was a one-acre garden protected by a paling fence and an eight-acre orchard with 1,100 peach, apple, white mulberry, and plum trees, from which brandy, cider, and silk could be made. A field of 50 acres lay on one side of a lagoon; 35 acres lay on the other. Two pumps rendered them useful for raising indigo. Also for sale were thirty head of cattle, seventy head of sheep, and a small stock of hogs. In addition thirty slaves could be purchased, including some of especial value—a driver to help supervise the other blacks, a bricklayer, two sawyers, and seventeen slaves good at either field or boat work. The remainder were children. It was said that a new owner, using water transportation, could make 15 percent on his money by selling corn and pork alone, both of which were in demand in Savannah. Allowing for exaggeration regarding profits, this pros-

29. Henry Melchior Muhlenberg, *The Journals of Henry Melchior Muhlenberg*, trans. Theodore G. Tappert and John W. Doberstein (Philadelphia, 1942–1958), II, 607, 664.

pective seller had described a plantation that, while not elegant, was neat and serviceable. It was probably one of the better places in its neighborhood.[30]

One key to the value of property was its accessibility to a stream that could take produce to market—in the above case, the Savannah River. Roads existed, but Georgians realized that "the rivers are their roads, on which they travel very comfortably and cheaply in boats, and on which one or two people can transport several hundred weight at a time."[31] Boats could enter small creeks and streams almost as easily as big ones. Little vessels laden with goods for the Indian trade, for example, commonly drew three or four feet of water.[32] Farmers often secured a double benefit by locating near flowing streams, for not only was transportation simplified but fertile lands frequently lay adjacent. Rice, corn, and heavy produce had to be grown near water carriage; otherwise the expense of delivering the harvest to market would have been "such as the Commodities will not bear."[33] DeBrahm exaggerated when he said that the cheapness and convenience of water transportation put land carriage almost out of use, but he was not wrong to emphasize the importance of boats to the well-being of the colony.[34]

The "piragua," a long, flat-bottomed boat, was the workhorse of vessels, carrying from twenty to thirty-five tons. It might have two masts with sails and a forecastle or cabin. The remainder of the boat was open without a deck. Piraguas with masts could spread their sails, but all were equipped with oars. The piragua had as many versions of its name as it had variations in its construction: pirogue, periagua, pettiagua, periawgoe, pirague, and pettiauger all appear in the records. It could operate in coastal waters as well as on rivers and creeks. "Droghers," locally called "droggers," were slow and clumsy coastal craft that were also frequently in and out of Georgia's rivers carrying heavy produce to market.

Smaller boats, operated by as few as two oars or by as many as ten,

30. Unsigned advertisement, *Ga. Gaz.*, Mar. 22, 1769.

31. Loewald, Starika, and Taylor, trans. and eds., "Bolzius Answers a Questionnaire," Pt. i, *WMQ*, 3d Ser., XIV (1957), 232.

32. Records in the British Public Record Office Relating to South Carolina (transcripts), XVIII, 137–138, Department of Archives and History, Columbia, S.C.

33. James Habersham to John Martin Bolzius, Sept. 25, 1747, Georgia Miscellaneous Collection, 1732–1796, Force Manuscripts, Library of Congress.

34. DeBrahm, *History of Ga.*, 49.

moved through the waters with freight and people. Many little vessels had awnings to protect their passengers from sun and rain. After 1760 Wright was a familiar sight on Georgia's streams, traveling with his party on the deck of the provincial scout boat shaded by an awning. Canoes moved people quickly from one point to another. In Savannah in 1764, Adrian Loyer, better known as a clocksmith and silversmith, hired canoes out by the day with blacks to row them.[35] For exceptionally heavy freight, such as lumber, flatboats were equipped with masts and sails. Samuel Douglass and Company of Savannah offered such a boat for sale in 1768. It was made of live oak and could carry about a hundred thousand shingles at once.[36]

The most useful stream in Georgia was the Savannah River, which was navigable from the ocean at Tybee up to Augusta and a little beyond. When the water was low, boats might be delayed in reaching their destinations, but year after year the river was usually reliable as a highway. A vessel carrying some ten tons of cargo, six sailors, and a steersman could leave Augusta and by steady progress be downstream in Savannah in four or five days, even though the river had so many bends that those who knew it reckoned the water distance from Augusta to Savannah at 250 miles (the land distance was only 130). The same boat required fifteen days to travel the more difficult upstream route from Savannah to Augusta.[37] The tide, when coming in, would help for 18 miles above Savannah, but from there on, for the next 6 miles, the vessel needed oars and vigorous rowing to reach Purrysburg, South Carolina. From Purrysburg to Augusta the river had fewer bends, and boats could spread their sails to supplement the rowing when the winds were right. Small craft carrying people but not cargo could move rapidly. In 1774 Hugh Finlay, a postal official on an inspection tour, boarded a wooden canoe in Purrysburg and arrived in Savannah (24 miles downstream) four and a half hours later, helped by the outgoing tide and the rowing of three blacks.[38]

Masters of boats preferred to sail close to the banks, where the current was weak. However, special hazards lay near the shore. As the backcountry opened, farmers clearing lands cut trees and toppled them

35. Advertisement of Adrian Loyer, *Ga. Gaz.*, Aug. 30, 1764.
36. Advertisement of Samuel Douglass and Company, *ibid.*, Sept. 21, 1768.
37. John Bartram, "Diary of a Journey," ed. Harper, Am. Phil. Soc., *Trans.*, N.S., XXXIII, Pt. i (1942), 28.
38. Finlay, *Journal*, 54.

into the water. When the river was low, logs sometimes wrecked vessels and spilled their cargoes.[39]

Farmers found the value of their lands enhanced when boats, big or little, could put in at the farm or at some place nearby. John and William Maxwell, who owned well-developed property in St. Philip Parish, advertised that "any vessel that can come over our bar may load with safety within 60 yards of the door."[40] Francis Arthur, who before his death in 1769 was a land trader, offered property either directly on river or creek landings, or situated two to seven miles away. He generally specified the distance between the farm and navigable water.[41] A stream need not be pretentious to be useful: Collins Creek on the south side of the Great Ogeechee River was navigable enough to be valuable when land there came up for sale.[42] Sometimes, though, a stream proved a disappointment. The Salzburgers moved their first settlement, Old Ebenezer, from the banks of a perfidious creek to a fine bluff on the Savannah River. The creek from which they moved ran a serpentine course, and its flow of water varied from swollen in wet times to shallow in dry. Overland, Old Ebenezer was only six miles from the Savannah, but by way of the creek, it was not less than twenty-five.[43] Provisions sent from Savannah sometimes had to be taken from a piragua in mid-journey and loaded into smaller boats for delivery at the Old Ebenezer landing, thus adding to the expense and intolerable inconvenience of maintaining the original settlement.

The Salzburgers of Old Ebenezer, situated as they were on the banks of an undependable stream, were among the first Georgians to value roads. Despite the erroneous assertion of DeBrahm that land carriage was almost unknown, roads were essential, because water transportation did not meet every need. Settlers in St. Paul Parish near Augusta who did not live directly on the Savannah River complained that they had "no convenient way of conveying their Heavy Produce but by carrying it in Wagons to some Landing on Savannah River where it may be taken off by Boats." They petitioned for a decent road from their area to the river "Opposite to the Boat Landing of Le Roy Hammonds and Company on the Carolina side being the upper-

39. Urlsperger, ed., *Ausführliche Nachrichten*, III, 573–574.

40. Advertisement of John and William Maxwell, *Ga. Gaz.*, Sept. 29, 1763.

41. Advertisement of Francis Arthur, *ibid.*, Sept. 29, 1763.

42. Unsigned advertisement, *ibid.*, Sept. 12, 1765.

43. P. A. Strobel, *The Salzburgers and Their Descendants* (Athens, Ga., 1953 [orig. publ. Baltimore, 1855]), 87.

most place where Boats can pass of any considerable Burthen."[44]

The earliest roads in Georgia were paths marked by blazes struck on the sides of trees. Many followed old Indian trails. The necessity to rely on these paths and the lack of good roads were trials. "The want of Roads is grievously complained of by almost every Man here," John Brownfield, a minor official, wrote in Savannah in 1737. "Several People are obliged to go to their Lotts thro' Swamps up to the middle in Water: which not only prevents their bringing any Crop home; but is the Cause that Men get violent Illnesses in Winter Time by being wet and cold as they pass through these deep Swamps." Corn that the trustees had purchased for the Savannah magazine rotted in the fields because it could not be brought to town.[45] As a result of these difficulties, the trustees by the early 1740s ordered a trail struck from Savannah up to Augusta and another cut from Savannah down to Darien, "so that droves of Cattle past it from one town to tother."[46] These roads sufficed for men on horseback, and where bridges were constructed— as they were outside Savannah and between Abercorn and Ebenezer —a cart or a wagon could pass too. When a road was run from Savannah to the Bethesda Orphan House, a distance of twelve miles, it traversed ten bridges, a remarkable phenomenon in Georgia in the early 1740s. Even ten years later there were few roads laid out and engineered.

The royal government faced the problem of roads squarely. The trust had had no strictly enforced policy regarding roads and riding paths. In 1755, however, the royal government gave the colony its first general law on the subject, some years after most of the other colonies had such regulations. The law required each public road to be twenty-four feet wide. Trees along the way were to be left standing, and any person caught cutting one down within ten feet of the roadway was to forfeit twenty shillings.[47] The tree-lined roadways envisioned by royal Georgians were actually built according to the planners' intentions, at least in places. On the route from Midway to Fort Barrington in the 1770s, a traveler found the road straight, spacious, and in excellent repair, "generally bordered on each side with a light grove ... all planted by nature, and left standing, by the virtuous inhabitants,

44. *Col. Records of Ga.*, XV, 429.
45. *Ibid.*, XXI, 470.
46. Ver Steeg, ed., *True and Historical Narrative*, 77–78.
47. *Col. Records of Ga.*, XVIII, 96–97.

to shade the road and perfume the sultry air."[48] It was intended that the roads be sufficiently broad to accommodate any horse-drawn vehicle. In the half decade before the Revolution, they were being widened from twenty-four to thirty-three feet, with a maximum of thirty-six authorized by law.[49]

Savannah was joined to distant parts by a usable road network in late royal times. To the north and west one could pass with ease through Ebenezer and on to Augusta. Toward the south a good road ran to a ferry on the Ogeechee River. It forked several miles beyond the ferry, with one branch going to Fort Barrington and the other to Darien. There were also good roads from Savannah to Queensborough and from Savannah to Fort Argyle. These arteries were joined by lesser paths and private lanes, often called cart roads, which forked off to homes and farms. As the backcountry became better settled, travelers saw many people as they passed along and received freely given help or hospitality, for "the many Plantations, and Settlements on these Roads mak[e] travelling very convenient, and easy for Man, Horse, and Carriages."[50]

The roads were often sandy, and sand was hard on horses, tiring them quickly.[51] Mud occasionally stopped vehicular traffic altogether. "It seems as if heaven and earth were combin'd against us," wrote Jonathan Cochran in 1775 from the Midway district, "for we have such an inundation of Rain and Water, that it is impossible to Cart." Cochran, a substantial planter and slaveholder and an occasional member of the assembly who once resigned from the lower house in order to give closer attention to his private affairs, noted with dismay that it had been raining two or three times a day for several weeks. He expected "the Roads wou'd Dry in some measure, and intended to get the assistance of my neighbours Carts and oxen to hurry down the Rice as fast as Possible, but can see no probability of it. My rolling Path is now impassible for any Carriage."[52]

The upkeep of public roads was a communal duty. All males between the ages of sixteen and sixty were liable for six days of repair work each year on the roads serving their homes and areas. Many

48. William Bartram, Travels, 10.
49. Col. Records of Ga., XIX, Pt. i, 280; DeBrahm, History of Ga., 49.
50. DeBrahm, History of Ga., 49.
51. Muhlenberg, Journals, II, 652.
52. Jonathan Cochran to Edward Telfair, June 20, 1775, Edward Telfair Papers, Perkins Lib., Duke Univ., Durham, N.C.

Georgians found this service obnoxious. There were instances when the commissioners charged with keeping the roads up did nothing and the work went undone. People liable for duty who defaulted had their names posted as violators subject to fine.[53] When in 1758 the Anglican church was being established, the road labor that the province demanded was cited as one reason why the church should collect only £30 sterling instead of £90 as the maximum vestry tax per parish. The colony, it was argued, already demanded much in "Labor and Taxes."[54]

Slaves and free blacks as well as white men were enrolled for road work. In 1758 a catechist who was teaching slaves to read, write, and follow the Christian religion reported that attendance at his classes was slight, since his students were doing their public duty.[55] William Gibbons, Jr., a planter and road commissioner, kept a sheet enumerating all the slaves liable to work on Newington Road, the lower part of the route from Savannah to Queensborough. This list gives the names of owners at the heads of columns and the names of their male slaves underneath. Slaves who were sick were so noted, and one black was shown to be lame.[56] Apparently gangs of assembled slaves made the white population nervous, for each white man was required to arrive for his service armed with a weapon and enough ammunition to fire twelve times.[57]

Roads often received unfavorable notice from grand juries, which made presentments twice each year, in June and December. The juries, upon receiving complaints of roads in bad repair or of work poorly done, presented the erring commissioners with a grievance. The presentment in theory was supposed to pressure the commissioners to amend faults or defaults.[58]

When a man or a woman wished to take a journey, horseback was the most common, and a relatively inexpensive, means of transporta-

53. *Col. Records of Ga.*, XII, 213–214; *Ga. Gaz.*, Jan. 18 and Aug. 30, 1769, Sept. 14, 1774.

54. Unsigned letter to the archbishop of Canterbury, read in committee Jan. 15, 1759, S.P.G. Papers, Ser. C, Pkg. 1, Pt. ii (Library of Congress microfilm, reel 2, 21).

55. Ottolenghe to Waring, July 12, 1758, MSS of Dr. Bray's Associates, Pt. H (L.C. reel 11, 335/207).

56. "A Return of all the Slaves liable to Work on the Newington Road" (ca. 1770s), William Gibbons, Jr., Papers, Perkins Lib., Duke Univ., Durham, N.C.

57. *Col. Records of Ga.*, XVIII, 732.

58. See the grand jury presentments, *Ga. Gaz.*, June 29, 1774, and June 21, 1775.

tion.[59] A person could buy a good riding horse for £4 or £5, "as long as one concentrates on necessity and not on show."[60] A more comfortable way to travel was in a riding chair, a buggy that usually carried one person but sometimes carried two. Chairs were common all over the colony, and we have an account of two meeting on a road outside Savannah in the 1760s. In one was Gibbons, who was going into town. In the other was Joseph Ottolenghe, formerly a catechist but at this time a member of the assembly. They paused to greet each other, but Ottolenghe had to move along quickly because he had a "young Horse in the Chair that would not Stop."[61] Phaetons, carriages, chaises, and chariots were also seen on the roads but were not nearly so common as chairs.

Both farmers and businessmen used carts and wagons as work vehicles. Carts were small and light; wagons were of many sizes. Heavy wagons like those used to haul lumber were drawn by four or more horses.[62] In 1774 a German wagoner who lived near Ebenezer decided that the upkeep of the road to Savannah was poorer than he had a right to expect, and he fearlessly denounced the commissioners responsible. The wagoner, Frederick Vansluckett, one of five or six men around Ebenezer who collected provisions and sold them in town, invited the commissioners to come and look at conditions for themselves; then "there will need no further application in my own." Despite Vansluckett's complaint, he did not suggest that the road was impassable. Using a wagon drawn by four horses, he regularly conducted his business over it, supplying produce for the tables of such gentlemen as would not now assist him, and making deliveries "in the dead of night, winter or summer, hail, rain, or shine, . . . at the risk of life, property and health."[63] His rather rhetorical complaint described roads as they really were in royal Georgia—sometimes badly kept, occasionally unpleasant to ride upon, but usually passable.

Roads were also reasonably safe from highwaymen, although instances where travelers were abused attracted public attention when-

59. Loewald, Starika, and Taylor, trans. and eds., "Bolzius Answers a Questionnaire," Pt. ii, *WMQ*, 3d Ser., XV (1958), 250.

60. *Ibid.*, Pt. i, XIV (1957), 232–233.

61. "A Memorandum of Agreement between Joseph Ottolenghe Esq and Willm. Gibbons as near as Willm. Gibbons could Recolect" (ca. 1760s), William Gibbons, Jr., Papers.

62. Advertisement of J. Bowman, *Ga. Gaz.*, May 11, 1774.

63. Letter of Frederick Vansluckett, *ibid.*, Oct. 5, 1774.

ever they occurred.[64] Even so, in 1775 a South Carolinian warm with the spirit of Revolution took a nap in his carriage on the king's highway between Savannah and Briar Creek. That he awoke undisturbed a little later proved that he had been safe from robbers. But he was not so sure that, in using the road, he was safe from the king. "I hope his Majesty will not be persuaded to get an Act of Parliament passed to constitute this treason," he said somewhat archly.[65]

Georgia's system of roads required bridges for small streams and ferries for large ones. Under the trustees, the president of the province and his board of assistants authorized ferries upon petition of potential users.[66] Under royal rule, the assembly authorized them as they seemed needed. Ferries in the royal period were usually leased for five years, and the ferry operators agreed to follow regulations laid down by the assembly. They were given an approved schedule of charges, including fees for every foot passenger, for every person and horse, for every wheeled carriage, and for livestock. Rates were posted at each ferry-house. Ferries operated from Ebenezer on the Savannah River to the bluff opposite on the Carolina side; from the center of Augusta to the Carolina bank; and over the Altamaha River at Fort Barrington. There were two ferries at Briar Creek, one at Mill Town, and another at the public road. The Great Ogeechee River was served by a ferry at Pine Bluff. The assembly required that those who leased ferries keep boats large enough to carry five horses at once and that they have servants or slaves sufficient to operate night and day.[67] Zubly set up a private ferry for public use at Middlesex on the Savannah River to improve land communications between Charleston and Savannah and to make a little money. Zubly's ferry lay just below Purrysburg. A traveler from Charleston could leave the public road three miles before it reached Purrysburg, go the short distance to Zubly's ferry, cross the river, and enter the public road from Ebenezer to Savannah twenty-two miles from the capital.[68]

Land transportation to Charleston was much used, but water con-

64. E.g., see *Ga. Gaz.*, July 28 and Aug. 4, 1763. A man had been attacked coming from a ferry, and Gov. Wright ordered a patrol of the area.

65. Gibbes, *Documentary History of the Revolution*, I, 237.

66. See *Col. Records of Ga.*, VI, 314, for a typical action by the president and his assistants. The action pertains to the Augusta ferry, which was not satisfying its customers.

67. *Ibid.*, XIX, Pt. i, 5.

68. *South-Carolina Gazette; And Country Journal* (Charleston), July 25, 1769.

veyance to South Carolina and other places outside Georgia was essential. The ocean was a mighty highway that Georgians valued and used. Boat passage from Georgia to South Carolina was easy to obtain and was a necessary link, particularly during proprietary times when Georgia's economic life was closely bound to its neighbor's. Throughout Georgia's first two decades, boats with skins from the Indian trade departed regularly from Augusta and passed down the river without stopping at Savannah. They moved out along the coast and up to Charleston with their cargoes. Savannah was home to virtually no locally owned vessels, and merchandise was almost always sent from Europe to South Carolina, where it was transshipped to Georgia.

Yet Savannah was endowed by nature to be an important port. At Tybee, where the river entered the ocean, there was fifteen feet of water at low tide and twenty-two at high. Ships of four hundred tons could cross the bar and enter smooth water. There was enough protected water to shelter four hundred vessels at once.[69] One of Oglethorpe's first and most useful projects was the lighthouse at Tybee, a ninety-foot structure of the best pine, set upon cedar piles with brick work about the bottom. The light was a beacon for ships at sea as well as a marker for people of the surrounding lowlands.[70] At one point Oglethorpe inspected the construction and, angered by unsatisfactory progress, imprisoned the man in charge and threatened to hang him.[71] Tybee Light, thus sped to completion, saved many vessels, but like most public structures of the pre-Revolutionary era, it was always on the verge of collapse. The first lighthouse blew down in a storm. Its replacement, built in 1741 and 1742, was likewise in danger of falling into the water.

The Savannah River itself proved a disappointment. It was forever forming or shifting sandbars, or mudbars, and in 1750 the river pilot, weary of running vessels aground while moving them down to the sea, declined to pilot any more vessels drawing more than ten feet of water.[72] The practice began of partially loading ships at Savannah, then moving them down the river to Cockspur Island, where additional cargo was taken on. Even ships loaded in stages sometimes grounded before reaching open water.

69. Ga. Hist. Soc., *Colls.*, I, 175.
70. *Ibid.*, 90.
71. *Col. Records of Ga.*, XXI, 116–117.
72. *Ibid.*, XXVI, 137.

The real dilemma over water transport in trustee Georgia, however, was not the inability of vessels to clear port satisfactorily but their failure to come in significant numbers. "No ships as yet come directly to this colony for freight," said Bolzius in 1751. "The products of this colony are shipped either from Port Royal (50 English miles distant from Savannah) or Charlestown. . . . We hope when the local surplus increases and more European goods are used here that ships will come directly to Savannah, as one did a year ago." [73] In the 1740s, if Georgia farmers had a surplus of stock or corn, or if they had cut a little lumber, they could not find an exporter for it. "The reason is obvious, we want some leading Staple Commodities to induce persons to send Vessels to us," said James Habersham. [74] Habersham and his business partner, Francis Harris, opened a Savannah mercantile house in 1744, when Georgia merchants still looked to their South Carolina connections to buy and sell for them. Habersham and Harris were far from being Georgia's first merchants, but they were doubtless the first to be resoundingly successful. In 1749 they undertook a risky and symbolic venture that weakened Charleston's hold on Savannah. They commissioned an English connection to charter a small ship loaded with British goods to come directly to Savannah. It was packed for a return voyage with rice, deerskins, staves, and other salable items. "This we believe is the first Ship ever charter'd to this Colony with a Design to be loaded with its produce for England." However, Habersham expressed doubts that a shipload of Georgia goods could be found for the return voyage but promised that "if we can't get loading enough here we purpose to procure what may be wanted from our Neighbours in Carolina." [75]

Habersham and Harris, Georgia's first merchants in direct foreign trade, marked a path that made them wealthy and that others followed. For as they began their new venture, the trustees were about to set aside the old land policies and the prohibition against slavery. Georgia would shortly have the salable commodity it needed to support an independent trade. Rice became the staple of commerce that brought ships in large numbers to Savannah (and later to Sunbury), that caused the waterfronts of the two towns to develop, and that led some

73. Loewald, Starika, and Taylor, trans. and eds., "Bolzius Answers a Questionnaire," Pt. ii, *WMQ*, 3d Ser., XV (1958), 232.
74. Habersham to Bolzius, Sept. 25, 1747, Ga. Misc. Coll., Force MSS.
75. *Col. Records of Ga.*, XXV, 390–391.

Georgians to buy or build their own ships, making Savannah a home port.[76]

As agriculture increasingly prospered in the 1760s and 1770s, the riverfronts at Savannah and Sunbury thickened with the masts of sailing vessels. In 1761 Savannah had loaded only 42 ships for the sea trade; four years later, 153 were loaded and packed.[77] The Stamp Act crisis of 1765 stranded 60 vessels in Savannah harbor, detaining them because there was no stamped paper upon which to issue sailing permits. When the stamps at length arrived, it was agreed almost by unanimous consent to sell enough paper to allow the vessels to clear port. But no stamp was ever sold for any other purpose. Georgians who had lived without trade during the proprietorship thus demonstrated their unwillingness to sacrifice commerce simply on a matter of principle.

The ocean was the highway that bound men as well as commodities to other parts of the world. From the docks at Savannah and Sunbury, ships carrying passengers set forth for England and the West Indies, for Charleston, Philadelphia, and New York. Passengers made sea voyages under typically poor eighteenth-century conditions and were often miserable. In 1770 Cornelius Winter, a young teacher who was in Georgia to instruct the slaves at Plantation Beth Abram, took ship for England on Savannah's most famous vessel—Captain George Anderson's *Georgia Packet*. Owned largely by Georgians, it made regular runs between Savannah and English ports. Aboard the *Packet*, Winter had a terrifying journey. The ship sailed during the Christmas season with an insufficient crew, because some had deserted and others had died without being replaced. Some seamen became ill after the ship left Tybee. Once at sea Captain Anderson "disguised himself in liquor." The day after Christmas, the *Packet* encountered a storm in which the sea broke over its decks repeatedly. Every sailor "expected it would have been a fatal night." Anderson, entirely drunk and completely relaxed, retired for the evening, but as the storm continued, he arose, busied himself, and proclaimed that the vessel's hope lay in its sound bottom. When the *Packet* finally came to England, Winter departed it willingly, not knowing whether "I was more tired of my situation or my company; both were bad enough."[78]

76. By 1773, 25 oceangoing vessels were owned or partially owned by Georgians. Ga. Hist. Soc., *Colls.*, III, 175.

77. *Col. Records of Ga.*, XXXVII, 142.

78. *The Works of the Rev. William Jay, of Argyle Chapel, Bath . . .*, III (New

Toward the end of colonial times, the short run to South Carolina was on the way to being regularized. In Savannah, Charles Dawson, a veteran of six years in the king's navy, proposed in 1774 to keep the *Sukey and Katie* constantly on the run to and from Charleston. For the overnight voyage, the vessel offered accommodations for passengers as well as for freight.[79]

In 1774 the Reverend Henry Muhlenberg embarked in Charleston for Savannah. Perhaps the most distinguished Lutheran clergyman then in the colonies, Muhlenberg was en route from his home in Pennsylvania to try to make peace among two disputing factions of Lutherans at Ebenezer. The heavily laden ship was on its final journey before being discharged from service. Its passengers included the no longer youthful Muhlenberg and his ailing wife, their daughter, an English woman and her son, eight other English passengers including a sea captain, four German women from Charleston, a group of slaves recently arrived from Africa, the captain, and a black crew. It carried cargo in addition to baggage. Muhlenberg hurried aboard and rushed to the cabin, where he found four bedsteads resembling cow cribs. "The lady and her little son took one, an old English sea captain . . . took the second, the third was taken by my daughter, and the fourth remained for my wife and myself." There was a great stench in the cabin, "as though rats had been decaying in it." Three other passengers entered and lay down upon chests and boxes. "My wife and I had only a narrow trough for both of us, so we divided the convenience between us; she stayed awake beside the crib from eight to twelve o'clock and let me lie in it, and from twelve to six o'clock I stayed awake and let her lie in it."[80]

Despite the discomfort and inconvenience, personal travel was reasonably reliable, much more so than some other features of life in the colony, including the mail service. In the early years of Georgia's settlement, as long as the Spaniards in Florida were a threat, good mail communications with South Carolina had especial value. Established avenues of contact with neighbors made Georgians feel less isolated and more secure. The first of a series of postal arrangements was instituted when the colony was only a year old. Oglethorpe arranged for

---

York, 1844), 34–35. This volume contains the "Memoirs Of The Late Rev. Cornelius Winter" (pp. 1–112).

79. Advertisement of Charles Dawson, *Ga. Gaz.*, June 1, 1774.
80. Muhlenberg, *Journals*, II, 594.

a rider to leave Charleston once every two weeks, pass through Ebenezer, and then go on to Savannah. Upon reaching Savannah, the rider
would reverse the route. The service was not dependable, however,
and was sometimes interrupted.[81] Isaac Chardon, a Charleston merchant, also hired a courier who conveyed letters to Savannah by water.
Rates were fixed by authorities in Savannah. Persons wishing to send
letters to Georgia left them at the Georgia and Purrysburg Coffee
House in Charleston, where the courier picked them up.[82] Throughout
the proprietorship, mail moved somewhat irregularly in and out of the
colony by courier or through arrangements with boat captains. Efforts
to keep land communications alive sometimes flagged but were resumed again. For several of the early years, Savannah was connected
by messenger with Frederica, but in 1741 the service was "put down
as useless."[83]

Sending mail to Britain required first getting it to Charleston, Beau-
fort, or Port Royal, where it could be entrusted to a ship captain. In
dispatching to England a collection of mail that included the official
proceedings of the trustee government, several packets from the Salzburg Germans, and some additional letters, Habersham had everything
nailed up in a box. The box was tied with a piece of red tape that was
also nailed, then sealed top and bottom with a wax impression.[84] When
Georgia's ports became busy with overseas shipping during the royal
period, captains of merchant ships collected mail at Savannah taverns
and business houses and started it on its journey. Even Governor
Wright preferred that the British government communicate with him
using merchant vessels rather than the mail packets, because the latter
took five or six months to get a letter to Georgia from London. Merchant vessels that came directly could do it in two.[85]

Within the colony itself, men resorted to private means to transmit
mail when there was no courier. After 1750 those who owned slaves
used them to deliver letters and messages. In Savannah, Robert Bolton
in 1763 offered to provide a black man and good horses to rush letters
to any part of the province for a fee.[86] This activity was typical of Bol-

81. Jones *et al.*, trans. and eds., *Detailed Reports on Salzburger Emigrants*, II,
10, 20, 43, 131, 151.
82. *Col. Records of Ga.*, XX, 32.
83. *Ibid.*, IV, 229, V, 485–486.
84. *Ibid.*, XXVI, 133–134.
85. *Ibid.*, XXXVII, 125, 144.
86. Advertisement of Robert Bolton, *Ga. Gaz.*, June 2, 1763.

ton, who had one of the most interesting careers in colonial Georgia. In addition to being Habersham's brother-in-law, he was a virtual factotum and man-about-town—a modest landowner, innkeeper, vendue master, shopkeeper, commissioner of the workhouse, a pillar of the Presbyterian church, and, in 1764, the first official postmaster of Savannah.[87] In that year the time appeared right to regularize the postal service. The British government in 1710 had provided for a colonial postal system, but it was not satisfactorily administered until 1753, when Benjamin Franklin and William Hunter became joint postmasters general for all the colonies.

As Savannah's postmaster, Bolton made plans to deliver mail locally and to give service every ten days to South Carolina. To accomplish this he turned to the assembly for financial assistance, but in vain. Disappointed, he relinquished the post in 1767, and James Whitefield, an unsuccessful merchant and nephew of evangelist George Whitefield, assumed the position and held it until 1770. He then balked and refused either to receive or take charge of further mail.[88] It is not surprising that the colony's postmasters found their duties wearisome, for the position carried no salary. In other colonies the printer of the newspaper was often happy to be postmaster, since the courier who carried the mail would also usually carry the newspaper. Furthermore, persons coming into the post office could be depended upon to examine the printer's wares while in the shop. In Georgia, James Johnston, who in 1763 founded and printed the *Georgia Gazette* in his place on Savannah's Broughton Street, refused to turn his shop into a post office; after Whitefield defaulted, however, Johnston agreed to handle local letters for a time but denied responsibility for them.[89]

Governor Wright, fearful that mail coming into Georgia would go undelivered, actively sought a postmaster. The position went to Alexander Thompson (or Thomson), collector of the port of Savannah—an officer of the royal government much under the governor's influence. Thompson received no salary but was paid 20 percent of the postage handled by the office. He received about £15 a year for his efforts. Thompson believed that people "of whom better things might be expected" were cheating him and suspected them of making private arrangements with riders to carry some letters secretly for personal

87. Ga. Hist. Soc., *Colls.*, VI, 23.
88. *Ga. Gaz.*, Sept. 16, 1767; *Col. Records of Ga.*, XXXVII, 510.
89. *Col. Records of Ga.*, XXXVII, 510.

profit. Under Thompson's supervision, a post to Charleston ran weekly, and a rider made the trip to St. Augustine, Florida, about once a
month.[90] The St. Augustine rider went by Sunbury, providing an important service for Georgia's second port of entry.

90. Finlay, *Journal*, 55, 57; advertisements of Alexander Thomson, *Ga. Gaz.*,
Sept. 28, 1774, and Mar. 29, 1775.

Chapter 3

Everyday Life: Part II

The postal system that developed in Georgia toward the end of colonial times was neither efficient nor well functioning. Still, it might have seemed so to the men and women who first settled in the province three or four decades earlier. Life in those early years was austere. For a substantial group of men sent "on the charity" by the trustees when the colony was two years old, there was a prescribed standard of subsistence. Each man received a watch coat, musket and bayonet, hatchet, hammer, handsaw, shovel or spade, broad hoe, narrow hoe, gimlet, drawing knife, iron pot and pothooks, and frying pan. There was a communal grindstone. Food was plentiful but plain, with every man being assigned a yearly allotment of 312 pounds of beef or pork, 104 pounds of rice, 104 of Indian corn or peas, 104 of flour, one pint of strong beer each working day and none otherwise, 52 quarts of molasses for brewing beer, 16 pounds of cheese, 12 pounds of butter, 8 ounces of spice, 12 pounds of sugar, 4 gallons of vinegar, and 24 pounds of salt. In addition, each got 12 quarts of lamp oil, a pound of spun cotton, and 12 pounds of soap. With downward adjustments in this formula, necessities were allotted to the men's mothers, wives, sisters, and children.[1]

To handle the allotments, trustee stores were erected at Savannah, Frederica, and Ebenezer, and they became Georgia's first significant

---

1. Ga. Hist. Soc., *Colls.*, I, 80. The schedule is taken from Francis Moore's *A Voyage to Georgia, begun in the year 1735 . . .* (London, 1744), reprinted in the cited volume. Moore was quoting from the trustees' "Rules for the Year 1735."

mercantile establishments. The storekeepers held enormous power, some said dictatorial power, over the inhabitants. They were far from the scrutinizing eyes of their employers, the proprietors in London, and equity often took second place to favoritism in the distribution of goods and the keeping of accounts. At times the goods sent by the trustees were shoddy or moldy. The meat was spoiled, the cloth was rotten, the cheese was filled with vermin. And although the storekeepers were seldom above reproach, their supplies were so flawed, their responsibilities so great, and the local needs so urgent, that only a Solomon could have satisfied the settlers. Finally the grievances of the citizenry and the suspicions of the trustees burst upon the most conspicuous of the storekeepers, Thomas Causton. A calico printer by trade, Causton was also bailiff in Savannah, and many complaints against him arose from his alleged tyranny in that office. In 1739 he was turned out of his store by the authorities in London, as much a casualty of the unpopular policies of the trustees as a victim of his own folly.[2] There were also privately owned stores for those with money to spend, but from 1733 until suppressed in 1740, the trustee stores were masters of whatever market there was.[3] The private establishments were puny allies of stronger interests in South Carolina.

All the institutions of Georgia's earliest years served a population demoralized by poverty and insufficiently supported by charitable and parliamentary largesse. Yet the causes for failure under the proprietors lay not in institutions alone, for many of the settlers were immoral idlers.[4] Some never cultivated any land at all and turned their heads "no ways but to the Ale house."[5] Failures of management united with the frailties of men to assure that some Georgians would be hungry and that many would eat badly, despite the provisions made for charity settlers. Even in Ebenezer, where the local leadership of Pastors Bolzius and Gronau was reliable, the shortage of meat was a matter of remark.[6] In Frederica, where conditions were usually better, people were once

2. Causton, in an attempt to vindicate himself, went to England in 1743 and was ordered by the trustees to return to Georgia. He died in 1745 on the return voyage.

3. Montaigut's store, a private venture, in 1734 was retailing goods in Savannah next to Oglethorpe's house. Phillipps Collection, 14200, Pt. i, 324, Univ. of Ga. Lib., Athens.

4. Oglethorpe looked upon the people of Darien as industrious but regarded Savannahians as idle. Ga. Hist. Soc., *Colls.*, III, 90.

5. *Col. Records of Ga.*, XX, 82.

6. Urlsperger, ed., *Ausführliche Nachrichten*, II, 74, 112, 149.

so hungry that they ate alligators.[7] Philip Thicknesse, a lad of about twenty who had been a student at Aynhoe School in England before coming to Georgia, considered himself fortunate to work for and live with Causton. There he never had a meal without bread and fresh meat; yet no other passenger who had arrived in Georgia with him could say the same. "Fresh Provision is Scarce and Dear. They live most upon Salt beef, and rice boil'd instead of Bread."[8]

Times were not substantially better until the 1750s, but not even the austere first two decades suppressed the Georgians' sense of hospitality. Hospitality was a characteristic they had in common with settlers in all the American colonies. Strangers, if respectable looking, were welcome in homes everywhere in the colony. Oglethorpe himself set an example by keeping "open house for all gentlemen comers and goers."[9] In the mid-1730s Sir Francis Bathurst, an impecunious Gloucestershireman who had fallen on hard times, worked in the fields of his farm near Savannah with Lady Bathurst and a son. The family had no money to buy livestock and lived in an inelegant two-room house twenty feet long and twelve feet wide. Yet the Bathursts, even in their low estate, shared what meager fare they had with visitors. As host, Sir Francis spread a breakfast of catfish, perch, and cold pork for one such guest. The visitor on that occasion brought two bottles of punch, which were drunk, and left the Bathursts two bottles of red wine as a gift.[10]

At Frederica, where the soldiers ate well at every meal, there was an altogether artificial prosperity and a genuine hospitality. In 1745 William Logan, scion of a wealthy Philadelphia merchant family, called on business and was taken in at once by officers of the regiment and gentlemen of the town. They welcomed him to their "club" and to their local entertainment. Upon his departure Logan carried away many gifts—two sheep, a hog, a steer, four turkeys, a quarter cut of beef, and a collection of pot herbs.[11]

Later on in royal Georgia, the wealthy had "Servants, that know how to spread a Table handsomely," but the welcome extended by the well-to-do was probably not more sincere than that offered by farmers

7. *Col. Records of Ga.*, V, 170.
8. *Ibid.*, XXI, 256.
9. Ga. Hist. Soc., *Colls.*, II, 42.
10. *Col. Records of Ga.*, XX, 356–357.
11. "William Logan's Journal of a Journey to Georgia, 1745," *Pennsylvania Magazine of History and Biography*, XXXVI (1912), 177–178.

in the backcountry, many of whom had little to share.[12] Two note-
worthy travelers, a father and son, visited Georgia in the 1760s and
1770s and left eloquent accounts of their experiences. John Bartram,
America's first native botanist and a celebrated man of great distinction, was kindly taken in by a family a day's journey from Briar Creek
in the 1760s. He not only shared in familial warmth but was given a
tour of the countryside.[13] Eight years later in the south of the province,
his son William, also a scientist of note, found the farmers hospitable.
At a modest plantation on the road to Darien, he was sheltered during
a thunderstorm by Donald McIntosh and was generously fed upon
venison; after being feted by people "remarkably civil and hospitable,"
he remarked: "Was there ever such a scene of primitive simplicity, as
was here exhibited, since the days of the good King Tammany!"[14]
William Bartram encountered warm welcomes everywhere—at the
home of Benjamin Andrew, a member of the assembly who lived on
a well-cultivated plantation near Midway; among the citizenry of Sunbury; and on St. Simons Island, where the man of the house lay on a
bearskin and smoked a pipe. There the host served a drink of honey
and water, strengthened with brandy.[15]

In Savannah, hospitality might have meant offering a cup of coffee
to a visitor, or it might have involved a social engagement with the
governor, who often extended dinner invitations.[16] The governor experienced or affected surprise when persons of respectability did not
visit him soon after arrival in the province.[17] Georgians respected their
last two royal governors (they neither liked nor respected the first),
but they never held the official residence in awe. They refused to call
it a palace and seldom called it a mansion, simply calling it "Government House." Georgians' eyebrows went up at the lavishness of Governor William Tryon's palace at New Bern, North Carolina.[18]

12. Ga. Hist. Soc., *Colls.*, VI, 182.

13. John Bartram, "Diary of a Journey," ed. Harper, Am. Phil. Soc., *Trans.*, N.S.,
XXXIII, Pt. i (1942), 24n.

14. William Bartram, *Travels*, 13.

15. *Ibid.*, 5, 11, 60, 61.

16. Muhlenberg, *Journals*, II, 601.

17. *Ibid.*, 679; John Bartram, "Diary of a Journey," ed. Harper, Am. Phil. Soc.,
Trans., N.S., XXXIII, Pt. i (1942), 23. Finlay, *Journal*, 58; William Bartram,
Travels, 4.

18. John J. Zubly regarded Tryon palace as a "sumptuous needless building."
Entry of Mar. 31, 1770, "Manuscript Journal of the Revd. John Joachim Zubly
from March 5, 1770, to April 9, 1781," Ga. Hist. Soc., Savannah. E. Merton Coulter

In contrast, Governor Wright lived rather informally. A visitor described dining with him in 1775. At the table were Sir James, Pastor Muhlenberg, and an influential Quaker, Joseph Maddock of Wrightsborough, with whom the governor had sometimes stayed. Wright toasted the king's health, conversed with his guests, and was twitted by Maddock about the Indians who were then discomfitting Wrightsborough. Maddock, who was struggling hard to be a pacifist, said: "You Englishmen have a great fortress . . . in your towns. You lock your thieves in chains. You set up two trees and put a crossbeam between them. You have ropes and you hang your thieves, and still, with all this fuss, you cannot stop your people from robbing and stealing." How much less, he asked, could the Quakers, who used no such instruments, do against the Indians? Maddock, sensing that the governor's hospitality was warm and sincere, showed his appreciation: "I love to be with you. I enjoy being with you. In fact, I could spend five more hours in your company today." The governor, who regretted that he could not spare the time, replied, "That would please me very much, but I have some absolutely necessary business to attend to today and cannot enjoy your society."[19]

Guests might generally expect to find comfortable accommodations in most places, for furniture was easily purchased. Even in trustee times, when many things were scarce, house furnishings were readily bought by those who could afford them. Newly arrived settlers, however, scraped along as best they could. Simple beds were sometimes made of sackcloth with one end open for stuffing with straw or flock.[20] Such basic beds and the bedsteads that supported them were inexpensive. The feather bed, however, was another matter. A good one with a pavilioned (canopied) bedstead was an item to pass along from one generation to another. Some furniture was made in the province—chairs, tables, beds, benches, and stools. The most common chair was the rush-bottom or straw-bottom straight chair, but Windsors, made of mahogany, red bay, pine, or walnut, were also popular. The Windsor chair had a back formed of upright rods surmounted by a cross-

seems to have been the first to note that Georgians usually referred to the governor's residence as a house. See Coulter's *Wormsloe: Two Centuries of a Georgia Family* (Athens, Ga., 1955), 93.

19. Muhlenberg, *Journals*, II, 680.

20. Phillipps Coll., 14208, 505–506; Loewald, Starika, and Taylor, trans. and eds., "Bolzius Answers a Questionnaire," Pt. i, *WMQ*, 3d Ser., XIV (1957), 247.

piece (often curved) and came with or without arms. High-backed chairs were often used and were sometimes of Windsor design. Mahogany was favored for the better kinds of furniture in Georgia, perhaps because it was imported; local wood, particularly pine, was used in making tables. Tables were described according to their shape or size—oval or square, large or small. Poor Georgians often had sand floors, but in the years before the Revolution, the Wilton carpet became for the wealthy a symbol of elegance unmatched by painted floor cloths or by rugs of plebeian manufacture. Other pieces of furniture, such as desks, chests of drawers, and bookcases, were described not by style but by the wood that went into their making.

Like other eighteenth-century Americans, many Georgians ate everyday meals off pewter dishes. Patrick Graham, who lived at Josephs Town on the river above Savannah, was first an officer in the proprietary government, then in 1752 president of the colony, and later a member of the council. By local standards he was a wealthy man. When he died in 1755 he left a large parcel of pewterware, worth £3, and earthenware dishes and plates valued at a pound. For guests and for celebrations, Graham owned silverware and good china. He left eighteen silver tablespoons, one soup spoon, twenty-one teaspoons with sugar tongs and tea strainer, and twenty-four ivory-handled knives and forks, plus china dishes. One of his most interesting pieces was a silver half-pint mug valued at fifteen shillings.[21] Silver was cherished and passed along to heirs and was occasionally ciphered or engraved for identification in case of loss or theft.[22] Less expensive and in broad use were various kinds of earthenware, such as delft, a tin-glazed pottery that often was white with blue or polychrome decoration, and, later in the century, queensware, a popular lead-glazed, cream-colored pottery first introduced by Wedgwood in the early 1760s.

Wills, which conveyed many of these items to new owners, often left bequests for "mourning." Habersham at his death provided money to buy suits of mourning for his nephew, Joseph Clay, and Mrs. Clay, and for his brother-in-law, Robert Bolton. The clothing was to be worn in memory of him. At times bequests might only cover the cost of a suit, but Habersham directed £25 sterling each to be given to Mr. and Mrs. Clay and £10 to Bolton, far more than enough to purchase

21. Estate of Patrick Graham, Esq., Mar. 6, 1756, Inventory Book F, 22, Dept. of Archives and Hist., Atlanta, Ga.
22. Advertisement of Henry Yonge, Jr., *Ga. Gaz.*, July 5, 1775.

a suit.[23] Frequently garments of the deceased were left to friends and relatives. In the 1750s Alexander Wylly, who later distinguished himself as Speaker of the Commons House and clerk of the council, was bequeathed the entire wardrobe of a Savannah merchant, Nevile Wainwright.[24] Another common bequest was a mourning ring to be worn in commemoration of the deceased donor. William Ewen of Savannah left one valued at ten guineas to Mary Jones, daughter of Dr. Noble Jones. He also bequeathed rings to two other women.[25] Ewen's ability to leave expensive gifts was due to his great talents. He had arrived in Georgia in 1734 as an indentured servant, and later worked as a potter. He became a wealthy citizen, a member of the assembly, and in 1775, president of the Council of Safety, which left him in charge of affairs after Governor Wright fled the colony in 1776.

In dress, a movement toward simplicity can be demonstrated partly by a decline in the use of wigs, or perukes. In 1739 Thomas Jones, employed in one of the trustee stores, was declared impudent for appearing without a wig before a military official. Jones was wearing a velvet cap instead.[26] This early incident suggests that the practical demands of the frontier, plus the warm climate, had wigs in retreat by the time the province was six years old, although later instances of their being worn may be cited for both trustee and royal Georgia. Inventories of estates from the royal period indicate a decline in the use of wigs,[27] and by the beginning of the Revolution, they had disappeared as a cus-

23. Will abstract of James Habersham, in Georgia Department of Archives and History, *Abstracts of Colonial Wills of the State of Georgia, 1733–1777* (Atlanta, Ga., 1962), 65, hereafter cited as *Will Abstracts*.

24. Will abstract of Nevile Wainwright, *ibid.*, 138; will abstracts of William Lavery, Mary Vanderplank, John Emmanuel, and John Pettigrew, *ibid.*, 76, 137–138, 45, 109–110.

25. Will abstract of William Ewen, *ibid.*, 46.

26. *Col. Records of Ga.*, XXII, Pt. ii, 132.

27. Inventory Books F, FF, and GG, *passim*. Inventories do not constitute scientific samples of usage, but it is worthy of remark that in 39 inventories between 1754 and 1759 useful for a study of wigs, 11 persons owned one or more. Yet of 79 such inventories between 1760 and 1765, only 6 indicated ownership of wigs. From 1766 to 1771, only 10 of 148 applicable inventories show wig ownership. Between 1776 and 1778, when there are 62 applicable inventories, no wigs are found. Had they been present, they would have been listed, since officers assigned to take inventories noted even empty bottles and cups without handles. Even if some Georgians had been buried in their wigs, it is certain that many persons would have owned more than one had they been common.

tomary form of dress. The formal attire they symbolized was also dis-
appearing, even among officers of local government for whom ceremony and appearance carried especial importance.

When James Whitefield's mercantile business went bankrupt in
1765, some persons said that "Jewelry and other Trumpery (by no
means suitable for this place)" had eased him onto the downward
path. Adornment and display were the exception, not the rule. Habersham, who could have afforded any clothing he wished, tended toward
the plain. "I would not be quite in, neither would I be quite out of the
fashion," he said.[28] In the 1760s he decided to have some simple but
proper clothing made in London, as he regarded Savannah tailors as
bunglers. He gathered up an old garment or two to send for size and
stuck a piece of cloth in a pocket to show the color desired. His samples
were lost in a shipwreck. Habersham dispatched a second bundle to his
friend William Knox, a Georgia resident from 1757 to 1762 and
then a well-placed official in London. "You are a most unfortunate
Adventurer [in] Coats," Knox wrote back to Habersham. "The second
you sent by Mr Hall is not arrived He having left it to be sent after
him from Charles Town. When it comes to my hands I shall set my
Taylor about it immediately, and get him [to] make you one as little
like it as possible."[29] Knox knew Habersham's preference in style, and
the Georgian received his new clothes in the summer of 1768. He
twitted Knox that they were too late for the king's birthday, adding
that while he approved the coat, he had reservations about the gay
waistcoat. However, to show his appreciation he wore it "the day after
it was landed, being Sunday."[30]

Clothing, although valued in Georgia as in other colonies, was none-
theless simpler than it was in England, for Georgians lived close to
nature. Scarcely a residence lay more than a stroll from forests teeming
with wildlife, which were hunted and trapped for sport and the dinner
table. People's lives were interlocked with animals: horses and oxen
for work and transportation; cows, sheep, and hogs for food. Like other
colonial settlers, Georgians kept cats and dogs for pets and, like eighteenth-century Englishmen, derived pleasure from the exotic appeal

28. Ga. Hist. Soc., *Colls.*, VI, 42, 61.
29. William Knox to James Habersham, Mar. 2, 1768, James Habersham
Papers, Ga. Hist. Soc., Savannah.
30. Ga. Hist. Soc., *Colls.*, VI, 75.

of birds. A newspaper advertisement of 1774 read: "Stolen from a Gentleman's house in Savannah, December 23d, supposed by a Negroe, A small Green Parrot, and a Yard Bitch of a brownish colour. Whoever gives information of either, or the thief, to Thomas Mills upon the Bay, shall receive a handsome reward."[31] Mills perhaps owned a small store in Savannah while also serving as the steward aboard the *Georgia Packet.* When Habersham in 1772 wanted a goldfinch and a linnet or two, he wrote to Governor Wright's daughter in England asking her to get them for him and to send them aboard the *Packet* in charge of Mills. "[B]y these little feathered Innocents, I may fancy myself conversing with you," he told the young woman. The birds were to travel in wire cages of iron, not brass, because brass was believed to contract a rust fatal to them.[32] Another Georgian, whose green parrot had flown its cage, placed an advertisement for it with instructions for the finder to bring the bird to the newspaper office and collect a reward. John Morel, a wealthy merchant with a country place on Ossabaw Island, liked water fowl. He offered to buy six pairs of tame summer ducks. The enthusiasm for birds as pets bridged social distinctions. Birds appealed both to patricians like Raymond Demere, a friend of Oglethorpe's and a commander of defense forces during the 1742 Spanish invasion of Georgia, and to persons of lower rank such as William Ely, a wagoner.[33]

What John Bartram called the greatest curiosity in Georgia involved the use of animals for food. In 1765 Bartram set out with a group of men to look at the cattle that were the source of fresh meat for the colony. After traveling twenty-five miles in the backcountry, much of it across poor ground, he and his party arrived at a cow pen. It was a "kind of house, or hut, near a good spring, in which four or five negroes, with one white man, generally live to look after a number of cattle of various kinds, that occupy a range of country of six to ten miles round." The attendants' principal duties were tending cows as they calved, assisting mares as they foaled, and bringing newborn animals to the pen if they needed attention. Some Georgians owned

31. *Ga. Gaz.*, Jan. 5, 1774.
32. Ga. Hist. Soc., *Colls.*, VI, 167–168, 209.
33. Unsigned advertisement, *Ga. Gaz.*, Feb. 23, 1774; advertisement of John Morel, *ibid.*, Aug. 3, 1768; estate of Raymond Demere, Aug. 22, 1766, Inventory Book F, 211; estate of William Ely, Apr. 23, 1777, Inventory Book FF, 55.

two or three cow pens some distance from each other. At the pens, Bartram noted, "the cattle are kept in distinct herds, and feed, both summer and winter, in their respective walks." The herdsmen were also "very dextrous in catching and training the wildest horses, and great profit is made to their masters by the sale."[34]

The trustees in the early years maintained large herds on farms operated by the trust's own indentured servants. When the farms were closed in 1743, all of the trustee herds were disposed of except one at Ebenezer, which was retained until sold to the Salzburgers in 1751. In 1744 the keeper of the cow pen at Ebenezer, Christopher Hopkins, drove twenty-four head of cattle to Savannah for slaughter. President William Stephens worried that the weather was too warm for the meat to be cured properly, so he and his assistants decided to have two or three cows killed at a time in the evening. They would cut the meat the next morning, "allowing the people of the town to serve themselves with what they had occasion for." They would sell the remainder to the workmen building Christ Church, with any unsold portions being preserved in barrels.[35]

The trustees did not supply meat free to the settlers in the 1740s; they charged the same prices as for meat delivered by private hands from South Carolina.[36] They preserved their cows from thieves with difficulty, for people were in "a general Combination to eat the Trustees Cattel" without paying anything for them. No Savannah jury would convict a man for killing a cow in the woods. Oglethorpe, realizing that the "Countrey cannot be supported without Cattel," employed hunters to catch the animals in the woods and deliver them to the cow pens for marking, "by which means I have already stopped the Stealing."[37] By 1750 the business of supplying meat had passed largely into the hands of private men whose pens were scattered across the upcountry. The royal government, in an attempt to suppress spoiled meat, required that all butcher's flesh be sold in supervised markets. There carrion could be detected and burned. The law could not always be

34. When Bartram described this cow pen, he was visiting both Georgia and South Carolina, and the pen mentioned may have actually been in the latter colony. John Bartram, "Diary of a Journey," ed. Harper, Am. Phil. Soc., Trans., N.S., XXXIII, Pt. i (1942), 26–27n.

35. Coulter, ed., Journal of Stephens, II, 91–92.

36. Ibid.

37. Col. Records of Ga., XXII, Pt. ii, 170–171.

enforced, however, for butchers sometimes sold beef, veal, mutton, lamb, and other meats at their houses.[38]

Georgians shopping in the 1730s would most likely have gone to the trustee store in Savannah, Ebenezer, or Frederica, although they could have gone to a number of small private establishments. In the 1740s private businesses became stronger, and traders could also lay out goods in the villages in a manner resembling the public markets of English towns. When traders came to Savannah by water, the trustee government, on threat of fine, required them to come ashore to dispose of their wares. They could not sell to citizens who rowed out to their vessels.[39] By the 1750s "Extortions Impositions and Irregularities" committed by some unscrupulous tradesmen had become unbearable; so the royal government created and regulated a public market in Savannah.[40] (The law also allowed sale of goods on the waterfront.) The market became a popular institution benefiting town and backcountry alike. For Savannah and the immediate countryside, it was the most dependable place to buy fresh produce. For the backcountry, it offered a fixed place and an orderly method for selling agricultural products. Under a 1755 law the market was near the center of Savannah, but in 1763 or 1764 it was moved to Ellis Square, nearer the docks (see the map of Savannah on p. 71). The start of business each day (except Sunday) was signaled by ringing a bell for five minutes at sunrise. In time this interval was seen to be insufficient, and after 1764 the bell rang for fifteen minutes.[41] The bell—at first on a pole and later in a belfry—was the object of the raillery of pranksters who stole the pole or broke into the belfry to ring it in the dead of night.[42]

The market itself was a series of stalls, or small shops, rented to persons with produce to vend. After the removal to Ellis Square, the market proper was sixty feet square with four little houses for truck at each corner. Stalls stretched from corner house to corner house. The square thus enclosed was entered through four passages, one on each side, and in the middle stood the bell. By law anyone except blacks might buy or sell freely. There was no business on Sundays, except that

38. Advertisement of David Zubly, *Ga. Gaz.*, Aug. 6, 1766.
39. *Col. Records of Ga.*, VI, 67.
40. *Ibid.*, XVIII, 80–81.
41. *Ibid.*, 576.
42. Advertisements of Hugh Ross, *Ga. Gaz.*, Aug. 25, 1763, and Dec. 30, 1767.

fish merchants might keep store, doubtless because their commodities spoiled quickly.[43] Transactions were made according to weights and measures in alleged agreement with a set belonging to the Exchequer in Great Britain. They were kept by the clerk of the market, and he could, as a matter of law, test weights and measures in any stall at the market or in the town at large against his exemplars. Hugh Ross, clerk of the market for most of its existence, wore out his wooden measuring devices and in 1770 asked the assembly for a new set. He wished them to be made of sturdier material—copper (for containers holding up to a bushel) and brass (for a yardstick).[44] Ross had clearly tried to do his duty in enforcing fair measures.

The market theoretically was a place where all kinds of goods or provisions might be sold, but in practice Georgians looked to it principally for vegetables, fruits, meats, poultry, and fish. Even so, it had no monopoly. Private merchants received and disposed of country produce, charging commissions that might or might not be more than the fees the clerk of the market assessed.[45] In royal times there were numerous private vendors in the province, many of whom had only small businesses. Bakers, for example, probably made bread at their homes and sold it there or in shops or stalls. A "shop" often meant nothing more than a room set aside in a residence. The law regulating bakers was among the best enforced of Georgia's colonial acts. George Baillie, the official commissary between 1763 and 1776, determined the market price of flour—and therefore of bread—and printed it regularly in the *Georgia Gazette*.[46] Every baker was required to mark his product with his initial or symbol and his price, so that violations of the rules of assize could be detected and punished by fine.[47]

Although trustee Georgia and royal Georgia were not far separated in time, the two eras differed markedly in the range of foods available. Under the proprietors, many Georgians ate simply, even meagerly. In

43. *Col. Records of Ga.*, XVIII, 81. The government was unable to enforce the market act absolutely. In violation of both it and the "slave code," blacks sold produce at the market in 1775 and even sold it on Sunday. Presentments of the grand jury, *Ga. Gaz.*, June 21, 1775.

44. *Col. Records of Ga.*, XV, 257–258, XVIII, 83.

45. Advertisement of Thomas Lloyd, *Ga. Gaz.*, Dec. 13, 1764; advertisement of William Moore, *ibid.*, July 16, 1766.

46. Advertisements of George Baillie, *ibid.*, Apr. 21, 1763, and Oct. 25, 1775. Between these dates the *Gazette* contains many of Baillie's official advertisements as commissary.

47. *Col. Records of Ga.*, XIX, Pt. i, 18.

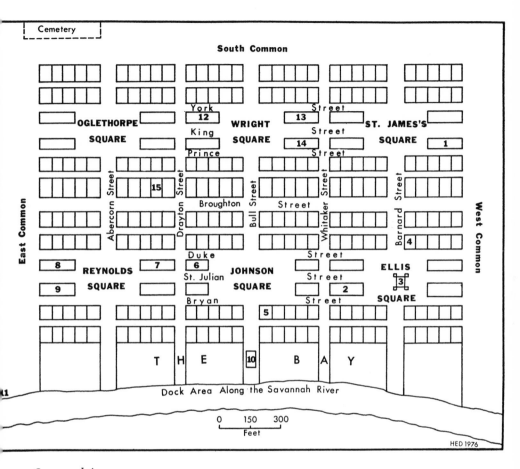

Savannah in 1770

*Principal locations are numbered (1) governor's house ("Government House");
(2) Independent Presbyterian Church (Zubly's meetinghouse); (3) Public market; (4) site of Machenry's Tavern; (5) James Habersham's house (this structure
could have been on the lot next door); (6) Christ Church; (7) Christ Church
rectory; (8) assembly house (colonial capitol); (9) filature (silk works); (10)
vendue house; (11) Fort Halifax (approximate); (12) courthouse; (13) jail;
(14) guardhouse; (15) James Johnston's printshop. (Based on a certified copy
of a map of Savannah dated February 5, 1770, Georgia Historical Society,
Savannah.)*

(Researched by Lilla M. Hawes; cartography by Patricia Jetmore.)

1741 the children at Bethesda orphanage had hominy twice a day, sometimes with, sometimes without, molasses. For dinner they had beef of their own raising with peas instead of bread.[48] Their external affairs were in the hands of James Habersham, even then a master at business arrangements, so we might suppose that these children fared better than the general public. In the royal era, however, matters were much different, and those with money to spend or goods to barter need not content themselves with mere wholesome simplicities. They could walk into a store on Broughton or Bull streets or the Bay, or a wharf store at the docks, and pick over numerous staples and an aromatic array of delicacies: pickled mackerel and herring in barrels, salmon in kegs, prunes, currants, raisins, preserved citron, ginger, sweetmeats, white and brown sugar candy, white wine vinegar, cheeses, sugar, and apples in barrels. Snuff came in glasses from Scotland; cut and pigtail tobacco arrived roundabout from England in paper packages. Ships brought merchandise from England, Scotland, and Ireland, and from Philadelphia, New York, and Boston. In royal times, one might buy directly off the ships as they lay docked. For example, in 1765 the *Georgia Gazette* advertised: "To Be Sold, On board the brigantine Chance, from Rhode-Island, now lying at Mr. Lloyd's wharf, Best Havana Refined Sugar, second sort ditto, New-England Rum, Cordials, Bristol Beer, Philadelphia Double Beer, Spermacoeti Candles, Wax ditto, English Shoes, Loaf Sugar, Barreled Fish, Cabinet Ware, Cheese, Potatoes, Apples, Cyder, Onions, and Castile Soap."[49]

From plentiful stocks, tea and coffee could also be bought. Coffee was the more popular beverage. Consumption was estimated in late royal times by a Savannah customs official, who calculated that of approximately 11,000 white persons in Georgia, 3,000 used around six pounds of tea a year; but 4,000 used some twenty pounds of coffee.[50] There were 1,000 children too young to drink either, he figured, and 3,000 white adults too poor to do so. Dr. Noble Wimberly Jones, physician, member of the assembly, and Revolutionary leader, was especially fond of coffee, particularly when tired. But fatigued or not, he drank it every morning and night, adding milk but no sugar.[51]

48. George Whitefield, *A Continuation of the Account of the Orphan-House in Georgia, From January 1740/1 to June 1742* ... (Edinburgh, 1742), 14.

49. *Ga. Gaz.*, Apr. 25, 1765.

50. *Col. Records of Ga.*, XXXVIII, Pt. i, 141, 142.

51. George Jones to John Grimes (n.d. except 1805), DeRenne Manuscripts Collection, Univ. of Ga. Lib., Athens.

Dr. Jones, unlike most Georgians of his day, confined himself to coffee and drank little that was alcoholic. What alcohol he did use was probably in the form of wine, drunk mainly by the well-to-do at mealtime. Although advertisements in the *Georgia Gazette* might give the false impression that wine was a popular drink, fairly little was used, not because of a lack of refined taste but because it was too expensive.[52] Even the wealthy could not afford claret unless it were smuggled. Of the wine drunk in 1769, 1770, and 1771, perhaps half was port and half was Madeira. Only about 160 of the 11,000 white persons in Georgia in those years drank as much as a pint a day.[53]

Wine never worried the authorities as much as rum, which was far more plentiful and was believed to destroy one's health. The trustees declared rum a public enemy after utterly failing to discourage its use by persuasion. Fear of rum was rampant on both sides of the Atlantic, and England itself passed a rum act in 1736. The trustees' fight against strong drink had an especial urgency, for the prosperity and perhaps even the survival of the young colony depended upon the industry of healthy men and women. Oglethorpe knew that he could not entirely suppress spirits and attempted to placate the populace with beer. On one occasion, he made sure that a convoy of piraguas bound for a common destination would remain together in transit by putting all the beer in one boat. This forced the other boat crews to keep up, for if they missed the rendezvous at night, they lost their share.[54] Still, beer did not quench the thirst for rum, and Georgians soon discovered that strong spirits could be bought inexpensively across the river in South Carolina. Workmen at Tybee Lighthouse found that "one day's pay would make them drunk for a week," when they spent it on South Carolina spirits.[55] Oglethorpe moved to have one South Carolina alehouse closed after fourteen workmen were drowned rowing to and from it.[56]

The proprietors were convinced that their stand against rum was right and could support their arguments with cases like that of John Milledge. "Millidge our best Carpenter is dead of a burning Feaver which on his Deathbed he confessed he contracted at the Indian Trad-

52. As an example, see the advertisement of John Patton, *Ga. Gaz.*, July 5, 1775.

53. *Col. Records of Ga.*, XXXVIII, Pt. i, 143.

54. Ga. Hist. Soc., *Colls.*, I, 112.

55. *Ibid.*, 89.

56. *Ibid.*, III, 84.

ing House; he drank there Rum Punch on the Wednesday, on Thursday was taken ill of a burning Feaver and on the seventh day, the Crisis of that Distemper, dyed."[57] Despite strenuous efforts to wean the people off rum and onto beer, rum could not be kept out of Georgia.[58] Local court officials would not prosecute rum sellers; they were unwilling "to be the Authors of Severity towards their Neighbours."[59] Vessels from South Carolina bound upriver on the Indian trade regularly passed Savannah laden with strong spirits. Magistrates in Savannah stopped some of the South Carolina boats and staved in their kegs, arguing that the river was Georgia's and that it could not be used to transport contraband. South Carolina saw these actions as an illegal interference with its Indian trade, and the cordial feelings it had entertained for Georgia in 1733 became strained within three years.[60] Never did the trustees come close to enforcing their edict proscribing rum. So complete was their defeat that after four years of trying, one former official in Savannah acknowledged that "if any man has but a shilling he lays it out that way, not buying shoes or stockings." Furthermore, he disclosed, even the magistrates drank.[61] In 1742 the proprietors ceased enforcing the act.[62] And four years later President Stephens reported from Savannah that rum was "generally drank by People of all Ranks: And 'tis certain, that during the Time of its being drank clandestinely, Abundance more of it was used than since; nor do we hear of so many Disorders as then: and 'tis evident the People of this part of the Province were never more healthy; not exceeding in a Year, one, two or three at most that have gone to their Graves in three Years past."[63]

Stephens, in his relief at not having to enforce the unpopular act any longer, might have been too sanguine, for drunkenness remained

57. James Edward Oglethorpe to the trustees, Aug. 12, 1733, Phillipps Coll., 14200, Pt. i, 106.

58. Thomas Christie to Oglethorpe, Dec. 14, 1734, *ibid.*, 325.

59. *Col. Records of Ga.*, IV, 62.

60. Records in the British Public Record Office Relating to South Carolina (transcripts), XVIII, 61–62, 83–101, Dept. of Archives and Hist., Columbia, S.C.

61. *Col. Records of Ga.*, V, 178–179.

62. The trustees were sensitive about the failure of their anti-rum law. They wished merely to wink at the law and suspend its enforcement without going through a repeal procedure. However, a formal act of repeal was drawn up but was never approved. *Col. Records of Ga.*, I, 54–56. Officials of the trust merely ceased enforcing the 1735 act. See McCain, *Ga. as a Proprietary Province*, 184–185.

63. *Col. Records of Ga.*, XXV, 137.

an acute problem. Moderate drinking carried no stigma, and religious men, as well as those who professed no religion, sold alcohol both at that time and later.[64] But intoxication was disapproved. In 1763 the *Georgia Gazette* offered a mock sermon (probably plagiarized) denouncing drunkenness. Paralleling admonitions against excessive drinking found in every American colony and in Great Britain, it ended gustily: "So much for this time and text; only, by way of caution, take this; a drunkard is an annoyance of modesty, the trouble of civility, the spoil of wealth, the destruction of reason, the brewer's agent, the alehouse's benefactor, the beggar's companion, the constable's trouble, his wife's woe, his children's sorrow, his neighbour's scoff, his own shame, a *waking-swill-tub*, the picture of a beast, and the monster of a man."[65] The *Gazette,* returning to the subject in a later issue, characterized the drunkard as a "*brewer's* pump to keep store cellars dry" and added: "Although he scarcely knows what a pulpit means, yet he is a most *religious* fellow, for the name of *God* is ever at his tongue's end; and he is particularly careful to teach his family the duty of *fasting*. . . . His *frugality* is very remarkable, for a shirt always lasts him a month. . . . He is a *Camel* in his draughts. . . . He is a *key* to the doors of workhouses, and keeps alive the charitable practice of burying the poor *gratis*."[66]

The newspaper's interest in drunkards was natural enough, for many of them were close at hand. Late in colonial times, 7,000 of Georgia's 10,000 white adults (male and female) drank an average of a half-pint of rum per day.[67] In addition, alcohol was consumed in the form of rye whiskey, beer, ale, cider, gin, arrack, peach and apple brandy, and wine.

Although much of the drinking was doubtless solitary, many activities in the colony were public and communal, including service in the militia and the keeping of the public roads. Citizens also labored together to clean the squares and commons of the towns and to control disastrous fires. Oglethorpe, observing that the common in Savannah was grown up with weeds almost as high as a man's shoulder, sent out orders "that upon Beat of Drum, this Morning, all Persons inhabiting

64. In 1764 three German deacons were licensed to sell alcoholic beverages at Ebenezer. *Ga. Gaz.,* Jan. 19, 1764.
65. *Ibid.,* Dec. 29, 1763.
66. *Ibid.,* Jan. 27, 1768.
67. *Col. Records of Ga.,* XXXVIII, Pt. i, 140. These figures are estimations of a customs official.

the Town . . . should appear at Sun-rising this Morning, and go to Work." The citizens did appear and before evening had "laid smooth some Hundreds of Acres." Oglethorpe joined the work party, and everyone, "without Distinction," did his share.[68] The responsibility of citizens for the cleanliness of towns carried over into royal times, although the duty was sometimes protested.[69]

The task of fire fighting, which fell upon the average citizen, was not protested and seems not to have been resented. Even in such carefully planned towns as Savannah, Ebenezer, Sunbury, Frederica, and Augusta (which sprawled for four or five miles along the southwesterly bank of the Savannah River), houses stood close enough together to justify fears of a general fire. In a matter of hours, a conflagration could do vast damage. In 1741 Stephens left Savannah for a few hours to ride to his plantation at Bewlie. As he arrived at the edge of town on his return, he "met with the lamentable News of a great Fire that happened about Three a-Clock in the Afternoon, and in a little more than an Hour's Time, burnt down five Houses, in the principal Part of the Town."[70] In 1758 the filature housing the silk-winding industry was entirely burned. Had there been a breeze, the whole town might have been lost. The powder magazine was near the filature, and its outer boards became so hot that resin streamed down them. But at last "some resolute People enter'd the Magazine, and their Example being follow'd by many," the powder was safely removed.[71]

To assist in fire control the government urged, and finally commanded, that all chimneys be made of brick, stone, or lime. Public wells were essential to fire fighting, and one was sunk in Savannah very early in 1733. Water was found before the digging had reached twenty-five feet. In 1765 one of the principal wells was at the intersection of Broughton and Barnard streets.[72] In addition to a well, fire control depended upon an engine (a manually operated pump), leather buckets, and willing hands. When there was a fire, the engine

---

68. *Ibid.*, IV, 433.

69. *Ibid.*, XIV, 452–454. In royal times the church beadle, in addition to his parochial duties, was Savannah's sanitation officer. *Ibid.*, XVIII, 754.

70. *Ibid.*, IV supplement, 119.

71. Ottolenghe to Waring, July 12, 1758, MSS of Dr. Bray's Associates, Pt. H (L.C. reel 11, 335/211).

72. Coulter, ed., *Journal of Gordon*, 46; presentments of the grand jury, *Ga. Gaz.*, July 4, 1765.

hurried to a well and pumped up water, and lines of men passed along bucketfuls to the blaze. In 1759 a move was begun to excuse fifteen men from some military duties in exchange for keeping the engine and working at fires.[73] But finally a man was employed merely to "play" the engine every two months or so and to repair it if it were broken. Sometimes the men who helped to test the engine were paid, but fire service was largely volunteered.[74]

In a province where the population was always small, and where men knew other people both through everyday enterprises and shared public undertakings, it was inevitable that suspicions would arise when anyone showed signs of leaving the colony suddenly. There was a great fear that men would flee their debts. Almost from the beginning, it was customary for persons to announce publicly their intention to depart Georgia. The proprietors required that no one leave without paying what he owed or making an agreement with his creditors.[75] Men usually notified the authorities of their intention to leave and also informed the public by posting a notice in a prominent place. In Savannah notices were commonly nailed up in Johnson Square. After 1763 they often appeared in the *Georgia Gazette*. A typical one read: "The subscriber intending to leave this province for a little time, gives notice, pursuant to an act of the General Assembly, that he is ready to answer to any suit, and give bail to any writ or summons that shall be issued against him."[76]

Such notices, of course, sought to prevent disputes arising over indebtedness. But even where wrangling arose, whether over money or other matters, the colonists seldom permitted that ultimate form of disagreement—dueling—to play a part in their lives, despite a famous duel in 1777 that took the life of Button Gwinnett and left Lachlan McIntosh wounded. In trustee times such affairs of honor were practiced, when practiced at all, among military officers.[77] The Gwinnett-McIntosh episode of 1777 was fought between two local leaders of the Revolution, men with military ambitions and aflame with martial ardor.

Personal hostilities more often found outlet in violent rhetoric,

73. *Col. Records of Ga.*, XVIII, 315–316.
74. Advertisement of Thomas Lee, *Ga. Gaz.*, Feb. 9, 1764.
75. *Col. Records of Ga.*, IV, 221, V, 503.
76. Identical advertisements of Josiah Powell and John Oliver, *Ga. Gaz.*, June 16, 1763; similar advertisement of Philip Mosses, *ibid.*, Jan. 26, 1774.
77. E.g., see *Col. Records of Ga.*, IV, 592–593, IV supp., 147, V, 372.

and although not everyone lit upon each provocation as an excuse to
tongue-lash his neighbor, some did. The Reverend John J. Zubly declared that "even in the opinion of [the] Apostle it is not always possible to be at peace with *all* men," though he agreed that "a wrangling
disposition" was unbecoming to Christians. Still, said Zubly, "there
may be circumstances in which to [be] altogether silent may hurt a
good cause."[78] Believing his own justifications, Zubly took up his pen
against a fellow divine, the Reverend Samuel Frink, rector of Christ
Church Parish in Savannah. Zubly's own rhetoric was pointed rather
than violent. But in criticizing Frink, he was addressing a master of
defamation. Frink disliked the Reverend George Whitefield, the evangelist, who was also one of Frink's predecessors as rector of Christ
Church. After his first arrival in 1738, Whitefield was often in the
colony in connection with Bethesda Orphan House, which he had
founded twelve miles from Savannah. Frink disliked the orphanage as
well as its founder. "His Orphan House has always been a Nest for
the Enemies of the Church. Ignorance and Enthusiasm its concomitant,
is the Characterisitck of all those that have received any Instruction
there. . . . I shall always look upon the disturbers of our tranquility,
to be the Vermin and Rats of any State." Frink regarded himself, however, as "a Lover of all, excepting those that oppose the Progress of
Christ's Kingdom down upon Earth." To Frink, Whitefield was a man
to be ridiculed not only for his "broad bottomed" approach to theology and to education but for his broad bottom. Whitefield was sensitive about his size, particularly in his later years. "I must say that I
never desire to see Whitfield in Georgia in the capacity of a Clergyman
any more. How to behave with regard to admitting him into the Pulpit
here in Savannah when he arrives I am utterly at a Loss. . . . Broad
bottoms are best at a distance."[79] Joseph Ottolenghe, the principal
author of the act establishing the Anglican church in Georgia, was no
less gifted at cruel rhetoric than his rector. In the midst of a business
dispute over the exchange of some lands, Ottolenghe wrote to William
Gibbons, Jr.: "I want none of your Favors, nor shall you have any note

78. John J. Zubly, *A Letter To The Reverend Samuel Frink, A.M., Rector of
Christ's Church Parish in Georgia, Relating To Some Fees demanded of some of
his Dissenting Parishioners* (Savannah, Ga.? 1770?).

79. Samuel Frink to the Rev. Dr. Burton, Aug. 4, 1768, S.P.G. Papers, Ser. C,
Pkg. 7, Pt. iii (L.C. reel 16, 236–239).

of Hand from me. If I owe you any thing arrest me. I want none of your dear purchased Indulgencies, but Justice."[80]

Dr. Redmond Burke, a professor of physic and student in surgery and midwifery, in 1774 found himself in dispute with some other doctors in Savannah. "You murderous tongues, so wanton in assassination of the basest kind, I wish I could find some expedient to calm your malevolence," Dr. Burke said to them. "Would you not creep forth in darkness, like certain stinking vermin, through fear or shame of light, an expedient might perhaps be found, but, as the stench of crushed bugs is more noxious than their feeble bites, may you still creep in darkness, nor ever daub my fingers. The only consequence I dread from your stupid rancorous backbiting is, that, when my friends tell me of it, they may misconstrue my silent scorn and call it pusilanimity. ... *Cave, cave, and vale, vale.*"[81] When John Pettigrew, a Sunbury businessman, died in 1755, he left the following instructions: "I have no exception to any person in town being at my Funeral, but John Hardy, carpenter who I despise on account of his bad character, and as I hate all villains as I do snakes, I desire that my Executors shall turn that Scoundrell from my funeral should he have the impudence to attend it."[82]

Among gentlemen, however, cool restraint was from time to time deemed more effective than abuse. In 1772, for example, Archibald Bulloch, Speaker of the Commons House, sent his neighbor, John Houstoun, a cold note protesting the mistreatment of some of his slaves by Houstoun and one of Houstoun's blacks. A son of the late Sir Patrick and Lady Priscilla Houstoun, Houstoun was a planter and prominent citizen who in a very few years would become a Revolutionary governor of Georgia. Wrote Bulloch: "Sir I am just now come to Town, and am informed, that in my absence, some Differences having happened between one of your Negroes and mine, occasioned you to . . . beat some of my Servants; and that your Negro not satisfyed with that afterwards met one of my Negro Girls, when going of an Errand from her Mistress, and beat her, so that the things she had in Charge, were thereby much damaged. Such Conduct naturally inclines

80. Ottolenghe to William Gibbons, Jr., Jan. 23, 1765, William Gibbons, Jr., Papers, Perkins Lib., Duke Univ., Durham, N.C.

81. Advertisement of Redmond Burke, *Ga. Gaz.*, Nov. 30, 1774.

82. Will abstract of John Pettigrew, *Will Abstracts*, 109–110.

me to conclude, that I am not informed of every particular relative to this Matter, and therefore wou'd be glad to have it from yourself."[83]

We cannot determine whether tumultuous rhetoric reduced the incidence of physical assaults by permitting the colonists to work off their hostilities verbally. Indeed, the story of crime and violence in general can only be sketchily reconstructed, because court records are lacking. The colonists themselves, however, thought they had severe problems with law enforcement, problems that did not diminish as the province matured. In 1772 the jail at Savannah was deemed "not secure enough to confine an Infant," and jailers sometimes found themselves either out of employment or in actual confinement for their failure to secure their charges.[84] The colonial government tried jails of several kinds. An early prison in Savannah was "built wholly of strong Loggs, with a Flat Roof of the Same," but by 1743 it was so rotten "that it cannot be upheld."[85] In the 1760s the failure of such structures to hold prisoners necessitated the use of one of the four caponiers at Fort Halifax in Savannah.[86] The caponiers were covered passageways across the fort's ditch, and the one used as a jail was little better than the log or wooden prisons. In 1766 William Sikes, a horse thief with a remarkable record of escapes from other prisons, was confined there. He was tried, convicted, and sentenced to be hanged, and his execution was desired by almost everyone except himself. To ensure that Sikes would keep his appointment with the hangman, Matthew Roche, the colony's acting provost marshal, employed guards to watch him, fearing that eight other horse thieves in the caponier might join him in a mass escape. For once the prison was secure; Sikes died on the gallows on January 9, 1767, at the end exhorting the provost marshal to write to his wife and four children in South Carolina reporting his death and urging them to lead upright lives.[87]

Except for roads that were out of repair, no issue so interested grand juries in royal Georgia as the jails.[88] Jurors were not merely concerned

---

83. Archibald Bulloch to John Houstoun, 1772, Archibald Bulloch Papers (photostatic copy), Ga. Hist. Soc., Savannah. The original is in the New York Public Library.

84. *Col. Records of Ga.*, VI, 164, XII, 155–156; Ga. Hist. Soc., *Colls.*, VI, 177.

85. *Col. Records of Ga.*, XXIV, 100.

86. *Ibid.*, XIX, Pt. i, 128–129.

87. *Ibid.*, XIV, 557–558; *Ga. Gaz.*, Jan. 14, 1767.

88. Presentments of the grand jury, *Ga. Gaz.*, Dec. 24, 1766, July 19, 1769, and Jan. 5, June 29, and Dec. 21, 1774.

because the prisons were insecure; they were displeased by the indiscriminate carelessness that threw minor offenders into the same cells with felons under sentence of death. The jurors also protested the incarceration of whites and blacks together. The jails themselves were foul enough to kill. Thomas Kingsman, an obscure citizen convicted of petty larceny, in 1774 contracted a fever from "breathing an impure and putrid air" in a small cell that he shared with many other prisoners and died while being removed to an infirmary.[89]

The only surviving consecutive court records reveal the kinds of cases and a few of the judgments rendered in one six-month period—from May 22 to November 11, 1740. The court heard a guilty plea on a misdemeanor involving the firing of a gun in Savannah (a fine of 6s. 8d. was levied), indicted two men for unspecified misdemeanors, provided for the administration of an estate, and established a mechanism for settling a dispute involving a seizure of goods at Augusta (the case was adjudicated by arbitration). Sitting three times as a court of claims, the magistrates considered land claims from 153 persons; a fourth sitting reviewed the accuracy of the first three. The court levied three fines for nonappearance. It indicted four men for riotous assembly in the Creek nation and for beating two constables. Only one of those indicted was in custody, but he was fined £6 13s. 4d. Dr. Patrick Tailfer, a Malcontent, was sued for wages by Peter Snow and George Johnson; Tailfer lost both cases. John Gardner, an Indian trader, pleaded guilty to "Endeavouring to Defame the Character of Frances the Wife of Thomas Wattle, by saying she had given him the Foul Disease." For his slanderous allegation, Gardner was fined 6s. 3d. The court acted upon several recognizances and tried two causes for debt.[90]

The most serious case tried during the six months involved a double murder. Joseph Anthony Manzique and William Shannon were found guilty of killing two trust servants at Fort Argyle, a small military establishment on the Ogeechee River where the Indians often crossed the stream. Judgment was passed on October 11, 1740, and the two died on the gallows outside Savannah thirty days later. Shannon had been a difficult member of Oglethorpe's regiment who had once been suspected of being a Spanish spy and who had been whipped and drummed out of the service. Manzique was a Spaniard, perhaps an

89. *Ibid.*, June 29, 1774.
90. *Col. Records of Ga.*, XXII, Pt. ii, 432–435.

itinerant doctor, perhaps a spy, with whom Shannon had taken up company. After the hangings, the body of Shannon was sent by boat to the mouth of the Ogeechee River downstream from Fort Argyle and hung there in chains, "this being such a Situation for a Gibbet, as would be conspicuous to all who passed to and fro."[91]

Public executions engaged the rapt and morbid interest of many Georgians, and at least once, a pickpocket appeared at the gallows to rob the spectators.[92] Hanging was by strangulation. The condemned person climbed a ladder at the scaffold, had the rope put around his neck, and was turned off the ladder. At times in the eighteenth century, condemned persons on the way to the gallows were coldly but accurately reassured that such a death was not too different from dying of apoplexy. During the trustee period, criminals served as hangmen for remission of their own punishments plus a small allowance. After 1755, however, a public executioner was necessary to officiate at the gallows and to administer corporal punishment.[93] The government could no longer find volunteers willing to be hangmen.

The most common capital crimes involving white felons seem to have been murder and horse theft, although death sentences were imposed for cattle stealing, sodomy, and robbing the king's stores. (Blacks were also executed, but for a somewhat different set of offenses.) Women were not spared. Alice Riley was the first woman to be hanged in Georgia. The province was only about two years old when she held the head of a sick man in a bucket of water until he drowned. She was pregnant when sentenced to death, and the hanging was delayed until after her son was born.[94]

The capture of criminals was haphazard, there being no police force. The night watch and militia patrols, sometimes composed of citizens serving reluctantly, made arrests as best they could. But many suspects were brought in by private citizens, who were paid for their service.

91. *Ibid.*, IV supp., 23–24, 27–28, XXII, Pt. ii, 433, 435.

92. Unsigned advertisement, *Ga. Gaz.*, Aug. 17, 1768. For interest shown in a multiple execution, see *Col. Records of Ga.*, IV supp., 366–367, 377, 381–382, XXII, Pt. ii, 199–201; *S.-C. Gaz.*, Aug. 4–11, 1739.

93. *Col. Records of Ga.*, VII, 218.

94. *Ibid.*, XX, 626. A discussion of the Alice Riley case may be read in Sarah B. Gober Temple and Kenneth Coleman, *Georgia Journeys: Being an Account of the Lives of Georgia's Original Settlers and Many Other Early Settlers from the Founding of the Colony in 1732 until the Institution of Royal Government in 1754* (Athens, Ga., 1961), 77–79.

In the 1760s Jacob Hood, who may have lived in or near Augusta, was rewarded for delivering three felons to jail.[95] Some criminals were taken by hue and cry or by variations of it. Richard White, Alice Riley's accomplice in murder, escaped from jail and was sighted by a group of workmen, one of whom cried, "Yonder Goes a man very fast." When the men pursued and overtook White, he fell on his knees "and with many Blows on his Breast baged his Life." Notwithstanding his pleas, he was "had immediately to the Gallows" and put to death. The men who caught him shared a reward of £50 currency.[96]

By the 1770s many people were convinced that horse thieves should no longer be hanged. Although horse stealing was a capital offense in England upon first conviction, the colonists reasoned that horses were kept in enclosures there, whereas in Georgia they were often either wild or loosely held. It was difficult to know whether a suspect had thought he was picking up a stray. Jurors, prosecutors, and witnesses usually interpreted the evidence in favor of the accused, and persons suspected of being notorious offenders were sometimes set free without any punishment at all. Some Georgians believed that if the law commanded a lesser penalty than death—the whipping post, for example—juries would be more willing to convict.[97] Some also believed that if horse theft were not a capital crime in the first instance, a man stealing a horse would be less likely to murder its owner to cover his crime.

The case of Joseph Prine, "a notorious Horse Stealer," brought the question to a head in 1773. Prine, who was confined in Savannah's jail, not surprisingly escaped. The jail was then in such a tumbledown condition that repairs were not even possible. The weight of a new floor would have brought down the prison. Prine was rearrested in South Carolina in February 1773 and returned to Savannah. There members of the council, the lower house, and the public undertook to save him by changing the law that provided death for first conviction. In the assembly a movement arose to rewrite the "Act to Prevent Stealing of Horses and Neat Cattle" with the intent to abolish the death penalty for first offenders. Such a change, however, would not have affected Prine; he had been sentenced under the old act. A

95. *Col. Records of Ga.*, XIV, 102. The keepers of the night watch in Savannah were paid a small stipend during the royal period. *Ibid.*, XV, 211–212, 250.

96. *Ibid.*, XX, 152–153, 225.

97. *Ibid.*, XII, 388.

group of gentlemen protested that if Prine were hanged, "he is snatched away at the dawn of mercy, he is wrecked within sight of the harbour. . . . That he dies not for having Stolen a Mare, but for having Stolen in 1772 instead of 1773." Two days before Prine was to die, the lower house asked the governor to extend mercy. The Commons House, in an unusual move, even recorded the votes of its members, who recommended clemency by a margin of eleven to ten.[98] The council unanimously advised the governor to pardon Prine on condition that he leave the province immediately and never return, upon penalty of death.[99] The date was July 21, the day before Prine was to be hanged, and it is almost certain that he was spared. Two months later Governor Wright assented to a new law abolishing the death penalty upon first conviction and substituting corporal punishment in its place. To sign it, the governor had had to overcome personal reservations founded in his concern that the new act was contrary to the laws of England.[100]

For noncapital crimes, the stocks, the whipping post, the branding iron, the ducking stool, and the jail were Georgia's instruments of correction, as they were elsewhere in the eighteenth century. Men stood in the stocks for drunkenness or for perjury; women were condemned to stand at the whipping post for stealing fowls. Servants were whipped for running away and for theft, and vagrants were often sentenced to ninety days in jail. Men guilty of manslaughter might be burned in the hand with the letter "M."[101]

The courts sometimes assigned a variety of penalties for the same offense. A single session of the Court of Oyer and Terminer and General Gaol Delivery in 1770 imposed different punishments on three persons convicted of the same crime—larceny. All three were modest persons, not hitherto conspicuous in the colony. John Ward was burned in the hand with the letter "R." Ann Galloway was sentenced to be privately whipped, and Thomas Johnston to be publicly whipped.[102] A person might be imprisoned for forgery, riot, debt, and a variety of other causes, including being loose, idle, or disorderly. In some cases a convicted person might appeal a verdict to England, but

98. *Ibid.*, XV, 385, 386, 460–461, XII, 378.
99. *Ibid.*, XII, 378, XV, 463.
100. *Ibid.*, XII, 386–389, XV, 535.
101. *Ibid.*, XXI, 249, 250, XI, 254, XX, 353; advertisement of William Graeme, *Ga. Gaz.*, Aug. 3, 1768; *ibid.*, July 6, 1774.
102. *Ga. Gaz.*, Jan. 10, 1770.

during the entire trustee period, only one appeal seems to have been made.[103]

The most strenuous efforts of the courts and the enforcers of the peace were insufficient to suppress crime in the towns or to control it in the backcountry. Savannah was troubled with thieves and rogues to the end of the colonial period; the backcountry offered them haven.[104] As early as the 1730s, Oglethorpe declared that "Felons Runaway Servants, Outlaws and Slaves from Carolina . . . have already molested the Inland Parts of the Countrey and thieving . . . is grown so common that great numbers of Hogs, and not a few Cattel, have been killed in the Woods." Thieves were also active in Savannah, he said.[105] Georgians liked to believe that the villains were not Georgians but were from Carolina or from colonies further north. South Carolinians, on the other hand, thought that outlaws operated across a territory extending from Georgia to Virginia. They believed there were two or three hundred of them, all in communication with one another.[106] A reputable British publication reported that Indians in the backcountry of Georgia and South Carolina in one instance assisted the process of law enforcement. In 1767 an especially cruel gang of criminals committed murders and other crimes in the area, and several were captured by the authorities and put to death. Two, however, fell into the hands of Indians who burned them at the stake.[107] In 1763 horse stealing was so common around Augusta that citizens there agreed to subscribe to a reward that led to the capture and execution of one thief. (When time came to pay, however, many of those who had offered money declined.)[108]

Some leaders in the province feared that malefactors in the backcountry might be not only marauders but squatters as well. Before the Indian cession of 1773, "idle People from the Northward" built huts on lands they expected to be ceded. The intruders, the government was informed, were persons of "no setled Habitations" who lived by hunt-

103. Coulter, ed., *Journal of Gordon*, 10–11.
104. *Ga. Gaz.*, Aug. 10, 1774.
105. *Col. Records of Ga.*, XXII, Pt. ii, 169.
106. *South-Carolina and American General Gazette* (Charleston), July 31–Aug. 7, 1767.
107. *London Magazine: Or, Gentleman's Monthly Intelligencer*, XXXVI (1767), 539.
108. *Col. Records of Ga.*, XIV, 546–548.

ing and plunder.[109] The militia and honest farmers occasionally combined to pursue these rogues but never succeeded in exterminating them. Till the end of the era, upcountry settlers were vexed and harassed by them.

Articulate Georgians sometimes suggested that the prevalency of crime bespoke the unhealthful status of their society, and they lamented their failure to control it. They were more successful in attending to the health of their bodies. There were attempts at providing medical care in the province from the first day of its existence, and Dr. William Cox, a surgeon, was among the first arrivals. Medicine as practiced in the great cities of England and Scotland was then subdivided into categories, the most prestigious practitioner being the doctor of physic, who had learned the medical arts in a university and was licensed. He did little work with his hands. Sometimes he did not even see his patients, but prescribed on the basis of symptoms described to him. Dr. Cox, as a surgeon, ranked lower in status than a doctor of physic, since for many years surgeons had been associated with barbers in Great Britain. Both bled patients, set bones, cut boils and ulcers, and drew teeth. Surgeons nevertheless were striving, with some success, to distinguish themselves from barbers. Lower in rank than the surgeon was the apothecary, or pharmacist, a storekeeper who sold medicines and recommended cures to his customers. In Great Britain, surgeons and apothecaries were usually called "mister," but in Georgia and other colonies, they were called "doctor." Another kind of medical assistant was the midwife—always a woman—who assisted at childbirth.[110]

Dr. Cox was the first settler to die in Georgia. He survived his arrival by only a few weeks, and Noble Jones, who also arrived in America in 1733 on the *Anne*, administered to the sick as best he could in his spare time. Jones was a man of vast energy and many talents, all of which combined to advance him to elevated rank during a career that spanned Georgia's entire colonial period. Just what his English medical training was, if any, we do not know. He was skilled at carpentry and surveying, was a successful planter, and, as the

---

109. *Ibid.*, XXXVIII, Pt. i, 6–7.

110. For studies on colonial medicine, see Richard Harrison Shryock, *Medicine and Society in America, 1660–1860* (New York, 1960); John Duffy, *Epidemics in Colonial America* (Baton Rouge, La., 1953); and Boorstin, *The Americans: The Colonial Experience*, 207–239.

years progressed, served as a judge, member of the council, and royal treasurer of Georgia before his death in 1775. But he was most celebrated as a doctor. In time he took his son, Noble Wimberly Jones, into his practice and supervised the young man's medical education himself. They became the two best-known doctors in Georgia, despite the undetermined training of the one and the home tutoring of the other.

The lines of demarcation that in British cities separated the doctor of physic from the surgeon, and the surgeon from the apothecary, tended to blur in Georgia. (They had blurred as well in the British countryside, where almost all health care was delivered by surgeon-apothecaries.) We have already seen that Dr. Redmond Burke identified himself as professor of physic and student in surgery and midwifery, thus assuming the titles of all the divisions of medicine except apothecary.[111] The list of men, virtually all called "doctor," who were apothecaries and surgeons, or physicians and apothecaries, is an interesting one, even though we may not know the exact sense in which the terms were used locally. New surgeons and apothecaries were being trained in Georgia throughout the colonial period as old practitioners took in promising youths as apprentices.[112]

Doctors went to the homes of their patients even when the sick lived some distance in the countryside. The partnership of Whitney and Williams, who called themselves both surgeons and apothecaries, accepted cases "any distance in the country."[113] Dr. Noble Wimberly Jones would go forty miles, traveling on horseback and carrying firearms.[114] Some practitioners persuaded a portion of the public that they could work near-miracles. Dr. John Patrick Dillon, who served St. George and St. Matthew parishes, claimed to have cures for a variety of ailments, some of which baffle medical science to the present day. In 1774 Dr. Dillon's performance was attested by forty-six subscribers, including John Adam Treutlen, who was soon to become the first governor of the state of Georgia. Treutlen and his fellow signatories testified that Dillon had cured "Consumptions, Consumptive Fluxes,

111. Advertisement of Redmond Burke, *Ga. Gaz.*, Nov. 30, 1774.
112. For example, Dr. David Brydie took in a son of Jonathan Bryan. William and Edward Telfair and Company to Telfair, Cowper, and Telfair, Jan. 15, 1774, Telfair Family Papers, Ga. Hist. Soc., Savannah; Robert Cumming Wilson, *Drugs and Pharmacy in the Life of Georgia, 1733–1959* (Atlanta, Ga., 1959), 16–18.
113. Advertisement of Whitney and Williams, *Ga. Gaz.*, Nov. 9, 1774.
114. Jones to Grimes (n.d. except 1805), DeRenne MSS Coll.

Dysenteries, Rheumatisms, Cancers of all kinds, Fistulas, Hysterick Affections, Convulsions, Epilepsies, Apoplexies, Hypochondrias, Caries of Bones; Cancerous, Cavernous, Fistulous, and Malignant Ulcers; Pleurisies, Gravels, etc."[115]

Of necessity, many Georgians resorted to self-medication. James Johnston's first issue of the *Georgia Gazette* advertised books on health and home remedies.[116] At least one prominent family owned a handwritten booklet entitled "Doctrine of Inflim Diseases," which was probably a useful guidebook for self-treatment. Apothecaries fitted up boxes of medicines "for plantation use, with directions."[117] Georgians could purchase a lancet for cutting fistulas and bleeding patients like the one used by Dr. Noble Wimberly Jones—an instrument with a small, sharp blade that slipped into a leather case no larger than the little finger of an adult person.[118] Sometimes clergymen trained themselves to double as doctors and bled patients.[119] While teeth might sometimes be pulled by doctors, lay persons used "Tooth Drawers," which they sometimes left at their deaths to be inventoried in their estates, particularly if they had large families or owned slaves.[120] Even William Stephens practiced self-medication, although he could have afforded the services of any doctor in Savannah. Stephens wrote that "under a little disorder with a Cold, I could not give that due attention to Business which I would, but was obliged to sit Idle good part of the day, near the Warmth of a Chimney Corner, which with a little Kitchen physick I have never failed with good Success to make use of, as a Remedy in such Distempers."[121]

Self-treatment reached its fullest practice in royal Georgia. Many settlers had slaves, children, and spouses to care for, in addition to

115. *Ga. Gaz.*, June 15, 1774.

116. Advertisement of James Johnston, *ibid.*, Apr. 7, 1763.

117. Advertisement of James Cuthbert, *ibid.*, Dec. 15, 1763; "Doctrine of Inflim Diseases," MS booklet on medication, with the ending date of Mar. 3, 1772, Telfair Family Papers. See also advertisements of Henry Lewis Bourquin, *Ga. Gaz.*, Nov. 10, 1763 and Johnston and Irvine, *ibid.*, Dec. 7, 1774.

118. Dr. Jones's lancet survives in the DeRenne MS Coll. For an advertisement offering lancets to the public, see advertisement of Cuthbert and Platt, *Ga. Gaz.*, July 12, 1775.

119. Muhlenberg, *Journals*, II, 669.

120. Estate of John Stewart, Jan. 4, 1766, Inventory Book F, 195–197; estate of Samuel Fulton, Feb. 27, 1777, Inventory Book FF, 36.

121. Coulter, ed., *Journal of Stephens*, II, 177.

themselves. Also, the population was then less concentrated around Savannah, Ebenezer, Augusta, and Darien. Earlier the proprietors had provided public doctors and midwives for the poor. They had no difficulty in finding enough midwives but were less successful in recruiting doctors who would work for the £20 a year they offered. In 1746 or 1747 Patrick Graham, an apothecary and surgeon, accepted the job of public doctor. He then held an assistant's position in the trustee government that required his frequent presence in Savannah anyway.[122] Savannah had an infirmary in trustee and royal times; in addition, doctors arranged other lodging for persons who were desperately ill or required continuous care. But except at Bethesda, where Whitefield's followers had an excellent infirmary, hospitals were not places where the sick went very cheerfully. In 1774 the hospital at Savannah, a woeful establishment "not fully answering the intended purpose," was used "for the reception of sailors and all indigent sick people."[123] This meant that persons who used it were either destitute or were strangers from distant parts.

We know only a little of the mortality rate in the province, but the coastal lowlands of Georgia and other southern colonies were unhealthful—"in the spring a paradise, in the summer a hell, and in the autumn a hospital."[124] The death rate was probably highest during the colony's first year. Of 114 colonists who left England in 1732 on the *Anne*, 29, or 25.4 percent, were dead within a year. Within ten years, 47 persons had died.[125] Elizabeth Stanley, a midwife who arrived in 1733, delivered 128 children, then returned to England in 1736 to lie in herself. She did not trust the other Georgia midwives. Of the 128 children she delivered, 40, or about 31 percent, were dead by October 1736.[126] Some responsibility for this mortality rate must rest upon Oglethorpe and the trustees. "Often, settlers were given plots of lands, not of their own choice where the soil might be fertile

---

122. *Col. Records of Ga.*, I, 495–496, II, 479.

123. Presentments of the grand jury, *Ga. Gaz.*, June 29, 1774.

124. Quoted in David Hawke, *The Colonial Experience* (Indianapolis and New York, 1966), 494.

125. Coulter and Saye, eds., *List of Early Settlers*, xii.

126. McPherson, ed., *Journal of Egmont*, 243. In South Carolina and probably in Georgia as well, infant mortality declined after 1750. Dr. David Ramsay of Charleston said that mothers had learned how to care for their children more hygienically. Shryock, *Medicine and Society*, 99.

and the water pure, but in localities favored by the Trust. Witness the two-year struggle of the Salzburgers to move from their inaccessible, low-lying, mosquito-infested area at old Ebenezer to higher ground."[127] It is likely that the rate declined once settlers were free to decide what best suited them. By the 1750s Pastor Bolzius was convinced that the physical labor required in opening the frontier was itself a preserver of health when one guarded against overheating or getting cold.[128]

Like much of the world of the eighteenth century, Georgia was assailed by epidemics, some mortal, some merely debilitating. After repulsing the Spaniards in 1742, many Georgians who had remained in the province or who had returned to it after the waning of the Spanish threat began "falling down daily ill in Feavers." The fever might have been malaria. It weakened many and invaded every corner of the province. It was regarded as a calamity, but apparently only about ten persons died from it.[129]

Smallpox did not become a frightful malady until after 1750, when slaves entered the colony. Slave ships arriving from Africa or the West Indies were thought to be the source of infection, and might actually have been so. In Georgia's forty-three-year colonial history, nine outbreaks of smallpox are identifiable; some were epidemics. Georgia's outbreaks never coincided with epidemics that attacked Charleston, which suggests that the source of infection was foreign. In any case, the efforts of both Georgia and South Carolina to isolate the disease were evidently effective.[130] In 1755, for example, a vessel arrived at the mouth of the Savannah River with smallpox aboard, and the captain was required to run his ship up a side creek to wait out a quarantine. His crew and passengers were restricted to a small area near where the ship was anchored. No person aboard could pass along anything to persons on shore except with a "long cleft Stick, and what may be so received must be dipped in Vinegar, and afterwards smoaked before the Person receiving the same do touch it."[131] A little later the province turned to regularized isolation for those infected with, or ex-

127. Ready, "Economic History of Ga.," 56.

128. Loewald, Starika, and Taylor, trans. and eds., "Bolzius Answers a Questionnaire," Pt. i, *WMQ*, 3d Ser., XIV (1957), 240.

129. Coulter, ed., *Journal of Stephens*, I, 114, 126.

130. Joseph I. Waring, "Colonial Medicine in Georgia and South Carolina" (paper read before the Ga. Hist. Soc., Savannah, Mar. 27, 1971), 17–18.

131. *Col. Records of Ga.*, VII, 137–138.

posed to, smallpox or other serious infectious diseases at sea. A house of confinement—a lazaretto—was built on Tybee Island.[132]

When the officers of the colony failed to arrest disease at the water's edge, they moved against it on land. In 1773 a sea captain named Bunner seems to have concealed the presence of smallpox on board his vessel; the ship cleared the gunner at Cockspur and arrived at Savannah. As the passengers came ashore, one of them, a young member of the Shick family of Ewensburgh, plainly bore the scarcely healed marks of smallpox. At once port officials indignantly ordered Captain Bunner to move his ship down to Tybee Creek, and all of the passengers were urged to hasten down to the lazaretto.[133] Also in 1773 Governor Wright received information that smallpox had broken out at White Bluff on the plantation of John Houstoun. Slaves who had been exposed were separated from those who had not, and sentries were placed at the plantation's outer gate.[134]

Sometimes all efforts proved ineffective. The attitude of the colonists toward death, though not callous, was conditioned by the fearful uncertainties of life. When the 1764 epidemic, which killed some two hundred white persons overall, carried off only about forty in Savannah, the toll was seen as light.[135] The accumulated sorrows of frequent deaths did, however, move the sensitive to grief and tears. After the loss of several friends and acquaintances, Zubly wrote sadly: "What a dying World—and I am Spard."[136]

Inoculation against smallpox caused almost as much turmoil in Georgia as the disease itself. Uproars were common in other colonies as well. Medical science was decades away from Edward Jenner's discovery of a safe method of immunization, and until the end of the eighteenth century, inoculation meant rather clumsily infecting a person with what was hoped would be a light case of the disease. Some inoculated individuals died or infected others and thus spread the disease. A method well known in the southern colonies and recom-

132. Advertisement of commissioners for building a lazaretto, *Ga. Gaz.*, May 13, 1767; *Col. Records of Ga.*, X, 399.

133. Joseph Clay and Company to Bright and Pechin of Philadelphia, Jan. 26, 1773, Joseph Clay Papers, Ga. Hist. Soc., Savannah; *Col. Records of Ga.*, XII, 348–349.

134. *Col. Records of Ga.*, XII, 367–368, XIX, Pt. i, 503.

135. Ga. Hist. Soc., *Colls.*, VI, 27; *Col. Records of Ga.*, XXVIII, Pt. ii a, 427.

136. "MS Journal of Zubly," Oct. 1, 1771 (?), Ga. Hist. Soc., Savannah.

mended by a London physician involved wetting a piece of string with the issue from a pustule of an infected person, drying the string, lancing the arm of the person to be inoculated, and fixing the dried string in or on the incision with a plaster. Inoculation in both arms was recommended "lest one of the plaisters should happen to come off; though if it were done only in one arm, . . . it would very rarely fail of success."[137]

The argument over inoculation increased in intensity in Georgia in 1764 as a result of the epidemic of that year. There was a tumultuous wrangle between those who regarded it as a dangerous spreader of the disease and those who thought it a lifesaver.[138] Dr. James Cuthbert, an inoculator, was the object of so much vilification that, to demonstrate that he had the true interests of the people at heart, he offered free medical service to those who could not pay. Nine months later, perhaps because he had been so much abused, he left Georgia and went to England.[139] Later, however, he returned and died in the colony in 1770. At the hands of Dr. Cuthbert and other men, some Georgians gained immunity as inoculation went forward under provisions of local law that legalized it in exceptional circumstances.[140]

Venereal diseases, subject to no inoculation and unaffected by the methods then used to treat them, produced no epidemics but did cause alarm. Venereal infections in the American colonies were commonly found in seaport cities. But Kenneth Baillie, Sr., a planter of St. John Parish, found the people on his plantation much injured by the havoc wrought by an infected overseer.

Eloped from the subscriber's plantation on the night of the 3d inst. Allan Bourk, a native of Ireland, a tall slender man, with long black hair, a sallow sickly complexion, and downcast look. He was employed by me as an overseer to an out-plantation, producing a certificate of his capacity

137. *S.-C. Gaz.*, Apr. 19–26, 1760.

138. E.g., see letter of "A Real Friend to the Province and People," *Ga. Gaz.*, June 7, 1764; letter of "A Lover of Truth," *ibid.*, June 21, 1764; and letters of "Who do ye think?" and "Candidus," *ibid.*, June 28, 1764.

139. Advertisement of James Cuthbert, *ibid.*, July 12, 1764; sailing notices, *ibid.*, Apr. 11, 1765.

140. *Ibid.*, Apr. 4, 1765; *Col. Records of Ga.*, XIX, Pt. i, 27. The first large-scale test of inoculation in America had been conducted in Boston in 1721. Some 240 persons were infected with smallpox virus. The death rate among those inoculated was 1 or 2%. The mortality rate among those who caught smallpox naturally was about 15%. Shryock, *Medicine and Society*, 56–57. Inoculation was used extensively in Charleston in an epidemic in 1738.

from a gentleman of Carolina, which I believe to be forged. During four months stay he infected every negroe wench on the plantation with a foul, inveterate, and highly virulent disease. That none may be imposed upon, and have their property ruined by such a diabolical villain, I take this method of making him publick. At his elopment he carried off a new mattress, a pair of sheets, and a blanket, with several other things.[141]

Rabies appeared late in Georgia, not until the 1770s. It was so terrible when it came that in February 1772, Habersham, then acting as governor, and his council ordered the destruction of every dog found at large in Savannah and surrounding villages. Ironically, it was a dog owned by Habersham's young son, John, that had bitten a twelve-year-old mulatto boy on the cheek; the child contracted rabies and died in agony.[142]

While smallpox, venereal disease, and rabies baffled the finest physicians, the apothecary shops of Georgia—with the apothecary or his assistants providing advice along with the potions they marketed—promised cures for common ailments. That some of the medicines hurried patients toward their graves can scarcely be doubted. This was especially true when they were combined with bleedings, purgings, blisterings, and sweatings, all then regarded as excellent remedies. The balms of the shops promised relief from ague, pestilential pleuritic fever, dry gripes, fluxes, and even yellow fever. Ague probably was malaria, fluxes were dysentery, and dry gripes was lead poisoning that came from drinking alcohol stored or distilled in lead containers. Pestilential pleuritic fever may have been influenza.[143]

At the apothecary shop of Dr. Lewis Johnson in Savannah, one might buy the "Family Medicines of Dr. Hill's," which promised relief for a myriad of complaints: bad digestion, disorders of old age, colds, coughs, asthma, consumption, gout, rheumatism, scurvy, sores, hypochondria, and nervous disorders, including faintness, low spirits, and fits. Dr. Johnson also sold two other imports from Great Britain—"Daffy's Elixir" and "Squire's Elixir," two favorites for home medication. He offered lancets and instruments for drawing teeth, along with scales, weights, and thermometers.[144]

141. Advertisement of Kenneth Baillie, Sr., *Ga. Gaz.*, Sept. 26, 1765.

142. *S.-C. and Amer. Gen. Gaz.*, Feb. 12–20, 1772; Ga. Hist. Soc., *Colls.*, VI, 163–164; *Col. Records of Ga.*, XII, 217–218.

143. Waring, "Colonial Medicine in Ga.," 4, 5, 8.

144. Advertisement of Lewis Johnson, *Ga. Gaz.*, May 13, 1767. The *Gazette* had many advertisements of apothecaries from its first year of publication to its last.

The trend observable in Georgia medicine extended far beyond healing and health; it was a trend toward greater simplicity. The distinctions between kinds of doctors, important enough in the urban areas of Great Britain, broke down in Georgia where even men of medicine considered them not worth insisting upon. On the frontier, people with no claims to medical training made purchases in apothecary shops and provided major health care to themselves and to others. The trend away from formality and rigidity and toward simplicity and self-reliance was found not merely in Georgia but in the other colonies. It reversed itself in time, but while it lasted, it manifested itself not only in medicine but in other ways, most notably in the ways that Georgians viewed their vocations and earned their livelihoods.

Chapter 4

Occupations

Although Georgia was finally to find its place in the mercantile system of the British Empire on the basis of agriculture, men and women of many occupations were either sent or permitted to emigrate there in the trustees' efforts to populate the colony and to provide for its needs. The original occupations of 827 persons who settled at trustee expense between 1732 and 1741 fell into 125 categories. Among these were 41 farmers, 49 husbandmen, 41 laborers, and 322 servants, all of whom probably found uses for their skills. But what of 5 locksmiths, 2 watchmakers, 3 tallow chandlers, 5 peruke makers, 5 miners, 4 hatters, a wool comber, and a heel maker? In addition, the original occupations of 528 settlers who paid their way comprised 46 categories, some useful on a frontier and others of no imaginable value.[1]

From the first year of settlement, the process of simplification already seen in medicine was discernible in other occupations. Georgians were being separated from the European guild system, which for many of them had defined their roles and skills. The guilds had been a part of British and European commercial life since the Middle Ages. Without doubt, their powers had declined by 1733. But there remained large numbers of guilds, or companies, with substantial powers, even if their monopolies were no longer complete. Each governed itself, disciplined its members, enforced its standards, and caused goods of bad manufacture to be discarded. Perhaps even more important, each

1. Coulter and Saye, eds., *List of Early Settlers*, xi–xii. Secondary works that have influenced this chapter include: Thomas Jefferson Wertenbaker, *The Old South: The Founding of American Civilization* (New York, 1942), 220–270, and Boorstin, *The Americans: The Colonial Experience*. Carl Bridenbaugh, *Myths and Realities: Societies of the Colonial South* (Baton Rouge, La., 1952), was helpful for this chapter as well as for others.

was a fraternal brotherhood bound together by secret rituals and articulated interests. Such companies—the drapers, shipwrights, wax chandlers, grocers, weavers, glovers, and bakers, to name a few—could not be successfully transported to a frontier colony where the economy centered upon the trustee store.

Often settlers who came to Georgia with skills learned in these ancient guilds became detached from their vocations altogether. Virtually none of them practiced his trade fettered by old rules. To fare well on a frontier, men needed adaptability more than regulation, freedom more than supervision.

The British guilds, like their counterparts elsewhere in Europe, took in apprentices to be trained for a period of years and at the end turned them out as journeymen. A journeyman could expect that intelligent application, good health, and good luck would in time make him master of his own shop. Georgia artisans often had apprentices and journeymen to assist them, as did artisans in other colonies, but no apprenticeship law was ever enacted in Georgia. The value of apprentices to masters can hardly be disputed, however. Advertisements for the capture of runaways attest their worth. "Absented himself from the subscriber since September last, Thomas Rolls, an indented Apprentice about 14 years of age, well known in and about town," wrote Adrian Loyer, a Savannah silversmith, in 1774. The advertisement offered five shillings for the delivery of Rolls to either Loyer or the workhouse.[2] Employers sometimes taught their servants trades, or agreed to teach them trades, without formal apprenticeships, as William Bradley, who for a time was in charge of the servants of the trustees, falsely promised to do for young William Sinclair, and as Andrew Duche, a potter, actually did for two servants in 1739.[3]

Georgians who engaged in carpentry, brickmaking, shipbuilding, blacksmithing, baking, hat making and such trades were seldom called artisans. They were usually called "mechanicks," a term that in the eighteenth century embraced most kinds of skilled craftsmen. Georgia mechanics faced competition from two sources—British-made goods

---

2. Advertisement of Adrian Loyer, *Ga. Gaz.*, Jan. 19, 1774. James Johnston often advertised for a printer's apprentice; for example, see *ibid.*, Apr. 28, 1763, and June 29, 1768. There are numerous examples of employment of apprentices and journeymen. In the *Gazette* for Nov. 15, 1764, an unsigned advertisement sought a journeyman tailor; on May 25, 1768, a carpenter and cabinetmaker desired an apprentice.

3. *Col. Records of Ga.*, XXIII, 139, XXII, Pt. ii, 291.

and, for much of the era, goods made by black slaves, who could make barrels, mend chairs, or shoe horses as well as free white men. Most colonists understood that they must buy manufactured goods from England, for they knew that they could not make some things themselves and that Britain's mercantile policy required the colonies to bolster the economy of the mother country. In Georgia, British policy was paraphrased: "The daughter (i.e., English America) must serve the mother (i.e., old England) first."[4]

Mechanics were free from slave competition until 1750. Thus in 1746 a group of carpenters, emboldened by the legal restraints on slavery, posted a sign in Savannah insisting that thereafter they would work only for wages set by themselves.[5] Their announcement was mere whistling in the wind, important only as a miscalculation of power by one special interest group, because the trustees would not allow the carpenters to fix their prices. But they well understood the value of the mechanics' class, and when the trustees permitted African slavery in 1750, they sought to protect white mechanics by decreeing that blacks would be used only in agriculture, with the single exception that they could be coopers.[6]

Even as the proprietors did so, white artisans in Savannah correctly assessed their threatened situation and met to organize the Union Society, "composed chiefly of mechanics" and devoted to the interests of that class.[7] As the years passed, the Union Society became concerned with things other than class interest. However, in 1760, ten years after it was organized, it used the departure of Georgia's second royal governor as an occasion to reiterate its support for several acts passed by the general assembly that affected artisans, including an act to "*prevent the introduction of negro artificers*" into the colony.[8]

The mechanics had pressed the assembly to enact that measure in 1758, one of its purposes being to hold down competition from slave mechanics. (Another was to help populate the colony; the act encouraged white artisans to settle by limiting their competition.) Despite its purposes, the law did not effectively protect white mechanics,

4. Loewald, Starika, and Taylor, trans. and eds., "Bolzius Answers a Questionnaire," Pt. ii, *WMQ*, 3d Ser., XV (1958), 231–232. Bolzius wrote this statement in 1751.
5. *Col. Records of Ga.*, I, 495.
6. *Ibid.*, 58.
7. Address of the Union Society to Gov. Ellis, *S.-C. Gaz.*, Nov. 15–22, 1760.
8. *Ibid.*

for large slave owners did not wish the legislature to limit the ways in which they might use their work force. The slave-owning interests apparently emasculated the original bill proposed in the assembly, and a mere shell became law. Five well-to-do Georgians initially led the attack, declaring that the measure, if passed as the artisans wished, would "indulge the Greediness and insatiable Thirst after Gain of a few Tradesmen of the Town of Savannah."[9] That the act passed at all was due to Governor Ellis.[10]

The bill as approved expressed a sentiment more than it secured a result, for it was filled with exceptions. It did not apply to slaves who lived on farms. Slaves were permitted to be shipwrights, caulkers, sawyers, coopers, porters, or laborers. Also, white handicraft tradesmen who owned one slave were in some cases permitted to use him in trade. Further, if white carpenters, joiners, bricklayers, plasterers, or other tradesmen could not be found for a job, blacks might be employed without limitation after compliance with a few procedures. Equally as important as the exceptions was the appointment of a board of commissioners with powers to fix the wages of white carpenters, joiners, bricklayers, plasterers, and other tradesmen. The men named as commissioners were from the same class as those who had earlier protested the entire measure; one of them, John Graham (later to be made lieutenant governor), had been one of the petitioners against it.[11] The life of the act was seven years, and when it expired, no attempt was made to extend it. It had been enforced without enthusiasm, and consequently white artisans were devalued by slave competition.

There was never effective legislation to keep masters from hiring out slaves, and they regularly did so. Sometimes they put slaves out

9. See the petition of Edmund Tannatt, John Graham, Alexander Wylly, Lewis Johnson, William Handley, and others, in *Col. Records of Ga.*, XVI, 269–270.

10. Address of the Union Society to Gov. Ellis, *S.-C. Gaz.*, Nov. 15–22, 1760. Ellis was a man of warm sympathies and was apparently concerned for slaves as well as for artisans. His attitude toward the former was noticed by Ottolenghe, who in 1758 wrote: "How often the present humane Governor and I have comiserate their [the slaves'] hard and forlorn Fate, and propose to find out some Relief for them, which would not be difficult, but who must give the Consent to such Regulations? Why the Legislative Body compos'd mostly of owners of Negroes, who would as soon consent to it as an Assembly of Lawyers would pass a Bill to curtail their Fees." Joseph Ottolenghe to the Rev. Mr. Waring, July 12, 1758, MSS of Dr. Bray's Associates, Pt. H (L.C. reel 11, 335/208–209).

11. *Col. Records of Ga.*, XVIII, 277–282.

to find work without supervision, expecting to profit from their earnings. But unless the owner kept a sharp eye on his blacks, he was likely to have the kind of difficulty acknowledged by planter James Bulloch in 1775:

Three Negroe Fellows . . . called *Polydore*, *Morris*, and *July*, well known in town as porters or jobbers, having absented themselves for several months, without ever coming near me, or bringing me, in all that time, one shilling of their earnings, I hereby promise a reward of five pounds to any white person, and fifty shillings to any Negroe or other slave, that will apprehend Polydore . . . and forty shillings to any white person, and twenty to any Negroe or other slave, for each of the other two, Morris, and July. Polydore frequently is up the river about Greenwood and Higginson's plantation where he has a wife; Morris and July keep commonly about town cutting and felling grass and jobbing sometimes by land and sometimes by water.[12]

Polydore, Morris, and July did menial work that threatened few white men. Yet they demonstrated the liberty that masters sometimes permitted their slaves, expecting, of course, a return on their hire. Slaves with many different skills went out to work and were a real threat to white craftsmen.[13] Even if owners did not hire out their slave mechanics, they used them on their plantations to perform tasks for which free white men would otherwise have been employed. No plantation was considered well managed if the people living on it could not do all the common things necessary for its operation. Slave artisans made and laid bricks for their masters; they plastered houses, sewed clothing, sawed and squared lumber, shoed horses, made simple tools in the forge, constructed barrels, did all kinds of carpentry, and even swept chimneys.[14] They thus lessened the market for white men who earned their livelihoods doing the same work. (Free black men,

12. Advertisement of James Bulloch, *Ga. Gaz.*, Aug. 2, 1775.

13. For examples concerning black carpenters, see *Col. Records of Ga.*, XIX, Pt. i, 504; unsigned advertisements, *Ga. Gaz.*, June 1 and Nov. 9, 1774.

14. Advertisements of William Ewen, *Ga. Gaz.*, Aug. 25, 1763; estate of Thomas Sacheverell, *ibid.*, Mar. 8, 1764; estate of John Spencer, *ibid.*, Sept. 13, 1764; John Eppinger, *ibid.*, Dec. 24, 1766; and Andrew Johnston, *ibid.*, Dec. 9, 1767. Also, for advertisements concerning a cooper, see *ibid.*, Oct. 22, 1766; for a bricklayer and plasterer, *ibid.*, Sept. 9, 1767; and for sawyers, squarers, and a seamstress and cook, *ibid.*, Jan. 17, 1776. The inventory of the estate of George Cuthbert shows that a slave blacksmith was assessed at £90. July 22, 1768, Inventory Book F, 343, Dept. of Archives and Hist., Atlanta, Ga.

on the other hand, were not a threat to white men's incomes, for there probably were never more than two or three dozen adult free blacks in Georgia at any one time before the Revolution.)

In 1751, as the province stood on the eve of a change of government, DeBrahm (who sometimes exaggerated) declared that the colony was deserted except for government employees and the Salzburgers.[15] Yet even in economic depression, the Salzburgers had realized that mechanics were necessary to support their principal activity, agriculture. At Ebenezer they encouraged artisans at a time when many craftsmen were engaged in agriculture and husbandry. "We now have the most necessary craftsmen, such as carpenters, shoemakers, tailors, blacksmiths, locksmiths, weavers, masons, tanners. Several carpenters also do lathe and cabinet work if necessary, and have the necessary tools. One of us can make do as a cooper, but saddle makers and carriage builders, as well as a potter, are lacking. . . . At this time bakers and brewers, knitters, clothmakers, glass blowers and so on are needed in the land."[16]

The shop of one artisan, James Love, a cabinetmaker who lived in Savannah in the 1760s, provides a glimpse into the general social and economic standing of a typical Georgia craftsman. In 1758 and 1759 Love was granted two town lots: one appropriate for a residence, on St. James's Square near what would shortly become "Government House," and the other, suitable for a business establishment, on the Bay overlooking the river. Love's standing in the community was modest, although his death in 1768 was an event significant enough to be noticed by the *Georgia Gazette*.[17] He had a wife and three sons and owned five hundred acres in St. Matthew Parish, as well as three slaves—two men and a woman. Someone in Love's home liked books or regarded them as an investment, for at his death he left about sixty volumes, a sizable private library. His walls were hung with seven pictures. In 1768 his estate, exclusive of real estate, was worth more than £500.[18]

Negro furniture makers might have cut somewhat into Love's mar-

15. DeBrahm, *History of Ga.*, 20.

16. Loewald, Starika, and Taylor, trans. and eds., "Bolzius Answers a Questionnaire," Pt. i, *WMQ*, 3d Ser., XIV (1957), 242, 246.

17. *Ga. Gaz.*, May 4, 1768.

18. Will abstract of James Love, *Will Abstracts*, 80; estate of James Love, Sept. 12, 1768, Inventory Book F, 353–356.

ket. Nature gave him an advantage over house furnishings imported from Great Britain, however—an advantage that accounts in part for the size of his estate. Lumber was dear in England but inexpensive in Georgia. Love could get walnut, maple, oak, pine, and hickory from local sources at favorable prices, perhaps even from his own land.

Love's shop was equipped with seven benches, two lathes, and a vise. In his work he used bed screws, casters, chisels, nails, brads, gimlets, hinges, moulds, and glue; and at his death he had ready for sale three mahogany desks and two chests of drawers, a high chest of drawers, another desk and bookcase, four bedsteads, two stools, two armchairs, thirty-two red bay chairs, and other items. He had made the sides and ends for eighteen bedsteads and the posts for twelve, and he had some coffins. Love owned several lots of wood ready to be worked—266 three-inch red bay planks; 3 red bay logs; 97 three-inch mahogany planks; 13 mahogany logs; some mahogany, plain pine, and featheredged pine boards; and some walnut.[19] Cabinetmakers in other provinces, such as Duncan Phyfe, Thomas Elfe, and Thomas Affleck, have been much praised for their craftsmanship. However, the work of James Love and other Georgia cabinetmakers like James Anderson, James Muter, and John Spencer remains unevaluated. If specimens survive, they have eluded identification.

Love made fine furnishings and little else. However, other men who called themselves carpenters or joiners also built furniture. Usually a joiner did finer and more ornamental work than a carpenter, but on the frontier distinctions between carpenters and joiners were blurred. When in 1744 Bolzius referred to "our ingenious Carpenter," he was praising the man's resourcefulness and adaptability. Five years later Bolzius was pleased that the joiners could make simple machinery.[20] Benjamin Goldwire, a carpenter in Christ Church Parish in 1766, was, in the fashion of the day, probably an architect of sorts as well as a builder, for his estate contained books on architecture.[21]

Among other trades, evidence survives about Georgia's colonial bakers. Elizabeth Anderson complied with the law both in imprinting her loaves and cakes with her initials or symbol and in fixing her prices under the act of assize. She baked for a time on the Bay but

19. Estate of James Love, Sept. 12, 1768, Inventory Book F, 353–356.
20. *Col. Records of Ga.*, **XXIV**, 302, **XXV**, 374.
21. Will abstract of Benjamin Goldwire, *Will Abstracts*, 62.

moved in 1774 to a house on Broughton Street next door to Lady Houstoun.[22] Less can be said of Nevill Smith, a baker of Frederica, or of Anthony Pages and John Johnston of Savannah. All three men, however, being in port cities, likely prepared ship bread for voyages along with other breads for local consumption. In Savannah, Joseph Williams, whose shop sat opposite the Lutheran church, supplied an additional service to his customers. Not only did he make bread and biscuit for sale, but between the hours of eleven and one each midday, he cooked anything for dinner that was sent to him, "and hopes to give entire satisfaction to those who may employ Joseph Williams." Williams might have moved to Savannah after closing down a business at Sunbury, where there were persons who owed him accounts in 1766.[23] John Barrell, a baker who emigrated from Bristol, pledged exactness to those in Savannah who gave him business; he not only baked but delivered.[24]

Butchers, like bakers, practiced their craft under law. There were restrictions on the quality, preparation, and sale of meat. For example, the government wished to prevent the slaughter of animals within the capital itself; so in 1764 it sought to have slaughtering sites moved at least a mile away from Savannah.[25]

Johannes Altherr of Savannah, a German butcher, in 1755 or 1756 owned a herd of cattle at Purrysburg, fifteen head of wild stock outside Savannah, and a corral of hogs on what was probably a river island. Altherr had a large boat and anchor, and it is likely that the boat, rowed by slaves, brought the livestock to slaughter as often as the market required. Altherr's tools embraced a collection of knives, two hatchets, a meat chopper, a wash basin, and 101 pieces of soap. He had 1,700 pounds of salted beef cured and ready for sale.[26] For a part of the colonial period, law required butchers like Altherr to comply with customer requests for small cuts. They faced fines if they refused to "cut and sell any Part or Quantity as the Buyer may want of Beef or a single Joint of Veal Mutton Lamb or Pork."[27]

22. Advertisements of Elizabeth Anderson, *Ga. Gaz.*, Dec. 14, 1768, and Aug. 17, 1774.
23. Advertisement of Joseph Williams, *ibid.*, June 4, 1766.
24. Advertisement of John Barrell, *ibid.*, Mar. 25, 1767.
25. *Col. Records of Ga.*, XVIII, 459, 575–576.
26. Will abstract of Johannes Altherr, *Will Abstracts*, 1–2; estate of Johannes Altherr, May 29, 1756, Inventory Book F, 27–31.
27. *Col. Records of Ga.*, XVIII, 576–577.

Butchers may have committed the care of their knives and cutting instruments to one of Georgia's few cutlers.[28] Or, in the flourishing spirit of self-reliance, the butcher may have cared for them himself. In any event, it is difficult to imagine a Georgia cutler earning a livelihood without the broadest kind of business. It would have had to include the sale and maintenance of wood saws, axes, and surgical lancets, as well as the utensils of housewives, cooks, tavern keepers, and ship captains.

Cutlers were among the rare artisans; mariners and sailors were among the plentiful. Agriculture depended upon the sailors and boatmen, who served on the inland and coastal waterways, and upon the mariners, who went to sea. Because shipping was the lifeline of the province, the government undertook to do all the things necessary to ensure its order and welfare. It provided for lights, pilotage, harbor masters, and collectors and also supplied inspectors and packers, who loaded the ships so cargoes would not shift in transit. Businessmen opened ventures related to water commerce—sailmaking, insurance brokerage, and wharf tending. The general assembly helped captains keep their crews, all of whom were assumed to be drunkards, by setting penalties for sailors who jumped ship or who declined to leave on a voyage when the time of departure came.[29]

With the legalization of slavery in 1750, local boats were operated in part by blacks. A very few black boatmen were free, but most were slaves who worked in shifts on coastal vessels that changed crews every eight or ten days.[30] The records are filled with reports of slaves who fled ship duty and of black sailors for sale. John Graham and Company, in a typical advertisement, put on the market "Three Sailors, who had been used to go in the schooner and boat."[31] John Stevens, a planter living at Josephs Town just upstream from Savannah, used harsh language to voice annoyance with rowdy black sailors who entered his property illegally:

Whereas the house and wine room belonging to the subscriber at Josephtown was, on Friday night last, broke open by some negroes, who took

28. Will abstract of Isaac Brabant, *Will Abstracts*, 16.
29. *Col. Records of Ga.*, XVIII, 781. Few things were more consistently mentioned than the drunkenness of sailors. For example, see Coulter, ed., *Journal of Stephens*, II, 164.
30. Alexander Thompson to Admiralty, Aug. 3, 1773, Adm. 80/131, P.R.O. (photocopies at the Univ. of Ga. Lib., Athens).
31. Advertisement of John Graham and Company, *Ga. Gaz.*, Feb. 8, 1769.

from thence a quantity of rum and Madeira wine; and whereas it has been a common practice for trading boats and others to land their people, and remain whole nights and days on the plantation, to the great prejudice of the subscriber; this is therefore to give notice to all trading boats and others, that, from and after this advertisement, any negroe or negroes who shall be found landing, or within the fences on the said plantation, not having a proper note from their owners, shall be whipped according to law, if in the day-time: And, for the better securing my property by night, I hereby give notice, that on Monday evening next I shall lay two spring-man-traps near my landing and dwelling-house, and keep fire arms ready in case of the least attempt.[32]

Shipbuilding was not of the same importance in Georgia as in New England or even in Charleston. Still, Georgia possessed tall trees for masts, oak timbers for the hulls of vessels, and pitch, tar, and turpentine for making boats watertight. Shipbuilding on the Savannah River employed some Georgians. In 1754 Peter Baillou, a Savannah shopkeeper, ordered built a square-sterned sloop of about forty tons, which he named *Luck of Providence*.[33] From its small size and style, one would judge that the *Luck* plowed the waterways of the province and perhaps served the South Carolina run. Later at least one boat was made at Augusta, a vessel that could carry six to seven hundred bushels of corn.[34] At Yamacraw, Robert Watts built a large ship to carry eighteen hundred barrels of rice; it went into service in 1775 for the Savannah mercantile house of Cowper and Telfairs.[35] Edward Somerville, a Savannah merchant, in 1760 sought and got a hundred feet of riverfront under Savannah Bluff for construction of a vessel; and in 1770 John Wand of Antigua undertook to build the *Elizabeth*, a large vessel, at Savannah. Wand procured through a London merchant some of the iron work, sails, cordage, and other materials to be used in the construction.[36] His need to buy necessary items elsewhere, at a cost of about £1,300, shows one reason why Georgia was not a major shipbuilding province. Nevertheless, an effort toward an organized industry commenced in the 1770s at Bewlie, the plantation that had once belonged to William Stephens and that later passed to John Morel.

32. Advertisement of John Stevens, *ibid.*, June 27, 1765.
33. *Col. Records of Ga.*, VI, 436–437.
34. Advertisement of Seth John Cuthbert, *Ga. Gaz.*, June 21, 1775.
35. *Ga. Gaz.*, May 17, 1775.
36. *Col. Records of Ga.*, VIII, 404; MSS concerning the ship *Elizabeth*, John Wand Collection, Ga. Hist. Soc., Savannah.

Daniel Giroud was ship's craftsman at Bewlie. In 1774 he advertised for carpenters who "will meet with good treatment and good wages, and will be paid off very punctually every month in cash."[37] Ten months later the *Bewlie* was launched, a vessel displacing about two hundred tons. Morel's craftsmen also cut and sold live-oak timbers for sterns, sternposts, transoms, bow timbers, futtocks, aprons, knees, and other things needed for making good ships.[38]

Georgians, however, largely missed an opportunity for selling oak to the king's navy. The navy found the planters indifferent, because their slaves could be used more profitably to grow indigo. The navy urged them to cut timber in winter "when their Indigo works would be put to stand"; but the planters would not commit themselves without skilled persons to supervise the conversion of the hardwood once it was fallen, and such persons were not available in the colony.[39]

In the building construction trades, which involved easier work with softer timbers, white craftsmen suffered little from the competition of British imports, for the obvious reason that no one could import a building. They did, however, face serious competition from slave laborers, many of whom were skilled not only in carpentry but in the important work of brickmaking and bricklaying. Even though houses were mostly wooden, there were crucial needs for brick in construction. Wooden foundations of buildings decayed or were eaten by termites, and wooden chimneys were forbidden by law. Too heavy to import except as ballast, a great many bricks were made locally.

John West was among the first in Georgia to set about brickmaking as a private venture, although in England he had been trained as a smith. West declared in 1738 that he could make (or "burn") 1,200,000 bricks a year in "noo ways in fearior to English and for half the price." Between January and August 1738, he made more than 200,000. His competitor and estranged former associate, Samuel Holmes, did not agree that West's product was of sound quality. He thought that West made the kind of bricks one might expect from a smith.[40]

Brickmaking was also practiced on many Georgia plantations. Virtually the only requirements were wood for a fire, good clay, forms in

37. Advertisement of John Morel, *Ga. Gaz.*, Feb. 23, 1774.
38. *Ga. Gaz.*, Dec. 28, 1774; advertisement of John Morel, *ibid.*, Oct. 11, 1775.
39. Charles Inglis to John Montagu, July 11, 1772, Adm. 1/484, P.R.O.
40. *Col. Records of Ga.*, XXII, Pt. i, 221–222, 244–245.

which bricks could be shaped, a kiln, and labor. Kilns could be built almost anywhere. Thomas Cook, a temporarily unemployed brick-maker of the royal period, stood ready to engage himself "with any gentleman" for the manufacture of brick, which meant that he would go to a distant plantation as readily as to a nearby brickyard.[41] In Savannah, Thomas Lee ran a brickyard using slave labor. One of the slaves was David, newly brought from Gambia in Africa. He spoke no English, but comprehended it sufficiently to assist Lee, which suggests that the craft of burning brick was universalized indeed.[42] Since bricks were a part of most buildings, bricklayers seldom seem to have been unemployed. Colonial wills suggest that good bricklayers accumulated modest estates, and some felt secure enough to form partnerships.[43]

Sawyers had no competition from Great Britain, for no one imported wood unless it was intended for specialized uses (like mahogany). However, free sawyers after 1750 survived competition from slave laborers only with difficulty. White men who called themselves sawyers in royal Georgia were likely supervisors at sawmills or were overseers on plantations where lumber cutting was a principal undertaking. Lewis Johnson, a man with extensive business interests, employed several white overseers in his sawing operation and advertised for one in 1767: "Wanted, An Overseer who understands the Business of Stave-Making, to take charge of a few negroes employed in that way." Staves such as these were used to make tubs and barrels, and that craft too was largely in the hands of slaves.[44] Sawing was laborious and was done by hand. A log was fixed upon a pen, and two men, one on each end of a whipsaw and one standing in a shallow pit, cut the log into boards. Hugh Mackay in the late 1730s worked seventeen of the trust's servants who spent a part of their time sawing. They labored "in the open air and sun, in felling of trees, cross-cutting and splitting of timber, and carrying it on their shoulders, when split, from the woods to the camp."[45]

41. Advertisement of Thomas Cook, *Ga. Gaz.*, Aug. 6, 1766.

42. Advertisement of Thomas Lee, *ibid.*, Dec. 3, 1766.

43. Will abstract of James Corneck, *Will Abstracts*, 31; will abstract of John Eppinger, *ibid.*, 45–46; advertisement of James Morrison and George Williams, *Ga. Gaz.*, Nov. 29, 1764.

44. Advertisements of Lewis Johnson, *Ga. Gaz.*, Apr. 29, 1767, and Oct. 18, 1764; advertisement of John Wood, *ibid.*, July 5, 1775. For an exception, see will abstract of Stephen Tarrian, *Will Abstracts*, 135.

45. Ga. Hist. Soc., *Colls.*, I, 187.

Rafts of shingles, staves, and cut lumber were often floated on the inland waterways. Lumber was a major export, borne to foreign markets principally by transient traders, for if Georgia farmers largely eschewed cutting oak for the king's navy, they were ready to have their slaves cut softer woods. The saw and the axe echoed in the forests and produced profit, even when the wood was only for local fuel. "To be sold for ready Money, at the Hermitage Landing, Fire-Wood at 4s. a Cord," read a notice of 1776.[46]

Painters suffered from the competition of black slaves, and they necessarily diversified their activities. A painter, who in England would have been a specialist, in Savannah would paint anything—houses, signs, or ships. Even though some advertised narrow specialties such as painting or gilding coaches and riding chairs, they could not have made a living at that unless they took on other kinds of work.[47] Painters (and sometimes carpenters) installed glass, for example, thus assuming a part of the traditional role of glaziers. They did not finish or polish the glass but only installed what was imported.

What of the crafts not associated with construction trades? What of the silversmiths, the watchmakers, the tailors, the saddlers, the potters, and other craftsmen who produced or kept in repair some item or items? There were silversmiths in Georgia even during the proprietary period, when the economy would have rendered their livelihoods marginal. By royal times some prosperous Georgians began to indulge a taste for plate and expensive table utensils, for jewelry in modest amounts, and for seals. William Sime came to Savannah from Great Britain and set himself up to please such individuals. At his business on Broughton Street, he worked as a goldsmith and jeweler. He made mourning rings and mounted and repaired swords and cutlasses. He also made and mended jewelry and ciphered countinghouse and office seals.[48]

Adrian Loyer, the Savannah silversmith, combined that craft with clocksmithing. His work embraced the "making or mending Clocks and Watches, Gold and Silver Work, Motto Rings, Lockets, and Hair

46. *Ga. Gaz.*, Jan. 3, 1776.
47. Advertisement of Robert Punshon, *Ga. Gaz.*, Apr. 26, 1769; unsigned advertisement, *ibid.*, Feb. 18, 1767.
48. Advertisement of William Sime, *ibid.*, Mar. 1, 1769. One silversmith in Georgia during the proprietary period was John Neild of Frederica. Neild did not rely on his craft for his total livelihood, for he was also a soldier. *Col. Records of Ga.*, XXIV, 387–388.

Work of all kinds, Guns, Swords, and Pistols, or any kind of Mathematical Instruments repaired and cleaned." Loyer brought over fine merchandise from London. So successful was he that he also imported Henry Finlayson, a British jeweler and silversmith, to assist him.[49]

Clocks and watches were common items. In 1735 two silver watches worth £6 each were presented as gifts to the captain of the colony's scout boat and to the captain of the Rangers.[50] Watches were housed in engraved cases of gold or silver and were either simple or repeating (striking). Clocks were plain, musical, chiming, or eight-day. Some men earned livelihoods specializing in watch and clock repair alone. But at Sunbury, Richard Wells made, as well as repaired, timepieces and took orders from the countryside. In Savannah, if one did not wish to deal with Loyer or Sime, he might go to James Green, William Watt, Robert Brown, or to Charles Bachelard, who had left the firm of Sime and Wright and had taken up business in a shop near the market in Ellis Square.[51] The public clock in Savannah, a timepiece that struck the hours, overlooked the town in trustee times, standing high at the end of the trustee store, "the most eminent and conspicuous place at present in Town." Loyer kept the town clock running during the royal period.[52]

There is no way of knowing how much of the money Georgians spent on watches, clocks, silverware, swords, rings, and jewelry went to support local artisans and how much went to Great Britain. A Georgian could order an item directly from the mother country with the cooperation of any merchant. Probably most of the money crossed the Atlantic. When, in the years before the Revolution, the Commons House of Assembly decided that its dignity required a mace, it did not consider employing a local artisan to make it. It turned instead to England, where Benjamin Franklin was the colony's agent. Franklin engaged the firm of William Pickett and in June 1770 paid about £89 for the finished item. It weighed about 154 ounces, was gilded and engraved, and rested in a red leather case.[53]

49. Advertisement of Adrian Loyer, *Ga. Gaz.*, June 7, 1775. Also see *ibid.*, Jan. 26, 1774.

50. *Col. Records of Ga.*, II, 95.

51. Advertisement of Richard Wells, *Ga. Gaz.*, Aug. 23, 1775; advertisement of Charles Bachelard, *ibid.*, July 13, 1774.

52. *Col. Records of Ga.*, XXII, Pt. i, 100, XVIII, 406.

53. "Bill to Dr. Franklin for a Mace" (paid June 21, 1770), Benjamin Franklin Papers, Keith Read Collection, Univ. of Ga. Lib., Athens.

It was not only for maces that Georgians looked to England. Tailors abounded locally, yet some of the wealthier colonists were dissatisfied with their work. Habersham, as already seen, considered them crude craftsmen. "All my clothes are miserably spoiled by the Bunglars here, and after repeatedly trying new Hands, I am forced to this Method of getting a decent Garb," he said, making arrangements to have his outfits made in London. During a part of the 1760s, Habersham lived next door to, and apparently rejected, two tailors in Savannah, William McDonald and Samuel Robinson.[54]

Of those among the 1,355 persons who emigrated to Georgia between 1732 and 1741 whose occupations can be determined, 23 called themselves tailors.[55] In royal times advertisements of tailors in the *Georgia Gazette* were numerous. Although some craftsmen in the 1760s and 1770s declared that they sewed according to latest fashion, others merely praised the neatness of their work. John McFarlein promised work "after the newest fashions in London," while David Gionovoly pledged "work done after the best manner, and with the greatest dispatch." Morgan and Roche simply offered "diligence and quick dispatch." Sinclair Waters and James Shannon promised "work done in the neatest manner, at the shortest notice, and on the most reasonable terms."[56]

Tailors often took in helpers. Jonathan Remington desired "two or three Journeymen Taylors, who are sober industrious men, and good workmen." Robert Pattison, who arrived from London and set up a shop with his name over the door down the street from James Johnston's printing office, desired "a smart white Boy or Negroe as an Apprentice."[57]

Wigmakers would have had greater difficulty in taking on apprentices, because, as noted, the use of wigs declined steadily. Wigmakers therefore not only made wigs but, as elsewhere, dressed natural hair; in short, they became barbers as well. "Richard Thompson, Peruke-

54. Ga. Hist. Soc., *Colls.*, VI, 61; advertisement of William M'Donald and Samuel Robinson, *Ga. Gaz.*, Sept. 3, 1766.

55. Coulter and Saye, eds., *List of Early Settlers*, xi–xii.

56. Advertisement of John M'Farlein, *Ga. Gaz.*, Dec. 6, 1764; advertisement of David Gionovoly, *ibid.*, May 13, 1767; advertisement of Morgan and Roche, *ibid.*, July 12, 1769; advertisements of Sinclair Waters and James Shannon, *ibid.*, Sept. 14, 1774.

57. Advertisement of Jonathan Remington, *ibid.*, Dec. 13, 1764; advertisement of Robert Pattison, *ibid.*, Oct. 25, 1775.

Maker and Hair-Cutter from London, Gives this publick notice, that he intends following his business, at the house of Mr. Christopher Ring in Broughton-street."[58] Thompson's advertisement made clear that in London he had both fashioned wigs and dressed natural hair and that he intended to do both in Georgia. Other wigmakers engaged in unrelated undertakings to improve their livelihoods. Thomas Mills made wigs at his shop on the Bay but also sold jewelry, glasses, hardware, toys, sweetmeats, currants, figs, walnuts, and hairpins, and gave cash for beeswax. John Doors was both a planter and a peruke maker.[59]

English competition in leather goods would have undercut Georgia tanners and leather workers except for the availability of hides. Not the least of the disadvantages for the tanner was the expense of setting up a shop. He required tools for cutting and scraping hides and a machine for making tannic acid from the bark of oak trees. He needed several vats, salt and lime, a great deal of water, and a house or shed of sizable proportions. In 1751 two indentured servants, John and Ulrich Neidlinger, and their wives, set up a tanning mill in one channel of the Salzburgers' gristmill. Bolzius computed the capital outlay involved in the project at more than £30. The Neidlingers, father and son, were in business for themselves, their freedom having been bought for them for £10. They were not the first tanners in Georgia, for William Moor had practiced the trade fourteen years earlier in Frederica.[60] Hides were easy to come by. Each time a cow died or was killed for food, the hide was either tanned or soon spoiled. Tanners could set up their operations near the towns where the animals were slaughtered for food or on plantations where they could get hides from nearby farms or cow pens.

In 1774 Lachlan McGillivray offered to lease a piece of land near Savannah where there was "a commodious dwelling-house, a good kitchen, and a large out house, with a number of tan vatts in good order, very convenient for carrying on the tanning business."[61] Such an operation would likely have been operated by a white man with slave

58. Advertisement of Richard Thompson, *ibid.*, Oct. 6, 1763.

59. Advertisement of Thomas Mills, *ibid.*, July 13, 1774; will abstract of John Doors, *Will Abstracts*, 42.

60. *Col. Records of Ga.*, XXVI, 200, XXII, Pt. i, 16. Before the Neidlingers began their operations, leather from Europe was sometimes received in Ebenezer as a gift. *Ibid.*, XXV, 215.

61. Advertisement of Lachlan M'Gillivray, *Ga. Gaz.*, Jan. 26, 1774.

assistants. "Run Away from the late Mr. Jones, tanner, at Mr. Ports's place, a Yellowish Negroe Fellow, middle aged, and pretends to have a hurt in his hand; his name Bentley, and has been used to the tanning business," read a notice of 1767.[62]

William Smith, a prominent planter at Smithfield, left in his estate a "parcel of Tanned Sole Leather, which will be sold in lots, to contain 50 or 60 sides in a lot."[63] The sale, conducted at Joseph Pruniere's store in Savannah, doubtless attracted some of the leather workers of the province—makers of saddles, harnesses, bridles, shoes, and leather work clothes. Simon Rouvier of Christ Church Parish considered himself both a tanner and a shoemaker; his brother John called himself a "cordwainer," the common name of the trade guild of shoemakers in England.[64] In Ebenezer in 1739 a shoemaker was given leather and other supplies on condition that he make shoes for the Salzburg orphan house for half price, but he died after working only five weeks.[65] Bolzius reported that the Salzburgers "are now again Destitute of a Shoemaker, and being in Want of Shoes at this time, I was forced to hire a Shoemaker who has agreed to make as many Shoes, as we shall want for the present, and the Rest of Leather shall be kept in good condition."[66]

During royal times shoemaking, like tanning, sometimes moved out of the towns and onto plantations. "A Sober industrious single Man who can make a good strong neat shoe, will meet with proper encouragement by applying to John Mitchell, of St. John's Parish," read a notice of 1774.[67] Mitchell, who owned almost 1,450 acres in the parish, probably wanted a man to make shoes for slaves. In 1774 there were more than fifteen thousand slaves in Georgia, all needing shoes in winter.

Most locally produced leather was used by saddlers, who made, sold, or mended a variety of items. Frederick Holzendorff, who at different

62. Advertisement of John Edwards, *ibid.*, Dec. 16, 1767. The slave referred to was sought in Georgia, although he had worked on a South Carolina plantation. Tanning operations were similar in both colonies.

63. Advertisement of Matthew Roche, *ibid.*, Oct. 22, 1766.

64. Will abstract of Simon Rouvier, *Will Abstracts*, 120; will abstract of John Roviere, *ibid.*, 121.

65. *Col. Records of Ga.*, XXII, Pt. ii, 159–160.

66. *Ibid.*, 219–220.

67. Advertisement of John Mitchell, *Ga. Gaz.*, Oct. 5, 1774.

times followed his craft in Savannah, Sunbury, and Newport, lined riding chairs with livery or saddle lace and made or mended harnesses, men's and women's saddles, pistol cases, saddlebags, cruppers, collars, mailbags, pads, bridles, girths, and silk whiplashes. From London he imported and offered for sale nails, buckles, chair reins, bits, whip thongs, harnesses, and chair lace—"in short all kinds of saddlery, and supposed to be the most complete assortment ever yet brought into Georgia."[68] Hugh Sym, a Charleston saddler who relocated in Savannah, carried on "the saddle and harness business in all its branches." He also made fire buckets and jockey caps.[69]

Sym's caps were special items, for Georgia men and women mostly wore imported headgear. English hats were noted for their low prices and good quality. Yet in the first nine years of the province, at least four hatters and one haberdasher settled there. It is certain that the hatters quickly abandoned their trade. In royal times there were milliners who specialized in hats and their trimmings, but beyond doubt, they sold, rather than created, their merchandise.[70]

Potters were as rare as hatmakers, even though Georgia showed early promise of becoming a seat of the former craft. History has adjudged that no southern province was noted for its pottery, yet in 1737 Andrew Duche, a French Huguenot born in Philadelphia, appeared in Georgia and discovered a deposit of superior clay near Savannah. He built a dwelling house, "with a large Kiln in a room annexed," and took in two servants as apprentices. Duche "baked off 2 Kilns of handsome Ware, of various kinds of Pots, Pans, Bowls, Cups, and Jugs, fit for many uses: and tho 'twas a large quantity; they are found so convenient, that he does not want Customers to take them off his hands. ..." Experimenting with fine clays to make something more unusual for "transporting," he produced a small teacup that, when held against the light, was virtually transparent. The quality of Duche's work excited comment inside the colony and out. "The Potter has the Model from his Lordship of the Flower Pot, and the Coffe cup from his Countess, both before him; which he has been chewing upon some days; but

68. Advertisements of Frederick Holzendorff, *ibid.*, Apr. 25, 1765, and Dec. 3, 1766.

69. Advertisement of Hugh Sym, *ibid.*, Aug. 15, 1765.

70. Coulter and Saye, eds., *List of Early Settlers*, xi–xii. See also advertisement of H. Rowning, *Ga. Gaz.*, Dec. 7, 1774.

has not yet fully told me what can be done in it," Stephens wrote to the trustees' accountant in London. Duche's career in Georgia, which had once seemed promising, was not ultimately successful. He cast his lot with the Malcontents and lost the goodwill of Stephens, who thereafter wished him well neither in his work nor in his designs to reform the colony.[71]

The colony could afford to dispense with its potter, but it could not have spared its blacksmiths. The smith was a man of versatility. In the absence of a gunsmith in trustee times, the public smith mended the firearms of the militia and of friendly Indians.[72] After 1750 the livelihoods of white blacksmiths were imperiled by numerous slaves who were competent at the forge. Still, whites were never eliminated from the craft. John Richards, for example, took up his trade in Savannah in 1766, offering to do a variety of tasks—ship work, gun work, plantation work, "all Work necessary to be done about a House. . . . As he is a young beginner, he hopes by close application to his business to give entire satisfaction to all who may be pleased to favour him with their custom."[73]

Artisans representing other well-known crafts also set up business in Georgia. John Wood was a tallow chandler and soap boiler, John Menzies served the colony as a bookbinder, and John Gallache was a gunsmith.[74] James Johnston's printing house supported a household into which nineteen children were born. Millers ground good flour at Augusta, and dozens of mills were worked all over the province. The Salzburg mill establishment was begun in the early 1730s and survived flood, questionable management, and in 1742 the invasion of a giant "crocodile" (actually, an alligator).[75] Georgians also did well as wheelwrights, carters, and wagoners. Surveyors were in demand, and their skills were tested continuously by the rigors of marking off

71. Coulter, ed., *Journal of Stephens*, I, 9; *Col. Records of Ga.*, XXII, Pt. i, 168–169, 331; Ga. Hist. Soc., *Colls.*, III, 102; and McPherson, ed., *Journal of Egmont*, 366–367.

72. *Col. Records of Ga.*, XXIV, 194.

73. Advertisement of John Richards, *Ga. Gaz.*, Dec. 24, 1766.

74. Advertisement of John Wood, *ibid.*, June 15, 1774; advertisements of John Menzies, *ibid.*, Feb. 16 and 23, 1774; will abstract of John Gallache, *Will Abstracts*, 56.

75. Advertisement of Alexander Fyffe and Company, *Ga. Gaz.*, Nov. 22, 1764; Urlsperger, ed., *Ausführliche Nachrichten*, II, 1944. The "crocodile" was crushed to death.

new farms in virgin prospects. Some employment existed for garden-
ers, especially in trustee times. Habersham later had an English gardener, and in 1768 Alexander Petrie offered himself to gentlemen who
wished to have gardens made or tended.[76]

In all the American colonies, some undertakings were discouraged
by British policy, among them the manufacturing of cloth. Spinning,
weaving, and knitting were done mostly in Georgia homes. There was,
however, a weaver at Ebenezer, and the Bethesda Orphan House at
one time embarked upon a short-lived project to make cloth.

By contrast wine-making was an industry that the British government encouraged. Efforts came to little, though, for Georgia wines
were not good. Stephens had envisioned a profitable arbor at Bewlie,
but many of his grapes dropped off before maturing. The wine from
those that ripened had "a Stronger Body than any I had yet met with,
a little rough upon the Palate, and with a bitterish Flavour."[77] Although nature seemed to encourage the cultivation of grapes, "there
is no Person, who will listen to her Addresses, and give her the least
Assistance, notwithstanding many of the Inhabitants are refreshed
from the Sweetness of her wild Productions."[78] A few men profited
from selling imported wines, although wines were not widely drunk.
The sole distillery in royal Georgia belonged to Andrew Elton Wells,
mariner, planter, port official of Savannah, and whiskey maker.[79]

There were useful and enjoyable pursuits that offered little chance
for earning a livelihood, such as hunting and fishing. Fish and game
were plentiful and sold for low prices. Men sometimes hunted deer for
their hides but left the carcasses to rot in the forest; the price of venison
scarcely justified getting it to market. Georgians liked to occupy themselves with business that promised large profits rather than small
ones, "since clothing and European goods and many other things are
very expensive."[80] For that reason, only a few white men earned liv-

76. Advertisement of Alexander Petrie, Ga. Gaz., Aug. 31, 1768.
77. Coulter, ed., Journal of Stephens, II, 5–6, 124.
78. DeBrahm, History of Ga., 22.
79. Will abstract of John Baptist Deloney, Will Abstracts, 39; will abstract of
Nicholas Horton, ibid., 70; will abstract of Andrew Elton Wells, ibid., 142. Wells,
a supporter of the Revolution in Georgia, was a brother-in-law of Samuel Adams of
Massachusetts.
80. Loewald, Starika, and Taylor, trans. and eds., "Bolzius Answers a Questionnaire," Pt. ii, WMQ, 3d Ser., XV (1958), 243.

ings as laborers or as porters. Both undertakings were largely abandoned to slaves who could be hired for the service. There was money, however, in the Indian trade and in work such as land brokerage and vendue mastering at public sales.[81]

In addition to the many craftsmen pursuing their trades in Georgia, there was a group of professional men whose skills, however crude, were valuable to the province. Throughout the colonial period, scribes and clerks found a demand for their services. In 1739 Oglethorpe declared that "writing for me is full one Man's work," and Stephens was troubled by the difficulty of finding a scribe both efficient and discreet.[82] Until 1763 there was no printing press in Georgia, and orders, regulations, laws, proclamations, broadsides, and even many business and governmental forms, were handwritten. Even after James Johnston established his press in Savannah, scribes could find employment. Correspondence had to be written at least twice, one copy being retained by the sender and the other dispatched to the recipient. Often two copies of correspondence were dispatched to the intended recipient by separate routes in hopes that one would arrive.

Clerks and scribes were sometimes men of limited education who frustrated their employers. "Our Clerk is very diligent, loves Writing and will copy almost Day and Night, therefore a valuable Hand, but cannot form a Sentence," said Habersham, who was secretary of the colony in 1751.[83] Others were persons of skill and intelligence who could cast accounts and render broad assistance. Stephen Biddurph, who at times taught school, opened a writing office in which he promised services worthy of a factotum: the advertiser "translates in most foreign languages; opens, closes, and carefully settles, either in the Italian or any other proper method of book keeping, all merchants, tradesmens, and others books; transacts expeditiously all manner of business pertinent thereto he is intrusted with, upon the shortest notice, on reasonable terms; complicated accounts properly stated and adjusted; all kinds of instruments in writing accurately drawn and en-

81. Samuel Savery ran a brokerage office at his house in Savannah, where he kept a book listing a large number of tracts of land for sale. A surveyor by trade, Savery assisted in the process of buying and selling. Advertisement of Samuel Savery, *Ga. Gaz.*, June 8, 1774. Among the prominent vendue masters were William Ewen, a member of the Commons House, and Robert Bolton.

82. Ga. Hist. Soc., *Colls.*, III, 98; *Col. Records of Ga.*, XXII, Pt. ii, 425.

83. *Col. Records of Ga.*, XXVI, 274.

grossed; musick copied." Biddurph decided that if he did not get enough encouragement in those pursuits, he would teach French and fencing.[84]

Lawyers were very unpopular with the authorities, particularly in trustee Georgia. Oglethorpe declared in 1739—and for once he probably saw merit in poverty—that the whole town of Savannah could "hardly pay the charge of one Chancery suit." There were "no lawyers allowed to plead for hire, nor no attorneys to take money, but (as in old times in England) every man pleads his own cause."[85] This arrangement pleased the trustees, for it gave their officers a latitude that a system burdened with legal niceties would not have allowed. It also gave the Malcontents another cause for complaint. Individuals out of sympathy with the government believed that the absence of lawyers exposed them "to as *arbitrary* a government as Turkey or Muscovy ever felt. Very looks were criminal, and the grand sin of *withstanding*, or any way *opposing* authority, . . . was punished without mercy."[86]

Uncomplimentary references to lawyers run through the literature of colonial Georgia, and the woeful preparation of Georgia's magistrates was often commented upon. A visitor from Pennsylvania, attempting to settle a business matter in Frederica in 1745, discovered that the judge of the Admiralty there, Captain Mark Carr, managed legal business with great caution, "not being much acquainted with Law."[87]

In royal Georgia the bar may have numbered fifteen attorneys, and practitioners were of three kinds—those who had been called to the bar at the Inns of Court in London; those who had served clerkships in England or in one of the colonies; and those who merely became lawyers without formal preparation.[88] Anthony Stokes, chief justice from 1769 until the end of colonial times, was himself a barrister who had little respect for most of the attorneys who appeared before him. Charles Pryce, who became attorney general in 1764 (although he was often absent, with his duties committed to a deputy), had never been

84. Advertisement of Stephen Biddurph, *Ga. Gaz.*, May 17, 1775.
85. Ga. Hist. Soc., *Colls.*, III, 95, I, 96.
86. Ver Steeg, ed., *True and Historical Narrative*, 58.
87. "William Logan's Journal," *PMHB*, XXXVI (1912), 170. See also *Col. Records of Ga.*, XXXI, 3.
88. See Alexander A. Lawrence's study of Anthony Stokes in Horace Montgomery, ed., *Georgians in Profile: Historical Essays in Honor of Ellis Merton Coulter* (Athens, Ga., 1958), 66.

called to the bar. He had been clerk to an attorney in Boswell Court.[89]

By far the greater number of attorneys was admitted to practice through "interest," which is to say, on the basis of self-preparation and their own interest; they knew little law. After Chief Justice Stokes arrived in the province, he was welcomed to membership on the council because no councillor except Noble Jones, also a judge, had "any" knowledge of the law. Jones, even as a judge, did "not pretend to a great deal."[90]

Georgians in royal times believed themselves badly used by attorneys. Lawyers in Savannah wanted "guineas to do a little writing," said one man who needed their services in 1775. And besides, "in this warm climate these gentlemen can only spend about three hours a day on brain work and must have the rest of the time for recreation, and even use the late hours of night for this latter purpose."[91] Despite the relative unpopularity of these men, they tended to be influential as well as prominent, and from their ranks came some of the colony's most vigorous leaders.

Many ordinary men became their own "lawyers" by consulting books. Others turned to offices where legal documents were prepared by specialists in writing rather than attorneys. Benjamin Prime, who had practiced law for a time in North Carolina, opened such an office in 1768 in Savannah. He set up shop opposite the building in which the assembly sat. For a fee, Prime wrote wills, deeds, mortgages, leases, letters of attorney, articles of agreement, and other legal documents.[92]

Among the business pursuits more or less frowned upon by the local government was tavern keeping. Taverners and innkeepers were suspected of shielding evil practices behind their doors, their importance to both social and commercial life notwithstanding. No private business except the Indian trade was more closely scrutinized by the authorities. In 1736 at Frederica, officials maintained a policy closely kin to harassment, decreeing that no "victualler or ale-house keeper can give any credit, so consequently cannot recover any debt."[93] Both trustee and royal officials regulated taverns and inns through licensing. To keep owners from moving from location to location, valid licenses

89. Memorandum of Charles Pryce, Esq., May 9, 1783, Ga. Loyalist Claims, A.O. 12/99 (microfilm at Dept. of Archives and Hist., Atlanta, Ga.).

90. *Col. Records of Ga.*, XXXVII, 467.

91. Muhlenberg, *Journals*, II, 675.

92. Advertisement of Benjamin Prime, *Ga. Gaz.*, Aug. 17, 1768.

93. Ga. Hist. Soc., *Colls.*, I, 96.

designated the street, lane, alley, road, bridge, ferry, village, town, or other place where the tavern could be legally operated. Persons trained to earn a living as mechanics could not normally keep a tavern or an inn, because these positions were reserved by law to persons without more acceptable means of employment.[94]

The government disliked the embarrassments inflicted upon it by tavern-related incidents. The Malcontents used Jenkins's Tavern, one of Savannah's flourishing public establishments, as a meeting place for criticizing the trustee government. Illegal rum was to be had at many Savannah taverns, as two servants conspicuously demonstrated on a Saturday evening in 1738. And the rattle of dice at Tisdale's establishment precipitated a scandal heard all the way to London.[95]

Yet taverns were significant institutions that proved useful to the government and people alike. Where else could important banquets as readily be held? In 1735 such events took place in Savannah at Mrs. Penrose's, which was not even licensed. Where else could people congregate in a neighborly spirit, including even officials of government, but at taverns like Jenkins's and Penrose's in Savannah, Bennet's in Frederica, Oaks's in Augusta, and others like them?[96] To some they might seem like disorderly establishments, but they had their uses.

After the opening of the backcountry, a traveler might find taverns, inns, or retailers of alcoholic drinks along most of the colony's principal roads. In 1764 and 1765 there were ten licensed taverns and twelve other places where alcoholic drinks might legally be bought in Savannah, and on the southwest road outside town, a traveler might stop at White's or Tebaut's. In or near Ebenezer, Martin Dasher and John Rentz kept taverns; John Wertsch and John Adam Treutlen, successful merchants, also sold drinks; and, three miles outside town, John Flerl also ran a place where drinks could be had. On the northwest road outside Ebenezer, there were three more taverns, and three more retailers of drink in St. George Parish along the road to Augusta. Sunbury was served by two taverns, Clark's and Williams's. Although thirty-seven establishments held licenses in the colony in 1764 and 1765, some important ones were apparently not included in the official license listing, which, for example, showed none at Augusta. Yet

94. *Col. Records of Ga.*, XVIII, 221–222.
95. *Ibid.*, IV, 122, XXXI, 3–4, XXIII, 503–506.
96. Phillipps Collection, 14207, 378–379, Univ. of Ga. Lib., Athens; *Col. Records of Ga.*, IV supp., 45.

James Jarvis had a tavern there both before and after the time the list was compiled.[97]

Small tippling houses were more of a danger to law and order than larger establishments, because small houses were for the most part "haunts for lewd idle and disorderly people, runaway Sailors Servants and Slaves."[98] On the road between Savannah and Augusta, a traveler stopped in 1775 at disreputable Nichols's Tavern, "where, to a very bad dinner, was added the oaths and execrations of as detestable a crew as horse thieves in general are. Was glad to get away."[99] Another traveler, pausing not far from Briar Creek, stopped "in the evening at a dirty tavern, where, however, we met with very civil usage."[100] Small, irregular establishments keenly interested colonial grand juries. Luke Dean, who had a small farm and a cow pen near Briar Creek, was presented in 1767 for keeping a disorderly house and "entertaining horse-stealers, and other persons of ill-fame." William Blackman, likewise a small farmer in St. Matthew Parish, found himself cited for "harbouring John Cornelious and James Moore, notorious horsethieves." At Sunbury tailor Richard Stephens kept a "very disorderly house, entertaining, enticing, and harbouring sailors and other riotous persons." The grand jury denounced Stephens as a "notorious drunken and debauched man, of abandoned principles, a nuisance to the town in general and his neighbours in particular."[101]

The frequent citation of disorderly places should not obscure the fact that there were some very proper taverns in Georgia. For example, John Bowles ran places in and near Savannah under the sign of the King's Arms, offering customers service "in a complaisant manner for their money." Bowles at times thought of himself as a taverner but in his will called himself a vintner, having apparently given up his tavern.[102]

97. *Ga. Gaz.*, Jan. 19, 1764, Jan. 24, 1765, and Feb. 4, 1767; advertisement of James Jackson, *ibid.*, Dec. 21, 1768.

98. *Col. Records of Ga.*, XVIII, 218.

99. Gibbes, *Documentary History of the Revolution*, I, 237.

100. John Bartram, "Diary of a Journey," ed. Harper, Am. Phil. Soc., *Trans.*, N.S., XXXIII, Pt. i (1942), 24n.

101. Presentments of the grand jury, *Ga. Gaz.*, July 22, 1767, and June 29, 1774. William Blackman was fined £50 in 1775 for keeping a disorderly house. *Ibid.*, June 28, 1775.

102. Advertisements of John Bowles, *ibid.*, Nov. 23, 1768, May 25 and Nov. 9, 1774, and May 31 and July 5, 1775; will abstract of John Bowles, *Will Abstracts*, 152.

When the assembly was in session, the population of Savannah temporarily increased, and taverns were crowded to overflowing with representatives and others who journeyed there on business. A young visitor at Robert Bolton's found that the house "abounded with boarders. . . . I generally endeavoured to be affable, but not forward; conversant, but not loquacious: short in my sittings after meals."[103]

Among the best-known establishments in Savannah during the 1760s was James Machenry's on Barnard Street at Ellis Square, the site of the public market (see the map of Savannah in chapter 3). Recalling that the homes of the governor and the president of the council cost no more than £500 each, it is impressive that Machenry's Tavern (including building, lot, and outbuildings) was assessed at £800 in 1768. Machenry also owned land on the Great Ogeechee River. But he and his wife, Ann, doubtless lived at their tavern and probably used their six slaves there as servants. Machenry kept nine or ten beds in his house, most of them large curtained ones, painted green, red, yellow, and blue and white. (Some of the bed "curtains" may have been mosquito netting.) He had at least nine looking glasses. The St. Andrew's Society was established at Machenry's in 1764, and other social and charitable organizations held meetings there.

Machenry created pleasant surroundings for his guests. It is easy to imagine his six china flowerpots filled with flowers. He had thirty pictures, six colored maps, and a Turkish carpet. He could seat forty-one persons simultaneously when he used every chair he owned. Twenty-four were matching green Windsors; he also had four high-backed Windsors. In his fireplace were brass-headed firedogs, and around the hearth, expensive fire implements. He owned ten tables, two tea boards, a corner buffet, a backgammon table and six packs of cards. In the kitchen was a hand mill for grinding coffee and an Indian corn mill for making meal. The kitchen was well supplied with utensils and serving dishes made of china, delft, stoneware, and pewter.

Compare the establishment of Machenry with the tavern of Abraham (later of Abigail) Minis, already mentioned, and the variety of the accommodations in Savannah becomes evident.[104] After the death

103. "Memoirs of Cornelius Winter," *Works of Jay*, III, 29; also William Bartram, *Travels*, 4.

104. Estate of James Machenry, June 4, 1768, Inventory Book F, 338–341. Machenry sometimes spelled his name McHenry. See will abstract of James McHenry, *Will Abstracts*, 84.

of Machenry in 1768, tavern keeping of a reputable sort continued at Creighton's and Jonathan Peat's, as well as at many smaller houses.

Despite the variety of ways in which Georgians could earn a livelihood, people were mostly dependent upon agriculture and related endeavors—the silk industry, the livestock business, and land trading. The establishment of a chamber of commerce in Charleston was noticed in Savannah, and the reaction was not uncritical. The advantages for trade should a similar organization be created in Georgia were clear enough. But a correspondent writing in the *Georgia Gazette* hoped that if such a thing were to occur locally, a chamber of agriculture would also be set up. The public would derive benefits from the establishment of both, and the writer stated that "I much fear, were either of them to take place without the other, the plan would be at least incomplete, if not (speaking generally) injurious."[105] Neither organization was established. Trade and agriculture—each, to use the term so often heard, "in all its branches"—found a natural balance between themselves that brought an increased prosperity to royal Georgia.

The most important consideration affecting agriculture during trustee times was the prohibition against slavery. Georgians might not keep black slaves, and there were few slaves of Indian blood, although Indian slavery was grudgingly allowed. Some planters around Augusta and elsewhere slipped slaves onto their plantations from South Carolina, but their use was not broad.

White settlers who first came to Georgia were given to understand that they would not need slaves. According to officials, the climate was radiant, and the silk and wine industries, with which settlers would be occupied, did not require backbreaking labor. But Georgia produced wine of poor quality, and the colonists soon discovered that there was more to producing silk than feeding mulberry leaves to worms. It was widely believed in Great Britain that in Georgia valuable mulberry trees grew everywhere. Although mulberry trees did grow wild, they were the black mulberry variety, which produced a leaf too sharp for the silkworm's taste. The white mulberry, with leaves suited to a silkworm's diet, had to be planted.

In 1741 Hector Beringer de Beaufain, an influential South Carolinian, told one of the trustees that while Georgia might be successfully

105. Letter of "An Humble Speculator," *Ga. Gaz.*, Jan. 26, 1774.

settled by white persons only, greater encouragements would have to be given "than what the Settlers there have now." [106] Bounties and gifts were insufficiently attractive. De Beaufain explained the arduous tasks to be considered:

The Best Corn land, is also the fittest for Mulberry trees, and that is Oak and hickory land, Swamps are too Wet, and Pine lands too poor; the better this land is, the thicker it is set with large trees and under them grow Underwood and Canes. The Planter who enters upon this land must first build himself a house or hutt, next he goes to clearing, which is done by hewing down the underwood, and then falling the trees and lopping off their Branches. When he thinks he has cut down as much as he can clean and enclose before Planting time, he cross cuts some of the Trees, and Splits them into rails for his fences, and then destroys the Rubbish that lies upon his field. [107]

Plows were difficult to use because stumps and roots caught them; so hoes were employed instead. On new plantations one might plow only after roots had been cut and had rotted in the ground for three or four years. Farm work was strenuous and de Beaufain feared that until a man became seasoned to the climate, he would "lay out more with the Doctor, than he can get by his work." [108]

Yet despite discouragements and difficulties, and because of bounties and official encouragement, the culture of silk held the enthusiasm of Georgians almost until the end of the colonial era. When Revolutionaries seized the house of Governor Wright in Savannah in 1776, among the objects they found in his cellar were "some Brass Kettles for Silk work." [109] They were, without doubt, relics of the day in 1771 or 1772 when the silk industry was discontinued in Savannah.

Farmers of trustee Georgia devoted their thoughts and labors, not to items for export (other than silk, a little lumber, and a few skins), but to those things needed to keep them alive—corn, peas, beans,

106. Phillipps Coll., 14212, 106. The quotation is from a long letter on agriculture that has been edited by Kenneth Coleman and published as "Agricultural Practices in Georgia's First Decade," *Agricultural History*, XXXIII (1959), 196–199.

107. Phillipps Coll., 14212, 107.

108. *Ibid.*, 113; Loewald, Starika, and Taylor, trans. and eds., "Bolzius Answers a Questionnaire," Pt. i, *WMQ*, 3d Ser., XIV (1957), 238.

109. Inventory of Gov. Wright's furniture, Nov. 1776, Misc. Bonds Book Y–2, 504, Dept. of Archives and Hist., Atlanta, Ga. The Salzburgers in and around Ebenezer carried on the silk culture after it had been discontinued elsewhere.

potatoes, and livestock. They measured their success by how much of these necessities they produced. A planter who was self-sufficient was lucky; one who had something to sell was luckier still.

Michael Burkholder, a German-speaking farmer who owned five hundred acres near Hampstead on the Vernon River outside Savannah, by 1742 came close to being the ideal planter envisioned by the trustees. There were others like him, mostly in the German community, but Burkholder stands out today because we know a fair amount about him. By hard work, intelligence, and diversification, he excited the imaginations of officials in Savannah, who wished that Georgia had many more like him. Burkholder was competent at several trades; he was a millwright, wheelwright, cooper, and carpenter. His eldest son and son-in-law were shoemakers and carpenters, and his eldest daughter a seamstress. Five younger children were training in those skills. In moderate weather the family worked the land, and in bad weather or in the heat of the day, they sought shelter and took up their crafts.[110] The Burkholders were models for their times. Less adaptable or less diligent men saw in their example a rebuke, particularly when they realized that they had not understood what was involved in coming to Georgia.

At the end of the trustee period, some men claimed to know why the Georgia experiment seemed to be failing. DeBrahm summed up the causes: the prohibition of black "servants"; the law against rum, in which he probably included the destructive effect upon the rum trade; and the kind of government the province had had, by which he meant the regulations under which Georgians had lived.[111]

Georgia agriculture began to flourish after 1750 when slaves were finally allowed and when men began to trade in land. Georgia turned to agricultural staples, particularly rice, indigo, and lumber, plus an assortment of other produce, and sold them for export. The goods exported at the customhouse in Savannah between October 10, 1767, and October 10, 1768, show how Georgia had developed:

Rice, about 13,358 barrels and 42 bags	Tar, 143 barrels
	Pitch, 451 barrels
Deerskins, 122 hogsheads, 2 casks, 2,090 bundles	Turpentine, 20 barrels
	Sago powder, 2,772 pounds

110. *Col. Records of Ga.*, XXIII, 439. Burkholder in time came to be spelled Burkhalter.

111. DeBrahm, *History of Ga.*, 51–52.

Raccoon skins, 282 bundles

Fox and otter skins, 2 bundles

Beaver skins, 27 bundles

Tanned leather, 2,644 sides

Pine lumber, 1,162,508 feet

Shingles, 2,754,450

Staves and heading, 574,610

Oars, 80

Handspikes, 340

Cedar posts, 405

Hoops, 4,000

Indigo, 16,928 pounds

Beeswax, 18 barrels, 1 keg, and 1 box

Cotton, 2 bags

Corn, 9,063 bushels

Rough rice, 1,121 bushels

Peas, 295 bushels

Potatoes, 219 bushels

Oranges, 6 barrels and 2 tierces

Pork, 471 barrels

Beef, 276 barrels

Hogs and shoats, 1,259

Fowls, 41 dozen

Horses, 102

Steers, 48

Hay and straw, 16 tons

Orange juice, 6 hogsheads

Raw silk, 541 pounds[112]

Rice comprised approximately one-third of the value of Georgia's exports.[113] Indigo and lumber also produced substantial incomes. Farm lands on tidal streams, where the rising tide pushed fresh water onto the rice fields, were especially valuable. Wealthy planters directed their overseers in systematizing their plantations. Habersham reduced everything "into a kind of regular System," then moved to Savannah and let his overseers manage matters.[114] Slaves planted rice in the spring and flooded the fields periodically during the growing season; when it was time for the rice to ripen, they drew off the water and left the grain to the sun. If good weather blessed the planter, his crop reached Savannah or Sunbury in the late fall and went aboard a ship to distant market. In a good year a planter might gross 25 or 30 percent on his investment.[115]

Relative prosperity finally arrived in Georgia because farmers and businessmen were free to pursue their best advantage. That advantage lay in agriculture and trade, each dependent upon the other. And agriculture's growth owed much to that institution earlier denied—African slavery.

112. *Ga. Gaz.*, Feb. 15, 1769.
113. W. W. Abbot, *The Royal Governors of Georgia, 1754–1775* (Chapel Hill, N.C., 1959), 23.
114. Ga. Hist. Soc., *Colls.*, VI, 39.
115. Abbot, *Royal Governors of Ga.*, 24.

Chapter 5

Slavery, Class Structure, and the Family

The pressures brought by the Malcontents for the admission of slaves did not budge the trustees. Georgia had been founded partially as a buffer for South Carolina, and a principal reason that black slaves had been prohibited was the hazard they might pose in case of invasion. If slaves could have rendered South Carolina safe, it was contended somewhat irrelevantly, then Georgia would not have been needed as a shield; South Carolina had thousands of slaves.[1]

Such arguments did not impress the Malcontents. It seemed to them that the proprietors had hatefully condemned them to austerity by denying them slaves, then had forced them to endure it with unclouded minds by forbidding spirituous liquors. The Malcontents believed they had "made shipwreck" of time and substance by coming to Georgia, and most of them departed.[2]

Officially, the proprietors were unperturbed by this defection, although in 1742 they entertained brief doubts about their ban on slavery. But once it was agreed to let the law stand, the trustees went ahead with enforcement, turning aside protests and ignoring the word from Georgia that men were "stark Mad" after slaves.[3] The proprietors

1. Ga. Hist. Soc., *Colls.*, I, 167. The word "slavery," as used throughout, refers to black bondsmen, because Indian slaves were not common in Georgia.
2. Ver Steeg, ed., *True and Historical Narrative*, 4, 8.
3. *Col. Records of Ga.*, I, 400–401, XXV, 72.

had long used every device they could to enforce their intent. Their agents seized slaves brought illegally into the province and sold them for the benefit of charity.[4] They welcomed statements from Georgia supporting their policy on slavery but turned deaf ears to allegations that colonists who declined to sign such statements were discriminated against.[5]

Finally, in 1750 circumstances secured what protests had not, and the trustees abandoned their much-embattled statute. The province was in serious economic distress. Even Pastor Bolzius of the Salzburgers, who had once opposed slavery, reconsidered reluctantly, tired of being criticized for his views. More important, there had been no parliamentary grant for Georgia for five years of the 1740s, and private benefactions after 1740 had virtually declined to nothing. The resources of the trustees were pinched. It was plain to see that new settlers would have to be attracted if the colony were to succeed. It was wholly unlikely that all of the new population could come from Europe. Men and women would have to emigrate from mainland colonies and the West Indies, where slavery was an old institution.

Faced with these weighty problems, the proprietors drafted a measure to repeal their act. Although no evidence survives to indicate that the draft bill was ever taken up by the Board of Trade or the Privy Council, or that it was approved by George II, the trustees nevertheless put it into effect on their own authority. It constituted the most benign slave code that Georgia had in colonial times. Masters were allowed to discipline their slaves if they did not endanger life or limb in the process. If a black person were murdered by a white, the murderer might hang. The measure also said that marriage and sexual relations between whites and blacks were forbidden and that duties and taxes collected on slaves would be applied to the advancement of religion, public works, and commerce. It demanded close supervision of slaves by white men. The relative gentleness of the code lay partly in what it did not say. It had no catalog of strictures governing slave conduct such as characterized slave statutes in the royal period. And it provided in a positive way that blacks should have religious instruction.[6]

4. Phillipps Coll., 14205, Pt. ii, 486–488, Univ. of Ga. Lib., Athens.
5. Ga. Hist. Soc., *Colls.*, II, 120.
6. The text of the draft bill is found in *Col. Records of Ga.*, I, 56–62. Georgians were consulted about its contents and the conditions under which blacks should be admitted.

White Georgians regarded slaves in varying ways, many of them contradictory. They considered them crafty, childlike, capable of mechanical skills, incapable of being instructed, affectionate toward their masters at times, and sometimes possessed of "secret rancor for having been snatched from their homeland and sold into everlasting slavery in a strange land."[7] White men sometimes believed that the goodwill of blacks could be bought with gifts of tobacco or other articles. But the harsh laws passed in the royal period proclaimed a belief in the necessity to crush any spirit of rebelliousness black people might evince. That they should be kept in eternal slavery was a principle determined early, "and no Christian gentleman may, in this respect, proceed according to his own judgment."[8]

The first slave code that Georgians wrote themselves was approved in 1755, a year after royal government was effectively established. Georgians took a South Carolina slave act passed in 1740 as a model in writing their law, and the end product was similar in content. The measure applied to all slaves—black, Indian, or of mixed blood.

A slave could expect death for a number of offenses: killing a white person except by accident or in defense of a master or overseer; insurrection or attempted insurrection; enticing or attempting to entice another slave to run away (if provisions for making the escape actually had been arranged); willfully burning or destroying rice, corn, or other grain; setting fire to tar kilns or naval stores; stealing another slave; and poisoning a person, slave or free. A slave might also be executed for maiming or wounding a white person upon the first offense and for merely striking him upon the third. For mischiefs, disobedience, or disrespectful behavior, offenders might be whipped, put in irons, or confined. Justices of the peace sat in judgment with small juries of freeholders. Any master whose slave was condemned and executed was paid by the government for his loss. Thus masters were encouraged to surrender guilty chattels.

Slaves could not do many things legally. They could not travel without written permission. They were forbidden to convene in groups off their plantations without supervision, buy or sell goods without

7. Muhlenberg, *Journals*, II, 675.
8. Loewald, Starika, and Taylor, trans. and eds., "Bolzius Answers a Questionnaire," Pt. i, *WMQ*, 3d Ser., XIV (1957), 245. In 1775 at Darien a group in which Lachlan McIntosh was a leader protested against slavery, considering it an unnatural practice. Lilla Mills Hawes, ed., *Lachlan McIntosh Papers in the University of Georgia Libraries* (Athens, Ga., 1968), 13.

tickets of authorization, or conceal other slaves guilty of a crime. Free men could not give or sell them alcoholic beverages without the permission of the master or overseer, or rent them rooms or houses, teach them to write, or permit them to beat drums, blow horns, or play other loud instruments.

The law also imposed some restrictions on slaveholders, at least in theory. Although it was forbidden to work slaves on Sundays (except household servants, and others in times of absolute necessity), masters did so with impunity. Slaves also could not legally be worked more than sixteen hours a day, and masters were to feed and clothe them adequately upon penalty of fine for failure to do so. It is unlikely, though, that these stipulations were enforced. For murdering or cruelly abusing a slave, a white person could be punished, usually by fine. The trustees in 1750 had required that one white servant capable of bearing arms be present on plantations for every four male slaves, but the 1755 act radically reduced the requirement. It allowed a master twenty slaves for each white servant capable of bearing arms, fifty for two white servants, and required an additional servant for each twenty-five slaves thereafter.[9] There is nothing whatever to suggest that such ratios were maintained, although grand juries would hold up to public scorn masters who worked slaves with no supervision at all. Probably Georgia was much like South Carolina; there it was thought that one white overseer could efficiently and safely manage about thirty slaves.

The slave code of 1755 was one of three such laws passed in royal times. In 1765 the assembly rewrote the 1755 measure, retaining some of the original language and all of the philosophy, only to have London disallow the new act on technicalities. In 1770 the assembly wrote the last of the general laws dealing with slaves in colonial Georgia. This act preserved the tone and intent of the 1755 measure.[10]

That the slave acts were harsh is beyond dispute. But passing laws is one thing; enforcing them is another. Many of the details of law enforcement in colonial Georgia, like much else, now lie beyond historical recovery, but evidence suggests that acts relating to capital crimes were not strenuously enforced. In its annual appropriations, the assembly usually anticipated that one slave a year would be exe-

9. For the 1755 act, see *Col. Records of Ga.*, XVIII, 102–144.
10. For the disallowed act of Mar. 25, 1765, see *ibid.*, 649–688; also, XVII, 419–420. For the 1770 act, see *ibid.*, XIX, Pt. i, 209–249.

cuted and paid for out of public funds.[11] Evidence does not allow a definite statement of the number actually put to death, but it can be shown that between 1755 and 1773—eighteen years—fifteen slaves were executed and two more may have been. There are gaps in the data, and it is probable that the number totaled more than seventeen.[12] Even so, slaves were not sent to the executioner in large numbers, and those sections of the slave codes concerning capital crimes were not strictly carried out. To execute a slave was to destroy property; few persons favored wholesale pursuit of such unprofitable severity. Rather than being frequent, executions were exemplary. To that end, the assembly refrained from requiring guilty slaves to die by hanging, the customary form of execution in Great Britain and the colonies. Instead, it said that a magistrate and his jury might order any kind of execution upon which they could agree. Although slaves were usually hanged, on at least four occasions before 1776, convicted slaves died by fire—one for arson, one for an attempted double murder by poison-

11. It was expected that the province would usually spend £40 a year reimbursing masters for executed slaves. This sum would only pay for one slave. See *ibid.*, XIII, 514, 645, XIV, 38, 101, XXXVII, 198a, and XXXVIII, Pt. i, 145.

12. Surviving tax acts show compensations made for executed slaves between 1755 and 1773 (with gaps). The tax act of Feb. 21, 1755, shows no slaves executed. [Charles C. Jones, Jr., and George Wymberley-Jones DeRenne, eds.,] *Acts Passed by the General Assembly of the Colony of Georgia, 1755 to 1774* (Wormsloe, Ga., 1881), 45–49. The colony was then still defining the measures it would use to control slaves during the royal era. The tax act of Feb. 8, 1757, also shows no slaves executed; neither does the tax act of July 28, 1757. *Ibid.*, 100–104, 130–135. The tax act of Mar. 27, 1759, shows one slave as condemned, but since the award was only for 11s., it is questionable whether the sum represents the cost of arresting him or was compensation for his execution. *Col. Records of Ga.*, XVIII, 349. The tax act of Apr. 24, 1760, shows no slaves executed. *Ibid.*, 392–408. The tax acts of Apr. 7, 1763, and Feb. 29, 1764, show no blacks executed. DeRenne Coll., Univ. of Ga. Lib. The tax act of Mar. 6, 1766, shows one or two Negroes put to death. T. 1/461, Pt. i, P.R.O. (photocopy at Univ. of Ga. Lib., Athens). The act of Apr. 11, 1768, indicates 9 executions, and the tax act of Dec. 24, 1768, shows 2. *Col. Records of Ga.*, XIX, Pt. i, 48–49, 121. The tax act of May 10, 1770, reveals no executions, while the act of Sept. 29, 1773, shows 3. *Ibid.*, 161–198, 481. Another source confirms that there were no more than 3 slave executions between 1770 and 1773. See Ga. Hist. Soc., *Colls.*, III, 177.

Four tax acts passed between 1755 and 1773 are not available to the historian; any or all of them may have contained information on executed slaves. See *Col. Records of Ga.*, XIII, 583, 692, XIV, 257, and XVII, 376. We cannot estimate the numbers of executions that occurred between 1774 and 1776, although the rate was definitely higher than it had previously been. Slaves were condemned in those years for arson, attempted murder by poisoning (the intended victims being Pastor and Mrs. Rabenhorst), and for insurrection and murder.

ing, and two for murderous insurrection. The arsonist was burned on the Savannah common.[13] Such a terrible form of execution was not unprecedented, having been resorted to in England and even in New York in 1712.

We also cannot measure the degree to which the slave laws regarding corporal punishment and confinement were enforced. Records do show that slaves charged with crimes were sometimes confined in the workhouse or jail, but the virtual disappearance of court records defeats attempts to estimate how frequently confinements occurred. Offending slaves were sometimes whipped, as provided by law. Men were paid for administering the punishment. Thomas Flyming, a small farmer in St. Matthew Parish, was paid one pound for "causing Corporal punishment to be inflicted upon Negroes."[14]

In general, masters disciplined their own unruly blacks. Difficult slaves were whipped, branded, or kept in irons. Flora, belonging to Elizabeth Deveaux, had "marks with a whip on her right arm." George Walker had two slaves escape at Briar Creek, one branded with a "C" on his shoulder; the other, a youth named Bob, wore large scars from whipping.[15] Blacks were sometimes branded for identification. Esther, who ran away from John Bowman on Skidaway Island, had "J. Bowman" on her breast. Bowman owned few slaves and was apparently determined to safeguard those he had. A slave who belonged to William McGillivray was branded with "CWMG" upon his breast.[16] Slaves kept in irons most often were those with prior escape records. "Run Away the 14th inst. from Mr. Forrester's saw-mill, on the way from Savannah, A Mulatto Boy, named Billy, . . . with an iron chain round his neck, which he endeavours to conceal by wrapping a cloth round it." Billy had run away two years earlier; he had made his way to a vessel, signed on as a sailor, and had gotten to St. Kitts before he was apprehended and returned to his master, George McIntosh of Sapelo Island.[17] Peter, a habitual escapee, ran away from Henry Parker of the Isle of Hope wearing an iron on each leg. He had been at large often enough before for his master to know that he called

13. *Ga. Gaz.*, Sept. 21 and Dec. 7, 1774; Muhlenberg, *Journals*, II, 575, 585.
14. *Col. Records of Ga.*, XIX, Pt. i, 186.
15. Advertisement of Elizabeth Deveaux, *Ga. Gaz.*, May 24, 1775; advertisement of George Walker, *ibid.*, May 11, 1774.
16. Advertisement of Edward Simmons, *ibid.*, July 6, 1774; advertisement of William McGillivray, *ibid.*, Jan. 11, 1775.
17. Advertisement of George M'Kintosh, *ibid.*, July 20, 1768.

himself "Boson" when away from the plantation.[18] Some planters kept iron caps with locks, at times with bells attached, for slaves who frequently ran away.[19]

Many of Georgia's slaves (there were fifteen thousand by 1773) came directly from Africa. African-born slaves tended to band together, perhaps because of their ignorance of the English tongue. A sensitive Georgian of the period wrote that slaves "never hear no other Discourses but what passes among themselves and no white People will have any thing to say to them but to abuse them with bitter Execrations and cruel Blows."[20] The pages of the *Georgia Gazette* were filled with advertisements for the sale of slaves arriving directly from Africa (see figure 3, following). Georgians made considerable distinction in price between those slaves who had been born in America or who had spent some years in America and those who came directly off a ship. The African blacks usually sold for less.[21] The vessels bore their human cargoes into the ports of Savannah and Sunbury and occasionally docked at plantations of merchant-planters. The merchants advertised slaves for sale under the names of the sections of Africa from which they had come—Senegal, the Gold Coast, Gambia, Sierra Leone, Guinea, Niger, Angola. Slaves from the Gold Coast, Gambia, and Angola were considered most desirable. Eboes from Nigeria—called "Hipponegroes"—were least valued and were regarded as suicidal.[22] "To be sold, on Tuesday the 28th October, 1766," read a typical advertisement, "A Cargo consisting of about One Hundred and Twenty Young and Healthy New Negroes, Just arrived, in the Ship Woodmanston, Capt. Benjamin Mason, in a short Passage of seven Weeks from the River Gambia." The selling firm was Clay and Habersham of Savannah. In the newspaper immediately under that notice was another from John Graham and Company offering about

18. Advertisement of Henry Parker, *ibid.*, Jan. 25, 1769.
19. Estate of Thomas Vincent, Sept. 30, 1768, Inventory Book F, 358; estate of Joseph Gibbons, Dec. 30, 1769, *ibid.*, 433, Dept. of Archives and Hist., Atlanta, Ga.
20. Joseph Ottolenghe to the Rev. Mr. Waring, July 12, 1758, MSS of Dr. Bray's Associates, Pt. H (L.C. microfilm reel 11, 335/209); Ottolenghe to Waring, Oct. 4, 1759, *ibid.* (L.C. reel 11, 335/218–219). Ottolenghe stated that "as for the Negroes of these Parts they are mostly Africans born." Henry Ellis attached a statement certifying the truth of the quoted contents of the letter.
21. Loewald, Starika, and Taylor, trans. and eds., "Bolzius Answers a Questionnaire," Pt. i, *WMQ*, 3d Ser., XIV (1957), 233.
22. *Ibid.*, 256.

140 new slaves from Gambia to be sold in Savannah the same day.[23] Although the largest number of sales advertised African blacks, some slaves came into Georgia from the West Indies. There many had experienced a harsher servitude than they would find in their new location.

Still, Georgia slavery was severe. One reason was that some masters —considered by contemporaries the worst of the lot—had come from the West Indies and based their methods on cruel experiences there. Such masters, and those who wished to keep their slaves free from Christian teachings, were considered affronts to religion and human compassion by some Georgians.[24] Also, part of the severity resulted from differences among the blacks themselves, differences that made slaves seem "strange" to one another. Slaves arrived at plantations speaking their native languages and behaving according to patterns learned in different lands. Communication even among themselves was circumscribed. Coming from different parts of Africa, they did not all speak the same language or dialect; many different kinds of speech were heard in the slave quarters on Georgia plantations. Nevertheless, unhappy captives huddled together out of necessity, seeking such comfort as they could find and the opportunity to speak the tongues they knew; at the same time, masters and overseers were forcing them to adjust to a new environment through work and discipline.

On plantations slaves lived in huts and sometimes had small garden plots that they could cultivate for themselves. Under the best of conditions, their work was hard. Plantation Beth Abram was the property of the Reverend Bartholomew Zouberbuhler, whose concern for his slaves was reflected in the generous benefaction left for them in his will. Yet even at Beth Abram, blacks complained of severe usage. A catechist from England who went to the plantation to teach, received "very heavy complaints" from the slaves that they were cruelly beaten, overworked, underfed, and left almost bare of clothes.[25] Of course, planters wished their slaves to remain healthy, but they also tried to maintain them at the least possible expense:

23. Advertisements of Clay and Habersham and John Graham and Company, *Ga. Gaz.*, Oct. 22, 1766.

24. Ottolenghe to Associates of Dr. Bray, Nov. 19, 1753, MSS of Dr. Bray's Associates, Pt. H (L.C. reel 11, 335/230).

25. "Memoirs of Cornelius Winter," *Works of Jay*, III, 30.

FOR SALE,

On Thurſday the 29th March, 1770,

A CARGO conſiſting of about 170 young
and healthy

NEW NEGROES,

CHIEFLY MEN,

All of whom have had the Smallpox,

Juſt arrived, after a ſhort paſſage of five weeks, in the ſnow Britannia,
Capt. Stephen Dean, from Gambia.

Savannah, Georgia, March 10. 1770.　　　JOSEPH CLAY.

IMPORTED from Antigua, in the Sloop Nancy,
and to be ſold by

COWPER and TELFAIRS,

Ninety odd choice Windward
Coaſt NEGROES,

Pick of a Cargo of Two Hundred and Fifty.

On Tueſday next the quarantain will be out, and they will immediately
thereafter be ſold.

3. Advertisements for Slave Sales, 1768 and 1770.

Merchants who sold slaves often advertised them under the name of the
distant places from which they had been brought. Blacks from Gambia (as
in the Joseph Clay advertisement above) were regarded as greatly desirable;
slaves from the Windward Coast were considered satisfactory. Eboes from
Nigeria were believed to be suicidal, were known to be difficult, and were
not generally sought after.

(From the Georgia Gazette, *July 6, 1768, and March 28, 1770.*)

The upkeep of the Negroes is cut very sparse. Year in and year out they receive nothing but Indian or Welsh or Turkish corn. . . . This corn they must crack themselves in iron mills. Very few receive salt for it, so they cook it in water without salt and lard. Instead of corn they may receive Indian beans, which are planted among the corn, and at certain times also potatoes. . . . They also get to eat the cracked rice, which is not sent to Europe. If they have benevolent masters, or prove themselves loyal, they may receive a little meat a few times a year. They love to eat meat, and sometimes roast mice or steal meat. Some have permission to catch fish on Sundays. . . . They love their families dearly and none runs away from the other. The separation of families is forbidden in our colony as something unnatural and barbaric; also Sunday work. In winter the Negroes must be kept warm, but in summer they go naked, except that the men cover their shame with a cloth rag which hangs from a strap tied around the body. The women have petticoats; the upper body is bare. The children of both sexes go about in summer just as they left the mother's womb. In winter Negro men and women have shoes, none in summer. One does not give the children any work beyond guarding the rice in the field from the rice birds, and possibly serving at table. They are spared from work so that they may grow big and strong.[26]

Winter clothing for male slaves usually consisted of a woolen camisole, or jacket (which served as a shirt), a pair of long pants, shoes, and a woolen cap. In cold weather slaves built fires in their cabins and had woolen blankets.[27]

While the attire and general treatment of blacks can be determined from reliable data, very little can be documented of the family life of slaves. Usually slaves took from the plantation population a mate of their master's choosing. They were considered married without ceremony and simply lived together.[28] But even in such unpromising circumstances, with their future uncertain and always determined by others, some slaves were probably able to achieve a degree of familial stability and cohesiveness.

Labor on rice plantations was especially difficult and hazardous to health. Slaves were frequently obliged to get up before sunrise to work in a barn warmed by a fire. They were then turned out to toil in the rice fields "half leg deep in water, which brings on pleurisies and

---

26. Loewald, Starika, and Taylor, trans. and eds., "Bolzius Answers a Questionnaire," Pt. i, *WMQ*, 3d Ser., XIV (1957), 235–236.

27. *Ibid.*, 236.

28. *Ibid.*

peripneumonies, and destroys numbers of them; and in the Summer, the quantity of water let into the Rice-fields makes it very sickly."[29] Slaves had assigned tasks to do and often did them under the supervision of another slave, called a driver. After the regular crops were harvested, they worked in the master's woods, cutting and sawing. Mortality among those on rice and river swamp plantations was higher than among those assigned to backcountry plantations. John Graham, Georgia's last royal lieutenant governor, owned about 26,500 acres of land and at one time possessed more than 250 slaves. From his account books, which were lost during the Revolution, he later recalled that mortality did not exceed two per year for each hundred slaves on his back plantations. On river swamp farms, the rate was three or four per hundred. However, there were more than enough births to replace those who died.[30]

Male field slaves in prime strength but without other skills were bought and sold for between £40 and £60 during much of the period; women field slaves brought slightly less. A craftsman—a cooper, blacksmith, or boatman—brought more. Slaves not in their prime sold for much less. In 1761 the inventory of William Butler, a large planter and slaveholder who had a plantation near the site of Fort Argyle on the Ogeechee River, valued a two-day-old infant at £5, female children at £8 and £12, old men at £15 and £30, a sickly female at £25, and an old woman at £12. A slave named Kit, blind in one eye, was valued at £30.[31] In Charles West's estate in 1768, Tissy, a sucking child, was figured to be worth £10; "old crazy Beck" was worth nothing and was carried as an incumbrance.[32] Slave values rose rapidly in the 1770s, but the relative values of healthy field slaves, craftsmen, children, and aged or ailing slaves remained as they had been in the 1750s and 1760s.

Blacks sometimes commented upon their condition in ways that were meaningful to themselves and that possibly were also a form of protest. Such an instance was reported in 1774.

29. Anthony Stokes, *A View of the Constitution of the British Colonies in North America and the West Indies* (London, 1969 [orig. publ., London, 1783]), 414–415.
30. Schedule of the lands and slaves of John Graham (1781), Miscellaneous Bonds Book KK–2, 286–297, Dept. of Archives and Hist., Atlanta, Ga.; memorial of John Graham (date uncertain), Ga. Loyalist Claims, A.O. 13/106, P.R.O.
31. Estate of William Butler, Sept. 14, 1761, Inventory Book F, 97–98.
32. Estate of Charles West, May 10, 1768, *ibid.*, 333.

During the intolerably hot summer months there is nevertheless a great deal of work to be done on the land. The master preferred to sit at home in the shade, but the Negro had to work outside in the heat of the sun. He often came into the house and saw his master reading the Bible or other edifying books and praying and writing. The Negro began to do the same thing and wanted to spend half the day in the shade over his devotions; and when the master instructed him from God's Word that one must work if one would eat, he made a wry mouth and declared that that kind of Christianity was not becoming or suitable to him, etc. Most of them retain their savage spite and cunning trickiness, like the gypsies in Europe; or as one Negro said, he would rather belong to the Moravian Brethren than to the High Church [Anglican] because the latter was always preaching about work and labor, whereas the former preached faith without works, and he was tired of working.[33]

That most blacks found a way to survive under such a harsh yoke testifies to their resilience; remarkably, many of them retained a distinct individuality in the midst of a society that officially discouraged it.

How did slaves react to their hard condition? We cannot estimate how many ran away or what all of their reasons for running away were. Advertisements in all surviving issues of the *Georgia Gazette* document about 450 individuals who fled, some more than once, but the figure means little because it is incomplete (see figure 4 for one such advertisement). The *Gazette* was not published for a time in 1765 and 1766, and the issues for a long period in the early 1770s have disappeared. In any event, not everyone who had a slave vanish would have advertised in the *Gazette*. Many masters lived a distance from Savannah and would have posted notices in the countryside rather than turning to the newspaper. Some who knew certain slaves well would not have advertised at all, being convinced they would return.

While advertisements in the *Gazette* reveal no pattern for escapes, they do suggest some of the reasons why slaves fled. Some had been sold and did not like their new masters. Others apparently left to be near acquaintances or relatives who lived elsewhere. Some were lured into escaping by other persons, and some evidently either did not like where they were living or wished to return to a place where they had previously lived.[34] Some, who bore whip marks, chains, or iron caps,

33. Muhlenberg, *Journals*, II, 638.
34. Advertisement of John Sacheverel, *Ga. Gaz.*, Apr. 19, 1764; advertisement

4. *Advertisement for Runaway Slaves, 1770.*

Runaway slaves upon recapture were customarily taken to the workhouse in Savannah or Sunbury, or to the jail in Augusta. This notice, variations of which appeared many times in colonial Georgia, was placed by the master of the workhouse in Savannah. If the runaways were not claimed after a period of time, they were sold.

(*From the* Georgia Gazette, *March 28, 1770.*)

might have been fleeing bad treatment. There were frequent reports that slaves had gone to Florida, a haven for runaways after the Spanish governor at St. Augustine pledged them their freedom and his protection there. Masters often suspected that their slaves had been enticed away by other persons—black, white, or Indian—who wanted them for their own purposes. Joseph Gibbons, a planter of Christ Church Parish, thought that Primus either had gone away with the Creek

---

of William Gibbons, *ibid.*, May 10, 1769; advertisement of Josiah DuPont, *ibid.*, May 24, 1775; advertisements of James Houstoun, *ibid.*, May 30, 1765, and Mar. 30, 1768; advertisement of Adrian Loyer, *ibid.*, Mar. 16, 1768; advertisement of Joseph Gibbons, *ibid.*, Feb. 17, 1768; and advertisement of Josiah Tatnell, *S.-C. Gaz.; And Country Jour.*, July 24, 1770. The Loyer advertisement apparently concerned a South Carolina slave who had escaped into Georgia.

Indians or had been picked up by backcountry settlers who would either work him or exchange him for horses in one of the colonies to the north. Elizabeth Deveaux believed that her runaway Flora had been enticed by sailors who were harboring her under the Savannah Bluff. Some blacks could not forget Africa and, in nostalgia for their native land, took canoes and set off hoping to reach "their own country."[35]

Masters who found themselves in possession of true troublemakers tried to sell them. "I find my Negroes have begun their old pranks," John Houstoun wrote to his brother-in-law, George McIntosh, in 1775. "I wish you would be good enough to make some Inquiry and find out whether the blame lies altogether on the Black side. If so I am of opinion Jacob and Pompey must at all counts be shipt off— this I'll do even if I get but £5 a piece for them."[36] Two escaped slaves of Lachlan McIntosh's were picked up and taken to the workhouse in Charleston, and McIntosh wrote to George Houstoun, John's brother, that he wanted them sold in South Carolina "*as soon* as possible to save any further Expense or risque." McIntosh stated that he "was determined to dispose of them, as they got acquainted with that Villain the Indian Doctor who conveyed them to the Nation and Lives in our Neighborhood altho they are the most Valuable Slaves I own, being both good Sawyers Squarers Boatmen and Shingle makers as well as Field Slaves, and no runaways untill they were decoyed away."[37]

Runaways, when picked up, were taken to workhouses in Savannah or Sunbury or to the jail at Augusta. A slave arrested in Savannah in the yard of Machenry's Tavern was confined in the workhouse, and in an action repeated many times in pre-Revolutionary Georgia, the warden publicized his capture in the *Georgia Gazette.* He thereby hoped to alert the owner that the slave had been found. The wording of the notice was typical: "Brought to the Work-house, a New Negroe Fellow, can't speak English, nor tell his master's or his own name, he is about five feet two inches high, bow-legged, has his country marks on his temples, and down his breast and belly, has on white negroe cloth

35. Advertisement of Joseph Gibbons, *Ga. Gaz.*, June 9, 1763; advertisement of Elizabeth Deveaux, *ibid.*, July 13, 1774; and advertisement of Joseph Weatherly, *ibid.*, Jan. 25, 1775.

36. Letter of John Houstoun to George McIntosh, June 30, 1775, Georgia Miscellaneous Collection (1732–1796), Force Manuscripts, Library of Congress.

37. Hawes, ed., *Lachlan McIntosh Papers*, 14.

jacket and breeches."[38] If a slave thus confined were not claimed after being advertised for a time, the warden of the workhouse might sell him. However, many runaways remained at large and in view for days or weeks after escaping.

No one can now know how many slaves were fleeing slavery itself and how many were running away as a result of local causes or individual preferences. Some could not adapt at all to slavery. They found themselves at such cross-purposes with the society enslaving them that, in effect, they declared war on their environment. Their numbers were probably as small as their actions were conspicuous. In 1765 a number of such fugitives banded together and withdrew into the swamps on the Savannah River. Sometimes they camped in South Carolina; sometimes they invaded Georgia to rob and harass plantations. White settlers led by planter Roderick Mackintosh fought them in a skirmish. At some point in this sequence of events, one of the slave leaders, named Ben, was captured.[39] Few facts survive concerning the episode, for it occurred while the publication of the *Gazette* was suspended during the Stamp Act crisis. Sometimes the militia pursued fugitives. Yet in 1772 bands of runaways operating from river swamps and islands above Savannah committed "Depredations on the Inhabitants in that Neighbourhood with Impunity."[40] Two and a half years later, a group of slaves newly arrived from Africa went on a rampage in St. Andrew Parish, slaughtered their overseer in the field, killed three more whites, and wounded others before being stopped.[41]

The rebellions are significant, for they demonstrate that some blacks could not accept slavery and showed it by actions quite different from individual protests. White Georgians felt real anxiety concerning their slaves, and with good cause. The revolt at Stono, South Carolina, in 1739 had cast a long shadow. That event claimed the lives of twenty-one whites and forty-four blacks. Stono was difficult to forget; still, the white colonists, ever quick to rationalize with or without justification, found reassurance in their conviction that the slaves had not re-

38. *Ga. Gaz.*, May 18, 1768.
39. *Col. Records of Ga.*, XIV, 292–293; tax act of Mar. 6, 1766, T. 1/461, Pt. i, P.R.O.
40. *Col. Records of Ga.*, XII, 325–326; also see XIX, Pt. i, 185.
41. *Ga. Gaz.*, Dec. 7, 1774.

volted on their own but had been prompted to it by the Florida Spaniards. At the time of Stono, Georgia had had no slaves. The fact is that Stono did not deter many Georgians from agitating for slaves, and after they got their way, they never ceased their efforts to buy more and more. Their exertions testify to the prevailing belief that, by and large, slavery was a tolerably "safe" institution from the white man's view.

Although the law decreed that movements of slaves should be restricted and controlled, there was actually great freedom of movement. The law said that slaves should carry tickets of permission as they traveled about, but it was winked at. They met together for funerals and celebrations, bought liquor, frequented taverns, and traded in commodities without permission slips. They sometimes even lived apart from "the immediate government and inspection of their masters or owners, or any other white person."[42] Complaints of grand juries about liberties that slaves enjoyed never moved the province to a strict enforcement of the slave acts.

Evidence survives reflecting instances of kind feelings and perhaps affection between slaves and masters. One slave desired to return to a master after some twenty years of separation.[43] Although too much can be made of the old image of the bereaved master standing, head bowed, with hat in hand at the grave of his beloved slave, such things may have occurred on occasion. However, in Savannah in 1774 deceased slaves were usually buried, not by their masters or indeed by any white man, but by other slaves.[44]

Masters sometimes freed faithful slaves by conferring a certificate of manumission.[45] A typical one read:

This is to satisfy to whom it may concern That this Black Man Mr. Moses Handlen is Free Man leaft by his Master Mr. Champernown Handlen, de-

42. Presentments of the grand jury, *ibid.*, July 13, 1768, Dec. 24, 1766, and Jan. 5, 1774; advertisement of John Houstoun, *ibid.*, Oct. 15, 1766; *Col. Records of Ga.*, XII, 147, 214.

43. Advertisement of James Herriot, *ibid.*, Nov. 22, 1775; Jacob Rader Marcus, ed., *American Jewry: Documents, Eighteenth Century* (Cincinnati, Ohio, 1959), 80.

44. *Ga. Gaz.*, Sept. 14, 1774.

45. Misc. Bonds Book J, 2–3; see will abstracts of the following in *Will Abstracts*: Isaac Barksdale, 10; Josiah Bryan, 19–20; George Cuthbert, 34; William Jones, 73; Bryan Kelley, 73; Charles Maran, 88; Charles Odingsell, 102; Margaret Pages, 105; Joseph Pruniere, 113; John Roviere, 121; and John Somerville, 129.

ceased in the year of our Lord 1760. This very black Moses Handlen is a very onnis Black man I knowed him from a Boy.
Witness my hand.   George Smith etc.[46]

The number of free blacks in Georgia was not large. In the 1760s the province anticipated taxes from twenty, but that estimate is only approximate.[47] Free blacks had some rights and could own or rent real property in the colony.

It has been debated whether slavery was a profitable institution for the South or whether it merely appeared to enrich the region while actually stifling its development. Georgians were convinced that slavery was a major reason that they had moved from poverty under the trustees to advancing prosperity under the king. For example, it was reported as fact that Hutchinson's Island, lying in the river before the town of Savannah, was sold in trustee times for £20 sterling. Toward the end of the royal era, after the arrival of slavery, it was said that the island could not be bought for £10,000 sterling.[48] Whether the figures are correct is immaterial today; they reflect the state of mind at the time. Men talked of unimproved lands that in six years increased in value from 5s. to 40s. per acre. And in late royal times, there were inhabitants in Savannah who would testify (with undoubted exaggeration) that before the passing of the trustee government, "almost every house there might have been bought for the consideration of doing the militia duty in the room of the first owner only."[49] Merchants were convinced that white Georgians regarded slavery as a sure road to prosperity, and they felt compelled to sell slaves along with other merchandise so as not to lose their planter customers to merchants who would.[50]

After the trustees agreed in 1750 to allow slavery, they had only two years remaining to make their influence felt. The proprietors required masters to permit "or even oblige" their blacks to attend in-

46. Misc. Bonds Book KK–1, 236. This particular instrument of manumission belonged to a black man who apparently had been freed in South Carolina.
47. *Col. Records of Ga.*, XIII, 518, XIV, 48.
48. Bernard Romans, *A Concise Natural History of East and West Florida* (1775), facsimile reproduction with an introduction by Rembert W. Patrick (Gainesville, Fla., 1962), 103–104.
49. *Ibid.*, 104.
50. Edward Telfair to William Thompson, Aug. 11, 1773, Telfair Family Papers, Ga. Hist. Soc., Savannah.

struction and worship on Sundays if a Protestant clergyman were conveniently available.[51] However, even in the German community, which had been the pillar of support for the trustees' antislavery law, slaves were worked on Sunday. The proprietors' intentions nevertheless found real expression in another form. In 1751 the trustees appointed Joseph Ottolenghe to be catechist for the blacks of Georgia.[52] A Jew converted to Anglicanism, Ottolenghe had been born and educated in Italy and had journeyed to London to be married, but was disappointed in his suit. After a dispute with an uncle who lived in England, he was cast into a British jail for debt. Attracted to Christianity by reading the New Testament, he was baptized a Christian according to the rites of the Church of England. During his imprisonment, he was befriended by members of the Anglican church in Exeter. For the rest of his life he maintained a firm attachment to the established church.

In Georgia, Ottolenghe was paid to teach the slaves reading, writing, and the principles of Christianity.[53] (He was to promote the silk culture at the same time.) The important thing about Ottolenghe's appointment was its officiality. His ministrations to the slaves were sanctioned by the trustees. Under royal government, the official attitude changed substantially. After the passage of the 1755 slave act, it was a crime to teach a slave to write. The provision was continued in the 1770 act and was law when the Revolution began. Some masters disregarded it, for prominent men conspicuously educated some of their slaves, and no one was ever prosecuted for doing so. Ottolenghe himself carried on his teaching until at least 1760, long after it was illegal.

To Ottolenghe and to others, the purpose of teaching slaves to read and write was to foster religion—specifically, to get them to use the Bible and the Book of Common Prayer. When he arrived in Georgia in 1751, he asked the rector of the church in Savannah to announce from the pulpit that slaves of consenting masters would be taught three times a week.[54] He disregarded advice that he become an itinerant catechist going from plantation to plantation and, instead, built a house in Savannah with a large room where his students assembled,

51. *Col. Records of Ga.*, I, 59. As previously noted, this "law" repealing the old act forbidding importation of slaves was never formally approved by the king. The trustees nevertheless sought to enforce it on their own authority.

52. *Ibid.*, II, 510.

53. *Ibid.*, I, 556.

54. Ottolenghe to the Rev. Mr. Smith, Dec. 4, 1751, MSS of Dr. Bray's Associates, Pt. H (L.C. reel 11, 335/201–202).

usually at night when their work was done and their owners could spare them. Many masters refused to have their slaves taught at all. For those blacks who came—sometimes there were fifty and at other times fewer than ten—Ottolenghe opened with prayer, then taught reading and instruction in the Lord's Prayer. Next came the catechism, followed by a homily. He taught some slaves to read, but poorly, for "Slavery is certainly a great Depresser of the Mind."[55]

The resistance of many masters to Ottolenghe's efforts was dogged, and the life of the catechist was difficult. Some masters thought they would be losers if their slaves were either converted or educated, asserting that Christian slaves were ten times worse than pagans. Some masters were as great heathens as their slaves, said Ottolenghe, and he was surprised that they even bothered to use "so many sophistical Arguments to obstruct the Instruction."[56] In the face of these discouragements, Ottolenghe found himself busier and busier with silk culture. By the early 1760s he had abandoned the slaves altogether.

After 1766 another attempt was made to educate blacks. The Anglican rector in Savannah, Bartholomew Zouberbuhler, who had accumulated substantial wealth in the brick business, left a part of his estate to support a catechist for slaves on his plantation. The slaves numbered fifty-two at his death in 1766.[57] The catechist was to live on the plantation, Beth Abram, and was to teach principles of Christianity along with reading and writing. He was also to work with slaves of other masters who were willing to have them taught. Zouberbuhler's will appointed trustees to administer the estate, but they made an error in judgment in selecting Cornelius Winter, a Methodist under the influence of George Whitefield, to come from England to settle at Beth Abram. Whitefield was disliked by important persons in Georgia, and Winter inherited the antagonisms. It might have been better had Zouberbuhler's trustees turned for assistance, not to Whitefield, but to the Society for the Propagation of the Gospel in Foreign Parts or to the Associates of Dr. Bray. Still, the financial support for the catechist was generous and secure; when Winter arrived in 1769 he was

55. *Ibid.* See also Ottolenghe to Waring, July 12, 1758, *ibid.* (L.C. reel 11, 335/206–212); and Ottolenghe to Associates of Dr. Bray, Nov. 18, 1754, *ibid.* (L.C. reel 11, 335/223).

56. Ottolenghe to Associates of Dr. Bray, Nov. 19, 1753, *ibid.* (L.C. reel 11, 335/230).

57. Estate of Bartholomew Zouberbuhler, Apr. 21, 1767, Inventory Book F, 253–254.

greeted by a supporter, James Habersham, who embraced him and said, "I will be your friend, if nobody else will."[58] Whitefield had cautioned Winter that he should be happy if he had as many blacks to teach as a ship's bed cabin would hold; and Winter must not wonder if, for attempting to work with the slaves, he were "whipped off the plantation." Winter noted a variety of reactions to him from men both white and black. "Some of the more sensible negroes facetiously said they were too wicked to be made good now. A few had their expectations raised by my coming, and seemed pleased with my errand. The white people in general conceived that I came there because I could not live in England, and I scarcely stirred out without hearing one and another say with the accent of contempt, 'There goes the negro parson.' "[59]

Habersham had been an advocate of admitting slaves into Georgia. He was also among those who saw to the education of some of his own. In 1775 a school with thirty black pupils and a Moravian teacher was functioning on one of his plantations.[60] He was convinced that there were other men like himself, "who would be glad to have their black servants become fellow-heirs with them, and partakers of the inheritance undefiled, and that fadeth not away."[61] Experience, however, showed that such men were uncommon. Winter felt that he lacked even the support of some of Zouberbuhler's executors.

Winter received threats of harm if he should go to the plantations of some planters; and a motion was made in the council to brand him a public nuisance, but it failed to pass.[62] After a year, the catechist left Georgia and returned to London to seek ordination to the Anglican ministry. His applications to the bishop of London were subverted by enemies he had made in Georgia and by implications drawn from his association with Whitefield, who had made the Anglican clergy a special object of criticism. Winter never returned to Georgia. Work among the slaves was carried on later by another catechist, the Reverend John Rennie.

As the American Revolution was about to begin, William Knox sent two Moravian missionaries to instruct his slaves at Knoxborough,

58. "Memoirs of Cornelius Winter," *Works of Jay*, III, 29.
59. *Ibid.*
60. Ga. Hist. Soc., *Colls.*, VI, 241.
61. "Memoirs of Cornelius Winter," *Works of Jay*, III, 39.
62. *Ibid.*, 29.

a plantation near Ebenezer.[63] Knox, who had earlier lived in Georgia, was then undersecretary of state for the colonies in London. His attempt was one of the final organized efforts to teach slaves in Georgia before the Revolution, and the outbreak of war assured its failure. Throughout the period after 1750, however, there were individuals who saw that some slaves learned to read and to write, among them Habersham, some of the Germans at Ebenezer, and the managers of Whitefield's orphanage at Bethesda. The purpose was always the same —to give the slaves skill in reading so that they might more easily learn the truths of religion.

Blacks in some numbers attended divine worship at white churches in Savannah, Midway, and Ebenezer.[64] But at the very end of the era, the slaves discovered impressive preachers in their own ranks and turned in ever increasing numbers to the Baptist church. George Liele, a slave born in Virginia, was converted to Christianity in Georgia by a white Baptist minister. Liele began preaching at his master's barn at Brampton, three miles from Savannah. His ministry in Georgia lasted some four years, and after the final British evacuation in 1782, Liele went to Jamaica, where he became pastor of a large church. His work had sown the seeds of the Baptist faith among Georgia blacks.[65]

Slaves provided not only the labor system upon which agriculture prospered but the base of the social structure as well. A slave had rights under the law barely sufficient to preserve his life, and he had no rights to preserve his humanity except against such extreme abuses as maiming and castration. Legally as well as actually, slaves were at the bottom of society.

63. Ga. Hist. Soc., *Colls.*, VI, 241.

64. Ottolenghe to Waring, July 12, 1758, MSS of Dr. Bray's Associates, Pt. H (L.C. reel 11, 335/209); Muhlenberg, *Journals*, II, 638; James Stacy, *History of the Midway Congregational Church, Liberty County, Georgia* (n.p., 1951 [orig. publ., Newnan, Ga., 1894]), 52.

65. [George Liele and Andrew Bryan], "Letters Showing the Rise and Progress of the Early Negro Churches of Georgia and the West Indies," *Journal of Negro History*, I (1916), 69–92; the Rev. George White, *Historical Collections of Georgia: Containing the Most Interesting Facts, Traditions, Biographical Sketches, Anecdotes, Etc. . . .* (New York, 1854), 313. Liele's chronology is confusing, but it seems clear that a movement of large numbers of blacks into the Baptist church occurred during the Revolution. Some were persecuted by white men for their faith, with the whites probably assuming that the blacks were assembling for seditious purposes.

Yet, except for slaves, Georgia's social structure was not rigidly fixed. Men, women, and families might rise or fall on the social scale, their place on it greatly influenced by their wealth. Wealth—or rather, the lack of it—had a great deal to do with the founding of the province. While Georgia was not important as a settlement for imprisoned debtors, it was a distinct place of hope and refuge for the poor. The industrious and struggling poor were recognized and honored (as was the farmer Michael Burkholder), but the idle poor were scorned in Georgia as in England. The errors made by the trustees in selecting some unworthy persons as early settlers were partially self-correcting, however. Many arrivals who avoided labor in Georgia, just as they had dodged it in England, speedily departed once the trustees' stores were closed.[66]

Although the trustees envisioned a colony of new beginnings, they never considered that the province would be without social distinctions. In 1734 they promised a desirable prospective settler that in Georgia he would have all the rights and privileges of an English "gentleman." These included the privilege of always doing military duty on horseback, of shooting and fishing in any part of the province not enclosed, and of not being judged at law unless four other gentlemen were on the jury.[67] Oglethorpe himself insisted upon distinctions. He allowed no trafficking between his officers and their soldiers.[68] No real nobleman ever settled permanently in Georgia (or in any other American colony with the exception of Lord Fairfax in Virginia), but by the end of trustee times, Georgians could become gentlemen and did so in three ways—by possessing a fortune, by holding important public office, or merely by enjoying esteem.[69] Georgia gentlemen skillfully emulated the behavior of the English gentry and were jealous of their

66. Ga. Hist. Soc., *Colls.*, I, 175–176.
67. *Col. Records of Ga.*, XXIX, 55.
68. *Ibid.*, V, 277.
69. Loewald, Starika, and Taylor, trans. and eds., "Bolzius Answers a Questionnaire," Pt. i, *WMQ*, 3d Ser., XIV (1957), 252. Before the Revolution, four baronets, members of the English petty nobility, lived in Georgia. They were Sir Francis Bathurst, who returned to England following Lady Bathurst's death in 1736; Sir Patrick Houstoun the Elder (d. 1762); Sir Patrick Houstoun the Younger; and Sir James Wright. The latter two departed Georgia after the Revolution and died abroad. Wright is buried in Westminster Abbey. Bathurst and the two Houstouns inherited their titles; Wright earned his. He was created a baronet by George III in 1772.

status. A minor official declared that Georgians in power, like edged tools, should not be meddled with.[70]

Nevertheless, social mobility characterized royal as well as trustee Georgia, for power and status were open to those who could certify themselves through wealth or remarkable abilities. One could not otherwise explain the rise to prominence of Habersham, a former Savannah schoolmaster; of Ottolenghe, the catechist who had been imprisoned in a British jail; of William Ewen and William Russell, who came as servants; of Francis Harris, who had started as a clerk in the trustee store; of John Adam Treutlen, who first came to notice as a schoolmaster among the Salzburgers; or of Edward Barnard, a former baker's apprentice.

Some men attempted to claim that they were gentlemen, only to have their pretensions shattered by others who had actually worked or insinuated their way into power. In the early days of the province, plots of land exceeding fifty acres were, perhaps not seriously, called "gentlemen's lots." Most of the recipients were "broken Tradesmen, and artisans."[71] Thus the title of "gentleman" was often debased. It was used at times by men who would have been hard put to defend it, and therefore some who had an undisputed claim to it declined its use.

As it became less a mark of distinction to be called a "gentleman," it became more important to be called "esquire" or "the honorable." As a title, "honorable" was mostly reserved for a small group of men who stood close to the governor as members of his council—the same men who comprised the upper house of the assembly. They were appointed by the king, usually upon the governor's nomination, and could be suspended by the governor, but seldom were.[72] Occasionally, "the honorable" was extended to judges. The title "esquire," written after the name, was more common. It went automatically to men who had been elected to the Commons House of Assembly and to holders

70. *Col. Records of Ga.*, XX, 176.

71. Ver Steeg, ed., *True and Historical Narrative*, 41.

72. Most councillors served for life or until they left the colony. However, both Noble Jones and Clement Martin, Sr., were removed from office following disagreements with the governor in the early royal era. Both were later restored. Jonathan Bryan was suspended by Gov. Wright for presiding over a meeting that criticized policies of the British government. Bryan was never restored to his seat on the council but was elected to the Commons House of Assembly. He was associated with the Revolutionary movement, and one of Georgia's older counties is named for him.

of office in government down through justice of the peace. (Most justices of the peace would have qualified as "esquires" in other ways; the "commission of the peace" was largely composed of men of standing.) The use of "esquire" as a title was also accorded to officers of the militia and, in no discernible pattern, to other men who were wealthy or prominent.

Titles were no more precise measures of status in Georgia than they were in other colonies. The use of "gentleman" might mean something, or nothing. A man who wrote "esquire" after his name was likely to be a person of real standing, and a man addressed as "the honorable" was certain to be. Even so, there were variations based upon wealth and personal influence within the latter designations.

Between the slaves at the bottom of the social ladder and the esquires and honorables at the top lay the remainder of the population. Rankings were nowhere formalized. There was no procedure for determining where the classes stood in relation to one another, but status was related to the possession or absence of wealth and to the esteem in which the various means of earning a livelihood were held.

Just above slaves in status stood the body of indentured servants brought to the colony from Europe, a portion of whose life and labor had been bought by a master. Indentured servants were commonly sold for seven years, although terms of indenture varied between four and fourteen. It was necessary to treat indentured servants better than slaves and to give them better food and clothing, for they had "from their infancy been accustomed to live in a different manner to what the negroes doe."[73]

The absence of blacks in the early years made a large number of white servants necessary. Many were indentured to the trust itself. These men and women farmed for the trustees, tended their cow pens, worked in their stores, operated mills, built bridges and roads, and did other work as directed by officials in the colony. The trust ceased employing servants for itself in 1743. Private individuals did not. They bought white servants, 2,492 of whom were privately held between 1733 and 1752.[74] Even so, there was a shortage of labor. Men called for more and more servants, a need seldom satisfied. Although white servants were better clothed and housed than slaves, they were not respected by masters, who expected them to malinger on the job, to

73. Coulter, ed., *Journal of Gordon*, 58.
74. Ready, "Economic History of Ga.," 275.

steal, and to attempt to escape. Habersham, who for a time supervised the servants bound to Whitefield, considered them a burden; he believed that less than half their expenses could be recovered from their labor. To lay out further resources on them, he said, was throwing away money in such a way as "could neither be justified to God nor Man."[75]

The trustees had hoped that servants would work out their indentures, then remain in Georgia to take up free land and add to the number of reliable freeholders. A few did; others bought their freedom before their time was out and became excellent citizens.[76] But the story of indentured servants in Georgia was mostly an unhappy one. As a labor system, the indenturing process did not work well. Untold numbers fled before their time had expired, their successful pursuit and capture hampered by clumsy processes of government. If a servant deserted at Ebenezer in 1750, for example, the owner had to take a copy of his indenture to Savannah to get it attested and sealed by a magistrate. By the time the procedure was complete, the servant was across the river in South Carolina.[77]

Some of the most sustained defamation surviving from colonial Georgia was used by masters in describing their servants. To William Stephens, some were whores and thieves and, in general, all were a "Sad crew."[78] To Noble Jones they were always sick, in trouble, or robbing him and running away. Jones put one of his in irons.[79] To Paul Amatis, the trustees' gardener, servants were concerned only with hunting, fishing, and other pleasures, and to John Bromfield, who was attacked by his servant with a sword, they were a hazard as well as a distress.[80]

Whether or not indentured servants were badly used, and some were, they were ill-regarded. The introduction of slavery, which made white indentured servants less necessary, did not elevate their status but actually lowered it, for masters no longer were dependent upon them. Toward the end of colonial times, the Savannah firm of William and Edward Telfair and Company was hard put to get rid of a con-

75. James Habersham to John Martin Bolzius, Sept. 25, 1747, Ga. Misc. Coll., Force MSS.

76. *Col. Records of Ga.,* XXVI, 51.

77. *Ibid.,* 82.

78. McPherson, ed., *Journal of Egmont,* 367.

79. *Col. Records of Ga.,* XX, 203.

80. *Ibid.,* 139, XXI, 255.

signment of servants that had just arrived by sea, probably from Great Britain. Finally seventeen were sold to the firm's general disadvantage (see also figure 5, following). The Telfairs despaired of selling five more who were nothing more than "a parcell of common Villains."[81] They might well have been anxious. Among the servants from that consignment there seems to have been a carpenter, John Carver, bought by Joseph Butler, a Georgia planter. Butler wrote Edward Telfair about his purchase:

As to the Servant man that you and the Capt. of the Vessell recommended to me for a Carpenter and Joyner, he Cant Joynt a plank nither has he Joynted One Since Ive had him. He is a Cursed fellow. I would not keep him One year for two hundred pounds Sterling. If you will give me Ten pounds for him, you may have him. I give you Twenty so that I am Willing to Loose Ten pounds by him to gitt rid of him, or Sell him for his 4 year to Some Sharp Master. If you think that Ten pounds Loss to me is not anough, for me to Loose, I am willing to Loose the Twenty So you Sell him to Some Sharp Master for 4 years. Pray Lett me know by the Bearour.[82]

Eleven nights later, the already dubious value of Carver's indenture vanished when he packed a bundle and ran away. The servant apparently escaped to South Carolina while Butler declaimed the news of his defection and called loudly for his arrest and delivery to the workhouse.[83] There is no record that Carver was ever apprehended. He was apparently never of the slightest use to the man who had purchased his services for four years.

The arrival of slaves all but eliminated the class of white men who had been simple laborers. Laborers in trustee Georgia had enjoyed a status slightly above that of servant, principally because they were not legally bound to any man. When slaves arrived, white laborers could scarcely compete, for employers could rent slaves by the day, week, or month even if they did not own them. Yet there still remained in royal Georgia a small class of white laborers, of whom Anthione Gautier of Savannah was one. It is impossible now to say exactly what kinds of work Gautier did for a living, but when he died, he owned a farm containing forty-five acres, a house and lot in Savannah, some small

81. William and Edward Telfair and Company to James Alexander, May 28, 1774, Telfair Family Papers.

82. Joseph Butler to Edward Telfair, May 12, 1774, Edward Telfair Papers, Perkins Lib., Duke Univ., Durham, N.C.

83. Letter of Joseph Butler, May 24, 1774, Edward Telfair Papers.

ABSENTED from on board the ship Mary, Capt. James Walden, lying at the subscribers wharf,

Six Indented Men Servants, viz.

JOHN HUMPHRIS, about 20 years old, 5 feet 4 or 5 inches high, with short black hair, and a swarthy complexion, had on when he eloped a suit of black broadcloth cloaths, born in London.

MICHAEL HERRING, aged 27 years, 5 feet 6 inches high, short hair, a dark complexion, had on a sailor's frock and trowsers, born in Ireland.

ROBERT COCK, aged 24 years, about 5 feet high, in a seaman's dress, curled hair, with a dark complexion, born in London.

RICHARD OWEN, a taylor by trade, aged about 40 years, 5 feet 6 or 7 inches high, had on a blue coat and light coloured waistcoat, born in Wales.

JOHN GRANT, aged 37 years, about 5 feet 7 inches high, had on when he went away a soldier's coat, born in Scotland.

EDWARD GRANVILLE, by trade a barber, aged 29 years, about 5 feet 7 inches high, with tied hair, pitted with the smallpox, had on a brown coat and breeches, with a white waistcoat, born in London.

Whoever will apprehend and deliver any of the above servants to the subscribers, or to the Keeper of the Gaol in Savannah, shall have twenty shillings sterling for each, with reasonable charges; and all persons are hereby forbid harbouring them, as they will, upon conviction, be prosecuted to the utmost rigour of the law.

May 24, 1774. WILLIAM and EDWARD TELFAIR and CO.

5. Advertisement for Runaway Indentured Servants, 1774.

The mercantile establishment of the Telfair brothers sold many indentured white servants. Often the servants confounded the indenturing system by fleeing. The six men referred to in this advertisement apparently fled as soon as the ship bringing them to Georgia touched dock in Savannah.

(From the Georgia Gazette, May 25, 1774.)

holdings in Purrysburg, South Carolina, plus a little personal property.[84] His real property in Georgia, except for the house, had probably been given to him by the government in Savannah.

Above the white laborer in status was the overseer who managed plantations where the owner was not resident, or where he was resident but did not wish to be in charge. Their usefulness is attested by advertisements for them in the *Georgia Gazette*. Often, but not always, single men were preferred, perhaps because of their availability for service at any time of day or night.[85] The status of overseers, like that of everyone else in the colony except slaves, was not rigidly fixed. While some were regarded as very lowly, others were bettering themselves and stood high in the estimation of their employers. Governor Wright had an overseer who, through his excellence, commanded a share of the crop. Habersham had one who was fast achieving that position.[86] Overseers usually were salaried and perhaps shared in the livestock.

On the other hand, Matthias Binder, who worked for William Gibbons, Jr., was perhaps an overseer but was sometimes called a laborer; he was little better off than one. Binder and his family lived on an island plantation belonging to Gibbons, and he and his son worked in the fields assisted by one of Gibbons's slaves. For their efforts the Binders received half the crop and garden produce, half the increase of the hogs and poultry (provided Binder supplied half the feed), and the use of the cattle. Binder received no money and had to keep up the plantation.[87] This arrangement differed little from the tenantry of a later day.

A more usual arrangement involved the payment of money. To oversee a plantation in the estate of Benjamin Farley in 1769, Gibbons employed William May, and their agreement was made formal by a

84. Will abstract of Anthione Gautier, *Will Abstracts*, 58; see also will abstracts of Christopher Wisenbaker, *ibid.*, 147, and Christian Campher, *ibid.*, 26.

85. For a sampling of advertisements seeking overseers, see the following in the *Ga. Gaz.*: unsigned advertisements, Oct. 11, 1764, May 13 and Sept. 2, 1767, Nov. 16 and Dec. 7, 1768, and Jan. 5, 1774; also those of Joseph Gibbons, Oct. 7, 1767; James Cuthbert, Sept. 7, 1768; John Mullryne, Feb. 9, 1774; John Morel, Feb. 23, 1774; Nathaniel Hall, Nov. 9, 1774; James Read, Mar. 29, 1775; and Theodore Gay, Dec. 13, 1775.

86. Ga. Hist. Soc., *Colls.*, VI, 133. The overseer of Gov. Wright was probably Joseph Weatherly, who was murdered, perhaps by slaves, in 1778 or 1779.

87. Agreement between William Gibbons and Matthias Binder, Mar. 15, 1760, William Gibbons, Jr., Papers.

document that both men signed: "Memorandom of Agreement between William Gibbons of the one part and William May on the . . . other. Said William May doth Agree to Oversee the Plantation of the Estate of Benjan. Farley the Term of one year from the 2 day February next. In consideration of which William Gibbons and Joseph Clay doth agree to pay him 25 pounds, and allow him a third part of the Hoggs he Raises on the plantation and also half of the Poultry, he the said May leaving the old stock whole."[88]

Although the law required that a white male overseer or supervisor be present on plantations where slaves were resident, it was occasionally ignored. Rather than trouble with overseers, some masters appointed a trustworthy slave to superintend the plantation. Such an arrangement was made by Pastor Rabenhorst near Ebenezer.[89]

In the middle position of the social hierarchy, above the servant, the laborer, and the overseer, stood the artisan class, or the mechanics. Artisans were of many kinds—carpenters, shoemakers, tailors, blacksmiths, masons, tanners, brickmakers, and so forth—and individuals within the class varied greatly in the successes they achieved. While James Love was a prosperous and respected cabinetmaker, almost nothing may be said of dozens of obscure men, such as Nevill Smith of Frederica, or John Johnston and Anthony Pages of Savannah, all bakers.

Artisans kept their place after a fashion and did not challenge their social betters for seats in the lower house of the assembly, even though we may be sure that they and other "common People" voted heavily in elections. They were willing to choose among gentlemen for assembly seats. They were also content for gentlemen to sit as churchwardens and vestrymen, not an empty honor since vestries were empowered to levy taxes for the expenses of the established church and for poor relief.[90]

88. Agreement between Gibbons and William May, Jan. 28, 1769, *ibid.*

89. Presentments of the grand jury, *Ga. Gaz.*, Jan. 5, 1774. The jury presented Samuel Douglass, Savannah merchant, for failing to keep an overseer on Skidaway Island and for allowing his slaves to keep firearms. Also see Muhlenberg, *Journals*, II, 616. Since Rabenhorst lived on his plantation, his arrangement did not violate the law.

90. Freeholders met each Easter Monday to elect the vestry and wardens of Christ Church Parish. The results for 1765, 1767–1772, and 1774–1775 show that men of the upper classes were always elected. Many of them, once elected, served until they died or left the colony. Twelve were chosen each year, and in the 9 years analyzed, only 26 individuals served in 108 slots. See notices of vestry

Artisans apparently did decide to fight for seats on the workhouse commission, however. At the same time and place that churchwardens and vestrymen were elected each year, the freeholders of Christ Church Parish also chose commissioners of the workhouse. The workhouse was the receiving place for runaway slaves and a house of confinement for some criminal slaves. Such an institution was marginally related to the interests of the mechanics, who saw slave laborers as a threat. Also, it is possible that, to artisans, seats on the commission came to possess a symbolic value beyond their actual worth.

Whatever their motives, members of the artisan class began to stand for election as commissioners; of the five men elected annually for one-year terms, in 1768 one was a mechanic, three were members of the upper class, and the fifth, Robert Bolton, was of debatable status. (A sometime shopkeeper, innkeeper, postmaster, and vendue master with ties to the middle class, Bolton was also certainly close to the upper class if kinship meant anything, for he was a brother-in-law of Habersham, who as president of the council ranked second only to the governor in local ceremonial matters.) In 1769 the upper class apparently rallied, for five of their own were chosen, if one includes the again victorious Bolton. Habersham himself was elected in that year, along with Ottolenghe, Edward Telfair, and William Young, all members of the upper class. In 1770, however, the mechanics asserted their strength, turning out all of the incumbents except Bolton and electing four of their own. In the elections of 1771, 1772, 1774, and 1775, they kept control of the board. Only Bolton, standing with a foot in each camp, triumphed in all of these seven elections.[91] We might deduce from the results (though not from anything written at the time that survives) that the mechanics had a sense of class consciousness and that they asserted it publicly, if somewhat less significantly than their fellow artisans in South Carolina and elsewhere.

Above the artisan class ranked the professional men—lawyers, medical men of the several kinds already discussed, schoolteachers,

---

elections, *Ga. Gaz.*, Apr. 18, 1765, Apr. 22, 1767, Apr. 6, 1768, Mar. 29, 1769, Apr. 18, 1770, Apr. 6 and 13, 1774, and Apr. 19 and May 17, 1775. Also see election notices in the *S.-C. Gaz.; And Country Jour.*, for Apr. 16, 1771, and May 5, 1772. For evidence that the "common People" voted in assembly elections, see *Ga. Hist. Soc., Colls.*, VI, 166.

91. See notices of election of commissioners of the workhouse, *Ga. Gaz.*, Apr. 6, 1768, Mar. 29, 1769, Apr. 18, 1770, Apr. 6, 1774, and Apr. 19, 1775; and the *S.-C. Gaz.; And Country Jour.*, Apr. 16, 1771, and May 5, 1772.

and clergymen. Again, classifications cannot be precise. Doctors such as Felix Pitt and John Patrick Dillon did not achieve a status comparable to Drs. Noble Jones, Noble Wimberly Jones, or Henry Lewis Bourquin. Pitt and Dillon had only their professions to commend them; the latter three had their professions plus positions in government.

The inhospitable attitude toward lawyers in trustee times slowly modified. In royal Georgia, lawyers of whatever preparation were important persons, and some of them found their way into government. The profession itself was held in esteem, and good training was especially valued. When Chief Justice William Simpson died in 1768, Governor Wright declared that his successor must be a *"Real Lawyer,"* a remark meaningful where numerous members of the bar had been admitted to practice through "interest."[92]

Clergymen enjoyed the respect attached to the recognized professions but were a bit below the highest rank, except in the Salzburg community and possibly at Midway. And like doctors, lawyers, schoolteachers, and clergymen, merchants also ranked above artisans, although they were not automatically of the highest class unless they qualified for admission in some other way.

To be associated with the land carried another kind of status in Georgia, a status that lay beyond considerations of wealth, office, and social rank. It had been the founders' earliest dream that Georgia become an ideal colony of agriculturalists. Oglethorpe had offered bounties upon certain crops when other inducements proved insufficient.[93] Governor Wright said that agriculture occupied the "whole strength and attention" of Georgians, and the traveler William Bartram believed that among the happy proprietors of Georgia's farms he had discovered a people both magnificent and joyful.[94] As a merchant, Habersham in 1747 was beginning to make the fortune that he would later add to as a farmer; as he saw it, the purpose of the merchant was to sell the produce of the planter for the enrichment of both.[95]

Even a subsistence farmer had status based upon his occupation, regardless of his poverty or affluence. Bartram once visited the planta-

92. *Col. Records of Ga.*, XXXVII, 376. Simpson's successor was Anthony Stokes.
93. Ga. Hist. Soc., *Colls.*, III, 88.
94. *Col. Records of Ga.*, XXXVII, 143; William Bartram, *Travels*, 10–11.
95. Habersham to Bolzius, Sept. 25, 1747, Ga. Misc. Coll., Force MSS.

tion, cow pen, and lumberyard of a moderately successful farmer on the Savannah River fifty miles from the capital. He came upon the husband and wife as they supervised milking at the pen. "I found these people, contrary to what a traveller might, perhaps, reasonably expect, from their occupation and remote situation from the capital or any commercial town, to be civil and courteous, and though educated as it were in the woods, no strangers to sensibility and those moral virtues which grace and ornament the most approved and admired characters in civil society." The newly married son of this couple had settled in a little house nearby on the river bank, where Bartram found the young man and his wife to be the fulfillment of an agrarian ideal: "What a Venus! What an Adonis! said I in silent transport; every action and feature seemed to reveal the celestial endowments of the mind: though a native sprightliness and sensibility appeared, yet virtue and discretion direct and rule. The dress of this beauteous sylvan queen was plain but clean, neat and elegant, all of cotton and of her own spinning and weaving."[96]

Writers like Bartram sometimes seemed more ingenuous than they were, since such exaggerated descriptions in praise of rural life had about them an element of literary convention. This does not mean, however, that such sentiments were insincere; there is ample evidence to show that Georgians actually held agrarian pursuits in elevated esteem. When in 1775 Governor Wright described the parochial committee then threatening his government as a "Parcel of the Lowest People," he was referring to the carpenters, shoemakers, blacksmiths, and other such persons serving on it, not to merchants and farmers.[97] Often merchants and farmers were the same people, for it was common, though not universal, for Georgians to be planters in addition to whatever else they did. Thus it was that the Joneses were physicians and planters; John Graham was a merchant and a planter; William Young was a lawyer and a planter; and Governor Wright and Chief Justice Stokes were officers of government and planters. Land was the most common resource in the province, and together with slaves, it was the most valuable and the most valued.

Not every member of the upper class was identified with agriculture, although most were. For example, William Graeme, attorney general and advocate general of the court of vice admiralty for Georgia, could

96. William Bartram, *Travels*, 310, 313.
97. Ga. Hist. Soc., *Colls.*, III, 228.

not pride himself on large agricultural holdings. He owned only six slaves, and three of those were children. Yet he moved in councils of influence and sat in the Commons House of Assembly, sometimes for Halifax and St. George, sometimes for St. Andrew.

Graeme, although not exceedingly wealthy, possessed a wardrobe commensurate with his rank. He owned a suit of scarlet regimentals, laced; a full-trimmed black coat and waistcoat; a sky-blue coat and waistcoat, laced; a blue coat and a laced scarlet waistcoat; a black coat and a waistcoat; a red coat with a black cloth waistcoat; and three other coats of brown, black, and grey. He also had a blue waistcoat and flowered gown and possessed the court attire of a barrister—a gown and full periwig. In a trunk he kept his two hats and an old wig, and he also owned stone and silver knee buckles, a gold-headed cane, a speaking trumpet, an officer's silk sash, a silver-hilted sword, and a pair of silver mounted pistols. There were other miscellaneous items of attire, including eighteen waistcoats and jackets, ten white shirts, ten cravats and stocks, and five night caps. He had several yards of rich, broad gold lace valued at £8.

Graeme's library held between seventy and seventy-five volumes mostly dealing with law, but it included a Bible, a Latin dictionary, and works of Shakespeare and Locke. He owned pictures of King George III and Queen Charlotte, as well as a number of other prints and pictures. In his cellar were brandy, rum, beer, two dozen bottles of French wine, and ninety bottles of porter.[98]

At his death in the early summer of 1770, Graeme was buried with military honors. The graveside service was attended by the grand master and brothers of the Masonic lodge and by the colonial light infantry company under Sir Patrick Houstoun. Gentlemen at the graveside "seemed deeply affected at the loss of so sincere a friend, and useful member of the community." He was remembered for his "ability, integrity, and faithfulness, in discharge of the duties reposed in him," and was declared to have merited universal respect.[99]

Graeme was an exception in that he was influential and yet virtually landless, for Georgians who received such accolades were usually men who owned many acres. In the 1750s there was a movement from the

---

98. Estate of William Graeme, Sept. 11, 1770, Inventory Book F, 479–487. Graeme's personal estate was valued at a little more than £772, not counting real estate.

99. *S.-C. and Amer. Gen. Gaz.*, July 18–25, 1770.

towns into the countryside. By the 1760s a country gentleman was expected to have a place in town in addition to his plantation home. He was likely to spend most of his time in town, going to the country to check on his overseer perhaps once in two weeks.[100] It was sometimes said that the upper classes had adopted habits of laziness. An uncomplimentary remark of the time said that gentle folk lay abed in the mornings, and if they were at work by ten, it was early for them.[101]

Agriculture and trade by the middle of 1760s had sufficiently enriched some persons to support such a style of life. On the other hand, for the years 1769, 1770, and 1771, estimates left by a customs official loosely suggest that approximately 30 percent of the adult white population lived at the subsistence level, too poor to buy even a pot of coffee or a cup of tea. The same estimates generally imply that some 70 percent of the adult white population lived above the subsistence level, although some were barely above.[102] Such a person was Adam Ranstatler, a poor but apparently respectable farmer who died about 1755. Ranstatler had been an indentured servant, but later he had been granted about a hundred acres of land near Vernonburgh. Despite his poverty, his occupation as an independent tiller of the soil entitled him to respect, even though his personal estate was worth only between £19 and £20. His possessions were simple. He had one luxury item— a teapot. Otherwise, he owned two pairs of breeches, a coat, a hat, and a pair of shoes. On his farm were twenty-six bushels of corn, three bushels of rice, thirty-two pounds of cotton, two sows, four pigs, three shoats, two cows and two calves, two heifers, an ox, and three beehives. In his house were found two iron pots, a skillet, a pan, a jug, a pewter basin, five plates, one dish, three pillows, and a churn. In addition, Ranstatler owned two guns, several working tools, a spinning wheel, a hoe, and a ploughshare.[103]

The spinning wheel suggests the presence of a wife, and her role in the household was no less important than her husband's. This was true even though the original policies of the trustees denied women the right to inherit or hold land. The idealized woman of trustee

---

100. John Bartram, "Diary of a Journey," ed. Harper, Am. Phil. Soc., *Trans.*, N.S., XXXIII, Pt. i (1942), 30; Ga. Hist. Soc., *Colls.*, VI, 39.

101. Muhlenberg, *Journals*, II, 679.

102. *Col. Records of Ga.*, XXXVIII, Pt. i, 141–142.

103. Estate of Adam Ranstatler, 1755, Inventory Book F, 7; *Col. Records of Ga.*, VI, 56–57, 375.

Georgia, not far different from the idealized woman in royal Georgia, was expected to realize her proper place in the home. When Lady Bathurst died in April 1736 at age 57, for example, she was interred in Savannah in the presence of people of the best rank, including Tomochichi and his spouse. She was eulogized as "a loving Wife, an affectionate Mother, and a true Housekeeper."[104] To John Wesley, the wives of the German pastors Bolzius and Gronau personified the ideal. "It appeared to be their delight as well as their custom to be the servants of all."[105] In 1775 Frau Rabenhorst, wife of a later German pastor, was described as "a Mary in faith and a Martha in charity, who seeks her salvation in humble solicitude and also ruleth well her own house."[106]

Girls were taught informally in homes and formally in schools, and the purpose of their educations was to prepare them to become pious and modest custodians of the domestic virtues. Girls' training among the Salzburgers was not unlike that received by females elsewhere in the province. At the Salzburger schools, they learned knitting along with their reading and writing. It was thought necessary to teach "in tender youth the arts of knitting, spinning, sewing, housekeeping, Christian manners and conduct, etc.," if Georgia were not to have a generation of slovenly mothers and housekeepers.[107] At Whitefield's Bethesda, girls learned the arts of managing a household, including knitting, washing, cleaning, and sewing. Some learned to spin.[108] All were taught religion.

Education for boys included instruction in religion and in the responsibilities of heads of households. It was expected that males would become providers for families rather than burdens upon society. A visitor to Ebenezer in the late royal period noticed at once the vocational intent of education: "And here the purpose is little more than that expressed by the Dutch countryman up in New York. This father

104. *S.-C. Gaz.*, May 8–15, 1736.

105. John Wesley, *The Journal of the Rev. John Wesley, A.M.*, ed. Nehemiah Curnock, Standard Edition, I (London, 1909), 375.

106. Muhlenberg, *Journals*, II, 677.

107. *Ibid.*, 669; Hermann Winde, "Die Frühgeschichte der Lutherischen Kirche in Georgia" (Ph.D. diss., Martin Luther University, Halle-Wittenberg, Germany, 1960), 137, hereafter cited as Winde, "Frühgeschichte der Luth. Kirche in Ga."

108. George Whitefield, *An Account of Money Received and Disbursed for the Orphan-House in Georgia. . . . To which is prefixed a Plan of the Building* (London, 1741), 1–2.

wanted to have his infant son baptized and the dominie asked what he was to be named. The reply was, 'Hans.' The dominie said, 'In High German that would be Johannes.' 'No,' said the father, 'he shall be called Hans. I don't want to make a *gentleman* out of him. I'm raising him for the plow and the farm.' "[109]

That some males failed to take their places as proper heads of households is attested by the failures who went to jail, to the whipping post, or to the gallows, as well as by the church levies for poor relief, assessed annually after 1758 in at least part of the colony. That women sometimes did not fulfill the roles expected of them was also a matter of unhappy record. There was no divorce; and some women, unable or unwilling to continue unhappy marriages, deserted their husbands and families. The pages of the *Gazette* contain advertisements of numerous men informing the world that they would no longer stand responsible for the debts of departed spouses.

Rebecca, my wife, having absented herself from me, this is therefore to give notice to all persons not to trade or traffick with her on my account upon any pretence whatsoever, as I will pay no debts of her contracting.

Samuel Germany, *of St. Paul's parish*[110]

Marriages sometimes remained long broken, perhaps perpetually so. For example, Olive, the wife of Daniel Derizous (or Derizoux), a planter of St. Paul, left him about 1760 and had apparently not returned when he died some fifteen years later. Unless she had died in the meantime, the marriage was still intact even though the home was not. Marriage bonds could be strained but not loosed by adultery and persistent drunkenness, and women were liable to quick condemnation for offenses for which men were granted easy indulgence.[111]

Evidence of great unhappiness within some marriages and signs that some women had not found contentment either as matrons or as

109. Muhlenberg, *Journals*, II, 669.

110. Advertisement of Samuel Germany, *Ga. Gaz.*, July 13, 1774. Also see the *Ga. Gaz.* advertisements of Henry Frederick Myers, Nov. 7, 1765; John Young, July 13, 1768; and Johannes Waldron, June 7, 1775.

111. Will abstract of Daniel Derizous, *Will Abstracts*, 40. It was a matter of only passing comment that the motion made in the Commons House to send for Whitefield's corpse was made by the greatest rake in the assembly. Ezra Stiles, *Extracts from the Itineraries and Other Miscellanies of Ezra Stiles, D.D., LL.D., 1755–1794, with a Selection from His Correspondence*, ed. Franklin Bowditch Dexter (New Haven, Conn., 1916), 602.

mothers had no effect upon the ideal enunciated for them. The ideal neither weakened nor changed in colonial Georgia, which perhaps suggests that many women filled the part that society assigned to them. But some able and vigorous females clearly considered the ideal too restrictive. In practice a few of them amended it by entering commerce, and by no means were all of them women who took over enterprises started by their husbands. Proscriptions for feminine conduct did not explicitly forbid women to be factors in commerce, and there is not the smallest sign that businesswomen were regarded with anything other than respect. Thus, while the feminine ideal was rigid, it was only an ideal. Society tolerated departures from it, particularly if attended by success. Indeed, in important matters such as silk production, both the trustee and royal governments welcomed women's participation. And while some of their work would have been done at home, some of it would logically have been done at the filature. It was even calculated at one time that if five hundred women in Georgia could be put to work at the silk business, the product of their labor would be worth £28,125 sterling.[112] Thus, although the ideal of self-sacrificing domesticity for women was not retreated from, even the government was anxious to see it bow to important economic considerations.

The business activities of women in royal Georgia are easily traced through the columns of the *Georgia Gazette*. Mary Garrety, Mary Wells, and Elizabeth Bedon taught school; Mary Martin, Mary Hughes, and Jean Campbell operated millinery and mantua-making shops; Jane Stutz took in boarders; and Catherine Clark sewed gowns, children's habits, and mantuas.[113] Abigail Minis ran the tavern of her deceased spouse. Gertrude Bolzius, who had impressed Wesley in 1737 as a housewife, had by 1763 raised cattle and made enough money to invest in a gristmill and sawmill.[114]

Women occasionally intervened in politics even though they had no vote. In 1768, in an attempt to secure the reelection of Sir Patrick

112. Extract of the "Journal of Mr. Habersham Mercht: at Savannah, in Georgia..." (June 11, 1751), 5, Habersham Family Papers, Perkins Lib., Duke Univ., Durham, N.C.

113. Advertisements in *Ga. Gaz.* of: Mary Garrety, Aug. 2, 1775; Mary Wells, Apr. 13, 1774; Elizabeth Bedon, Aug. 2, 1769; Mary Martin, Jan. 12, 1774; Mary Hughes, Oct. 1, 1766; Jean Campbell, Aug. 27, 1766; Jane Stutz, Nov. 22, 1775; and Catherine Clark, May 18, 1774.

114. Will abstract of John Martin Bolzius, *Will Abstracts*, 14.

Houstoun the Younger to a seat in the Commons House of Assembly, two women of high rank, Mrs. Heriot Crooke and Mrs. James Mossman, got into a riding chair and canvassed for votes near Vernonburgh, where Sir Patrick was a candidate. They aroused resentment, not because they were women involved in a man's business but because they spoke unflatteringly of John Mullryne, another member of the Commons House. Sir Patrick lost the contest to Philip Box but was returned the following year for St. Andrew Parish.[115]

Even so, the ventures of women into commerce and their forays into public life were not in accord with what society expected. The family was the critical unit of society, and the roles of both men and women within it were firmly fixed.[116] True, there were families that were torn by disputes. But even the most tumultuous disagreement that can now be reconstructed showed family strength as well as weakness. Clement Martin, Sr., a member of the council for most of the royal period until his death in 1775, was locked in a long and rancorous wrangle with his son, Clement, Jr. The elder Martin alleged that his son had cheated him out of £6,000. The men attempted to settle their differences through arbitration conducted by four prominent Georgians—James Read, George Baillie, Joseph Clay, and Button Gwinnett.[117] The arbiters failed. The elder Martin finally died full of hatred for his son, bequeathing him his maledictions and six fowls from off a dunghill; the son, who died the same year as his father, departed life with much bitterness toward his father's family.[118] Martin's dislike for his son seems to have grown out of the quarrel over the money and not out of the irregular life that young Clement had led. The son, at least as early as 1755, was cohabiting with a woman named Elizabeth Jackson; five children survived the long and unsanctioned liaison.[119] By 1775 she seems to have died or departed. Clement, Jr., when dying, was convinced that only unity and harmony, which he had not had with his father's family, could save his brood of illegitimate children. "I most

115. *Ga. Gaz.*, May 11 and 18, 1768; *Col. Records of Ga.*, XIV, 590, X, 913.

116. Samuel Frink to the Rev. Dr. Burton, Jan. 7, 1768, S.P.G. Papers, Ser. C, Pkg. 7, Pt. iii (L.C. reel 16, 204–207).

117. Misc. Bonds Book R, 435–437.

118. Will of Clement Martin, Sr., Will Book AA, 212, Dept. of Archives and Hist., Atlanta, Ga.; will of Clement Martin, Jr., *ibid.*, 190–193.

119. Conveyance of Clement Martin to Elizabeth Jackson, July 7, 1755, Misc. Bonds Book R, 205.

earnestly recommend to them to live together in the strictest Union as I am convinced their own good and happiness depends almost totally on their keeping together and assisting each other."[120]

Although the province had early made provision for the care of orphans, its people believed firmly that, if possible, kinsmen ought to remain together in times of distress. In 1742 William Stephens wrote that "poor [James] Landrey of Highgate, who lost his Wife lately in this Common Sickness, was this day taken off himself also in the same, leaving 5 Children, who for their parents sakes, (that deserved so well by their Industry) have a Just Claim to what Assistance can well be, for their Encouragement to follow the Example given them; the Eldest Boy and Girl being about 18 or 19 years of Age, 'tis hoped will be aiding towards the three little ones, and with a little advice be enabled to live comfortably together."[121]

Bequests in colonial wills usually postulated the holding of families together even when the wife was not in charge of finances. Whether a widow exercised real control over an estate depended upon the will of her deceased spouse. Sir Patrick Houstoun the Elder, who died in 1762, believed that Lady Priscilla was strong enough to manage a household with several young children (the eldest male, Sir Patrick the Younger, was still a minor). John Barnard of Wilmington Island near Savannah also felt that his wife, Jane, could manage matters after his death. On the other hand, Thomas Peacock and James Andrew, both wealthy planters of St. John Parish, entrusted their wives to keep the family together but preferred that the management of their estates be left to guardians or executors.[122] They may have felt that the supervision of large plantations and numerous slaves was no proper occupation for a woman, but they clearly expected their widows to fill the essential role of keeping the families united. Both the Peacock and Andrew families were members of Midway Congregational Church, where familial spirit was strong and where families sat together at worship with "Children in the Lap."[123]

120. Will of Clement Martin, Jr., Will Book AA, 192.

121. Coulter, ed., *Journal of Stephens*, I, 122.

122. Will of Sir Patrick Houstoun, Bart., Will Book A, 83; will of John Barnard, *ibid.*, 26–27; will of Thomas Peacock, *ibid.*, 428–429; will of James Andrew, *ibid.*, 398–400.

123. James Stacy, *The Published Records of Midway Church*, I (n.p., 1951 [orig. publ., Newnan, Ga., 1894]), 16.

Georgia, then, was a province where the founders expected social distinctions to exist. A structure evolved based not upon old patterns of inherited position or rank but upon wealth, vocation, and, to a degree, merely upon the character of individual men, women, and families. Except for slaves, the class structure was not fixed. Individuals could rise or fall in status, and Georgia, like the other colonies, was rich in men who had arrived poor, bearing insignificant credentials, but who rose to the top levels of the social structure. There were more of these men in the early decades than in the later, for society was becoming more rigid as the Revolution approached—but not rigid enough to be a general cause for discontent.

The role of women was indicated by a declared ideal, but that role, too, was not absolutely fixed in Georgia any more than it was elsewhere in America. The frontier situation valued results. Women who succeeded in business were respected rather than discountenanced.

Families were the crucial unit of society, and both men and women were expected to assume recognized roles within the household—the man as husband, provider, and head of the house, and the woman as wife, mother, and housekeeper. It was assumed that a couple would prepare their children to assume proper and useful roles in society. Many families performed as society wished, and members of immediate families often assisted one another after the head of the house was gone.

The society that developed was, for whites, more open than the European societies from which they had come. It was made so by free land, by the absence of an ancient aristocracy, and by the spirit of self-reliance that evolved as Georgians opened their frontier. To a visitor in 1774, Georgians seemed rather independent in spirit, "more easily led than driven."[124] A closed society, or even a highly inflexible one, would not have answered their needs.

124. Muhlenberg, *Journals*, II, 636.

Chapter 6

Culture and Amusements

Colonial Georgia has often been thought of as a crude frontier, a primitive spot on a barely developed shore. Little cultural life has been envisioned there—few books, little music, little art. There are good reasons, of course, why such an attitude has persisted. For one thing, Georgia has suffered in comparison with its more cultured neighbor, South Carolina; the society of Savannah was never that of Charleston. For another, there are few physical remains, since books, prints, and paintings have largely disappeared. Only a fraction of colonial buildings now stand. And as buildings disappeared, so too did vital documents. Few purely personal diaries and letters—the kinds of papers that provide insights and lively anecdotes—are extant. Most of the documents that survive are governmental or quasi-governmental in nature.

Even so, the records tell an interesting tale. While we find all of the vigorous outdoor activities that passed for recreation and amusement on the American frontier, gentility and learning are discoverable too, along with the healthy curiosity of colonial Georgians. We must conclude that these people led rather full lives.

Any unusual event attracted a crowd.[1] The government itself sponsored a number of ceremonies to entertain the populace and, even more important, to instill in the people a sense of community. The ceremonies were linked to the throne, the royal family, the govern-

1. Muhlenberg, *Journals*, II, 613.

ment, and to great events in the history of the British people. Such occasions drew Georgians of every rank and station.

Events held in Savannah were often spectacular and were repeated in lesser measure in Frederica, Augusta, and other towns. In the time of the trustees, celebrations were less elaborate and less expensive than they later became. The colony was poorer then, and the Malcontents and other citizens were in no mood to rejoice. The officials, however, did their duty as they saw fit and arranged public rejoicings on the anniversaries of King George II's accession to the throne (June 15), his coronation (October 11), and his birth (October 30). Oglethorpe's birthday was celebrated on December 21. The festival days of the patrons of England and Scotland, Saints George and Andrew, were also times of jubilation.

The British flag was ceremonially raised on such occasions. Trustee officials assembled the people at the flagpole with the militia drawn up, hoisted the flag as cannon roared, and toasted the king, the royal family, the proprietors, and sometimes Oglethorpe. The militia drank standing in ranks. At Frederica in 1745, in ceremonies held for the king's birthday, the people gathered on the parade ground. At noon soldiers appeared under arms and "went through their Exercise with a great deal of Regularity." The people then moved to the fort for the discharging of guns, after which an elaborate dinner was served.[2]

Under the royal governors, when most people were wealthier and their spirits better, the ceremonies were more impressive. Formal processions were added. They were no haphazard, straggling things but were worthy of a dignified and self-confident government. The order of precedence was established by law and set forth in detail by a herald of the College of Arms. The herald, Joseph Edmonson Mowbray, decreed that provincial officials and their wives would march in order of rank, with the governor leading, followed by the lieutenant governor, the president of the council, members of the council, the Speaker of the Commons House, the chief justice, treasurer, associate judges, baronets, the attorney general, the judge of admiralty, the secretary of the province, and, finally, the members of the Commons House of Assembly.[3]

2. "William Logan's Journal," *PMHB*, XXXVI (1912), 168.

3. Stokes, *View of the Constitution of British Colonies*, 190. That this order of march was used in Georgia can scarcely be doubted. The order of precedence was preserved in the writings of Chief Justice Stokes, who walked in many such processions.

In 1764, to mark the twenty-sixth birthday of George III, Governor Wright ordered flags hoisted at Fort Halifax, at Fort George in the river on Cockspur Island, and on vessels in the road and harbor. At noon he appeared at the council chamber, where he was met by the council and others; they all then proceeded to Fort Halifax and there drank the king's health as guns thundered. Afterward "His Excellency gave an elegant entertainment at the Council-chamber to the Council, publick officers, and a great many other gentlemen. The evening concluded with illuminations, bonfires, and other publick rejoicings."[4]

Ceremonies like this one were well attended. In 1772 the crowd at the king's birthday exercises was not as large as it might have been, because the Commons House of Assembly had been locked in a dispute with the governor over whether he, as representative of the crown, could veto the lower house's choice of a Speaker. Still, the crowd was big enough to satisfy those who wished it to be large.[5] In Augusta the same year, crowds were not notably smaller. However, the military part of the celebrations seemed casually done to a visitor newly arrived from the Indian country.[6]

The most elaborate of the ceremonies was held but once. On February 10, 1761, a new king was proclaimed for the first and only time on Georgia soil. In Savannah military units stood in salute before the council chamber as guns fired. At length, the windows of the chamber were flung open, and the clerk proclaimed the accession of George III. Cannon fire split the air. The proclamation was then handed over to the provost marshal, and Wright led everyone to the marketplace and to Fort Halifax, where the ceremony was repeated. People in Sunbury, Frederica, and Augusta took part in the celebrations, for festivities were ordered in those towns as well as in Savannah.[7] The usual round of ceremonial occasions supplied entertainment for many Georgians.

In addition to festivities intended to instruct a populace in the spirit of patriotism, other observances were occasioned by lesser causes than nations and kings. The arrival of a royal governor was reason for rejoicing. To mark the coming of the first one, John Reynolds, in 1754, the lower classes in Savannah set fire to the guardhouse and very

4. *Ga. Gaz.*, June 7, 1764.

5. Ga. Hist. Soc., *Colls.*, VI, 183.

6. David Taitt, "Journal of David Taitt," in Newton D. Mereness, ed., *Travels in the American Colonies* (New York, 1916), 563.

7. *Col. Records of Ga.*, VIII, 490–494, XXVIII, Pt. i b, 497–498.

nearly burned the old council chamber as well.[8] These outpourings were eclipsed when the unknown Henry Ellis arrived some three years later to succeed Reynolds, who by then was too well known in a negative sense. Nine-tenths of the people of Savannah hailed the new lieutenant governor.[9]

In lesser rituals, other branches of government held semipublic observances. The Commons House of Assembly, after formally opening its sessions, gathered in the Anglican church in Savannah to hear a sermon from the rector. The courts of the province commenced with religious ceremonies involving processions through the town.[10]

Weddings and funerals brought Georgians together in happy and solemn times. In 1744 the Reverend Thomas Bosomworth, who was to prove one of the worst Anglican rectors the colony ever had, was married to Mary Musgrove-Matthews, an Indian woman of mixed blood who had great claims against the colony. In short order, they were to create an ugly tumult, but at the time of their wedding, that unhappy development could not be foreseen. The wedding feast was celebrated in almost general fashion, few being uninvited. President Stephens offered his house for the occasion, and workmen built three long tables from which to serve a cold repast "of all such kind of provisions as this place could afford, boyled, Roasted and Baked, brought ready dressed." The party began about seven in the evening, and wine and drink were plentiful. "Dancing likewise was one Ingredient in Merry Making, for which a Fiddle was prepared; and they that were disposed to such Exercise, found themselves partners, 8 or 10 Couple at a time. In short nothing happen'd in the whole Company (large as it was) that gave any offence, every body taking their own time to go home when they pleased; but the Dancers kept the latest hours, as tis rarely seen otherwise."[11]

Funerals were often held in early evening. The warm climate dictated that bodies be quickly buried, and in the dusk friends and neighbors gathered as bells tolled. Funeral processions wound their way through the streets to the cemetery. If the deceased had been of military rank, muskets were fired; if he had been a member of an organi-

---

8. *S.-C. Gaz.*, Nov. 7, 1754.

9. *Ibid.*, Apr. 28, 1757.

10. *Ga. Gaz.*, July 8, 1767; Phillipps Collection, 14203, Pt. i, 51–52, Univ. of Ga. Lib., Athens.

11. Coulter, ed., *Journal of Stephens*, II, 137.

zation, its membership might come to the service. Sermons were delivered either in the church or at the graveside, and some ministers, like the Reverend George Whitefield, conducted services at each place.[12]

The lamentations following Whitefield's own death illustrate what colonial Georgians saw in funerals. Whitefield had died while on a preaching journey in New England, and his body was buried at Newburyport, Massachusetts. Georgians who had loved him, assisted self-consciously by some who had not, arranged for a public mourning service in Savannah. One member of the assembly even tried to send for the corpse. An admirer described the exercises in Christ Church: "All the black cloth in the stores was bought up; the pulpit and desks of the church, the branches, the organ loft, the pews of the governor and council were covered with black. The governor and council in deep mourning convened at the state-house, and went in procession to church, and were received by the organ playing a funeral dirge. Two funeral sermons were preached, one by Mr. Ellington . . . ; the other was preached by Mr. Zubly. All the respect showed to his memory at his death, kept my sensibility alive."[13]

Sensibilities of Georgians were served in varying ways by a plethora of organizations. It has been said that residents of neighboring Charleston formed more private societies than people anywhere else in America; clubs could exist there for virtually any reason, and some South Carolinians belonged to several. In other colonies, especially in the South, organizations also flourished. In Georgia they met a variety of needs. They sought the special interests of their members or served the public good, or both. The Union Society, when established in 1750, consisted mostly of craftsmen concerned with their interests as a class. The society took St. George, patron saint of England, as its protector and held its annual gatherings each St. George's Day in April. Its quarterly meetings were usually at public taverns. Tradition

---

12. *George Whitefield's Journals (1737–1741) to Which Is Prefixed His "Short Account" (1746) and "Further Account" (1747)*, facsimile reproduction of William Wale's edition (1905), with an introduction by William V. Davis (Gainesville, Fla., 1969), 397, hereafter cited as *Whitefield's Journals, 1737–1741*.

13. "Memoirs of Cornelius Winter," *Works of Jay*, III, 31. See the Rev. Edward Ellington's sermon, *The Reproach of Christ, the Christian's Treasure. A Sermon Occasioned by the Death of the Rev. George Whitefield . . . Preached At Christ Church, Savannah, . . . On Sunday, November 11, 1770* (London, 1771).

says that the society was started by five men, three of whom were Benjamin Sheftall, Richard Milledge, and Peter Tondee. Milledge and Tondee were carpenters at that time and Sheftall a small merchant. Tondee later ran a famous tavern, at which the society sometimes met. Yet the Union Society did not remain an organization of mechanics, for after a time, men who were not artisans joined it and shared its leadership—such men as Dr. Henry Lewis Bourquin, William Gibbons, William Young, Jonathan Bryan, and Dr. Noble Wimberly Jones, in addition to men like William Ewen, who had once been a potter but who no longer followed a mechanic's trade.

Still, men of more genteel professions never crowded out the mechanics. The officers elected on St. George's Day, 1769, were of mixed vocations. The senior steward was William Young, lawyer. Other officers were Joseph Parker, silversmith; Samuel Farley, lawyer; James Anderson, carpenter or cabinetmaker; and Benjamin Goldwire, who had grown up in a carpenter's household and had inherited some of his father's tools.[14] After a few years, the society was supporting a charitable endeavor, offering schooling for ten children a year. Its officers evidently managed its funds well, for in 1774 it had money to lend.[15] As pre-Revolutionary tensions sharpened, the Union Society became active in politics and rallied behind Jonathan Bryan, a member, when Bryan angered Governor Wright in 1769 by presiding over a meeting to discuss nonimportation of British goods. For this act Bryan was expelled from the council. The society responded by presenting him with a handsome piece of plate, hailing him as "a real Friend to his Country in general, and the Province of Georgia in particular."[16]

After 1750 festival celebrations on St. George's Day were sponsored every April by the Union Society. But observed with equal fervor each November was the Scottish St. Andrew's Day. Perhaps the model for St. Andrew's clubs everywhere in the colonies was the one established in 1729 in Charleston. Only a few years later in trustee Georgia, a club was set up in Savannah, organized by the Malcontents, who were almost all Scotsmen. For diplomatic reasons, William Stephens reluc-

14. *Ga. Gaz.*, Apr. 26, 1769.
15. Advertisements on behalf of the Union Society, *ibid.*, Nov. 16, 1768, Aug. 16, 1769, and May 25, 1774.
16. *Ibid.*, Sept. 20, 1769; advertisement of the Union Society, *ibid.*, Mar. 14, 1770. That Bryan was a stubborn man is attested by Urlsperger, ed., *Ausführliche Nachrichten*, II, 2083–2084, and by "Memoirs of Cornelius Winter," *Works of Jay*, III, 30.

tantly joined them in observing St. Andrew's Day and even lent support to their celebrations, but he disliked the proceedings as long as the Malcontents remained in Georgia.[17] At Frederica the observance of St. Andrew's Day was a considerable event. In trustee times it was customary to ask all gentlemen of the town to a dinner and "to make all they can drunk." To avoid intoxication, one visitor in 1745 hid on a vessel in the harbor and thus escaped the notice of more riotous celebrants. But on the following day the festivities were renewed, and the visitor was "very much disturbed" when a group of drunks tried to break in his door to get him to join them.[18]

In Savannah a new St. Andrew's Club was founded in 1764 at Machenry's Tavern. The former organization founded by the Malcontents had lapsed in the 1740s; so it is almost certain that the new one had no connection with it. The new undertaking was a charitable group for the relief of the poor and doubled as a dining society; it opened its membership not only to Scotsmen but "to every gentleman, of what nation or profession soever." On November 30, 1764, the day "The St. Andrew's Club at Savannah in Georgia" was inaugurated, its thirty-odd members offered entertainment for the gentlemen of both the upper and lower houses of assembly and others.[19]

The club was not totally welcome in Georgia even in the 1760s, for that decade was marked everywhere by quiet but deep suspicions between Britons of English and Scottish descent. The earl of Bute, a Scotsman, held high office in Great Britain, and it seemed to many that Scots were securing office and preference everywhere. Inevitably, a reaction took place among other persons who wished office or preferment for themselves or their friends. In Georgia it was feared that the St. Andrew's Club might become an instrument of exclusiveness and factionalism.[20] Criticism was gradually quieted, however, and gentlemen of varied backgrounds were received into membership, one of the most faithful and convivial of whom was James Habersham, a Yorkshireman. "Tomorrow I am to dine with a merry Saint, St An-

17. *Col. Records of Ga.,* V, 398, 413, IV, 40, 235–236.
18. "William Logan's Journal," *PMHB,* XXXVI (1912), 176.
19. *Ga. Gaz.,* Dec. 6, 1764; unsigned advertisement, *ibid.,* Nov. 22, 1764. The first officers of the St. Andrew's Club were: Patrick Mackay, president; William Simpson, vice-president; Dr. Andrew Johnston, treasurer; Henry Preston, clerk; and Simon Munro, assistant.
20. Letter of "A.B.C.," *ibid.,* Dec. 13, 1764; letters of "Scoto-Britannico-Americanus," and "X.Y.Z.," *ibid.,* Dec. 20, 1764.

drew, I am a member of the Society, and as I am told our Friend John Graham will preside there, I am of Opinion, he will send many of the Saints Votaries away with Sare Heads. I do not mean that our Friend John likes Sare Heads, because I know him to be one of the most temperate and at the same time one of the best Hearted Men in this Province, but for the Honor of his Saint and Country, I think he will on this Occasion particularly exert himself."[21] The club patronized the best taverns. In addition to Machenry's establishment, it also met at Mrs. Goffe's, Creighton's, and at Lyon's, and gathered at the courthouse in 1769 and in 1774, when it entertained the governor.[22]

The Freemasons in Georgia go back almost to the founding of the colony, certainly back to 1734, and they promoted a spirit of fraternity and mutual assistance. At the beginning they were not altogether popular and were accused of clannishly joining together not only for mutual support but for unseemly and drunken antics. Stories were told in Savannah of loud revels, and men gossiped of Masons reeling homeward at two o'clock in the morning.[23] Even so (or perhaps for that reason), membership was coveted.[24] The order eventually included many prominent Georgians. Sermons for the Freemasons became a tradition. In 1737 the lodge in Savannah heard a sermon from the Reverend John Wesley, who was afterwards thanked for his efforts at a dinner.[25] In 1739 the Reverend William Norris preached to them at the church, from whence a procession of Masons marched to dinner at a tavern—a procession led by men bearing wands and wearing red ribbons on their breasts, followed by a group in white gloves and aprons.[26]

Upon Lieutenant Governor Ellis's arrival in 1757, the Freemasons, led by their youngest brother, marched to his house to present an address. In the entourage were Habersham, Noble Jones, Sir Patrick Houstoun the Elder, John Graham, Noble Wimberly Jones, Thomas Vincent, and Charles Watson, all influential enough to help Ellis in many significant ways. The address delivered to Ellis avoided topics

---

21. Ga. Hist. Soc., Colls., VI, 154–155.

22. Ga. Gaz., Dec. 6, 1769, and Dec. 7, 1774.

23. Col. Records of Ga., V, 179, XX, 481.

24. For example, Francis Percy, son-in-law of Sir Francis Bathurst. Ibid., XX, 238.

25. "Journal of Thomas Causton, Esq. 1st Bailif of Savannah," Phillipps Collection, 14203, Pt. i, 41.

26. Col. Records of Ga., IV, 361.

of religion and politics but professed interest in the welfare of the province and pledged cooperation in securing it.[27] The Freemasons kept a schedule of meetings throughout colonial times, almost always at taverns or public houses, and they invited all brothers in the province to join in their regular processions to the church and to enjoy the feasts afterward.

Among other provincial organizations was the Georgia Society, founded to reward persons who might make helpful discoveries affecting silk and indigo. The organization also promoted trade, relieved misfortune, and encouraged education. In 1759 it sought a schoolmaster to teach school in Savannah for three years at a salary of £45 a year.[28] Still another was the Society of St. Patrick, which formally existed in Georgia before 1773.[29] (St. Patrick's Day—March 17—had been observed much earlier.) The Thunderbolt Club was probably made up of persons who lived in or near the village of Thunderbolt, five miles from Savannah.[30] Two other organizations must remain largely subjects of conjecture. Members of the Ugly Club dined in "harmony and festivity" in Savannah in the years before the Revolution, but if they had any purpose other than easy fellowship, no record has preserved it.[31] Similarly, the Amicable Club, sometimes called the Amicable Society, had purposes not known, although its members asserted themselves in behalf of "American rights" in the decade before 1775.[32] Clubs with odd names were a fixture in all the southern colonies. In Charleston a citizen might join the Meddlers, the Laughing Club, the Fancy Society, or the Beef-Steak Club, among others probably not too different in tone and character from Georgia's Ugly Club or Amicable Society. Hospitality apparently abounded in these clubs (up to a point) as well as in society at large. In Frederica the garrison

27. Address of the Freemasons at Savannah to Henry Ellis, *S.-C. Gaz.*, Apr. 28, 1757; Papers of the Savannah Masonic Lodge, 1756–1757 (photocopies), Force MSS, Georgia Miscellany, Library of Congress. A list of members in 1756 is included in the papers. Solomon's Lodge Number 1 in Savannah is the descendant of the original Masonic lodge in Georgia.

28. *S.-C. Gaz.*, Apr. 28, 1758, Apr. 21, 1759, and Oct. 25–Nov. 1, 1760.

29. *S.-C. Gaz.; And Country Jour.*, Apr. 6, 1773.

30. Letter concerning the Thunderbolt Club, *Ga. Gaz.*, Aug. 6, 1766; advertisement of the Thunderbolt Club, *ibid.*, Aug. 3, 1768.

31. Advertisements and notices of the Ugly Club, *ibid.*, Feb. 22, 1769, Sept. 20, 1769, and Jan. 5, 1774.

32. Advertisement of the Amicable Club, *ibid.*, Sept. 21, 1768; notice of the Amicable Society, *ibid.*, Sept. 6, 1769.

officers had a fellowship, usually open to guests, which they called "club night." They visited the homes or quarters of members in rotation for conversation, food, and drink.[33]

Clubs were not within everyone's reach and were only one vehicle to fellowship and relaxation. People made parties out of short journeys; in 1773, when committees of the upper and lower house went downriver to inspect Tybee Light, they took along food and liquor from the taverns of Minis and Tondee.[34] Any curiosity drew an audience. For eight days in the summer of 1765, numbers of Savannah people converged upon the plantation of Noble Jones, where the attraction was an agave plant in luxuriant blossom, bearing thirty-three branches.[35]

The out-of-doors was attractive to colonial Georgians, as to all the American colonists. The festival days and seasons of the Anglican church—Christmas, Easter, Whitsunday—were popular times for cricket, quoits, and football. Pleasure was taken in simple things such as walking, riding, swimming, exploring, hunting, and fishing. In the 1770s at the plantation of Benjamin Andrew near Midway, a late-afternoon fishing party casting from the banks of a creek amid a grove of magnolias, myrtles, and sweet bay trees, caught fish the size of a man's hand.[36]

Horse racing was popular but never to the degree that it was in South Carolina. There a prominent Charleston merchant once complained that ships' captains could not get their vessels loaded because the races were such an irresistible diversion. Never did the *Georgia Gazette* publish odds on the races as did the *South-Carolina Gazette*. Indeed, the first races in Georgia were rather shabby things. In 1740 the Malcontents organized them between the gate of Savannah's public garden and the middle of Johnson Square, a distance of a little more than a quarter of a mile. The animals pressed into the race were not fine horses but ordinary ponies and work animals. Stephens, unsympathetic toward the sponsors of the events, was not pleased with anything about the races, yet conceded that they attracted numerous spectators.[37]

Horse racing was occasionally pursued for money and pleasure in

33. "William Logan's Journal," *PMHB*, XXXVI (1912), 171, 172, 174, 175, 176.

34. *Col. Records of Ga.*, XIX, Pt. i, 487–488.

35. *Ga. Gaz.*, July 11, 1765.

36. William Bartram, *Travels*, 11–12.

37. *Col. Records of Ga.*, IV, 604–606.

royal Georgia. In 1763 at Sunbury, races were run for two days for several purses, and in the evenings, social assemblies were held in the long room of Williams's Tavern there. Cudgel playing was organized as a supplementary diversion.[38] Horses also ran on courses near Savannah, and in 1760 Noble Jones gave his son, then absent on military duty, an account of such a contest: "Yesterday the great Horse race between Mr. John Maxwell and Mr. John Fitch was run, when the former's horse beat. Mr. Sabb had the misfortune of having his leg broke."[39]

Lotteries, a form of entertainment intermixed with speculation, were popular in many of the American colonies as well as in Great Britain, but they never amounted to much in Georgia. In 1763 what Governor Wright called a "very trifling private Lottery" was begun and seems to have been the only one of consequence ever conducted.[40] The assembly immediately acted and declared lotteries illegal.[41] Had Georgia been an older colony, lotteries might have been more important, for they had enjoyed the approval of the British government in earlier times. The Virginia Company, for example, was authorized by the king in 1612 to conduct lotteries to help support that colony. However, by the middle of the eighteenth century, the attitude of the British government had begun to change. In 1769 Georgia and the other royal colonies received instructions from London to disallow all lotteries unless approved by the king. The order had little effect in Georgia, because locally conducted ones were already illegal. However, a few tickets were sold in Georgia for drawings held in other places.

Gambling was much more prevalent and was denounced as a destructive force. In all of the American colonies, it was discountenanced as a lamentable practice, and there are plentiful accounts of men ruined by it. Although illegal in Georgia, gambling could not be suppressed. Indeed, some men seemed to mock the law, not troubling to

38. *Ga. Gaz.*, Oct. 13 and Dec. 8, 1763.
39. Noble Jones to Noble Wimberly Jones, Aug. 20, 1760, Noble Wimberly Jones Papers, Ga. Hist. Soc., Savannah.
40. *Col. Records of Ga.*, XXXVII, 417.
41. *Ibid.*, XVIII, 608–619. The 1763 lottery did not go well. See *Ga. Gaz.*, May 26, June 2 and 30, Oct. 13, and Dec. 1 and 8, 1763. Late in the royal period, a Charleston merchant sent a few tickets to friends in Georgia for sale in behalf of a northern charity. The Rev. J. J. Zubly declined to handle the tickets, but Joseph Clay, the merchant, sold a few.

conceal their violation of it. In 1744 John Dawson, with apparent impunity, took a newspaper advertisement to declare that, while drunk, he had been cheated at gambling and had given a note to cover his losses. He warned all persons against taking the note, for he was determined not to pay it.[42] Three years later the Revolutionary government that controlled Georgia at the time said that gambling was still a prevalent evil and attempted to suppress it.[43]

Some Georgians, perhaps relatively few, liked games that were not necessarily games of chance—skittle alley, shuffleboard, billiards, backgammon, and cards. At Machenry's Tavern the proprietor kept a backgammon table and had six packs of cards.[44] He would have been unwise to permit his guests to gamble, for detection would have made him liable to fine. The *Georgia Gazette* advertised playing cards, backgammon boards, and billiard tables for sale.[45] Yet a sampling of estate inventories does not suggest that many homes had games. Of the 329 surviving inventories that are applicable, only 14 record games.[46] In parts of the province, such amusements were utterly disapproved of; in the German settlements, for example, the Lutheran pastors, who did not regard moderate drinking as a sin, considered card playing a moral offense.[47]

But organized religion had nothing against pastimes like reading. The ever observant DeBrahm, in Georgia regularly after 1751, said reading and conversation were common diversions, that libraries flourished, and that bookstores had the newest editions and sold them promptly. "There is scarcely a House in the Cities, Towns or Plantations, but what have some Choice Authors, if not Libraries of religious,

42. Advertisement of John Dawson, *Ga. Gaz.*, July 20, 1774.

43. *Col. Records of Ga.*, XIX, Pt. ii, 51–52.

44. Estate of James Machenry, June 4, 1768, Inventory Book F, 340, Dept. of Archives and Hist., Atlanta, Ga.

45. Advertisement for the sale of a billiard table, *Ga. Gaz.*, May 16, 1765; advertisement of Samuel Douglass and Company, *ibid.*, May 11, 1774; advertisement of Gershon Cohen, *ibid.*, Sept. 14, 1774; advertisement of George Houstoun and Company, *ibid.*, Nov. 16, 1774.

46. The 329 inventories from which this information is derived are found in Inventory Books F, FF, and GG. The inventories disclose no evidence of games in homes between 1754 and 1759. Between 1760 and 1765 only 4 estates show games, and between 1766 and 1771, 8 show games. Between 1776 and 1778 there were only 2 listed. Several inventories contained in the books did not apply for purposes of this tabulation.

47. Muhlenberg, *Journals*, II, 636–637.

philosophical and political Writers." Even people who had no special education often read "good Authors." DeBrahm was surprised "at the good and sound Judgments and Argumentations of Men, whom He knew had been brought up entirely to Mechanism without any more Education than reading and writing."[48] He probably did not overstate the amount and kinds of reading done in royal Georgia, but he could scarcely have made the same observation about proprietary times.

The colony had been founded in part for purposes that were idealistic, and the bulk of reading matter in Georgia between 1733 and 1752 was religious, even narrowly religious, in nature. Many boxes of books, donated by private persons and organizations in England and selected for their uplifting qualities, were sent to Georgia. One shipment, dispatched in 1735 aboard the *Simond* and designated for Frederica, tells a great deal about all such benefactions. It included 722 volumes, but there were only nine different types of books: the Bible and New Testament (46 copies), the Book of Common Prayer (51), the Bishop of Man's volume on the Lord's Supper (25), the *Christian Monitor and Companion to the Altar* (50), the *Christian Monitor and Answer to Excuses* (50), hornbooks (100), primers (100), ABC books with the church catechism (100), and the *Friendly Admonition to the Drinkers of Brandy* (200).[49]

Books of religious instruction and schoolbooks were sent by the thousands. Some were used in schools, others were put in libraries controlled by parsons, and many were given to settlers. In 1755 Joseph Ottolenghe seems to have given a New Testament to Noble Jones. The book was small enough to fit in the palm of the hand, and it slipped easily into a man's coat pocket. Printed in Oxford in 1753 and inscribed by Ottolenghe in 1755, it bears Jones's bookplate and autograph, and on two blank pages in the back, a prayer is written in his hand.[50] This inexpensive little volume was typical of thousands sent to Georgia in its first decades.

The house of the Anglican rector in Savannah had enough bookshelves to hold a sizable library, and a large one had been accumulated there by the end of the trustee era. The Associates of Dr. Bray sent a

48. DeBrahm, *History of Ga.*, 24.
49. *Col. Records of Ga.*, III, 124–125.
50. New Testament of Noble Jones, preserved in the DeRenne MSS Coll., Univ. of Ga. Lib., Athens.

complete library in 1736, and thirteen years later, the library of Dr. Crow, late rector of St. Bartolph's, Bishopsgate, London, was dispatched from England. Most of Dr. Crow's collection, which contained works in English, Latin, and Greek, probably found its way into the public library run by the parson in Savannah.[51] In 1757 the Commons House of Assembly took notice of the parson's books and declared that fifty-six folio pages were required to catalog them.[52]

The parson's library in Savannah was not the only library in proprietary Georgia. At one time there was one of a sort at Frederica, and the Salzburgers at Ebenezer also had an important collection.[53] A library for Augusta was created in 1751 when the trustees sent 166 volumes aboard the *Charming Nancy*. The books had been given by several benefactors in 1732 and doubtless had been in storage for almost twenty years. In view of the proprietors' purposes, the Augusta catalog was what one would have expected. It listed:

Book of Common Prayer, 22 copies
Holy Bible, 7 copies
Companion for the Sick, 12 copies
Whole Duty of Man, 13 copies
Faith and Practice of a Church of England Man, 12 copies
Help and Guide to Christian Families, 20 copies
Showing How To Walk With God, 50 copies
The Great Importance of a Religious Life Considered, 6 copies
The Young Christian Instructed, 12 copies
Spelling books, 12 copies[54]

DeBrahm said that by the early 1760s, there were five good libraries in the colony with books in thirteen languages—three libraries in Sa-

---

51. *Col. Records of Ga.*, IV supp., 65, XXXI, 325, XXXIII, 412–413; Wesley, *Journal*, ed. Curnock, I, 321–322; Urlsperger, ed., *Ausführliche Nachrichten*, III, 580.

52. *Col. Records of Ga.*, XIII, 142–143. It would be hazardous to estimate the number of volumes in the parson's library using only the 56 folio pages required for its cataloging. However, the library at Whitefield's Bethesda contained some 1,200 volumes and took a bit more than 23 pages to catalog. For evidence that the parochial library in Savannah was still intact shortly before the Revolution, see letter of William Ewen, *Ga. Gaz.*, Dec. 21, 1774.

53. *Col. Records of Ga.*, IV supp., 159–160.

54. *Ibid.*, III, 359–360. The trustees also ordered Plato's works in Greek and Latin and his *Republic* in French. *Ibid.*, II, 139.

vannah, one at Ebenezer, and one that he curiously described as being 96¾ miles from the sea on the Savannah River.[55] The last had to be at Augusta.[56]

The library at Ebenezer had been formally organized by 1738. Its shelves were filled with religious works, the Bible being the most popular volume there, followed by Johann Arndt's *True Christianity*, a famous devotional work of German theology.[57] The Salzburgers had had numerous books in their settlement before the formal organization of their library, and after its establishment, it not only supplied the Ebenezer Germans but sent books on loan to nearby communities and plantations, to Savannah, and even to the Congarees and other places in South Carolina. The Ebenezer collection was principally in German but had some works in Latin and English.[58] The language, religion, and culture of the Salzburgers set them apart in Georgia, and they wished that their library contained more books explaining the differences between the religious sects, works to help them keep their bearings in a strange land.[59] Titles of 104 of their books, identifiable today, establish the religious orientation of the collection. There are, for example, four titles by Arndt, fifteen by August Hermann Francke, one by

55. DeBrahm, *History of Ga.*, 24. We cannot satisfactorily identify the 3 libraries that DeBrahm said existed in Savannah. Certainly the public library in care of the parson was one, but what were the other two? Did Whitefield's library at Bethesda count, even though it was 12 miles from Savannah? Was DeBrahm referring to the private libraries of Thomas Burrington or Zubly, to which many friends of these men would have had access? Did he mean the holdings of the Georgia Library Society? Any one of these would have been considered a good library.

56. Berry Fleming, comp., *199 Years of Augusta's Library: A Chronology* (Athens, Ga., 1949), offers a solution to the mystery of the 96¾ miles. On pp. viii–ix he says: "Reading these words in Savannah, with the speedometer on my car registering Augusta at some hundred and twenty miles away, I had to discard my immediate guess that he [DeBrahm] was talking about Augusta . . . ; the distance to Augusta by river was considerably more. . . . Remembering an old map of Georgia I had seen, printed in 1807, I wondered if DeBrahm could have fixed upon his 96¾ miles through some early cartographical distortion. . . . On a chance, I measured the 1807 air-line from 'the Sea' to Augusta. It was 2⅝ inches. The map scale was 60 miles to 1⅝ inches. This, as you see for yourself, puts the distance to Augusta at 96.92 miles. Which, considering the discrepancy of .17 mile may have been easily due to taking our sights on different tides, seemed close enough."

57. Winde, "Frühgeschichte der Luth. Kirche in Ga.," 143–144.

58. Jones *et al.*, trans. and eds., *Detailed Reports on Salzburger Emigrants*, I, 12–13; Winde, "Frühgeschichte der Luth. Kirche in Ga.," 144, 145.

59. Urlsperger, ed., *Ausführliche Nachrichten*, III, 580.

Samuel Urlsperger, and several by other Lutheran writers.[60] By the
end of the Revolution, nothing was left of the collection; it had been
destroyed by fire, that nemesis of many colonial libraries.

The collection that Whitefield assembled at Bethesda also disappeared in a conflagration, but before its destruction in 1773, it was one
of the best in Georgia. In the 1760s Whitefield took a step long envisioned and attempted to convert his Bethesda orphanage into a college. (It actually did become an academy.) In preparation for the
college, he enriched the library already present. Before the collection
burned a few years later, it had 1,200 volumes.[61] It is likely that many
of the works were donated. But books of which Whitefield disapproved
did not find a place on the shelves; of more than 45 works he was
known to dislike, not one made its way into the Bethesda library.[62] Of
the 1,200 volumes, approximately 900 were of a religious nature. They
included almost every sort of religious work available in the 1760s
and 1770s—dictionaries, encyclopedias, lexicons, commentaries, study
guides, concordances, expositions, biblical translations, sermons, and
theological and philosophical works. Twenty-nine volumes had to do
with church and biblical history, and almost every religious denomination was represented. There were 25 volumes by the Wesleys and
26 by Whitefield. The remaining 25 percent of the library—more than
300 books—consisted of the following:

I. Dictionaries, encyclopedias, etc.		45
II. History and biography		108 [103]
a. British history, 55		
b. American history, 10		
c. Natural history, 8		
d. Ancient and general history, 30		
III. Geography and travels		10
IV. Literature, poetry, and mythology		75
V. Music (mostly hymns)		23
VI. Education (theoretical and practical)		3
VII. Science		19

60. Winde, "Frühgeschichte der Luth. Kirche in Ga.," "Appendix II," 216–
225.

61. Catalogue of the Bethesda library, Jan. 1, 1771, Inventory Book F, 505–
529.

62. Robert V. Williams, "George Whitefield's Bethesda: The Orphanage, the
College and the Library," Florida State University Library History Seminar No. 3,
Proceedings (Tallahassee, Fla., 1968), 65–66.

Bethesda's collection of 1,200 volumes in 1771 seems respectable enough when compared with Harvard's 5,000 (in 1764), William and Mary's 3,000 (1776), Yale's 4,000 (1766), Princeton's 1,281 (1760), King's (Columbia) 2,000 (about 1760), Pennsylvania's 1,670 (1832), Brown's 250 (1772), and Dartmouth's 355 (1775). The books at Bethesda were also somewhat balanced in subject matter, although not quite so well balanced, for example, as a famous gift of perhaps 1,000 volumes that the eminent Bishop Berkeley gave to Yale in 1733.[64]

The culture and the learning that Georgians received from books, however, did not depend upon the Bethesda library. The public apparently had no access to it, although without doubt some friends of the institution did. More important were the books in public libraries and in homes. DeBrahm was correct when he said that books were common. A few were possibly decorations, others were inherited rather than chosen, and some may even have been investments, because of their value. An impressive percentage of Georgia homes in the royal period contained books or other reading matter. Of 328 applicable inventories surviving from the royal era, 188 indicate ownership of reading materials.[65] We may conclude that while Georgians were not bookish, many of them read.

63. *Ibid.*, 61–63. These figures are approximate.
64. *Ibid.*, 63, 64.
65. The statistics break down as follows:

Years	Inventories listing reading materials	Inventories listing no reading materials
1754–1759	21	18
1760–1765	44	36
1766–1771	91	56
1776–1777	32	30

The study is based upon Inventory Books F, FF, and GG (23 inventories with no applicability to this tabulation have been discounted). These figures, while impressive, should be interpreted cautiously. They do not mean that slightly more than 57% of Georgia's homes had reading materials in royal times, because the inventories do not present a perfect sample. The persons whose estates were in-

Quite as important as the distribution of books are the kinds and the quantity an average household had. This information generally cannot be garnered from the inventories, however, for the officials who made them usually recorded only that a deceased person had owned a "parcel" of books without specifying how many or what they were. For example, Michael Burkholder, the model farmer referred to in chapter 4, owned a parcel of German books valued at 20s. James Fraser, an influential and respected citizen who lived in or near Augusta, died in 1755 and left a bookcase and books valued at £60.[66] The latter private library must have been impressive, the former hardly so at all.

The device of listing parcels rather than titles, though customary, was not universal. Some inventories recorded titles, permitting our examination of a number of small collections as well as some large ones. John Robinson, a mariner, owned five volumes—Dryden's *Poems*; John Cleland's *Fanny Hill; or, The Memoirs of a Woman of Pleasure*; Sir John Narbrough's "Journal," printed in *An Account of several late Voyages and Discoveries to the South and North*; *Letters from the Dead to the Living* by Elizabeth Rowe; and the *Practising Attorney*. The latter suggests that Robinson, like many other Georgians, was his own legal consultant. Mary Wannell, apparently a Savannah housewife, had two small Bibles and a psalmbook, altogether valued at two shillings. Many small collections were like hers, consisting mostly of a few basic religious works. William Clothier, only recently arrived from St. Kitts at the time of his death in 1769, owned seven volumes of *The Spy of Paris*, five books on travel and architecture, and three other volumes.[67]

Thomas Burrington, who was clerk and sometimes a member of

ventoried were mostly male and were individuals of above-average means to a large extent. Although inventories were required, many estates were doubtless overlooked. It is reasonable to assume that estates not inventoried more often than not belonged to poor persons or to those located some distance from Savannah; in short, persons who would have been less likely to own reading materials. These considerations, however, do not disturb the conclusion that books were more commonly held than might have been supposed. It is also true that the estates of many poor people contained reading materials and that the estates of many individuals of above-average means did not.

66. Estate of Michael Burkholder, Apr. 15, 1762, Inventory Book F, 107; estate of James Fraser, Feb. 25, 1755, *ibid.*, 5.

67. Estate of John Robinson, Dec. 18, 1758, *ibid.*, 71; estate of Mary Wannell, Jan. 12, 1757, *ibid.*, 42; estate of William Clothier, Mar. 1, 1769, *ibid.*, 385.

the Commons House of Assembly, possessed a private library of approximately 425 volumes in four languages. His might have been one of the three Savannah libraries referred to by DeBrahm. Men often lent their books to friends, and Burrington, as a public man, probably did so. Most of his volumes were in English, several were in French, and some were in Latin and German. Not surprisingly, approximately 200 had to do with law. The remainder, about 225 volumes, concerned religion, history, travel, and belles lettres, and included works by Horace, Seneca, Cato, Ovid, Shakespeare, Milton, Pope, Smollett, and Swift. Burrington owned dictionaries, the *Spectator*, the *Tatler*, *Tom Jones*, and *Tristram Shandy*.[68]

The library of the Reverend John J. Zubly struck a learned visitor as a "fine collection of old and new books, the like of which I have seldom seen in America." The guest noted that "the external appearance of his library and study is hardly inferior to that of the most famous in Europe. The books all stand up straight according to the *principium indiscernibile* like trees that cast their fruit and leaves in autumn and cover the ground with them, for here, too, one found innumerable printed leaves, whole and half tracts, manuscripts, etc., on the floor." The room was like the libraries of other scholarly men "whose studies are said to have presented the same appearance because they would never permit the scrupulous housewives to do any cleaning in them lest they cause disorder."[69]

Button Gwinnett, one of three Georgians to sign the Declaration of Independence, had 21 volumes on several subjects—law, husbandry and agriculture, religion, grammar and spelling, and belles lettres. Councillor Grey Elliott owned about 200 books in several languages. The Reverend C. F. Triebner, one of the Lutheran pastors at Ebenezer, possessed more than 600. At his death in 1768, Chief Justice Simpson left more than 220 books, of which 55 to 60 percent were on the law. Newdigate Stephens, favorite son of President Stephens, had some 60 volumes, of which about 45 percent dealt with religion.[70]

68. Estate of Thomas Burrington, July 30, 1767, *ibid.*, 282–288.

69. Muhlenberg, *Journals*, II, 596.

70. Estate of Button Gwinnett, Aug. 25, 1777, Inventory Book GG, 9–10; estate of William Simpson, Mar. 21, 1769, Inventory Book F, 392–397; estate of Newdigate Stephens, Apr. 18, 1757, *ibid.*, 48; advertisement of William Ewen and Robert Bolton, *Ga. Gaz.*, Apr. 11, 1765; memorial of the Rev. C. F. Triebner, received Sept. 25, 1783, Ga. Loyalist Claims, A.O. 13/37, P.R.O. (microfilm at Dept. of Archives and Hist., Atlanta, Ga.).

The practical concerns of this life occupied much of Georgians' attention, however, and in their attempts to master the frontier, they acquired or had access to books that showed them how to do useful things. The varied subjects included agriculture, architecture, cookery, bookkeeping, gardening, the culture of indigo, the breeding of silkworms, and many other topics.[71] Bolzius thought Jethro Tull's book on agriculture had been sent to him by Providence. "The Horse Hoing Husbandry, was fallen into my hand, which I perused with great Pleasure, and communicated the Contents thereof, relating to our sort of Land, to our people in several Meetings." Instructing the Germans from the book produced promising results. It "brought them in the way of ploughing by mutual Assistants their old Grounds, to such a good Effect, that there is now in large Fields a most pleasant Hope of a good Crop."[72]

At some time during or before 1763, a subscription library was organized in Savannah. Such libraries in American towns were usually patterned upon the Library Company of Philadelphia, founded by Benjamin Franklin and his friends in 1731, or upon English models. In Philadelphia members paid a fee for belonging, and a committee controlled purchases. Charleston followed suit in 1748 when seventeen citizens formed the Charles Town Library Society. The membership grew rather rapidly, as did the book holdings. By the 1770s the library had almost two thousand volumes. Under the rules initially laid down, a committee of twelve members met the first Wednesday of each month (sometimes more often) to compile lists of books to be purchased. Members borrowed books and pamphlets by submitting requests to the librarian.[73] The rules of the Georgia Library Society were probably similar, but they do not survive. It is impossible to say with certainty even where the collection was housed in its early years. Near the end of the colonial era, however, a library room existed in the courthouse, and the society met there.[74] The society depended upon dues paid by its members, as attested to by this notice:

71. *Col. Records of Ga.*, XXXI, 119, 170; advertisements of James Johnston, *Ga. Gaz.*, Apr. 7 and Nov. 10, 1763; advertisement of John Wood, *ibid.*, May 17, 1775.

72. *Col. Records of Ga.*, XXIV, 359.

73. Rules of the Charles Town Library Society, *S.-C. Gaz.*, Apr. 16–23, 1750.

74. Notice of the Georgia Library Society, *Ga. Gaz.*, Nov. 8, 1775.

Savannah, Feb. 10, 1767.
This evening, at a meeting of the Library Society, it was unanimously resolved, that every member who does not pay up his arrears, on or before
the first Tuesday in April next, shall be expelled: It is therefore expected,
that every person concerned will pay a due regard to this notice. The Society
will meet at Mr. Creighton's on the said Tuesday evening in April, at six
o'clock, for the above purposes.

By Order of the Society,
George Baillie, Secr.[75]

In 1774 the Georgia Library Society began to disband and was succeeded by the Savannah Library Society. The new organization needed
a minimum of fifty subscribers from the town and vicinity but found
itself with seventy and the likelihood of attracting more.[76] The Savannah Library Society bought some or all of the volumes of the older
group and met at the courthouse, a circumstance that suggests its books
were housed there. The librarian was Richard Davis, most likely the
brother-in-law of Henry Yonge, surveyor general of the province,
member of the council, and a brother of the bishop of Norwich.[77] That
Davis was a highly literate man can scarcely be doubted. After 1779
he was clerk to Chief Justice Stokes.[78] Davis's efforts to recover all the
books of the old society for the use of the new group afford the only
information available about the catalog of those two organizations. In
1775 he advertised for the return of volumes that had been withdrawn
from the old society and were still in possession of its members. The
list contained not a single title on a religious subject. Otherwise it was
somewhat balanced. More than two dozen historical works were missing from the shelves, including the third and fourth volumes of Paul
de Rapin's famous Whig *History of England.* Other works were the
*Dictionary of Arts and Sciences, Poems by Several Hands, Royal and
Noble Authors,* Charles Rollin's *Method of Teaching and Studying
the Belles Lettres,* Voltaire's *State of Europe,* Alexander Pope's translation of the *Iliad,* Montesquieu's *Spirit of the Laws,* the *Critical Re-*

75. *Ibid.,* Feb. 25, 1767.
76. Notice of the Library Society, *ibid.,* Nov. 23, 1774.
77. *Ibid.,* Dec. 7, 1774, and May 24, 1775.
78. Memorial of Alexander Thompson, Sept. 9, 1788, Ga. Loyalist Claims,
A.O. 13/36 a; petition of Richard Davis, *ibid.,* A.O. 13/34. Davis was loyal to
the crown during the Revolution and was murdered by blacks in Jamaica after
the war.

view, *Elements of Criticism*, the *World*, four volumes of *Debates in the House of Commons*, books of essays and travel, and works by Addison, Pope, Swift, and James Thomson, popular poet and playwright and author of *Rule Britannia*.[79]

The range of these titles is not surprising. Advertisements of booksellers in Georgia regularly offered such works for sale. Indeed, some of these titles were in James Johnston's book advertisement that appeared in the first issue of the *Georgia Gazette* in 1763. Johnston ran the best book shop in the province but not the only one. Books were stocked along with other goods by such merchants as Morel and Telfair; Kelsall, Darling, and Munro; Inglis and Hall; Alexander Fyffe and Company; Samuel Douglass and Company; and William and Edward Telfair and Company. Besides histories and belles lettres, these and other stores sold large quantities of religious writings, schoolbooks, and practical works like almanacs. *Tobler's Almanack* was available each year and forecast the eclipses, tides, sunrises and sunsets, moonrises, and the weather; advised on the best times for planting; and provided the dates of the regular sessions of court. The money-minded could consult a table that computed interest for them at 8 percent. *Tobler's Almanack* for 1764, printed and sold by Johnston, was probably the first volume ever produced in Georgia.[80]

The founding of the *Gazette* in 1763 itself added a valuable dimension to life in the province. The assembly fully understood that the printer required encouragement, and it arranged for Johnston to receive government assistance while his venture was in its infancy. The surviving issues of the *Gazette* (and a huge majority does survive) show that Johnston was a competent printer, although not among the very best (see figure 6, following). He would not have been expected to be innovative or to have had vast typographical resources at his disposal. His approach both to printing and to editing was consistent with other rather conservative colonial editors. Much of Johnston's news was picked up from other newspapers. With few exceptions he kept editorial silence in reporting local events. Like other colonial printers, he opened his columns to letter writers expressing many

79. Advertisement of the Library Society, *Ga. Gaz.*, May 24, 1775. In several instances the titles cited were issued in many volumes, and only scattered ones were missing.

80. A copy of the 1764 almanac, a booklet of 12 unnumbered pages, is in the DeRenne Coll., as are editions for 1766 and 1770.

THE GEORGIA GAZETTE.

NUMBER 4.   THURSDAY, APRIL 28, 1763.

EUROPEAN INTELLIGENCE.

LONDON, December 23,

WE are informed that Gen. Howard's, Col. Lambert's, and Col. Frederick's regiments, are to embark from Portugal for Minorca, to garrison that island, and a regiment from Gibraltar to go on the same service. The French troops are soon to evacuate it.

Sir Richard Lyttleton is appointed Governor, and Col. Barre, member of parliament for Wycomb, Lieutenant-Governor of Minorca. And the Earl of Darlington, master of the Jewel-Office, is the room of Sir Richard Lyttleton.

Transports are preparing to carry a number of French prisoners to their own country for an equal number of ours, the necessary articles for that purpose being settled.

It is said the King of Portugal has settled penfins upon the Prince of Buckebourg and some English General officers in confideration of their services this war.

Yesterday the Duke of Rutland received by the mail the agreeable news from Germany, that the Marquis of Granby, who had been very ill for some time, was in a fair way of recovery.

The Queen has sat for her picture to the celebrated Miss Reed, who draws her Majesty in a sitting posture, with the young Prince in her lap.

A very fine chariot, of most exquisite workmanship, is making in Long-Acre, which is designed as a present to the French King, from a great personage.

The Duke de Nivernois has delivered no passports for British ships since the signing of the preliminaries, and will deliver none. All these passports have been sent to the Earl of Egremont, and all applications to obtain them must be made at his Lordship's office only.

All the passports given for private persons by the Duke de Nivernois, have been, and always will be, delivered gratis.

Letters from Madrid of the 28th assert, that the Spanish troops on their march, returning out of Portugal, paid ready money for every thing they had from the subjects of Portugal.

His Majesty has been pleased to appoint Lieutenant-Colonel Vaughan, of the 94th regiment of foot, to be Lieutenant-Colonel to the 46th regiment of foot, Murray's, in the room of Lieutenant-Colonel John Young, who retires.

The tin-plate workers belonging to the ordnance, are shortly to prepare a model of a building for the exhibition of our grand fireworks, which are to be played off at the conclusion of the general peace.

A particular state of all the garrisons in England, and its dependencies, is taking, together with the number of men at present retained; and we hear that they will be raised to their full complement.

It is said a royal country seat will shortly be presented to his Royal Highness the Duke of York by his Majesty.

Dec. 25. The obsolete terms of Whig and Tory are now revived with as much acrimony as in 1680, the divisions in the ministry are very great, and seem still to increase.

a brave people as the British nation could be wheedled or bullied into a peace by any external power; because we don't know of any such power but what may have been brought by to their interest upon solid and reasonable terms. How then are we to account for this extraordinary phenomenon in politicks? Must we call it a general frolick, or shall we say, Quos Deus vult perdere, dementat. Indeed we don't know what to make of it; but of this we are certain, that Dutchmen, after such a successful and glorious war, would have made a better peace."

St. James's, Jan. 10. This day the Right Hon. Humphry Morrice, Esq; Comptroler of his Majesty's Houshold, and Sir John Philips, Bart. were, by his Majesty's command, sworn of his Majesty's Most Hon. Privy-Council, and took their respective places at the board accordingly. Lond. Gaz.

London, Jan. 11. By letters dated the 27th of December we learn, that the Marquis of Granby was so well recovered that he was preparing to set out for England.

On the 30th ult. the regency of Hanover issued orders to prevent the inlisting of the disbanded men for foreign service, and, if necessary, to employ force to compel the foreign rollers to quit the country.

From Paris they write, that, to prevent future broils, a King of the Romans will soon be elected; and that the Archduke Joseph will be the person. Three camps are talked of to be formed in the spring, for disbanding the troops; one in Alsace, another in Flanders, and the third in Provence. The sons of those employed in husbandry will be sent home, and only those kept who have no home.

Letters from Saxony tell us, that the Prussian soldiers are permitted to chuse wives among the young women of Saxony, and the magistrates of the place to which the girl belongs are compelled to give her 300 crowns for her fortune.

We hear from Rome, that the Pope lately assembled a consistory of several cardinals, about the expulsion of the Jesuits from France, but the result of it was not yet made publick.

Jan. 12. By yesterday's mail we learn, that the cold is set in so severe, that the march of the British troops from the county of Bentheim to Williamstadt is stopt by it.

Last night the corpse of the late Earl Granville was carried from the Jerusalem-Chamber to Westminster-Abbey and interred by the Lord Bishop of Rochester in great ral pomp and solemnity, in the north isle of Henry the VII. chapel, by the remains of his mother and his first lady.

All the arches of London bridge are stopt up by ice, and at Rotherhith several booths are built on the Thames.

On Monday last the Right Hon. the Lord Mayor sent a considerable quantity of coals for the use of the poor prisoners in Newgate.

Jan. 13. A minister from the Elector-Palatine arrived at Ratisbon the 22d ult. and it was generally thought he was come to sign a neutrality with the Baron de Plotho, the Prussian minister, in the name and on the part of the Elector his master.

The Right Hon. the Earl of Bute, in confideration of the rigorous season, which has deprived the industrious working watermen of their natural subsistence, has been pleased to give 100 pounds to be distributed amongst them by the mil-

---

6. *The Nameplate and a Portion of the Front Page of the* Georgia Gazette, *April 28, 1763.*

The Georgia Gazette *was published weekly from 1763 until 1776 with only one major interruption. The issue of April 28, 1763, came out at the end of James Johnston's first month of publication. The newspaper commonly had four pages but sometimes had more.*

(*Courtesy of the Georgia Press Association, Atlanta.*)

points of view. He carried verse, some of it local and much of it bad, as well as essays on moral subjects.

The advertisements in the *Gazette* tell more about everyday life in the province than the news columns do. They were a great convenience, for no longer was it necessary to post important notices at the well, the market place, or the pump in Georgia's towns. An advertisement in the *Gazette* was more efficient. However, Johnston's advertising rates were expensive enough to prevent the newspaper from becoming a bulletin board for everyone. He charged three shillings for a short advertisement carried in three consecutive issues, and more for longer notices.[81]

At first the *Georgia Gazette* appeared each Thursday but later changed to Wednesday. Johnston printed on pages measuring 7¼ by 11¼ inches, divided into two columns. The *Gazette* commonly ran to four pages but sometimes was as long as six or eight with occasional supplements. Its founding gave the colony something it badly needed —a well-focused local instrument of communication.[82] We cannot know the number of paid subscribers, but the subscription rate was high, usually 10s. a year—more than a nominal sum considering that *Tobler's Almanack* could be had for 9d., and a complete set of laws passed in 1768 for only 2s. 6d.

Georgia was well served by newspapers in the years before the Revolution, having access to four that printed Georgia news and advertisements. Besides the *Georgia Gazette*, Charleston's three newspapers—the *South-Carolina Gazette*, the *South-Carolina and American General Gazette*, and the *South-Carolina Gazette; And Country Journal*—had readers in Georgia. In the style of the day, Johnston never promoted his paper exclusively but helped his customers buy subscriptions to publications produced elsewhere. In 1766 Governor Wright read not only the Georgia and South Carolina newspapers but also the *Pennsylvania Gazette* and doubtless many others as well.[83]

The attention that Georgians gave to art was less widespread than that expended upon books and newspapers. Yet it was not inconsequential. Inventories reveal that pictures, paintings, and decorative

81. The price cited here is based upon a bill that Johnston submitted to William Gibbons, Jr., paid on Feb. 6, 1772. William Gibbons, Jr., Papers, Perkins Lib., Duke Univ., Durham, N.C.

82. Louis Turner Griffith and John Erwin Talmadge, *Georgia Journalism, 1763–1950* (Athens, Ga., 1951), 1–6.

83. *Col. Records of Ga.*, XXXVII, 114, 115, 119, 124, 145.

maps, although not common, were also not rare. Of 328 applicable inventories, 64 record some kind of decorative art.[84] People who bought pictures often chose prints or maps. In 1761 Johnson and Wylly were selling prints by Hogarth at their store on the Bay in Savannah. Inglis and Hall were still selling them six years later. In Augusta in 1765, Brown, Struthers, and Company stocked pictures and maps.[85] Machenry's Tavern had thirty pictures and six colored maps, and numerous Georgians owned pictures of King George and Queen Charlotte. These were prints, not paintings, for they were usually valued at 10s.[86] William Ewen, one of the leaders of the Revolution, owned such a print of the king and without doubt had displayed it in his home in earlier days, along with twenty-eight other prints that he had. When he died in 1777, still in the forefront of the Revolutionary movement, the persons who inventoried his estate appraised the twenty-eight prints at £5 but listed the one of his majesty separately and assigned it a value of absolutely nothing.[87] Georgians had some expensive and impressive paintings, too. As early as 1739 one of the Salzburger benefactors in Germany sent a portrait of himself to Ebenezer.[88] Although no professional portrait or miniature painters were resident in the province, some persons arranged to have likenesses made of themselves and their families, usually employing artists from Charleston. Jeremiah Theus, a Swiss who worked in Charleston, enjoyed a broad patronage in Georgia.[89]

84. The inventories break down as follows:

Years	Inventories listing decorative art	Inventories listing no decorative art
1754–1759	7	32
1760–1765	16	63
1766–1771	31	117
1776–1778	10	52

85. Advertisement of Johnson and Wylly, *S.-C. Gaz.*, July 4–11, 1761; advertisement of Inglis and Hall, *Ga. Gaz.*, July 8, 1767; estate of Brown, Struthers, and Company, Feb. 22, 1766, Inventory Book F, 223.

86. Estate of James Machenry, June 4, 1768, Inventory Book F, 339. For examples of the types of prints owned, see estates of Mary Bryan, Aug. 18, 1766, Inventory Book F, 204; John Perkins, May 20, 1767, *ibid.*, 263; Bartholomew Zouberbuhler, Apr. 21, 1767, *ibid.*, 255; and William Simpson, Mar. 21, 1769, *ibid.*, 393.

87. Estate of William Ewen, Aug. 25, 1777, Inventory Book GG, 3.

88. Urlsperger, ed., *Ausführliche Nachrichten*, II, 144.

89. In 1971 a collection was displayed at the National Portrait Gallery in Washington, D.C., that included portraits of some colonial Georgians. The works

Musical instruments, unlike works of art, were seldom listed in colonial inventories, a fact that is mystifying, for instrumental music was neither esoteric nor arcane.[90] In the royal period advertisements often refer to the availability of violins, lutestrings, and flutes, and the few instruments mentioned in inventories were usually small, hand-held ones of this type.[91] By 1763 a pipe organ was in use at St. Paul's Church in Augusta, where a competent musician was on the bench.[92] Two years later Edward Barnard of Augusta donated a pipe organ to Christ Church in Savannah, its first. Barnard was an indefatigable supporter of the Church of England and a pillar of St. Paul's. Rising from humble beginnings as a baker's apprentice, he was by 1765 a large planter and slaveholder, a sometime Indian trader, and a worthy member of the assembly who could well afford such a gift. The organ in Savannah was first played at public services on November 17, 1765, with John Stevens, Jr., at the console.[93] Stevens, a native of England, was probably organist at Christ Church for two or three years. He later played with some distinction at St. Michael's Church in Charleston and died in 1772.

Music among the Salzburgers was a popular and approved form of entertainment—one of the few approved forms. The Lutheran canon as interpreted at Ebenezer disallowed most kinds of games; so the Germans turned to music for pleasure as well as for inspiration under the leadership of the pastors. They were experts in unaccompanied singing, although in 1740 they had been briefly tempted to send to

---

were attributed to Henry Benbridge, an artist based in Charleston in the 1770s. James Habersham used the services of Theus. In 1772 he commissioned 7 works from him and paid £320 for them in South Carolina currency. Ga. Hist. Soc., *Colls.*, VI, 197. A portrait of Habersham by Theus, circa 1772, hangs in the Telfair Academy of Arts and Sciences, Savannah, Ga.

90. One finds not a single musical instrument listed in the inventories between 1754 and 1759; only one from 1760 to 1765; 6 from 1766 to 1771; and 2 from 1776 to 1778—only 9 in all out of 328 applicable inventories. It is possible, of course, that elderly persons who felt themselves near death gave their violins or lutes to younger musicians whose fingers were more capable of making music. The statistics are based upon Inventory Books F, FF, and GG, *passim*.

91. Advertisements of Simon Munro, *Ga. Gaz.*, Dec. 29, 1763; Inglis and Hall, *ibid.*, Oct. 1, 1766; Samuel Douglass, *ibid.*, Nov. 1, 1769; and Gershon Cohen, *ibid.*, Sept. 14, 1774.

92. Vestry of St. Paul Church to the Rev. Dr. Burton, Mar. 20, 1763, S.P.G. Papers, Ser. C, Pkg. 7, Pt. iii (L.C. reel 16, 116–118).

93. Bartholomew Zouberbuhler to S.P.G., May 1, 1766, *ibid.* (L.C. reel 16, 73); *Ga. Gaz.*, Nov. 21, 1765.

Europe for a harpsichord. They suppressed that urge as impractical because they needed other things more and applied themselves to unaccompanied harmonization.[94] One visitor in 1774 said they sang "in a way to gladden one's heart, even the most difficult of the Halle melodies," an accomplishment that could be credited to Bolzius. The pastor believed that singing lessons prevented "little mistakes" from creeping into music and, therefore, taught the Salzburgers as long as he lived. Sometimes he prayed, "God, let this practice do for Christ's sake!"[95] In Savannah before the organ arrived, the church tune was set by a person paid to do it, and at Midway Congregational Church, Parmenas Way, a prominent person in the church and the colony, raised the tune and got free use of four seats for doing so.[96]

Singing seems to have been the most common musical expression. DeBrahm asserted that colonial Georgia was never at any time debauched by European luxuries such as balls, masquerades, operas, and plays, an assertion that, even allowing for his prejudices, we may accept.[97] Yet Georgians did not disdain to dance at the Bosomworth wedding in 1744. There were balls, dances, and even dancing schools in royal times.[98] In the 1770s brilliant assemblies that involved dancing were held in the courtroom of the courthouse, the protests of Chief Justice Stokes notwithstanding.[99] Infrequently masquerades were also held. The governor himself sometimes lent his patronage to a cultural event such as a public reading, or a farce, like the one performed at Lyon's Tavern in Savannah in 1768, entitled "Lethe, or Aesop in the Shades." "Among a Variety of entertaining Characters are the Fine Gentleman and the Fine Lady, with a Song in Character. Between the Acts, Musick, Vocal and Instrumental. To begin precisely at seven o'clock. Tickets to be had at the Exchange and at Mr. Crighton's Tavern, at Half a Crown each. No Person to be admitted without a Ticket."[100]

On the king's birthday in 1766, Georgians heard what probably was the first concert given in the colony. The event also took place in the long room of Lyon's Tavern with Stevens, the Anglican organist,

94. Urlsperger, ed., *Ausführliche Nachrichten*, I, 2597.
95. *Ibid.*, III, 660; Muhlenberg, *Journals*, II, 646.
96. *Col. Records of Ga.*, VI, 101; Stacy, *Records of Midway Church*, I, 16.
97. DeBrahm, *History of Ga.*, 24.
98. Advertisement of Medley D'Arcy Dawes, *Ga. Gaz.*, Sept. 25, 1765.
99. Ga. Hist. Soc., *Colls.*, VI, 166–167.
100. *Ga. Gaz.*, June 22, 1768.

presiding and probably performing. He had by then been playing at Christ Church for six months and had organized the concert. We cannot know what music was played, how many musicians were involved, or who they were, but there is evidence to show that afterward a birthday ball was held.[101] Although they could not be considered as concerts, presentations of music in taverns and at assemblies were sometimes provided by slaves.[102]

Georgia, then, long before the start of the Revolution, was a colony where those men and women who were white and free lived on a plane above the purely fundamental. If balls and masquerades did not flourish, they were not unknown. If there was not a vigorous musical tradition (except among the Germans), Georgians nevertheless enjoyed music of their own making. The government itself was committed to a regular schedule of public celebrations, events that, when added to the round of church fasts and feasts, lent rhythm and order to people's lives. Clubs and societies bound men together in amiable fellowship, and wholly apart from clubs, hospitality was freely extended to strangers and friends. Devotion to outdoor activities—sports, walking, hunting, fishing, exploring—was consistent with a climate warm in summer and mild in winter. Books were an appendage to life in which many found fulfillment. While numerous Georgians were totally illiterate, and others could only sign their names, books were owned and read. In cultural attainments, Georgia was of course neither New England nor South Carolina. But as the Revolution approached, the people living in this forty-three-year-old province, the first half of whose history had been spent in poverty and the second half in the modest acquisition of wealth, increasingly enjoyed the pleasures, comforts, and amenities that money could buy.

101. *Ibid.*, May 21, 1766.
102. Advertisements of James Alexander, *ibid.*, Jan. 13, 1768; Alexander Wylly, *ibid.*, Oct. 25, 1775; and James Robertson, *ibid.*, Jan. 17, 1776.

Jerusalem Lutheran Church, the oldest public building in Georgia still standing, was built in 1767 and 1768 on a bluff overlooking the Savannah River some twenty miles above Savannah in what is today Effingham County. The completed structure was the most prominent building in the then thriving Lutheran community of Ebenezer. Today only the church and its cemetery remain from colonial times, the town having disappeared. The church, however, is still regularly used for Lutheran religious services. Originally, the cupola was surmounted by a metal swan, the symbol of Martin Luther. Tradition says that British soldiers shot holes in the swan during the American Revolution. In the 1950s a replica of the original swan was installed atop the cupola. The church is of locally burned brick, and some of the bricks show the hand prints of the persons who made them more than two centuries ago.

(See reverse.)

7. *Jerusalem Lutheran Church, Effingham County, Georgia.*

(Photo by Kenneth Rogers, 1957; courtesy of the Atlanta Journal-Constitution
Magazine.)

Religion

Chapter 7

A year before the *Anne's* passengers arrived at Yamacraw Bluff, the trustees turned to the Society for the Propagation of the Gospel in Foreign Parts for assistance in advancing the practice of religion in Georgia. The S.P.G. had been founded in 1701 and sought rather openly to help the Church of England dominate religious life in the colonies, a fact resented by dissenters both in England and in America. To promote the Christian religion in general and its special interest in particular, the S.P.G. sent missionaries to many colonies and paid their salaries until local methods of support were devised.

The financial resources of the S.P.G. were behind much of the effort exerted by the Anglican church in Georgia, for with exceptions, the society's funds paid a part of the expenses of the Anglican clergymen in the province.[1] To its discredit, the S.P.G. must bear part of the responsibility for the quality of ministers sent, because the society had a large hand in their selection.

With one exception and with many variations in degree, the Anglican clergymen in Georgia were either fractious, overzealous, youthful and inexperienced, discouraged, narrow, immoral, made useless by Revolutionary ferment, or were in their posts too brief a time to demonstrate their strengths or weaknesses. Not only were most of them poorly chosen, but they were few in number. For long periods the province was served by one priest. The parishes, or charges, were of such size that a man could serve only some people with no hope of reaching all.

---

1. The S.P.G. did not pay the salaries of Charles Wesley, George Whitefield, or Christopher Orton during the proprietary period.

John Wesley, who really had wished to convert the Indians rather than to be a parish priest, had the latter role forced upon him by local necessity and the strong desire of the government. His parish was more than two hundred miles long. "What will become of This Poor People, a few of whom now see the Light and bless God for it, when I am Called from Among them, I know not." Indeed, said Wesley, he did not know what would become of them while he was there, for his assignment "laughs at the Labour of One Man."[2]

Unless a Georgian lived in Savannah, he would not have had easy access to an Anglican clergyman during much of colonial times. (After 1750 a priest sometimes was at Augusta.) Clergymen of other denominations might have been expected to supply the gaps, and to a degree, they did. Before 1770 the devoted ministers of the Salzburgers served their Lutheran flock exceedingly well, but theirs was a specialized ministry separated by language from the majority of Georgians not fluent in German. The Presbyterian ministry of J. J. Zubly in and around Savannah was an important religious force, and the Congregationalists of the Midway district and St. John Parish received dedicated leadership from the Reverend John Osgood. Notice should also be taken of the Jews; the Moravians, whose departure spelled Georgia's loss and the good fortune of Pennsylvania and North Carolina; the Quakers at Wrightsborough, a community struggling with self-discipline; the Baptists, who arrived late but whose numbers increased in the 1770s; and the scattered ministries of other nonconformists like the Presbyterian John MacLeod, at Darien until 1741, and the Lutheran John Ulrich Driesler at Frederica. After 1740 Whitefield's Bethesda orphanage was a religious as well as an educational influence. The Bethesda enclave was Methodist in fact but for the most part Anglican in affiliation—quarrelsomely Anglican, but Anglican nevertheless.

The Church of England was established by law in 1758. The act of establishment meant that all citizens, regardless of religious preference, were subject to taxes for its support and for poor relief. No one was compelled to attend its services, however, and the government itself early encouraged some dissenting clergymen by granting glebes for their support.

From the very beginning, the official policy of the government was one of religious toleration for everybody except Roman Catholics,

2. *Col. Records of Ga.*, XXI, 220–221.

but there were few of them in Georgia.[3] The prejudice against them carried over from attitudes brought from England, sharpened by the threat to security posed by Catholic Spaniards in Florida and Catholic Frenchmen and Spaniards in Louisiana.

That hard feelings against communicants of the Church of Rome were real and not a pose was shown by the malice with which Protestant Georgians accused one another of being secret papists. John Wesley was so accused. But even more remarkably, Henry Parker, who was president of Georgia after Stephens stepped down, was so charged in 1751 in an anonymous letter to the trustees. Inquiry was made, and it was discovered that, although Parker attended the services of the Church of England, he had never been seen to receive Holy Communion. Parker quickly asserted that he had been in a Roman Catholic church only once in his life, and that was out of curiosity. However, his mother late in life had become a communicant of Rome even though one of her deceased husbands had been a priest of the Church of England. The charges against Parker were made about the time that he subscribed to the qualifying papers in preparation for becoming president. To lay the issue to rest, he signed the Oath against Transubstantiation, which had earlier been ignored in the qualifying process. He also made plans to receive Communion.[4] Thereafter public officials routinely signed the Oath against Transubstantiation at the same time that they executed the Oaths of Allegiance, Supremacy, and Abjuration. In it they swore that they "do believe that there is not any Transubstantiation in the Sacrament of the Lord's Supper, or in the elements of Bread and Wine, or after the Consecration thereof by any person whatsoever."[5]

The intention was to prevent Roman Catholics from immigrating, and it was very nearly realized. However, the government did not feel threatened by the very few Roman Catholics who actually lived in Georgia. Four were reported in 1747.[6] In the inventories of estates for 1770, one finds that Lucretia Triboudite, a well-known woman in Savannah, owned a crucifix, cross, beads, and a parcel of French books,

3. *Ibid.*, I, 21.
4. *Ibid.*, XXVI, 324–326.
5. White, *Historical Collections of Ga.*, 38–41.
6. Reba Carolyn Strickland, *Religion and the State in Georgia in the Eighteenth Century* (New York, 1939), 43.

all suggesting that she might have been Roman Catholic, possibly conspicuously so. There is no sign that she was troubled by the state, even though she was prominent as a shopkeeper and businesswoman.[7]

In practice, few colonies were more liberal in their official views of religion than Georgia. Aside from the prohibition against Roman Catholics, which was largely self-enforcing, one searches in vain for signs of persecution of dissenters for religious reasons, with one possible exception. Toward the close of colonial times, the Reverend Daniel Marshall, a Baptist, was arrested while conducting services in St. Paul Parish, an arrest probably made on someone's whim and justifiable under no religious statute of the province.[8] He was in jail only briefly.

In any discussion about churches and ministers, a number of questions must be asked and, insofar as possible, answered. Did Georgians go to church? Were they instructed in their faith, whatever sect they adhered to? Did Georgia differ religiously from the other southern colonies it most closely resembled? And perhaps most important, did religion make a difference in the lives of the people and the life of the society in which they lived?

The 1740s was the decade of the Great Awakening in America. The fires of religion burned hot, and men and women found themselves aflame with religious passions. One of the preachers who stirred souls to life up and down the American seaboard was George Whitefield, whose home base was in Georgia at Bethesda. Indeed, many of Whitefield's sermons were preached to raise money for his orphanage. Whitefield possessed one of the most remarkable voices ever to speak from a pulpit. He assembled crowds of such size that they could only be addressed out of doors. In Philadelphia, Benjamin Franklin conducted an experiment during one of Whitefield's outdoor performances and concluded that the minister could be heard by more than thirty thousand persons at once. Franklin, recalling a Whitefield service, commented on the preacher's considerable talents. "I had in my Pocket a Handful of Copper Money, three or four silver Dollars, and five Pistoles in Gold. As he proceeded I began to soften, and concluded to

7. Estate of Lucretia Triboudite, Feb. 27, 1770, Inventory Book F, 448–449; advertisement of Lucretia Triboudet, *Ga. Gaz.*, Feb. 21, 1765.

8. The Rev. Abraham Marshall, "Biography of the Late Rev. Daniel Marshall," *Georgia Analytical Repository*, I (1802), 25–26. Marshall was regarded by some persons, including Zubly, as an irritating individual who created commotions. It is likely that he was accused of disturbing the peace or some similar infraction.

give the Coppers. Another Stroke of his Oratory made me asham'd of that, and determin'd me to give the Silver; and he finish'd so admirably, that I empty'd my Pocket wholly into the Collector's Dish, Gold and all."[9]

Under such an influence, flames were kindled at Bethesda that lifted men and women to pentecostal ecstasies, particularly when Whitefield appeared for visits. We can assume that there also were real religious experiences in the congregations of all the ministers in the province, even the insufficient ones, although such things are difficult to document. Yet, even allowing for the seriousness and piety of some of the Lutherans and Congregationalists, the constancy of many of the Presbyterians, Jews, and Quakers (and while they were in Georgia, the Moravians), the zeal of the late-arriving Baptists, and the devotion of some of the Anglicans, can we say that colonial Georgians by and large were people of deep personal religious commitments? The overpowering testimony from lay people and ministers alike is that they were not.

There were three principal difficulties with religion in Georgia. The number of ministers in the province was small; so there were some colonists who wished to have the services of a clergyman but did not. On the other hand, many persons who did have a minister to serve them were not interested. Furthermore, some of Georgia's clergymen were ineffective. Concerning Georgians who were not interested in religion, we can appreciate a statement made in 1735 by the Reverend Samuel Quincy, then rector in Savannah. Quincy reassured the authorities in London that they need not worry about unwanted Roman Catholic missionaries coming in and making converts. "Religion," he said, "seems to be the least minded of anything in the place."[10] Of course, Whitefield could assemble large congregations, for people wished to hear one of the great forensic personalities of the day. But they did not exert themselves mightily to hear other clergymen, although some would have if they had had more opportunity.

When Joseph Ottolenghe arrived in Georgia, a false report spread that he was a minister, and he found himself pressed to visit the back-

9. *Whitefield's Journals, 1737–1741*, 8; Leonard W. Labaree *et al.*, eds., *The Autobiography of Benjamin Franklin* (New Haven, Conn., 1964), 177–179. Franklin's estimate has been questioned, but he proved that Whitefield could be heard by large crowds. See also Albert D. Belden, *George Whitefield—The Awakener: A Modern Study of the Evangelical Revival* (New York, 1953), 233.

10. *Col. Records of Ga.*, XX, 208, XXVI, 104.

country. Unqualified to go, he sent them books instead. The Reverend Bartholomew Zouberbuhler strongly felt that there were souls waiting to be added to the flock in places distant from Savannah, but he, for all his concern, could only attend those closest to the fold. Likewise, the Reverend Samuel Frink was convinced that there were people in the parishes around Savannah who had "but very little more Knowledge of a Saviour than the Aboriginal natives," but he could scarcely spare a day from his parochial duties to visit them. Zubly thought that "vital Religion" was in a low state everywhere, and Joseph Clay, a Savannah merchant and a devout layman who preferred Anglican clergymen to all others, was by 1771 so disgusted with the quality of the Anglican ministers he saw that he was ready to welcome almost any kind of Christian preacher.[11] "Unless God in his infinite mercy and goodness, uses some extra means in our favour, this land, I may say land of darkness and ignorance, (more particularly if applied relative to the people in the back woods, many of whom I dare say never saw a Bible in their lives, or ever heard a gospel sermon, and most of whom can neither write nor read,) must be left without teachers at least of the gospel of Jesus Christ." Clay said that if the persons responsible for dispatching Anglican clergy to the colony were judged by the quality of the men generally sent, one would conclude that "their only care was to see that they were not religious men."[12]

Although the government during trustee and royal times strove to advance religion both for its own sake and as an aid to acceptable behavior and social order, Georgians who showed themselves entirely uninterested in churches bore no stigma. In 1758, while the Church of England was being established, those individuals most interested in it had to contend with a party in the assembly "such as Care for no Churches at all."[13]

11. Joseph Ottolenghe to the Rev. Mr. Smith, Dec. 4, 1751, MSS of Dr. Bray's Associates, Pt. H (L.C. reel 11, 335/201–202); Samuel Frink to the Rev. Dr. Burton, June 29, 1769, S.P.G. Papers, Ser. C, Pkg. 7, Pt. iii (L.C. reel 16, 240–247); Massachusetts Historical Society, *Proceedings*, 1st Ser., IX (1866), 218–219.

12. "Memoirs of Cornelius Winter," *Works of Jay*, III, 39.

13. Unsigned letter to the archbishop of Canterbury, read in committee Jan. 15, 1759, S.P.G. Papers, Ser. C, Pkg. 1, Pt. ii (L.C. reel 2, 17–25). This letter, written in behalf of Ottolenghe by an unknown person, quotes at length from a letter written by Ottolenghe himself on Aug. 12, 1758, and describes some of the circumstances surrounding the passage of the bill establishing the Church of England in Georgia.

We cannot now determine just how large this group was. But in addition to that not inconsiderable number of people to whom religion was inconvenient or unattractive, or both, there were large numbers of Georgians who simply had no access to a clergyman. Moreover, there were others who did, but who were disgusted by the unsuitability of many of the ministers. Clerical behavior was often irregular and confusing and sometimes revolted ordinary as well as pious people. Yet not all clergymen were equally weak or derelict; a few, especially the Lutherans, were exemplary.

From the beginning the Salzburgers stood somewhat aloof from the other Georgians. For the support of their ministry, they had gifts sent by friends in Germany, principally by persons connected with the famous orphanage near Halle, and by the Society for the Promotion of Christian Knowledge in Great Britain, in addition to funds raised locally. The Lutheran ministers in the colony were true sons of German Pietism, a spiritual movement that had its most important center at Halle. Pietists, in approaching religion as they did, were reacting against an earlier era when Lutheran pastors prided themselves upon cold and lofty disquisitions. The everyday Lutheran layman of that era was rich in exegetical screeds, poor in the simple and engrafted word. The Georgia pastors were a part of the reaction against such an approach. Their ministries were intimate, practical, and rather gravely judgmental. Between 1734 and 1776 the Lutherans of Georgia had five ministers, the most remarkable of whom was John Martin Bolzius. Except for his role as a leader of those who opposed the legalization of slavery (for which he was soundly lambasted), he was one of the few prominent men in Georgia to escape serious criticism from his contemporaries. Until his death in 1765, he led his followers with firmness and wisdom, exhorting them to hard work and demonstrating how to achieve good results in agriculture. At his right hand was the Reverend Israel Christian Gronau, his assistant, who served him without apparent jealousy or stress until Gronau died in 1745. Gronau's replacement, the Reverend Hermann Henry Lemke, arrived in Georgia the following year. Like Bolzius and Gronau before him, he had been a student and teacher at the orphanage outside Halle. In 1752 still another minister arrived from Germany—the Reverend Christian Rabenhorst—and for the first time, the Germans in Georgia had three pastors.

It was remarkable that two had hitherto sufficed, for they served not only Jerusalem Church at Ebenezer but also smaller ones erected in the countryside at Zion, Bethany, and Goshen.[14] The pastors also went once every six weeks to Savannah and occasionally to Purrysburg, South Carolina, to preach and to administer Holy Communion to Lutherans there. Lemke lived only three years after Bolzius died in 1765, and for a brief time, Rabenhorst served his widely scattered German flock alone. But in 1769 the Reverend Christoph Friedrich Triebner arrived—the last German minister to be assigned to Georgia. During the ministry that he and Rabenhorst now shared, the Lutheran church in Georgia fell into discord. Triebner and Rabenhorst quarreled not only about procedures but about church property and resources; they and their adherents split the Germans into factions. Triebner's group was led by his brother-in-law, John Gaspar Wertsch, and Rabenhorst's faction was principally headed by John Adam Treutlen. In Ebenezer an ugly dispute arose over possession of the church building itself, the end result of which was that the two factions no longer worshipped jointly.[15] By then the quarrel had gone beyond issues and involved property, position, and pride.

The Reverend Henry Melchior Muhlenberg, patriarch of the Lutheran church in America, came to Georgia from Pennsylvania in 1774 to mediate the dispute and, if possible, to repair the rupture. On paper he settled the disagreement, concluding that Triebner was the greater offender; almost immediately, however, the onset of the American Revolution revived the discord. Triebner conspicuously embraced the British cause, while Rabenhorst declined to do so. Rabenhorst died on December 30, 1776, but because of the war and the divisions left by the dispute, Triebner never again presided over a united congregation. The disagreements among the Germans after 1770 should not obscure their achievements under their three earliest ministers. Rabenhorst, too, probably would have been a sufficient pastor had Triebner never come to Georgia. The half-decade of wrangling at the close of the colonial era actually was untypical of Georgia Lutherans, yet it stood as a conspicuous reproach to them.

Religious groups that were small and isolated managed their affairs better than larger and more prominent ones. The practices of the Moravians were above criticism, except to officials intolerant of their

14. Muhlenberg, *Journals*, II, 652.
15. *Ibid.*, 601.

pacifism. Perceiving that their firmly held principles were odious to others, the Moravians decided "to remove from this Place."[16]

The Quakers of Wrightsborough came to Georgia after 1768 and by 1775 had a township of 124 families, which implies a total population of 600 or more. They established a monthly meeting that judged and reproved frolicking, dancing, profanity, fornication, excessive drinking, undue or unexplained absences from meeting, and other unseemly offenses, while maintaining a society almost certainly characterized by love and unity.[17]

The Jews were numerous enough to have had a synagogue, but their differences prevented their building one. The Reverend Samuel Quincy in 1735 reported that there were two kinds of Jews in Georgia, Portuguese Jews and German Jews, and that they differed markedly in customs and behavior. The Sephardic and the Ashkenazic Jews thought their differences too important to be set aside as accidents of geographic origin.[18] Each group had its own congregation, which met in members' homes. Both factions stood above scandal and were respected for the propriety of their conduct.

As noted, the Congregationalists settled in the Midway district south of Savannah in what in 1758 became St. John Parish. They organized a church remarkable for the sustained quality of its leadership. By 1771 the white population numbered about 350, and from them the Reverend John Osgood drew his Midway congregation. The church had perhaps 150 members in the 1770s. Midway was not a town but a crossroads, and people came to service from the nearby countryside and from the town of Sunbury. Services were sometimes also held in Sunbury, but Midway was, and remained, the religious center of St. John Parish. Osgood was pastor at Midway from its founding until his death in 1773. He had come with the original settlers from South Carolina, where he had been born in 1710 and ordained in 1735. By the time his ministry began in Georgia in 1752, he was a dignified, middle-aged man of experience, probity, and wisdom. Before 1770 Osgood

16. *Col. Records of Ga.*, XXI, 365.

17. Hitz, "Wrightsborough Quaker Town and Township," *Bull. of Friends Hist. Assoc.*, LXVI (1957), 16; Minutes of Wrightsborough Monthly Meeting, Nov. 4, 1773, June 4 and Sept. 3, 1774, Apr. 4, May 6, and June 3, 1775, May 4 and Oct. 5, 1776, and Feb. 1 and Mar. 1, 1777, Quaker Collection, Guilford College, Greensboro, N.C.

18. Phillipps Coll., 14201, 66–67, Univ. of Ga. Lib., Athens; Urlsperger, ed., *Ausführliche Nachrichten*, I, 2277.

had an assistant. For a time he was the Reverend John Alexander (later to be ordained an Anglican priest), and between 1767 and 1770, he was the Reverend James Edmonds. Osgood remained Midway's undisputed religious leader until his death, after which an occasional supply preacher filled the pulpit.

The Puritan heritage of the Midway Congregationalists was hardly evident by the middle of the eighteenth century. Osgood himself was moderate rather than severe, "chearful but not light, solid but not sad." He kept open communion with other Christians, and as he lay upon his deathbed in 1773, he asked those friends and relatives gathered about him to sing one of the great hymns by Isaac Watts. It included the lines: "Religion never was design'd / To make our pleasures less."[19]

The people of Midway took their religion seriously but made no effort to suppress worldly interests, particularly those relating to land policies, government, and Indian relations. That they had a capacity for toleration and compromise is evident in a letter they wrote in 1773 to Dr. John Witherspoon, president of the College of New Jersey at Princeton, describing the qualifications they desired in a minister to assist and, if necessary, to replace the ailing Osgood: "And we desire and request that he may be a man of moderate Principles, Sound in the Articles of Faith, and one who receives the Westminster Confession thereof, a moderate Calvinist. That he may be so far as can be discovered seriously and devoutly religious and of a regular life and conversation. And though we are desirous that in point of church government, he be of our particular persuasion and profession, yet should there be any small difference of opinion, as to any particular mode or manner of administration not essential, we hope a mutual condescention and forbearance will prevent any disagreement, contrary to the peace of the Gospel."[20]

In Savannah a relatively small but influential congregation of Independent Presbyterians had a truly remarkable pastor, Zubly. The Church of Scotland had no hand in founding the church; in fact, Zubly was probably not even a Presbyterian. Born in St. Gall, Switzerland,

19. John J. Zubly, *The Faithful Minister's Course finished; A Funeral Sermon, Preached August the 4th, 1773, in the Meeting at Midway in Georgia, At The Internment Of The Rev. John Osgood, A.M. Minister of that Congregation* (Savannah, Ga., 1773), 17, 18, 23, 30. Osgood's selection of this hymn and these quoted lines, in particular, were remarked upon at his funeral services.

20. Stacy, *Records of Midway Church*, I, 154.

in 1724, he was educated in the *gymnasium* there and was ordained at the German church in London before his twentieth birthday. The Independent Presbyterian church was truly independent, connected with no outside ecclesiastical organization. The year of its founding is traditionally given as 1755, the year that forty-three dissenters from the Church of England, subscribing to the doctrines of the Church of Scotland, petitioned for a church lot. They asked the governor and council for property upon which to erect a building, and in keeping with the local policy of assisting dissenters, the government granted it.[21] The church building was brick and was complete within three years. It faced Ellis Square, near the spot where the public market was soon to be relocated. Zubly took charge of the congregation in 1760 and was its first and only minister before the Revolution. He usually preached in English but also used his native German for persons who spoke that tongue in and around Savannah. In addition to his service to the Independent Presbyterian Church (with seventy communicants in 1773), Zubly also ministered to seventy German Calvinists outside Savannah and occasionally preached in South Carolina. Although he could be gentle and kind, he had a hard and unyielding side to his nature, and in the late 1760s, there was a near schism in his church.[22]

Zubly's own account of the episode contends that the dispute was over membership requirements. He had attempted, he said, to open the doors wide enough to admit anyone who professed belief in the Westminster Confession, but some in his congregation apparently wished additional tests to be imposed. Others, however, disputed Zubly's interpretation and said that opposition to his personality—not his principles—was the cause of the trouble.[23] His adversaries in 1769 proposed to start a competing Presbyterian church in Savannah. The venture finally came to nothing, and on paper at least, the congregation remained united. It is unclear how the quarrel was finally re-

21. *Col. Records of Ga.*, VII, 183. The names of 10 of the petitioners may be identified. They were among the lay persons in colonial Georgia whose religion may be definitely determined. The petitioning Presbyterians included Jonathan Bryan, James Edward Powell, Robert Bolton, James Miller, Joseph Gibbons, William Gibbons, Benjamin Farley, William Wright, David Fox, Jr., and John Fox.

22. "Memoirs of Cornelius Winter," *Works of Jay*, III, 29. Also see letter-to-the-editor dispute between Zubly and Lachlan McGillivray in *Ga. Gaz.*, Mar. 16, Mar. 23, Mar. 30, Apr. 6, and Apr. 20, 1768. The disagreement was over a tract of land.

23. Stiles, *Extracts from Itineraries*, ed. Dexter, 601.

solved. Zubly's critics, however, had not been obscure worshippers on the back bench but men to be reckoned with: Councillor John Graham, Councillor Lewis Johnson, Attorney General William Graeme, Commissary General George Baillie, James Cuthbert, John Simpson of Sunbury, Indian trader Lachlan McGillivray, and three men who at times sat in the Commons House of Assembly—John Rae, John Jamieson, and John Glen. In addition, the prominent firms of Inglis and Hall and Cowper and Telfairs handled subscriptions for the new meetinghouse, which in the end was never built.[24]

In 1773 Zubly reviewed for a friend the Christian ministries then active in Georgia, and his appraisal was generally accurate. In addition to his own ministry, the Church of England had twelve parishes, but ten had no rectors; the only Anglican priests doing parochial duty were at Savannah and Augusta. Midway Congregational Church maintained a branch of sorts at Sunbury; however, both houses of worship were served by the single clergyman from Midway. The Salzburgers had two ministers. A society of Presbyterians on the Altamaha River (doubtless at Darien) seemed about to get a minister but had none then. Zubly wrongly doubted that there was a Baptist church in Georgia, for Georgia's first Baptist church had been established the year before by the Reverend Daniel Marshall at Kiokee Creek above Augusta.[25] The late-arriving Baptists, from whom much was to be heard later, entered quietly and almost unnoticed.

This survey emphasizes a fact already implicit in much that has been said: to serve 33,000 Georgians, there were in 1773 only seven regular ministers—two Anglicans, one Congregationalist, two Lutherans, a Baptist, and Zubly. Roughly, that would be one clergyman for each 4,700 persons. Services were held, of course, at Bethesda, where nonparochial clergymen officiated. The Jews and the Quakers (of whom Zubly said nothing) conducted their own worship. Even so, Bethesda

24. Advertisements in *Ga. Gaz.*, Apr. 26, May 3, May 10, and July 12, 1769. We can assume, but not prove, that most of the persons associated with this venture were Presbyterians.

25. Mass. Hist. Soc., *Procs.*, 1st Ser., IX (1866), 215–216. Zubly did not mention the Scotch-Irish at Queensborough except to say that they had no settled ministry. Little can be said about the clergymen who at times served among them. Thomas Beattie was there for perhaps 2 years after 1769, and William Ronaldson attempted a ministry just before and during the Revolutionary War. A minister named John Beattie died on his way to Queensborough in 1774. Substantial numbers of Presbyterians at Wrightsborough and at Briar Creek were served only by supply pastors.

served mostly a group outside Savannah, and the Jews and the Quakers together accounted for only a small part of the population.

In a province where most people were unserved, DeBrahm said that the prevailing religion was "what is cultivated by the Church of England." [26] Lacking a broad witness borne by any other denomination, and given the official status of the Anglican religion after 1758, we may be sure that had they been asked, a great many Georgians would have said that they adhered to the Church of England.

The story of the establishment of the church in Georgia is a remarkable one without exact parallel in any other province. Usually, if establishment had not already occurred by 1758, it did not occur at all. Establishment was no easy thing to bring about in Georgia, although it was finally done voluntarily and without external pressure. A move to establish the Anglican religion was begun in 1755 in the first session of the assembly under royal rule. A bill passed the lower house but did not survive in the upper. A similar thing happened in 1757. [27] In 1758, however, an act of establishment was finally passed and became law. Ottolenghe, then a member of the Commons House, seems to have been its principal mover, assisted by Edward Barnard of Augusta and Henry Yonge. Ottolenghe wrote an account of what happened and not unnaturally made himself the "hero" of the story.

According to him, there were three alignments in the Commons House—Anglican churchmen, dissenters, and men who had no feeling for any church. Spotting a division among the dissenters, he strove to turn their disagreements to the advantage of Anglicanism. The Germans and the Congregationalists "differ'd so much from each other as both differ'd from the Church of England," Ottolenghe said, and he set about keeping them from uniting. He succeeded. After fourteen days he and his allies passed the establishment measure through the lower house and sent it on to the upper, where all the members except two were dissenters.

The upper house cut the bill to shreds and sent it back to the lower chamber with the words "Church of England" struck out, which convinced Ottolenghe that the measure, if passed in that form, would

26. DeBrahm, *History of Ga.*, 37.
27. The 1755 citations may be found in *Col. Records of Ga.*, XIII, 55, 60, 62, 63, 66, XVI, 55, 62, 65. For those for 1757, see *ibid.*, XIII, 126, 127, 156, 157, 159, XVI, 179–181.

establish "every whimsical Sectary in Georgia." But again fortune favored him. The altered bill arrived back in the Commons when that body was already angry with the upper house over another matter. Ottolenghe made it appear that changing the church bill was yet another affront. The Speaker of the lower house appointed him to represent that chamber's interests in a conference committee with the upper house, and he shrewdly arranged for the appointment of two dissenters to his committee, knowing that they would be required to advance the opinions of the lower house rather than their personal convictions. Thus he expected them to influence dissenters in the other chamber. If his account of what happened is correct, he was right, for the strategy worked.[28]

It is not difficult to accept Ottolenghe's version of events, as far as it goes. But it does not even approach the heart of the matter. Why, for instance, did Georgia establish the Church of England at such a late date and why at all with so many dissenters in the assembly? First of all, the Church of England did have influential and dedicated supporters both in the assembly and in society at large, and they worked indefatigably to bring about establishment. Only two organized groups provided opposition—the Lutherans and the Congregationalists. The Presbyterians, who might have offered spirited resistance, did not have effective leadership in Savannah until Zubly arrived in 1760, two years later. Furthermore, the act reassured dissenters on three points. Anglican clergymen were forbidden to exercise "any Eclesiastical Law or Jurisdiction whatsoever," a matter of great importance because dissenters everywhere feared church courts.[29] Also, establishment did nothing to interfere with dissenting churches, and their members were free to conduct worship services as before. But there was a third, less obvious, but exceedingly substantive, comfort for dissenters. Churchwardens and vestrymen were to be elected each Easter Monday, and the law made all Georgia freeholders and householders (that is, most male taxpayers) eligible to vote, including dissenters. The Lutherans were a substantial majority in what the new law designated as St.

28. Details and quotations concerning the establishment are taken from an unsigned letter to the archbishop of Canterbury, read in committee Jan. 15, 1759, S.P.G. Papers, Ser. C, Pkg. 1, Pt. ii (L.C. reel 2, 17–25). The committee that assisted Ottolenghe in representing the Commons House's views consisted of James DeVeaux, William Francis, Henry Yonge, Noble Wimberly Jones, and John Milledge. *Col. Records of Ga.*, XIII, 294.

29. *Col. Records of Ga.*, XVIII, 271–272.

Matthew Parish. The law left them free to honor the letter of "establishment" while violating the intent, and they quickly set about doing just that, certainly with the knowledge and probably with the encouragement of the civil authorities in Savannah. From 1758 until about the spring of 1766, the Lutherans of St. Matthew met each Easter Monday at their big church in Ebenezer to choose their own church deacons for the coming year; after the elections a justice of the peace swore in the deacons as churchwardens and vestrymen.[30] Thus for a number of years this substantial body of dissenters wryly complied with the law by installing its own leadership under the titles of the "establishment" in St. Matthew. They ran matters completely to suit themselves with no more than a wink in the direction of Anglicanism.

It is probable that if the dissenters had not been assured of the right to vote, the establishment bill would never have passed. Early in the assembly's process of approving the measure, and before its success was assured, representatives from the German community approached Ottolenghe, the floor manager, and requested "Favours in the Bill as might give them Ease."[31] The process of permitting the Lutheran deacons to be churchwardens and vestrymen was doubtless the "favor" settled upon. In granting dissenters the vote in vestry elections, the assembly bypassed South Carolina's precedent (in which only Anglican churchmen could participate) and embraced instead the example of North Carolina, where dissenters enjoyed such rights. With the Lutherans early pacified, much effort was subsequently expended to persuade them that they were "of the Establishment."[32]

Had the Lutherans foreseen the events of the following fifteen years, they might well have united with the Congregationalists to defeat the establishment bill. But as long as Pastor Bolzius lived, the "arrangement" worked. At some time in 1766, a few months after Bolzius's death, it began to come apart. A large portion of what occurred was

30. *Americanisches Ackerwerk Gottes; oder zuverlässige Nachrichten, den Zustand der americanisch englischen und von salzburgischen Emigranten erbauten Pflanzstadt Ebenezer in Georgien betreffend, aus dorther eingeschikten glaubwürdigen Diarien genommen, und mit Briefen der dasigen Herren Prediger noch weiter bestättiget*, Pt. IV (Augsburg, 1767), 8–9; Muhlenberg, *Journals*, II, 625, 630, 644.

31. Unsigned letter to the archbishop of Canterbury, read in committee Jan. 15, 1759, S.P.G. Papers, Ser. C, Pkg. 1, Pt. ii (L.C. reel 2, 18).

32. Mass. Hist. Soc., *Procs.*, 1st Ser., IX (1866), 216.

doubtless the result of a series of accidents caused by the imprecise use of language in making out land grants and conveyances; but the Lutherans, ever suspicious, could not be sure. They suspected, and were finally convinced, that a small group of Anglican zealots in Savannah, probably consisting only of two well-placed men, was trying to take over Lutheran church properties and give them to the Anglican church. Ottolenghe was under heavy suspicion as one of the perpetrators. Shortly before Ottolenghe's death in the summer of 1775, no less a personage than Habersham, the council president, plainly implicated him in helping to arrange the wording of the grant for the Jerusalem Church property in Ebenezer so that it could be subject to Anglican seizure. Of that one instance of deliberate manipulation of legal language to their disadvantage, the Lutherans could very nearly be certain. And other incidents of the period from 1761 to 1775 led them to entertain additional doubts that seemed reasonable at the time. Habersham's statement was supported by a hornet's nest of hints and circumstantial suggestions pointing toward Ottolenghe. (Habersham also implied that one other influential person was involved.) It was ironic that Ottolenghe had always professed to be a great friend of the Georgia Germans; at length, it was concluded in the German community that he was indeed their friend so long as they did exactly as he said.[33]

We cannot be sure who Ottolenghe's helpful assistant in Savannah might have been, but evidence points to Henry Yonge. Yonge was a sponsor of the establishment act in the 1758 assembly, a member of the conference committee that approved its final form, a brother to the Anglican bishop of Norwich, a sometime church officer in Christ Church Parish, after 1771 a member of the council, a lawyer familiar with legal documents, and, most important of all, surveyor general of the province. As surveyor general, he was in a position to influence the language in which grants for property were written.

The event that set off the property disputes occurred on August 11, 1761, when Joseph Gibbons, a Presbyterian, "for Love and good Will I bear to Religion in General," bestowed upon the German Protestants living in and around Savannah a lot in the suburb of Yamacraw upon which to build a church. For the token sum of five shillings, he conveyed the property to six prominent Lutherans who were to act as

33. Muhlenberg, *Journals*, II, 602, 604, 607, 624, 629, 630, 681, 682.

trustees—Michael Switzer, Sigismond Bilts (Biltz), John Shick, Gaspar Gerbert, Frederick Herb, and Solomon Shad. The conveyance was not recorded until April 30, 1764, almost four years later. Its language was to cause much trouble, since it conveyed the property "for the use and Benefit of the German Protestants and their Successors," nowhere mentioning that the Protestants should be Lutherans.[34] Although that point had little apparent significance when the conveyance was written in 1761, it took on enormous meaning on February 20, 1767, when seven prominent Lutherans applied to join the Anglican church, stating that they represented 206 other like-minded Germans living in and around Savannah. Since after their change of religion they would still be German Protestants—but of the Anglican rather than the Lutheran persuasion—the wording of the conveyance would permit an easy transfer of property, as well as membership, to the Church of England. Among the seven petitioners who signed their names, two— Shick and Herb—were trustees to whom Gibbons had originally committed the lot. The petitioners informed the rector, vestry, and wardens of Christ Church Parish (one of whom was Yonge) that they already had a chapel fitted up, and the message was relayed to the London offices of the S.P.G., along with Christ Church's endorsement. It was proposed that an Anglican priest who spoke German should come to Georgia to minister to the would-be converts and to instruct the German children.[35] Few, if any, of the 213 petitioners completed their spiritual journey to Anglicanism, for when their paper reached the S.P.G. offices, the society availed itself of private information that reinforced its decision not to send a German-speaking priest to Georgia. The information came from a private person who reported that the petition had grown out of a dispute in the German community, apparently over either Pastor Lemke or Pastor Rabenhorst. In addition, the society was convinced that the Germans had enough money to support their own minister without assistance.[36]

34. Conveyance Book C, II, 805–806, Dept. of Archives and Hist., Atlanta, Ga.; Mass. Hist. Soc., *Procs.*, 1st Ser., IX (1866), 216.
35. Petition of German Protestants to the rector, churchwardens, and vestry of Christ Church, Savannah, Feb. 20, 1767, and letter of the rector, churchwardens, and vestry of Christ Church to the Rev. Dr. Burton, Feb. 23, 1767, S.P.G. Papers, Ser. C, Pkg. 7, Pt. iii (L.C. reel 16, 219–225).
36. Minutes of the Standing Committee, May 11, 1767, *ibid.*, Ser. E (L.C. reel 1).

The wording of Gibbons's conveyance was almost certainly an accident, since no one could have foreseen its consequences. But accident or not, it was pivotally important, for the Lutherans immediately saw that they had been cruelly lied to. All of the efforts made to convince them that they were "of the Establishment" were founded upon a sham, for as soon as an issue at law became involved, the law coldly regarded them as dissenters. Very quickly, the expedience of swearing in the Lutheran deacons under Anglican titles in St. Matthew Parish was discontinued. However, the distress caused by the imprecise wording of legal documents was only beginning.

In 1767 there began a second chain of events that convinced the Lutherans that their church stood to lose almost every piece of property it had. Several valuable tracts of land and their appurtenances were involved, two of them granted before the Anglican church was even established. In that year the Lutherans began to build an expensive brick church at Ebenezer—a structure so solidly put together that it is still in use more than two hundred years later. It is the oldest public building in Georgia still standing (see figure 7, facing p. 193). The church took two years to build, and when it was finished, John Gaspar Wertsch, acting in his role as deacon, went down to Savannah to get a grant for the property upon which it stood. Yonge ordered the property surveyed in 1768, and the grant was registered in 1771. Since Wertsch was apparently the sole custodian of the grant document, and since many of the Germans could not have read the English very well anyway, it was some time before its meaning was grasped. The grant said that the Ebenezer property was to be used for the worship of God "according to the rites [and] Ceremonies of the Church of England."[37] A rigorous investigation of the matter was slow in coming and did not achieve decisive focus until 1774. However, when it was completed, it was clear that not only was the church property and cemetery at Ebenezer reserved for the Anglican church, but every piece of Lutheran church property in Georgia, except the little church at Zion and a new lot on Wright Square in Savannah that had been bought in 1771, was at least arguably subject to annexation by the Anglican establishment. The threatened properties included the church and land at Goshen, the church and land at Bethany, and the mill system built at huge ex-

37. Register of Grants Book H, 56, registered Apr. 2, 1771, Surveyor General Department, Office of the Secretary of State, Atlanta, Ga.

pense outside Ebenezer, which helped fund Lutheran churches and schools, the houses and salaries of ministers and schoolmasters, and the assistance provided to widows, orphans, the sick, and elderly.[38]

The full realization of what had happened could not have come to the Georgia Lutherans at a worse time. For when they finally understood their predicament, their two pastors, Triebner and Rabenhorst, were locked in their bitter dispute that split the community into large factions. There was concern that Triebner would apply to the bishop of London for holy orders, be ordained deacon and priest in the Anglican church, and then take over the property. Some persons professed also to have doubts concerning Rabenhorst, although it was Triebner who was most under suspicion because of his special relationship with Ottolenghe. Ottolenghe had in fact repeatedly proposed to him that the "dispute could be settled more agreeably and with greater impartiality by a number of *gentlemans* in Savanna rather than in Ebenezer." In addition, Triebner, Wertsch, and forty of their supporters had petitioned Governor Wright and the council for help, a process regarded by some as inviting outside intervention. In time, however, such appeals became absolutely necessary; accordingly, urgent representations were made by Lutheran leaders to Wright, Chief Justice Stokes, Habersham, and Councillor Clement Martin for aid in getting the legal papers rewritten to secure the property to the Lutherans. All four men were warmly sympathetic. Governor Wright gave his "word of honor" that it would be done. The property was indeed retained, although it is not clear whether the documents were actually changed or whether the beginning of the Revolution rendered the issue moot.[39]

That such an unfortunate series of complications would embitter the Lutheran community and touch the sensibilities of other Georgians was in no way apparent early in 1758 when the establishment act was passed. For although the measure was not strong enough to please Ottolenghe entirely, the fact that it had its strongest support in the

38. *Ibid.*; also Register of Grants Book B, 518 (Feb. 2, 1761), for Bethany; *ibid.*, 500 (Jan. 16, 1761) and Plat Book C, 25, for Goshen; Register of Grants Book A, 268 (Jan. 12, 1757); Register of Grants Book B, 149 (Sept. 20, 1759); *ibid.*, 150 (Sept. 20, 1759); and Register of Grants Book A, 415 (July 25, 1757). The latter 4 grants comprised the 1,025 acres of the Lutheran mill property. Surveyor General Dept., Office of the Sec. of State. Also see Muhlenberg, *Journals*, II, 599, 600, 602, 605, 606, 620, 627, 628, 629.
39. Muhlenberg, *Journals*, II, 601, 602, 604, 606, 631, 678–681, 684.

popularly elected Commons House of Assembly suggests that most Georgians were satisfied with it. In addition to what it said about religion, it had beneficial civil implications. The parishes created by the act were also subdivisions of government. Even in parishes where there were no Anglican churches, and that always included the majority, the vestrymen and wardens were civil officers who had important things to do. In Christ Church, they were justices of the peace, superintendents of the watch, supervisors of fire protection, overseers of sanitation, and supervisors of the cemetery. They levied church taxes and used the money both to help run the Anglican church and to assist the poor. In parishes where there was no Anglican church, we might assume that all the money collected was for poor relief, although it cannot be proved that any money was ever collected in such places.

The act of 1758 divided Georgia into eight parishes. After the English fashion, each comprised a fairly large geographical area. Christ Church Parish thus not only embraced the town of Savannah but extended some distance up and down the Savannah River and south and southwesterly to the Ogeechee. St. Matthew Parish included Ebenezer and much of Georgia's German population. Above St. Matthew lay St. George Parish, which included the district of Halifax and where, in a little more than a decade, Queensborough would become a settlement of importance. St. Paul lay above St. George, with Augusta as its principal settlement. South of the Ogeechee River were St. Philip, St. John (including Midway, Sunbury, and much of the colony's Congregationalist population), and St. Andrew. St. James in 1758 consisted of Great and Little St. Simons islands, with Frederica as the principal settlement. (In 1765 Jekyll Island was added to St. James.) Four additional parishes were created in 1765 in the area between the Altamaha and the St. Marys rivers—St. David, St. Patrick, St. Thomas, and St. Mary. These latter four were scantily populated before the American Revolution.

At the moment of establishment, there were only two functioning Anglican churches in the province—Christ Church in Savannah and St. Paul's in Augusta. Their vestries could levy no more than £30 annually in taxes, and vestries in parishes without a church could levy no more than £10.[40] The sums raised by such taxes could never be large.

40. *Col. Records of Ga.*, XVIII, 267–269.

In fact, the citizens of Georgia never bore the entire cost of establishment at any time, because the Society for the Propagation of the Gospel continued to contribute to the support of Anglican clergymen, and Parliament in the 1770s also supplied some funds.

Vestry elections were regularly held on Easter Mondays. In 1769 the church commissioners scheduled them at the parish courthouse for St. George Parish, at the muster field in Sunbury for St. John, at the muster field for St. Andrew, and at the fort in Frederica for St. James. The Lutherans of St. Matthew, having by then had their fill of their earlier arrangement, no longer permitted the election to be held in Jerusalem Church. It was scheduled at the Ebenezer muster field.[41] In Christ Church and St. Paul parishes, elections were by law held in the church.

The legal position of the Anglican church after 1758, as well as the fact that it was always an important religious force, assured that the quality of its clergymen would be a matter of importance. Little need be said of the first Anglican pastor in Savannah, the Reverend Henry Herbert. Authorized to perform religious and ecclesiastical office in the province, he arrived with the first settlers, served briefly, fell ill, and died at sea on a voyage back to England.[42] The first minister to enjoy a stipend from the S.P.G. was Samuel Quincy, a Bostonian who had been ordained priest by the bishop of Carlisle. Quincy was the first in a succession of unsatisfactory Anglican ministers resident in the province. Under his leadership, the believers who communicated at the altar of the Church of England reportedly numbered only three at one juncture, while much of the population enjoyed itself at Sunday shooting. In addition, Quincy shocked many persons by abandoning his duties altogether, turning them over to a wheelwright who for six months read the prayers, comforted the sick, and buried the dead. Not surprisingly, all of this constituted "behaviour the Trustees could not excuse." Quincy, realizing that he had sacrificed his moral authority, discovered an impediment to further service—his wife refused to join him in Georgia. He finally asked to be relieved of his duties and also requested the names of those Georgians who had criticized him. The trustees readily granted the first request but charitably declined the second, resting his resignation upon his own desires. Quincy's rector-

41. Advertisement of the church commissioners, *Ga. Gaz.*, Jan. 18, 1769.
42. *Col. Records of Ga.*, XXXII, 49–50.

ship, begun in 1733, thus ended under a cloud in 1735.[43] He later served with distinction in South Carolina.

Quincy was succeeded by the Reverend John Wesley, whose famous ministry was to end unhappily within two years. Wesley arrived on February 5, 1736, and his chief concern was the salvation of his own soul. He thought that through instructing Indians uncorrupted by compromising teachers, uncommitted to any church party, and unskilled in devious argumentation, he might arrive at truth. The Reverend Benjamin Ingham, who arrived with Wesley, joined with the Moravians and actually succeeded in teaching a few Indians. However, Wesley's desire to serve the Indians was never more than a wish, for he found himself in Savannah involved in a parochial charge that included all the usual duties—reading prayers, celebrating Holy Communion, conducting weddings and baptisms, exhorting the faithful, comforting the sick and sorrowing, and burying the dead.[44] His ministry, technically divided between Savannah, Frederica, and other parts of the province, was mostly carried out in Savannah. Wesley brought energy to his duties, but his enthusiasm offended some persons. Even before he had left England, the trustees were aware that he was associated with the Methodist sect, although Wesley was a strict adherent to the Anglican communion. The Methodists were suspect partly because they considered themselves guided by the Holy Ghost in every step they took.[45] In Georgia, influenced by the Moravians as well as by his own prior associations, Wesley believed that God directed each detail of living and dying. In November 1736, for example, after burying the only son of a grief-stricken woman, he concluded that God, in His mercy, had rescued her from debilitating sorrow by sending her a violent fit of rheumatism.[46]

Wesley's churchmanship pleased some Georgians but confounded others. He conducted his ministry according to what he thought were the customs of the primitive church, holding frequent celebrations of Holy Communion for a people accustomed to receiving it no more

43. McPherson, ed., *Journal of Egmont*, 103, 207–208, 216; *Col. Records of Ga.*, XXIX, 165.

44. Of course, John Wesley later became one of the most influential leaders in religious history. Scholars have sometimes reasoned that the power of his later ministry derived from the character-building disappointments and misfortunes he experienced in Georgia. Wesley, *Journal*, ed. Curnock, I, 174n.

45. McPherson, ed., *Journal of Egmont*, 107.

46. Wesley, *Journal*, ed. Curnock, I, 298.

than two or three times a year. He baptized by Trine Immersion, in which the individual presented was submerged totally in the water three times, once for each member of the Holy Trinity. Asked to baptize a child of one of the bailiffs of Savannah, he was displeased when the parents refused to have the child immersed. He said, however, that he would merely pour the water if the parents certified that the infant was weak. The mother replied, "Nay, the child is not weak; but I am resolved it shall not be dipped." [47] The child was then baptized by another person. In another incident, a young Englishman who worked in the storehouse in Savannah presented himself to Wesley as a candidate for matrimony, and although the clergyman did not actually oppose the marriage, he declined to perform the ceremony. The young man, thwarted by vague objections, got himself quickly to Ebenezer, where he sought to be married by the German pastors. [48]

However, it was neither Wesley's strictness nor his concept of duty that finally undid his ministry in Georgia. A group of devout persons in his flock came to him often for prayer, communion, and study, and among them was Sophie Hopkey, a niece by marriage of Thomas Causton's. Causton was at the height of his powers. Miss Hopkey was eighteen years old, and Wesley was thirty-three. That he was smitten with her and fell in love appears probable from his *Journal*. Suddenly, however, she married another man, William Williamson. When she subsequently appeared at the altar to receive Holy Communion, Wesley denied it to her, arguing legalistically that she had not complied with the requirement that those intending to communicate had to give advance notice in writing to the officiating clergyman. "I foresaw the consequences well," Wesley wrote, "but remembered the promise in the Epistle for the day, 'God is faithful, who will not suffer you to be tempted above that ye are able; but will with the temptation also make a way to escape, that ye may be able to bear it.' " [49]

The consequences were serious and swift. On August 8, 1737, only one day after Mrs. Williamson had been turned away, a warrant went out to all constables, tithingmen, and others in Savannah to arrest the priest and bring him before one of the bailiffs on the charge of defaming Mrs. Williamson. Her husband asked damages of £1,000. Wesley was apprehended the following day. He denied that he had defamed

47. *Ibid.*, 210–211.
48. Urlsperger, ed., *Ausführliche Nachrichten*, I, 999.
49. Wesley, *Journal*, ed. Curnock, I, 376.

Mrs. Williamson and declined to comment upon his actions, since that was an ecclesiastical matter and, as he stated, "I could not acknowledge their power to interrogate me." [50] A grand jury under the influence of Causton subsequently indicted him on ten counts. Wesley, doubting that he could get a fair trial in Savannah—and, in fact, unable to get an early trial at all, although he requested one—posted a notice announcing his intention to depart. Legal actions were immediately taken to prevent his leaving, but on the evening of December 2, 1737, he quietly slipped away by boat.

Until Wesley's ministry was spoiled by the clash with Causton's family, it gave satisfaction to many of his parishioners and was probably acceptable to most. The year after his departure, William Stephens praised him as a man "of unquestionable Abilitys to perform the Ministry committed to his Charge; and I never observd any due Respect wanting towards him from the generality of the people, till that unhappy Breach between him and Mr. Caustons Family." [51]

John's brother Charles fared little better during his short stay in Georgia. Arriving in 1736 with John, Charles had been appointed minister at Frederica, secretary to Oglethorpe, and secretary of Indian affairs. At Frederica he was caught up in a damaging dispute into which his inexperience betrayed him. Two women confessed to Charles that they had committed adultery with Oglethorpe, and he believed them. They then went to Oglethorpe and told him that Wesley was spreading the story that they had had intercourse with him. Oglethorpe, too, believed this tale. Charles Wesley's usefulness in Georgia was at that moment reduced, and although the relationship between him and Oglethorpe was later repaired, his short career in Georgia was not a happy one. After less than six months, he willingly left the colony on July 26, 1736. [52]

John Wesley was succeeded by Whitefield, who came to Georgia in 1738 presumably to conduct a ministry. Yet the most remarkable thing he did was to found Bethesda orphanage. When Whitefield came, he was only a deacon in the Church of England, which meant that he could preach, baptize, and solemnize marriages but could not celebrate Holy Communion. In order to equip himself for a full minis-

50. *Ibid.*, 377.

51. *Col. Records of Ga.*, XXII, Pt. i, 167.

52. Wesley, *Journal*, ed. Curnock, I, 188–189n; *The Journal of the Rev. Charles Wesley M.A. Sometime Student of Christ Church, Oxford. The Early Journal, 1736–1739* (London, 1909), 7–67.

try, he was obliged to return to England, for there was no bishop in America to ordain him priest. On his first visit Whitefield was only in Georgia from May to August 1738, manifesting "his great Abilities in the Ministry" with sermons that greatly moved his congregation. The people overflowed the courthouse, where the services were then held. He left for England in late August, and the Reverend William Norris arrived in Savannah the following October, so that the province was served by a priest while Whitefield was away.[53]

Once Whitefield arrived in London, the trustees, who had desired him to be a parish clergyman in Georgia, began to perceive that he was more interested in establishing an orphanage there. Even so, no conflict between it and an active ministry was at first foreseen. The trustees agreed that when Whitefield returned to Georgia, Norris would be transferred to Frederica, and Whitefield would be missionary to Savannah at a salary of £50 a year. The trustees also commissioned Whitefield to embark upon a preaching journey in England to take him through the dioceses of London and of Bath and Wells to raise money for the Georgia orphanage. In the meantime, he had been ordained by the bishop of Gloucester in the Cathedral Church of Christ in Oxford.

As Whitefield began his English tour, he discovered that many churches and pulpits were closed to him. He had preached widely in England before his first journey to Georgia, lambasting the Anglican clergy as unconverted heathens and hypocrites, and he had done all this with an eloquence that stunned the innocent and guilty alike. (The following year, in a characterization more typical than wise, he continued his rhetorical habits, saying that a religious book written by the bishop of London was sufficient to send thousands to hell.) As English church doors closed against him, Whitefield increasingly took to preaching out-of-doors, an art he perfected. After his fund-raising journey was completed, Whitefield appeared once more before the trustees and, to their astonishment, returned their commission for raising funds, proclaiming it worthless. He also rejected any salary as minister for Savannah while claiming the trustees' grant of five hundred acres for the orphan house, which by then was already functioning in Savannah, in a limited way, under the direction of Habersham.[54]

In Savannah, meanwhile, Whitefield's followers were voicing com-

53. *Col. Records of Ga.*, IV, 148, 150, 212.
54. *Ibid.*, XXXIII, 21, IV, 529, V, 166.

plaints against Norris. Habersham, a layman who had read public prayers during the weeks after Whitefield's departure and before Norris's arrival, began to make public odious comparisons between Whitefield and Norris, to the discredit of the latter. It seemed that Norris's character "must be pulled to Pieces and mangled, that another, whom they are fond of, may shine with greater Lustre." To show contempt for the minister, another of Whitefield's friends attended Norris's services and read a book as he preached. When Whitefield himself returned to Savannah, he charged Norris with promulgating heresy during his absence. He also denied him Holy Communion for playing cards "when he should be going about doing his duty."[55]

So intense was the bitter feeling that Stephens was relieved when Norris left for Frederica to assume that ministerial charge. While serving there in 1739 and 1740, Norris acquired a reputation for bad temper and stubborn conduct; his reputation reached a low point when a German maid who had served him was found to be pregnant. There was conflicting testimony concerning the identity of the father of the child, but many persons in Frederica blamed Norris and ostracized him. Some couples merely proclaimed themselves married rather than have their union solemnized by one they believed to be a fornicator. To some Norris was guilty beyond doubt; to others he was merely a dogged, sour, captious, and disagreeable man.[56] Few lamented his departure in 1740. His exit left Georgia once more with but a single Anglican minister—Whitefield. (The Reverend Edward Dyson, a military chaplain who at one time performed religious duties, had become a drunkard and died.)[57]

Whitefield himself was not to serve long at Savannah. His appointment was dated May 16, 1739, and a year and a half later, on December 29, 1740, he gave up his parochial duties, finding them "inconsistent with my other affairs." He had informed the trustees almost a year earlier that he intended to serve a limited time. He had, in fact, much disturbed them with menacing letters sent to London, threatening to inform the world "how little is to be seen for all the money good people had contributed" for Georgia.[58] The vexation that the

55. *Ibid.*, IV, 219, 229–230, 528–530, V, 377.
56. Phillipps Coll., 14206, 190, 294; *Col. Records of Ga.*, V, 501. Also see Phillipps Coll., 14206, 292.
57. *Col. Records of Ga.*, IV, 42, 198–199, 414, V, 80, 171.
58. *Ibid.*, I, 348; *Whitefield's Journal, 1737–1741*, 503; *Col. Records of Ga.*, V, 291.

trustees felt at Whitefield's threats culminated in a meeting assembled to consider what their attitude toward him should be. Dr. John Burton, one of the original trustees, complained that Whitefield was attempting to be "totally independent of every body." Whitefield had refused a salary as clergyman in Savannah, Burton believed, so that he could resign as parish minister as soon as it suited his fancy. Burton had never regarded Whitefield as an honest man after he accepted a commission to solicit money, actually collected some, and then put down the commission as worthless. That procedure had rendered Whitefield unaccountable to the trustees for dispersing the collected funds. Burton was also convinced that the sole purpose of Whitefield's orphanage was to breed Methodists. Another trustee called Whitefield a "fool" but thought it would be ill-advised to reply to him in angry terms, because he might then abandon the orphan house idea and throw the orphans back upon the trustees. He felt that Whitefield was sincere, but too enthusiastic. Most of the trustees believed that Whitefield would not denounce them to the public until he received an answer to his letter.[59]

By the time Whitefield stepped down from his pastorate, his dream of an orphan house had been realized in the countryside twelve miles outside Savannah. On November 3, 1740, a procession of wagons and people on horseback and foot evacuated the temporary facility in Savannah and moved to the rural location. A collection of orphans had been assembled from all over Georgia and from the Eastern seaboard as far north as Pennsylvania. In establishing Bethesda Orphan House, Whitefield created the institution that he served happily for the remainder of his life. His electrifying preaching was thereafter done in part to solicit funds for it. Toward the end of his life he declared that for nearly thirty years he had been called by Providence to be a "presbyter at large," that is, a traveling preacher.[60] The funds collected

59. *Col. Records of Ga.*, V, 332–334.

60. George Whitefield, *A Letter to His Excellency Governor Wright, giving an Account of the Steps taken relative to the converting the Georgia Orphan-House into a College; together with the Literary Correspondence that passed upon that Subject between his Grace the Archbishop of Canterbury and the Reverend Mr. Whitefield. To which also is annexed the Plan and Elevation of the present and intended Buildings and Orphan-House Lands adjacent* (London, 1768), 9. For an interpretation of Whitefield's reasons for establishing Bethesda, see Neil J. O'Connell, O.F.M., "George Whitefield and Bethesda Orphan-House," *Ga. Hist. Qtly.*, LIV (1970), 41–62. O'Connell argues that not only did the orphanage serve Whitefield's own purposes, but that Georgia might not have needed it. An

meant much to Bethesda, but Bethesda also meant much to him. To justify his preaching journeys, which involved unwelcome intrusions into the parishes and congregations of other ministers, an itinerant had to have a charitable cause for which to solicit support. Bethesda was Whitefield's cause.

At Bethesda itself, Whitefield's friends devoted themselves intensely to what they believed were his principles. While many of the people there were at least technically Anglicans, it seemed to persons in Savannah who favored the Church of England that they were destructive dissenters. To Whitefield's followers the central difference between themselves and other Christians was a matter not of creed or theology but of rapturous experience arising from conversion. Whitefield was a preacher who stirred passions and moved men and women to emotional upheavals. His converts valued those experiences as assurances that they had achieved the truest religious condition. Dr. Burton had asserted that Whitefield desired the orphan house as a place to indoctrinate Methodists, and to devoted Anglicans in Savannah, Bethesda sometimes seemed a fortress from which hostile dissenters attacked the Church of England in retaliation for its suspicions about the dissenters. For example, when Whitefield's successor arrived in Savannah in late 1741, the leaders at Bethesda tested him severely. The minister was the Reverend Christopher Orton, a man of twenty-four who had been ordained only three months earlier. He arrived on December 3, 1741, in company with a clerk, Thomas Bosomworth, and three days later began his duties as Anglican pastor. His efforts much pleased Stephens. "Wild Sectaries," however, were soon spreading word that Orton had not truly been called to preach the Gospel. On January 11, 1742, after only thirty-nine days in Georgia, Orton was beset by Habersham and four others from Bethesda, who interrogated him brutally. He failed to convince them of his soundness, and after their questioning, they charged that he was not a Christian. They denounced him for preaching false doctrine, for not understanding the articles of the Church of England, and for daring to preach without having been called by the Holy Spirit.[61] Habersham and Jonathan Barber, a Presbyterian minister at the orphanage, were fined in court

orphanage was already in operation at Ebenezer, and the trustees had earlier devised other methods of caring for orphans.

61. *Col. Records of Ga.*, XXXIII, 179–180; Coulter, ed., *Journal of Stephens*, I, 29–30.

in Savannah for their part in the episode, and the trustees in London rebuked Habersham, expressing dismay that a man of so much misguided zeal should have the care of children. The trustees ordered the magistrates in Savannah to undertake frequent visits to Bethesda to observe the instruction of the children and to remove them if they were being improperly taught.[62] Orton's ministry was brief. He died only nine months after his installation, a victim of the plague of 1742.[63]

For a time there was no Anglican clergyman in Georgia, and services were conducted by a lay reader. But by the end of 1742, Bosomworth, the clerk who had come with Orton, decided to go back to England to receive ordination. Until then he had enjoyed an acceptable reputation. Shortly after his departure, however, it became known that he was a man of serious shortcomings and that his indiscretions had been concealed by his friend, Orton. With Orton dead, Bosomworth's imperfections came to light, and by the time he returned to Georgia, he was a tarnished man.[64] He nevertheless officiated as minister for more than a year, in the meantime marrying Mary Musgrove-Matthews, an Indian woman of mixed blood who had previously served the provincial government and who was intent upon pressing for payment. After a time Bosomworth cast aside his clerical calling altogether and sued for his wife's claims. Together they created an uproarious disturbance in Savannah, which before it was settled, caused untold consternation and resulted in the disgrace of Bosomworth.[65]

This unattractive priest was succeeded by the Reverend Bartholomew Zouberbuhler, the only colonial Anglican clergyman who enjoyed unqualified success in Georgia and the only Anglican minister to have a long tenure. Zouberbuhler declined to be drawn into tumults, and for twenty years (1746 to 1766), he retained the affections of his people. He was not an Englishman but came from St. Gall, Switzerland, Zubly's birthplace. Zouberbuhler's father was pastor of a Swiss congregation in South Carolina, and the younger man early attracted the notice of Alexander Garden, the bishop of London's commissary in South Carolina. Zouberbuhler went to England and was ordained deacon and priest in 1745 in the Chapel Royal at Whitehall. In 1746

---

62. Coulter, ed., *Journal of Stephens*, I, 37; *Col. Records of Ga.*, XXX, 491–492.

63. Coulter, ed., *Journal of Stephens*, I, 119. Orton died Aug. 12, 1742.

64. *Ibid.*, 228.

65. See E. Merton Coulter, "Mary Musgrove, 'Queen of the Creeks': A Chapter of Early Georgia Troubles," *Ga. Hist. Qtly.*, XI (1927), 1–30.

he came to Georgia to take up his duties in Savannah. He arrived in the *Judith*, the same vessel that brought Pastor Lemke to the Salzburgers and aboard which Causton had died while returning from England.[66] Spotted fever had taken a heavy toll on the vessel, and during a crisis when a part of the crew was incapacitated, Zouberbuhler had navigated the ship. For twenty years afterward he steered the affairs of the Anglican church in Savannah with a skillful hand. In 1750 he reported an increase in real religion in his parish, while lamenting his inability to serve more people than those in his immediate congregation.[67] Also in 1750 he at last moved public worship out of the courthouse and into Savannah's first real church—a move postponed because the building had taken six years to construct. In 1765 the structure was expanded with additional pews and a gallery to hold the organ given by Edward Barnard.[68]

Zouberbuhler was much esteemed in his own time. His parishioners held him in high regard, and the trustees were afraid of losing him. "He has perform'd his Duty so well hitherto, and so much better than any of his Predecessors, that the Loss of him could not easily be repair'd."[69] In the twelfth year of his ministry, the Church of England was established, and by the time of his death on December 10, 1766, he had proved to be not only a faithful custodian of his parish but also a prudent manager of worldly affairs. He was a man of some wealth, and a substantial part of his estate went toward educating the slaves on his plantation.[70]

Zouberbuhler's final years in Savannah were trying. His health steadily deteriorated, and six years before his death, he knew that he ought to lay down the rectorship of Christ Church Parish. Yet he would not leave his pulpit until a replacement arrived. For a brief

66. *Col. Records of Ga.*, XXXIII, 311–312, XXV, 8.

67. Bartholomew Zouberbuhler to the Rev. Dr. Philip Bearcroft, Dec. 20, 1750, S.P.G. Papers, Ser. B, Vol. 18, No. 197.

68. *Col. Records of Ga.*, XXIV, 238, XXVI, 13–14. See also Gawin L. Corbin, "The First List of Pew Holders of Christ-Church, Savannah," *Ga. Hist. Qtly.*, L (1966), 74–86. Not all of the pew holders were Anglican. James Edward Powell, Lewis Johnson [Johnston], and Robert Bolton were Presbyterians, as probably were others. Perhaps some status was attached to having a pew, and in a practical sense, the holder was assured of a seat from which to hear visiting preachers.

69. *Col. Records of Ga.*, XXXI, 249–250.

70. Estate of Bartholomew Zouberbuhler, Apr. 21, 1767, Inventory Book F, 256. The estate was appraised at £2,583 18s. 6d., but the total figure should actually be larger, since real estate holdings were not counted.

moment in 1761 one appeared—the Reverend William Duncanson, sent by the S.P.G. But a single interview was enough to convince the vestry and the wardens that Duncanson was unfit, and Zouberbuhler was forced to remain in his post.[71] Meanwhile, St. Paul Parish, learning of Duncanson's availability, called him to Augusta, where the rectorship was vacant. Duncanson was not there six weeks before he was disgraced as a drunkard and a vile talker. He was shortly under a peace warrant from a man he challenged to fight, attempted to horsewhip, and menaced with a loaded pistol. A little later he was accused of seeking to debauch his landlord's daughter. Denying everything except that he drank moderately in the evenings to lift his spirits, Duncanson passed unlamented from the scene.[72]

It is easy to sympathize with the vestry at Augusta in its willingness to accept a man who had been rejected elsewhere. St. Paul Parish had had difficulty in getting and keeping ministers ever since its founding in 1750. The first had been the Reverend Jonathan Copp, a Connecticut native and Yale graduate who had arrived in 1751. Within four months of his installation, he was the object of complaints, and he presided poorly over a troubled scene. Following his departure in 1756, the rectorship was vacant for several years, and the church and the parsonage, both erected at much expense, were given over to nonparochial uses. During Indian wars and alarms both buildings sheltered refugees from the backcountry. By 1761 the church was in such poor condition that it appeared beyond repair, but in time services were held there again.[73] The desperation of the St. Paul vestry was evident not only in the Duncanson affair but in arrangements made following his departure. The Reverend William Teale was employed in 1764, as there was no other candidate at hand. Teale served only four or five months and surrendered the parish reluctantly upon the arrival of the Reverend Samuel Frink. Teale, it developed, might not have been a proper minister at all, since the legitimacy of his ordination was in doubt.[74]

71. Vestry minutes of Christ Church Parish, Savannah, Sept. 4, 1761, S.P.G. Papers, Ser. C, Pkg. 7, Pt. iii (L.C. reel 16, 103).

72. Vestry of St. Paul, Augusta, to S.P.G., Feb. 8, 1762, S.P.G. Papers, Ser. C, Pkg. 7, Pt. iii (L.C. reel 16, 109–112); William Duncanson to Bearcroft, May 20, 1762, *ibid.* (L.C. reel 16, 88–95).

73. *Col. Records of Ga.*, XXVI, 301, XIII, 613.

74. Frink to Burton, June 1, 1765, S.P.G. Papers, Ser. C, Pkg. 7, Pt. iii (L.C. reel 16, 131–134); William Teale to Burton, June 4, 1765, *ibid.* (L.C. reel 16,

The Reverend Samuel Frink was a convert to Anglicanism who demonstrated all the unattractive aspects of a convert's zeal. He was the son of a Congregational minister in New England and a graduate of Harvard, class of 1758. When as a young man his intention to convert to Anglicanism became known, he assailed those who criticized him as "enemies spiteful and malicious, such as no Man would suppose could possibly exist on this Side the infernal Regions. . . . I would remind such Persons, that after Death, comes the Judgment."[75] This excessive language gives an accurate clue to his temperament. He had no high regard for his assignment in Augusta; yet he gave no great offense during his service there. In January 1767 he moved downriver to Savannah, where he was given the pulpit left vacant by the death of Zouberbuhler. There, after a year, he tartly declared that he had been better off financially in Augusta. Hoping to get money from the assembly for the clergy of the established church, he began consulting with members of the Commons House to move "this thing."[76]

After a time and with even greater determination, Frink undertook something that no clergyman in Georgia had ever done before and that none dared ever to do again. The surplice fees for conducting religious services were not large, but if they were his (as Frink believed), he wanted them. His reasoning was simple. He was rector of the established church in Christ Church Parish and was therefore the "official" clergyman; thus all pay for services should go to him, even though dissenting ministers may have officiated. Frink had solicited precedents regarding wedding fees to support his contention. In North Carolina, Anglican clergymen collected fees for weddings they had not performed, and even in Georgia, Governor Wright seems to have felt that Anglican clergymen should have preference in performing weddings. Where he could, the governor made out wedding licenses to Anglican clergymen, who sometimes endorsed them over to dissenters in exchange for half the fee. This practice, however, was not

---

136–138); vestry of St. Paul, Augusta, to Burton, Nov. 12, 1764, *ibid.* (L.C. reel 16, 122–123).

75. Samuel Frink, *The Marvellous Works of Creation and Providence, Illustrated* (Boston, 1763), v–vi, quoted in Clifford K. Shipton, *Sibley's Harvard Graduates: Biographical Sketches of Those Who Attended Harvard College in the Classes 1756–1760, with Bibliographical and Other Notes,* XIV (Boston, 1968), 271.

76. Frink to Burton, Jan. 7, 1768, S.P.G. Papers, Ser. C, Pkg. 7, Pt. iii (L.C. reel 16, 204–207).

universal, for there were not enough Anglican clergymen in Georgia to make it so.

Shrewdly, Frink did not move to establish firm local precedents on his own behalf. He took an indirect route. The sexton of the Anglican church was a minor official responsible for, among other things, having graves dug and funeral bells rung. The assembly, and later the wardens and vestry, had indicated fees for him in connection with these two activities; so Frink moved to seek payment for his sexton for duties not performed. Two lawsuits were brought, and one of them, intended for a precedent, was tried before a Court of Conscience in Savannah, apparently on the first Thursday in May 1769. It involved one of the most prominent men in the province, Joseph Gibbons, Jr., a wealthy member of a powerful family and a Presbyterian. Gibbons's connection with the case grew out of a kindness on his own part, and until the suit was filed, the whole matter had not touched his vital interests. A poor man had died, and Gibbons, for charitable reasons, had taken care of him during his last illness and at his death had had him buried at his own expense. At the funeral the sexton of the Presbyterian church had rung the Presbyterian funeral bell. On April 12, 1769, a legal summons went out for Gibbons, requiring him to appear before the Court of Conscience to answer charges that he owed fees to Frink, who presumably wished to collect the money and remit it to his own sexton.[77]

In the Court of Conscience, Frink appeared in person and sought to have Gibbons pay two charges: 3s. 6d. for digging the poor man's grave, and 3s. 6d. for ringing the funeral bell. Gibbons did not contest the fee for digging the grave. There was only one cemetery for white Protestants in Savannah, and Frink's sexton had probably arranged for the grave to be dug. Gibbons did, however, refuse to pay the other fee, since the Anglican bell had not been rung at all, and no bell had been rung by the Anglican sexton.

Both the judge and the jury were subjects of comment following the trial. Ottolenghe, the judge, had unwisely declared his opinion on the merits of Frink's cause before the court ever met. The jurymen were William Ewen, Thomas Lee, and Jonathan Peat. Ewen was a dependable supporter of the Church of England and was at that moment one of the vestrymen of the parish. He had never served before

77. At about the same time, Frink brought a second suit, this one against a ship captain who had buried a seaman in Savannah as a dissenter.

on a Court of Conscience jury. Thomas Lee was the clerk of the Anglican church. Ewen and Lee voted a judgment in Frink's favor, leaving Peat, a local taverner, in the minority. Ottolenghe quickly showed that the case was indeed a precedent by asserting that the sexton had a right to fees for burials anywhere in the parish whether he attended or not, even if they were on private plantations. Ottolenghe added that dissenters had no right to a bell of their own and said that Frink was to blame for not having pulled the dissenters' bell to the ground.[78]

For once the *Georgia Gazette* cast aside its impartiality and joined in the controversy. The newspaper account was more of an editorial than a news item and no doubt reflected the views of printer James Johnston, who was probably a Presbyterian. The item read:

If a parish sexton is entitled to a fee for every burial, it will be a double hardship upon such parishes as are chiefly inhabited by Dissenters, such as St. Matthew's, St. John's, and St. Andrew's parishes. And if any Justice should have a right to pick a jury of choice, he is more than morally sure that they concurred with him in prejudging the matter before it comes to a hearing; a trial in that case will be worse than a mere formality.

It is also thought, that to decide such a matter is above the jurisdiction of the lowest court in the province; for though a suit for three shillings and sixpence comes properly enough within the compass of small and mean causes, yet to establish a precedent of this nature, that will be pleaded all over the province, is not a trifling matter.[79]

The *Gazette* predicted that, despite the ruling, many Georgians would refuse to pay people "that do no work for them."[80]

Zubly, already irritated that Frink had refused to officiate at the funeral of his child, rose to the attack. The two ministers had been polite when Frink first arrived, but after that Frink had shunned Zubly, refusing to walk beside him in funeral processions. In a public letter to Frink, Zubly stressed that the Presbyterians had a bell of their own. But "it seems we are not to make use of it unless we pay a fine of three shillings and sixpence for the non-usage of your's." Deploring Frink's haughtiness, Zubly recalled his felicitous relationship with the deceased Zouberbuhler. "Your worthy predecessor sometimes did not look it beneath him to accept of my services, and what his opinion was of me and my conduct on his dying-bed (which often makes us view

78. *Ga. Gaz.*, May 10, 1769; Zubly, *Letter to Frink*, unpaginated.
79. *Ga. Gaz.*, May 10, 1769.
80. *Ibid.*

things in a truer light) some worthy gentlemen still living may possibly remember." Zubly said he would have remained silent but for the ominous prospect that fees were about to be assessed against dissenters all over Georgia.[81] Indeed, other people interpreted the issue exactly as Zubly did, for the Commons House took up the quarrel and passed measures to give Presbyterians and Jews their own burial grounds. These actions would have removed non-Anglicans from the jurisdiction of the rector of Christ Church Parish. When the bills reached the upper house, consideration of both was postponed until a date in June when the assembly would not be sitting, the governor having by then prorogued it for the king's birthday. The upper house then passed a bill of its own that would open the existing cemetery to all persons except Roman Catholics and that would allow the Anglican rector 3s. 6d. when he attended funerals, 2s. 6d. when he did not. This measure made the lower house indignant. One assemblyman, an Anglican, moved that the bill "be thrown under the table." The lower house, however, mocking the earlier example of the upper chamber, instead scheduled the measure to come up on the king's birthday.[82]

Apparently, Frink was not disturbed by the uproar in the assembly, for even as the matter was debated there, he went ahead with a third suit, this time against a widow who had recently lost her husband. The outcome is not wholly clear, but the case appears to have been either dropped or thrown out of court.[83]

Opinions were indeed inflamed, but the proroguing of the assembly on May 10, 1770, before any final action could be taken, forestalled an immediate solution. During the following year the assembly was involved with other business, including a rancorous pre-Revolutionary dispute over the powers and prerogatives of the Commons House itself, a wrangle that in April 1771 resulted in the sudden dissolution of the assembly. Even so, hard feelings concerning the fees had not subsided. In July 1771 Noble Wimberly Jones, who had been Speaker, indicated that if the assembly were called again, its members would probably take some action. As for himself, he said, although he had not com-

81. Zubly, *Letter to Frink*, unpaginated.
82. Mass. Hist. Soc., *Procs.*, 1st Ser., IX (1866), 217; *Col. Records of Ga.*, XVII, 563, 575. For the passage of the Presbyterian burial bill, see *Col. Records of Ga.*, XV, 95–96, 100, 115, 137, 142, 151. For the passage of the Jewish burial bill, see *Col. Records of Ga.*, XV, 145–146, 149, 151–154, 165–166, 168, 172.
83. Zubly, *Letter to Frink*, unpaginated; Mass. Hist. Soc., *Procs.*, 1st Ser., IX (1866), 217.

mitted himself earlier, in the future the entreaties of his neighbors might prompt him to take a more active role than his best interests dictated. By that Jones meant that since he was already involved in a continuing dispute over colonial rights, he would prefer not to plunge into another area of controversy, but he might do so. As Jones communicated those views in a letter to Benjamin Franklin on July 8, 1771, Frink, far from backing down, was keeping up local pressures to collect on behalf of his sexton.[84]

He was never to feel the wrath of the assembly, however. It never sat again during his lifetime. When Jones gave his views on the matter, Frink had less than four months to live. He died at the age of thirty-six on October 4, 1771, after a short illness. It is of more than passing interest that even at the end of his tumultuous public life in Savannah, he retained the loyalty of his principal church officials and the affections of many people in Christ Church Parish. The church could not hold the mourners who appeared at his funeral.[85] Frink was buried in the church cemetery in Savannah under an epitaph proclaiming him "in life and manners grave and pius. In conversation pleasant and facetious. In heart sincere, of candid and gentle disposition. . . . But as his faith was built upon reason so his zeal was tempered with moderation. He particularly excelled in the great Christian graces of charity and hospitality."[86] This tribute is remarkable in its own right and affirms the truth of Dr. Samuel Johnson's famous dictum which holds that in lapidary inscriptions, a man is not upon oath.

Frink did win one victory for the Church of England in Georgia that could have been important had not the Revolution come. He goaded the church commissioners into setting aside glebe lands, which resulted in the establishing of a church in St. George Parish.[87] It also appeared that additional Anglican clergymen would soon be arriving. Indeed, the Reverend John Alexander, a former dissenter who had been or-

84. William B. Willcox *et al.*, eds., *The Papers of Benjamin Franklin*, XVIII (New Haven, Conn., 1974), 167–168, 171.

85. Noble Jones and William Ewen, churchwardens of Savannah, to S.P.G., Oct. 10, 1771, S.P.G. Papers, Ser. C, Pkg. 7, Pt. iii (L.C. reel 16, 180).

86. *Some Early Epitaphs in Georgia, Compiled by the Georgia Society of the Colonial Dames of America*, with a foreword and sketches by Mrs. Peter W. Meldrim (Durham, N.C., 1924), 110. The tombstone incorrectly gives the date of death as Oct. 4, 1773.

87. Frink to Burton, July 6, 1770, S.P.G. Papers, Ser. C, Pkg. 7, Pt. iii (L.C. reel 16, 163–166).

dained an Anglican priest, had already served a brief and unhappy ministry at Sunbury in St. John Parish; and when Frink died in October 1771, the Reverend Timothy Lowten had been attempting to serve St. John and occasionally St. Philip parishes since the previous April. When Frink died, Governor Wright was in England. After a delay Habersham, president of the council, in November 1771 placed Lowten in the vacant pulpit at Christ Church, leaving St. John again unserved. Lowten, a young man about whom opinions were divided, made only a faint mark in Savannah. He was dead by 1773.

Augusta in the meantime had been served by the Reverend Edward Ellington, but he left in 1770 to serve Bethesda as president. He was followed in Augusta by the Reverend James Seymour, formerly a Savannah schoolmaster who had gone to England to be ordained. With him had gone his relative and fellow schoolmaster, Alexander Findlay. When Findlay returned to Georgia, he was dissatisfied with arrangements made for him in St. George Parish and refused the assignment. Instead he took a parish in South Carolina.[88] St. George had never had a regular rector, and it did not get one until January 1774, when the Reverend John Holmes was installed. Holmes found that about half his flock professed to be Presbyterians, but he thought them to be poor ones at best, either ignorant of religion or badly instructed.[89]

The last minister of Christ Church Parish before the Revolution, succeeding Lowten, was the Reverend Haddon Smith. By 1774 revolutionary ferments were so sharp that Smith never officiated in circumstances that could be considered normal. For example, William Gibbons, a Presbyterian, advertised his wish to rent out the pew he held in Christ Church "during the Reign of the Rector."[90] Smith's tory principles probably offended Gibbons, who was among the Georgians protesting British policies. Several articles appeared in the *Georgia Gazette* denouncing Parliament's acts of 1774, and Smith answered them sharply under a pseudonym that did not hide his identity for long. The Provincial Congress tested him severely by ordering him to observe July 20, 1775, as a day of fasting, using such prayers as it should direct. When he declined, he was forbidden to officiate further in the church, and a layman was named to read prayers. A few days

88. Alexander Findlay to S.P.G., Sept. 2, 1771, *ibid.* (L.C. reel 16, 21–22).
89. John Holmes to S.P.G., Feb. 1, 1774, *ibid.* (L.C. reel 16, 24–26).
90. Advertisement of William Gibbons, *Ga. Gaz.*, Dec. 14, 1774.

later Smith and his family slipped down the river to Tybee Island and from there took a ship to Liverpool.[91]

Another priest, the Reverend John Rennie, had arrived in 1774 to instruct the late Zouberbuhler's slaves, the same duty done earlier by Cornelius Winter. Rennie also conducted services in St. Philip Parish. After Smith's flight, Rennie served some of the Christ Church parishioners, but he too was quickly in difficulty, because he adhered to the unaltered liturgy of the church. By mid-1775 invocations for the king and the royal family were unacceptable to those in actual power, and Rennie was forbidden to read prayers or to preach, although he continued to perform baptismal, matrimonial, and burial rites. Finally in 1777 Rennie, like Smith before him, gathered up his family and fled.[92]

In such ways the American Revolution drove all the most conspicuous ministers of the Church of England into flight. Seymour, a tory, was destined in time to abandon his pulpit in Augusta. The ministries of other sects were also in difficulty. After 1773 Osgood was dead, and his Congregational pulpit at Midway was vacant. Even the death of Rabenhorst at Ebenezer in 1776 did not heal the divisions there, and feelings against Triebner were such that, although he preached thereafter in the Lutheran community, he was afraid to officiate in Jerusalem Church.[93] Zubly was in trouble because of his seeming equivocations upon the subject of colonial rights. Only in the backcountry were some frontiersmen discovering a kind of faith and worship congenial to them. Two intrepid Baptist ministers, Daniel Marshall and Edmund Botsford, were beginning to gather Georgians into the Baptist fold.

Was Georgia different from the other southern provinces in matters of religion? Some of the same elements are found in all of the southern colonies. From Maryland southward, for example, the parishes of the Anglican church were rather large, and there were numerous vacant pulpits. In South Carolina in 1770 about half the parishes had no

91. Memorial of Haddon Smith, Jan. 15, 1784, Ga. Loyalist Claims, A.O. 13/36 a (microfilm at Dept. of Archives and Hist., Atlanta, Ga.); *Col. Records of Ga.*, XXXIX, 417.

92. Memorial of John Rennie, Mar. 31, 1783, Ga. Loyalist Claims, A.O. 13/36 a.

93. Andrew W. Lewis, ed., "Henry Muhlenberg's Georgia Correspondence," *Ga. Hist. Qtly.*, XLIX (1965), 433.

incumbents. Everywhere the backcountry was insufficiently churched, where it was churched at all. We find also that, with a good many exceptions, the citizens of other colonies wore their religion casually. In Maryland and Virginia religion was as much a social as a spiritual affair, perhaps more so. The church was a place where people saw their friends and neighbors each Sunday. In all the southern colonies there were a few good clergymen like Zouberbuhler, some bad ones like Frink, and some, like Seymour and Lowten, who were passable. There were many scheming or time-serving clerics but few as crafty as Frink, who in pursuit of his own interests risked bringing the wrath of the assembly down on the established church. Another shared characteristic is that the Anglican church in Georgia, as in other colonies, performed some of the functions of local government. The vestrymen were civil officials as well—justices of the peace, members of assembly, councillors, and royal officials.

In light of the problems of religion in Georgia, what was its impact upon the people and the society? A not inconsiderable number of colonists led godly and upright lives, and their faith made them hopeful if not quite happy. In addition, the philanthropic reasons for which, in part, Georgia was founded had a basis in religion, and many of the settlers who immigrated would not have done so had their freedom to worship not been assured. This was positively true of the Germans, the Quakers, and the Moravians and was possibly true of the Congregationalists. Religion also affected education and intellectual life. Some of the most important libraries were donated by people reputed to be religious and were run by pastors. The best schools in the German- as well as the English-speaking parts of the province operated under the supervision of religious leaders. Many of their teachers were clergymen or men who later became clergymen. Bethesda, both an educational center and a charitable organization, was founded and functioned as a militantly religious institution. The education of slaves grew out of the activities of Christians who desired that black people learn to read and write so as to share more fully in the Christian faith. In the ranks of such persons one would place Habersham, Knox, Ottolenghe, and, of course, Zouberbuhler.

Ultimately more important than any of these factors, religion made a difference in a crucial if intangible sense because Georgia was officially a Christian colony. In actual fact it always was; by law it was after 1758. Although the teachings of the Christian faith were not followed in those times to any greater degree than in any other, religion served as an exemplar and an arbiter and established standards that doubtless had a real if unmeasurable impact upon human conduct. The common people of Georgia must have valued the standard, for if they had not, the assemblymen whom they elected could neither have established religion in 1758 nor have retained it thereafter without effective political protest. Establishment was not something imposed from the outside but was a matter internal to Georgians, a matter of local business. There are signs that the Anglican church was starting to come into its own a bit more as Revolutionary tensions heightened. Dissenters were also showing an increasingly lively interest in religion. All of the differing Christian denominations in Georgia might have found themselves better promulgated than before, had not political considerations spoiled a number of ministries and radically altered the entire state of affairs.

Yet political considerations did intervene. The result was that almost everywhere many Georgians who had lived beyond the reach of ministers for years were, as the Revolution began, more unchurched than they had been in decades. The people found their ministers fled or dead, their pulpits silent or suspect, and their formal religious structure damaged. As colonial times ended, little more of religion survived than the ideal itself and what men and women could discover and practice for themselves with reduced benefit of clergy.

Chapter 8

Education

Most education in provincial Georgia adhered to no formal structure. Mothers trained their daughters at the hearth to become wives and mothers in turn. The wife of William Spencer, for example, was a conscientious stepmother to her husband's daughters and taught them "to be good House Wifes and also expert at their Needles."[1] Fathers taught their sons to earn a livelihood at the anvil, in the fields, or at the workbench. Boys were trained as apprentices so that their trades could support a family. The home instruction in medicine that Noble Jones gave to his son was similarly an apprenticeship—an education that was practical and thorough even though unsupported by a university degree.

Education, formal and informal, preserved and fostered the understood values of the state and of society. Formal education, particularly that part supported by the government, advanced religion while teaching reading and writing, skills that had important vocational as well as religious uses. Formal education for white children was commonly available in Savannah and Augusta except in the earliest days and was available as well among the Germans and at the Bethesda orphanage. It was less accessible in rural areas, where it had to be arranged for, often with difficulty. The records are largely silent upon the subject, but apparently formal instruction was rare in the backcountry, where only an estimated 14.5 percent of Georgia's population lived when the Revolution began.[2] The literacy rate in the province can only be guessed at, but it seems to have been rather high considering the times.

1. *Col. Records of Ga.*, XXVI, 7.
2. Bridenbaugh, *Myths and Realities*, 121.

From the beginning most of the Germans could read.[3] And in 1768 the Reverend Edward Ellington made an observation at Augusta that probably had a wider application. He said that people who lived in town could generally read and write but that those who lived some distance in the country usually could not.[4]

At first the trustees made insufficient provision for education. Not until the colony was three years old did effective formal instruction begin in Savannah. While the proprietors had not delayed a moment in sending a religious ministry to the province, they seemed to give little official thought to schools, perhaps because they believed that merely setting aside lands for the support of schoolmasters at Savannah and Frederica would attract the teachers the colony needed.[5] Such was not the case. The lure of land alone was insufficient to secure good teachers. Indeed, the earliest schoolmaster in Savannah was a failure. William Waterland, a dealer in textile fabrics, had arrived with the first settlers. He was a brother to the king's chaplain in London but was a drunkard whose bad habits had lost him his brother's regard. The trustees gave Waterland a bailiff's commission but soon discharged him for misbehavior. As a schoolteacher he was equally a misfit, and by 1734 he was gone. Another teacher, John Burnside, a writing master at Fort Argyle, was granted a license in 1735 to teach in Savannah; if he did so, no record remains.[6]

Beginning in 1736 and for some years thereafter, the problem of finding schoolmasters for Savannah seemed to be self-solving. In 1736 a succession of highly motivated young men began to arrive who were willing to teach without compensation. Charles Delamotte came with John Wesley and in 1738 was succeeded by Habersham, who had appeared with Whitefield. Delamotte, son of a Middlesex magistrate, emigrated at his own expense to teach "reading, writing, and the principles of Christianity." For a time he was relatively happy working in Savannah with his friend Wesley. But after Wesley departed, Delamotte inherited the prejudices against the parson and began to think

---

3. Jones *et al.*, trans. and eds., *Detailed Reports on Salzburger Emigrants*, II, 44.

4. Edward Ellington to the Rev. Dr. Burton, June 30, 1768, S.P.G. Papers, Ser. C, Pkg. 7, Pt. iii (L.C. reel 16, 227–228).

5. *Col. Records of Ga.*, III, 388, 390.

6. *Ibid.*, XX, 128, 308; Coulter and Saye, eds., *List of Early Settlers*, 56.

himself persecuted. He lasted only seven months by himself before returning to England.[7]

Delamotte's successor was Habersham, who worked without pay between 1738 and 1740. He was modestly supplied with necessities by the trustees. Once the plan for Whitefield's orphanage was afoot, however, he left the public school to work full time at Bethesda, relinquishing his teaching post to John Dobell. Prior to succeeding Habersham, Dobell, who had also arrived with Whitefield, instructed French-speaking children at Highgate outside Savannah.[8]

In 1741 Dobell went back to England for a visit and, presumably, for conferences with the trustees. The proprietors were beginning to realize that if a school were to be maintained at Savannah, they had to offer a schoolmaster more than a plot of land and the barest necessities of life. Thus in late 1741 it was agreed to pay Dobell a salary, and he returned to Savannah to resume his duties as schoolmaster.[9] (In addition he was made registrar of Georgia and paid a second stipend.)

Out of this arrangement, an institution evolved that was advanced for its time but not unprecedented—a free school that any child could attend without charge. It had not been the trustees' intention in 1741 to set up such a school. They had expected that only poor pupils would be educated without charge and that all others would pay tuition. But this placed Dobell in an intolerable position, for it was he who was expected to decide who could afford to pay and who could not. In his distress he turned in June 1742 to President Stephens, Stephens's assistants, and the Anglican minister. Dobell asked them "to determine what certain Number of Children shall have the Benefit or Freedom of the said School, and who those Children are; that you receive the Application of the Parents or Guardians of such Children, and give me Orders to receive into the School all such poor Children as you shall think proper to admit, which shall be faithfully obeyed."[10]

Stephens and his assistants agreed to do what Dobell had asked. But in doing so, they did not reckon with human nature. Poor parents and

---

7. *Col. Records of Ga.*, V, 84; Phillipps Coll., 14203, Pt. i, 106–108, Univ. of Ga. Lib., Athens. A bit later in England, Delamotte left the Anglican church and became a Moravian.

8. *Whitefield's Journals, 1737–1741*, 152.

9. *Col. Records of Ga.*, XXX, 430.

10. *Ibid.*, VI, 35.

guardians now decided that there was a stigma attached to applying for free education, and many refused to do it. Enrollment declined sharply, and the trustees reacted decisively. They increased Dobell's salary (though it remained small), forbade him to take money from any parent or guardian, and opened the school to all children without charge.[11]

Dobell and the men who succeeded him during the trustee period labored under the supervision of the Anglican minister in Savannah, a customary arrangement in the eighteenth century. The minister had a hand in examining and sometimes in instructing the students. Dobell's relations with the Reverend Christopher Orton during the months that Orton occupied the rectory were excellent. He continued teaching after Orton's death and during the rectorship of the tumultuous Thomas Bosomworth. Yet he felt overworked. Although he was a satisfactory schoolmaster, the other work he did for the government to piece out his income was poor. In 1746 he abruptly left Georgia.

To keep the school open, the government turned inadvisedly to Peter Joubert, a man much criticized for intemperance during his tenure as schoolmaster. He was drunk so often and was so neglectful that the Anglican minister, who by then was Zouberbuhler, had him removed.[12] The next master of the free school was only a slight improvement. Edward Holt was an unpleasant and disputatious man whose bizarre behavor resulted in much criticism and who was once suspended and possibly jailed. At one juncture a private person started a competing school and "got the major part of the Children." In November 1750 Holt's promise to reform restored him as schoolmaster, but in 1752, when the trust was about to be dissolved, he was offered his and his wife's passage home to England.[13]

In the era of the trustees there probably were more or less regular schools at Vernonburgh and at Acton, both of which would have been something like the one at Savannah. There was also a public school at Augusta.[14] Whether the institution in Savannah remained free to

11. *Ibid.*, II, 408.
12. *Ibid.*, XXXI, 421.
13. *Ibid.*, VI, 343–345, 354, XXVI, 267, II, 520.
14. The names of all the schoolmasters in royal Georgia are not known, but licenses were issued to Thomas Eastham (in 1754), Valentine Bostick (1755), Edmund Bermingham (1758), Robert McClatchie (1762), John Holmes (1766), and Alexander Findlay and James Seymour (1768). These men all served in Savannah. In 1757 John Gordon was licensed for Augusta. Peter Gandy was a

students during the royal era is not clear. Probably it did not. It is possible that some poor students were educated in it without charge while parents or guardians with money paid tuition. For if an education were totally free, why did the Union Society and the St. Andrew's Club advertise that a few needy pupils might secure instruction at their expense? [15]

In general there were three kinds of schools in colonial America, although the boundaries between them were frequently vague. These were English schools, sometimes called "common" or "petty" schools; Latin grammar schools; and academies. English schools stressed reading in the native language, plus writing and arithmetic. The Latin grammar schools emphasized the Latin and Greek languages and their literatures but also offered instruction in English, mathematics, and other subjects. Academies were not well defined. One scholar has said that an academy offered what its master could teach, what its students could learn, or what its sponsors would support—or some compromise among the three. [16]

Georgia had schools of each of these three kinds plus some (particularly in the German community) that did not fit any of the definitions. Probably most of the government-sponsored schools in royal Georgia were of the Latin grammar type.

Each of Georgia's three royal governors was instructed to see that white children were taught reading and religion, and the royal government made a conscientious effort to keep public schools functioning up to the beginning of the Revolution. [17] For a time after 1768 the one in Savannah was run by Alexander Findlay and James Seymour, two men educated at the University of Aberdeen in Scotland. (Both

---

public schoolmaster in Savannah, and Joseph Brooks and Theobald Maigheneaux were public schoolmasters in Augusta. Commissions Book B-1, Dept. of Archives and Hist., Atlanta, Ga., for licenses of: Eastham, Nov. 25, 1754; Bostick, June 25, 1755; Gordon, Dec. 9, 1757; Bermingham, Jan. 5, 1758; McClatchie, Oct. 9, 1762; Holmes, July 2, 1766; Findlay and Seymour, June 26, 1768. Also see *Col. Records of Ga.*, XXVIII, Pt. iia, 384; Ellington to Burton, Feb. 10, 1770, S.P.G. Papers, Ser. C, Pkg. 7, Pt. iii (L.C. reel 16, 234–235).

15. For example, advertisements, *Ga. Gaz.*, Nov. 23, 1768, Feb. 22, 1769, and Mar. 9 and Dec. 7, 1774.

16. This description of the kinds of schools found in 18th-century America is adapted from Lawrence A. Cremin, *American Education: The Colonial Experience, 1607–1783* (New York, 1970), 500–505.

17. *Col. Records of Ga.*, XXXIV, 69–70, 298–299, 483.

later were to become Anglican clergymen.) In April 1770 their institution was visited and examined by Governor Wright, the Reverend Samuel Frink, President Habersham and other members of the council, members of the Commons House of Assembly, and other gentlemen of "liberal education." This inspection seems to have been the only one of its kind ever held, and Findlay and Seymour probably invited it for reasons of their own. The visitors were pleased with the "plan of education," the fruits of which they saw as the young scholars recited speeches selected by the masters that were "well calculated to ingraft in their tender minds a deep sense of religion, honor, and virtue."[18]

We cannot say whether places other than Savannah and Augusta regularly had such a public school; there were at least brief periods when the school was closed in Savannah.[19] Still, we may glimpse the inside of the Savannah school—apparently a Latin grammar school— as it appeared when Robert McClatchie was public schoolmaster there. McClatchie was licensed to teach in 1762 and died four years later. He personally owned much of the equipment, including the pine benches and the writing tables used by the children at their studies. He had cards for teaching beginners the alphabet and a book of directions explaining how to use them. He was well stocked with writing paper and had 825 Dutch quills, several papers of ink powder, a pewter inkstand, a two-foot measuring stick, a mahogany ruler, a pine chest, two cases of mathematical instruments, 114 Latin and Greek volumes, 31 English books, and other pamphlets and books. McClatchie also owned 56 copper plate impressions.[20] It is possible, of course, that some of these items were for his personal use, but this catalog gives the impression that the contents of a schoolhouse were being inventoried. In McClatchie's school the Anglican rector doubtless handled the religious instruction.

German-speaking Georgians had their own rather deliberate approach to education, which, in its end result, was not calculated to be much different from that of the English-speaking public schools. The Salzburgers also sought to serve the values of society, encouraging both

---

18. *Ga. Gaz.*, Apr. 18, 1770.

19. Presentments of the grand jury, *ibid.*, July 13, 1768.

20. Estate of Robert McClatchie, Dec. 26, 1766, Inventory Book F, 231, Dept. of Archives and Hist., Atlanta, Ga.

religion and vocation. A boy should be educated in Christianity, they believed, but it was also essential that he write a good hand, understand grammar and arithmetic, and know something of geography and history, all of which would help him to take a proper place in society. As the Revolution approached, it was all the more important that German-speaking boys be properly prepared, since the best farm land around Ebenezer had been taken and many of them would have to seek their livelihoods elsewhere.[21]

The energy and resourcefulness of these Georgia Germans was such that during much of the colonial period they had three, at times possibly four, functioning schools—one at Ebenezer to serve the town and vicinity and two or three others on outlying plantations at Zion, Goshen, and Bethany. Before 1745 there had been a little German school at Frederica. They all ran hand-in-glove with the Lutheran church. The plantation school at Zion met in the little church there, separated from the sanctuary by a partition. The pastors rigorously supervised the schoolmasters and often taught themselves. So firm was the Salzburgers' commitment to education that they had a school in operation within months after the first arrivals set foot in Georgia in 1734 and almost before they had anything else. They built a "little house" for a school near Old Ebenezer, and when winter came and the house was cold, they moved classes into a home. In summer they kept the classes going, rescheduling them from the sweltering afternoon hours to the more pleasant times of early morning.[22]

The German schools were aided by grants from the Society for the Promotion of Christian Knowledge in Great Britain. But income also came from the earnings of the complex of mills on Mill Creek outside Ebenezer—mills owned by the Lutheran church in Georgia—and from the contributions of faithful settlers, from gifts from Germany, and from tuition collected from parents. Toward the end of the era, those who could pay nothing could apply to the church council for assistance for their children.[23]

The Germans employed exacting schoolmasters. In 1749 a child was kicked by a horse and subsequently died, but in the frenzy of his

21. Muhlenberg, *Journals*, II, 669.

22. *Ibid.*, 661; Jones *et al.*, trans. and eds., *Detailed Reports on Salzburger Emigrants*, II, 22, 25; Urlsperger, ed., *Ausführliche Nachrichten*, I, 1040, 2073.

23. Muhlenberg, *Journals*, II, 664.

final hours, he deliriously recited pieces of poems and parts of the ABC book drilled into him by a strict master.[24] Teachers included the ministers; John Adam Treutlen; two noted physicians, Dr. Christian Thilo and Dr. John Ludwig Meyer; and in 1764, a female teacher named Heckin (at Ebenezer), among a good many others.[25]

The teachers made but small allowance for tender age. In 1742 a schoolmaster holding classes in a plantation kitchen required that children recite their poems for him and exacted the greatest accuracy even though the children were very small.[26] The Lutheran pastors had difficulties with their schoolmasters, but none so serious as those the English authorities in Savannah had with Peter Joubert and Edward Holt. Bolzius disliked schoolmaster Treutlen, who, while a young man, was regarded as high-handed, overly superior, and incorrigible in having his own way;[27] however, Treutlen taught German and English six hours a day at Ebenezer to general acclaim during 1758 and 1759, leaving the schoolroom after a time to enter what became a successful mercantile business.

He and other German masters taught both languages if they could, for from the beginning the trustees had desired that the Salzburgers learn English. Bolzius and Gronau heartily concurred, and about 1734 Christopher Ortman was appointed to teach it. Yet his English was so Germanic that Oglethorpe, upon hearing it, ordered him restrained at once from teaching English to any child.[28] Ortman carried on for a time longer as instructor in German and was finally removed, not for what he did to the king's English, but for affronts to Bolzius. In the meantime, the pastors had engaged a young man, Henry Bishop, to teach English. Bishop had been a student in the charity school of St. Dunstan in West London and had come to Georgia as a servant to the trustees.[29] He was faithful in exercising the children but was so weak in discipline that he could not make his charges respect him. To rectify this shortcoming, the pastors themselves went into his classroom to lend a hand. At length Bishop married a German girl, and they later moved to South Carolina. He was succeeded by Henry

24. Urlsperger, ed., *Ausführliche Nachrichten*, III, 542.
25. Winde, "Frühgeschichte der Luth. Kirche in Ga.," 136–138.
26. Urlsperger, ed., *Ausführliche Nachrichten*, II, 2113.
27. Winde, "Frühgeschichte der Luth. Kirche in Ga.," 137–138.
28. *Col. Records of Ga.*, XXII, Pt. ii, 183.
29. *Ibid.*, II, 74.

Hamilton, a periwig maker, who let down standards even further.[30] Thereafter English was taught by anybody who could be prevailed upon to take the task.

For several years there was another important educational institution at Ebenezer—an orphanage that was functioning by 1738, modeled after the famous house near Halle from which both Bolzius and Gronau had come. Besides serving as a home for orphans, the Ebenezer institution was a hospital and a hostel for strangers. Some of the German children who lived and studied there worked in the fields that belonged to it. After 1744, however, when families began to take the orphans into their homes, the orphanage declined in importance and was later closed. There was undisguised self-interest in this development, for children old enough to work were a valuable asset in a colony without slavery.

During the years in which the orphanage was an important institution, Bolzius and Gronau saw to it that the children's schedule was divided between religion and work. Students rose before five and bathed and dressed while a hymn was sung for them and a bit of scripture read. There followed a short homily, a prayer, and one or two verses of a hymn. Light chores were done while breakfast was being cooked; some children who had lessons were allowed to study. After a hot breakfast the children went to school until noon; after lunch they worked until school reopened at two. Classes ended at four, and more work followed. The children's labors were always light and intentionally so. The elders did not see chores as important in themselves but, rather, as exercises to build good habits. In the evening before bedtime, there were prayers, recitations of the catechism, and private devotions.[31]

The Salzburgers enjoyed a particular distinction in that they ran the only educational system in Georgia designed to serve both the town and countryside. In non-German Georgia, another pattern was becoming discernible similar to that found in other southern colonies. Public schools existed in towns, and private schools functioned alongside them. But private schools were also found in rural areas serving children not otherwise reached. This interesting mixture of public and private education developed as a result of need and opportunity, with

30. *Ibid.*, XXV, 4; Urlsperger, ed., *Ausführliche Nachrichten*, II, 363.
31. Urlsperger, ed., *Ausführliche Nachrichten*, I, 2207–2208.

private schools by far the more numerous and broadly dispersed. Some country families took in tutors for their children, for private schools in the countryside were never plentiful enough to serve all needs.

Joseph and William Gibbons ran a rather noted private institution in the country. It was apparently an English, or "common," school. The Gibbonses owned plantations not far from Savannah and alternated their boarding school between themselves every other year. In 1763 it had been functioning for at least a year under schoolmaster John Portrees. Portrees, in agreeing to continue teaching there again, advertised for a half-dozen scholars to study writing, English grammar, and the practical aspects of mathematics—geometry, mensuration, arithmetic, plane and spherical trigonometry, navigation, and surveying. William Read, son of Councillor James Read, attended for a time but, finding the master tyrannical, ran away and returned home. His father thereafter put him in a private institution in Savannah designed for "select young gentlemen," for whom classical masters had been brought from Europe.[32] Other families or groups of families ran private schools in the country. John Baker, related by blood or marriage to many of the Midway people, seems to have been the principal sponsor of one, and the Bourquins, Foxes, and McLeans at Little Ogeechee appear to have supported another.[33]

It is impossible to say how many private schools there were in Georgia. The existence of more than thirty can be documented. Among others, James Beverly operated one at Sunbury, and David Hughes taught in St. George Parish; John Daniel Hammerer had kept school in Augusta and among the Cherokee before he moved to Savannah. In Ewensburgh, schools were operated in residences by C. S. Etty, Richard Rogers, and Joseph Daniel.[34] Of the rather numerous private institutions in Savannah, some seem to have been of the English, or "common," type, while others were Latin grammar schools. Latin apparently was fairly well known, for about the time that Zubly and Frink

32. Gibbes, *Documentary History of the Revolution*, II, 248; advertisement of John Portrees, *Ga. Gaz.*, June 16, 1763.

33. Advertisements of John Baker, *Ga. Gaz.*, June 8, 1768, and May 4, 1774; advertisements of Henry Bourquin, John Fox, and John McLean, *ibid.*, Apr. 6 and Aug. 10, 1768.

34. Will abstract of John Pettigrew, *Will Abstracts*, 110; will abstract of David Hughes, *ibid.*, 71; advertisement of C. S. Etty, *Ga. Gaz.*, Feb. 23, 1774; advertisement of Joseph Daniel, *ibid.*, July 13, 1774; Ga. Hist. Soc., *Colls.*, VI, 149. Hammerer's school in Augusta could have been the public school.

were exchanging insults in the controversy over fees for Frink's sexton, a lengthy riddle in Latin was posted on a building where a dissenting minister had preached. The *Georgia Gazette* reprinted it without bothering to translate. When Zubly soon after attacked Frink in a published letter, he too offered the riddle without putting it into English.[35]

In Savannah there were private schools serving not only vocations and religion but also less fundamental aims of society—military defense and, increasingly toward the end of the era, social skills. There were schools for adults, schools for women, and schools that met in the evening. Instruction was offered in subjects as diverse as bookkeeping and the fine points of military drill (including loading and quick firing, the different facings, wheeling by grand divisions, forming the hollow square, and the proper salutes for general officers with colors, pike, or drum).[36] Gentlemen might learn self-defense; or from the same schoolmaster, adults and children of both sexes might learn "all the celebrated dances that are used in polite assemblies."[37] These schools differed scarcely at all from their counterparts flourishing in Charleston in the 1760s and 1770s.

One of the best schools in the province was Whitefield's Bethesda, standing alone in the countryside outside Savannah. It was a good school for several reasons. After 1740 it had continuity of location, facilities, and leadership. Few institutions outside the German-speaking communities offered such advantages, and they particularly lacked continuity of leadership. Whitefield's preaching missions supplied the school's income. Bethesda, an orphanage as well as a school, was controversial in its early years, in part because of the personal and religious antagonisms that accompanied Whitefield wherever he went and, equally as important, because it fell afoul of the balance in education that colonial society expected. Whitefield himself understood, at least in theory, what needed to be done at Bethesda, for he early declared his intention of having his scholars there learn both religion and a trade. Besides being a Christian institution, it was to be a "Publick Nursery for Planters and Mechanicks."[38] Less than three months

35. *Ga. Gaz.*, Feb. 15, 1769; Zubly, *Letter to Frink*, unpaginated.

36. Advertisement of Alexander Fullerton, *Ga. Gaz.*, July 23, 1766; advertisement of Thomas Lee, *ibid.*, Feb. 24, 1768. An interest of schools in military preparedness may further be seen in an address to Gov. Ellis in *S.-C. Gaz.*, Apr. 28, 1757, and in Gibbes, *Documentary History of the Revolution*, II, 252.

37. Advertisements of John Revear, *Ga. Gaz.*, June 29 and Aug. 31, 1768.

38. *Col. Records of Ga.*, XXII, Pt. ii, 359.

after Whitefield enunciated these aims, however, a regimen was de-vised that emphasized religion at the expense of vocational preparation.

The school children rose about five and knelt in prayer for a quarter of an hour, "during which time they are often Exhorted what to pray for, particularly that Jesus Christ would Convert them, and Change their Hearts."[39] At six everyone went to church to sing a psalm and to hear a lesson. The services lasted about an hour, and around seven Bishop Ken's "Morning Hymn" was sung, followed by extempora-neous prayer. During the next hour adults and children ate breakfast together. Here graces were said, one or more hymns were sung, the business of the day was discussed, and assignments made; sometimes too, the children were questioned or exhorted. From eight to ten the students worked at vocational tasks—carding, spinning, picking cot-ton or wool, sewing, and knitting—and at chores like cleaning, cut-ting wood, and fetching water. Others worked at a trade. At ten school began. Reading and writing were taught, and the scriptures were emphasized. Formal instruction was accompanied by singing and prayer, "not by Form, but out of their [the teachers'] own hearts." All took the noonday meal together, and until two in the afternoon, every-one did "something usefull, but no time is allowed for Idleness or play, which are Satans darling hours." Everyone at Bethesda was said to be extraordinarily quiet. From two until four classes were resumed, and from four to six the children went back to their work assignments. The evening meal began at six, "when the Master and Mistress's at-tend to help them, and Sing with them, and watch over their words and Actions." At seven everyone went to church for about an hour's sing-ing and preaching, and around eight the children were instructed in religion (by Whitefield if he were present). His purpose was "to ground the Children in their Belief of Original Sin, and to make them Sensible of their damnable State by nature." At nine the children went to their rooms accompanied by an adult, who would pray and sing with them again. Before going to bed "each Boy, as in the morning, is seen to kneel by his Bedside, and is order'd to pray from his own heart for a quarter of an hour, Some person instructing them how." At ten al-most everyone else went to bed, although some occasionally sat up an hour or two longer for private devotions, meditation, or conferences.

This kind of monastic piety made some of the children hysterical.

39. The quotation and what follows on the regimen of the orphanage is from Phillipps Coll., 14204, 417–419.

In London, Benjamin Martyn, secretary of the trustees, in 1743 read a published account reporting that the children were often kept praying and crying all night and that one of the youngest, being asked what he wanted, "said he only wanted Jesus Christ." Martyn sent a rebuke to Habersham, then temporal manager at the orphanage. "Religion should be shewn and recommended to them in an amiable Light, nor should they be fill'd with ill grounded Terrours, which must probably give their Minds an Enthusiastick Turn, or by bending them too much one way, make them hereafter fly back another with greater Force, and may gave them a Distaste even to Religion it Self."[40] Eventually education at Bethesda, although never losing its dedication to religion, achieved a sense of balance that pleased the royal government as much as the earlier imbalance had dismayed the trustees.

This judicious proportion was displayed at length in anniversary day ceremonies in 1771. The governor journeyed from Savannah to watch the exercises and to hear Peter Edwards, one of the students, proclaim that education had practical as well as spiritual aims. The students, said Edwards, learned duty to God and country while learning also to "move in a superior sphere of life" and to be useful to mankind. Edward Langworthy, the tutor, who was regarded in the province as a very good classical scholar, expounded further:

It is undoubtedly the indispensible obligation of every one entrusted with the business of education to satisfy the public with respect to their abilities and intentions, and therefore I hope to convince you that no pains will be spared, no time lost, that whatever is useful in the Sciences, or ornamental in life, will *here* be inculcated both by precept and example. Authors in the several branches of knowledge will be regularly read and the sacred scriptures constantly explained: These can bestow understanding upon all men; they are the universal logic, since none can read them without either acquiring a greater exactness of thought, or being invited to contract a greater rectitude of manners.[41]

Seldom were the purposes of education better stated in colonial Georgia, and by the time this little speech was made, Bethesda, its difficult early days behind it, enjoyed the near patronage of some of the most influential figures in the province. In January 1770, Whitefield managed to draw much of the government itself from Savannah, where the legislature was in session, to one of his assemblies. He staged a

40. *Col. Records of Ga.*, XXX, 491–492.
41. *S.-C. Gaz.; And Country Jour.*, Apr. 16, 1771.

procession with his scholars in flat caps and black gowns, and Governor Wright was escorted to a great chair in the chapel with a tapestry hanging behind it. It was wondered, apparently with a straight face, whether the governor's seat more nearly resembled a bishop's throne or a prebendary's stall. The music was harmonious and striking as His Excellency proceeded to his place and took his seat with the council on either side of him, the Speaker of the House and some of his colleagues conspicuous upon benches nearby. The chief justice was also present.[42] No other educational institution in provincial Georgia would have been comfortable with so pretentious a show.

In Bethesda's earliest years there was not the smallest hint that the institution would ever patronize or be patronized by powerful men in the local government. The institution had a host of enemies, and the local Anglican minister had every reason to regard it as a stubborn stronghold of wrongheadedness. The magistrates in those early days were equally astonished and appalled when Whitefield, interpreting the role of his orphanage broadly, embarked upon a campaign to bring under his care every orphan in the province, including some already well provided for by other arrangements. So excessive was Whitefield's zeal that the trustees brought him down to earth and made it clear that the magistrates alone could say which orphans went to Bethesda and which were to be otherwise cared for. So strong was feeling in some quarters during the early years that the institution could not escape the ultimate charge of Protestant demagoguery—that its policies were popish.[43]

Several observations should be made about Bethesda's first decade. Questions were often asked at the time about whether the sums that Whitefield raised on his preaching ventures were properly used. They were sometimes bluntly phrased, implying that the evangelist was using the resources for his own advantage, but no proof of these suspicions has ever been produced. Reports of severe discipline of children at Bethesda may have had slightly more substance. Despite the criticisms directed at them, the managers oversaw the building of magnificent facilities. A "great house," the tallest building in Georgia, dominated other structures lying around a quadrangle. Close at hand on a salt water creek was a wharf at which the orphanage schooner and other vessels tied up. The population varied, but even before the

42. *Ga. Gaz.*, Mar. 21 and 28, 1770.
43. *Col. Records of Ga.*, V, 359–360, XXIII, 240–241.

facilities were complete, Bethesda was the largest institution in Georgia, sheltering nearly 150 persons, counting servants, staff, and tradesmen. Sixty-one were orphans or other destitute children.[44]

There was no way such an establishment could be ignored in a province that was poor in both money and population. In time the government revised its earlier negative appraisal of Bethesda, and by 1751 officials in Savannah were prepared to concede that children there were well cared for.[45] Indeed, the relationship between the orphanage and the government thereafter became exceedingly close. Habersham left Bethesda and gained wealth as a Savannah merchant. He became increasingly influential in government councils, but the interests of Bethesda never failed to concern him, not even when his duties as president of the council were heaviest. Everything we know about Habersham suggests that he was the same man from the beginning of his career to the end—able, unswerving in loyalty, and religious. The Habersham who was fined in 1742 for assailing the Anglican pastor at Savannah as a near-heretic—which, in Habersham's terms, meant that the pastor did not practice religion the same way it was practiced at Bethesda—was the same man who presided over the council in 1764 when Whitefield launched a plan to make Bethesda a college, a move that, if successful, could have broken important ground in education in the South.

Bethesda would have become the only college south of the College of William and Mary in Virginia. Whitefield had originated the idea long before 1764, but the signing of the Treaty of Paris in 1763 made the time seem propitious for action. The ratification of the treaty was followed by the creation of two new British colonies south of Georgia—East Florida and West Florida. Not only did they secure Georgia's southern frontier, but they ensured friendly neighbors who might be willing to send their children to college in Georgia. On December 18, 1764, Whitefield memorialized the governor and the council and asked for two thousand acres of land to improve and expand the original plan for Bethesda. The purpose would be the "Education of Persons of superior Rank who thereby might be qualified to serve their King, their Country and their God either in Church or State." Whitefield played strongly upon local pride, suggesting that not only Floridians but students from northern colonies would be entering the

44. Ga. Hist. Soc., *Colls.*, I, 201.
45. *Col. Records of Ga.*, XXVI, 116.

province for education. They would bring money, thus strengthening the economy, and Georgia gentlemen would no longer need send their sons northward for an education. The outward flow of capital would be slowed.[46]

Without a day's delay, the governor and council voted the two thousand acres. The legislature speedily lent its endorsement, and Whitefield believed that his plan would easily be fulfilled.[47] It was his intention to seek a charter from the king in council, and he felt secure because he had the help of Lord Dartmouth, the friend of Methodists, who was shortly to become president of the Board of Trade. Two months after receiving encouragement and help from Governor Wright, the council, and the Commons House, Whitefield paid the debts of the orphanage, placed out all the children except two or three, printed an audit in the *Georgia Gazette*, and left Savannah by boat.[48] By slow progress he made his way to London, arriving there in July 1765 in time to see Dartmouth installed in his important new position.

But Whitefield reckoned without his enemies in the Church of England, whom he had often attacked as unconverted hypocrites. Years earlier he had engaged in rancorous dispute with Thomas Secker, then bishop of Oxford. By 1765 Secker was archbishop of Canterbury, and he now placed himself squarely in the path of the proposed charter. He called attention to the fact that Whitefield had no intention of making the college an Anglican institution. Nevertheless, Secker might have lost his fight had not a change in government removed Lord Dartmouth from power. Inevitably, Whitefield's petition was referred to the archbishop, and Secker suggested key alterations, probably knowing he was asking two things that Whitefield would never accept— that the charter require the president of the college to be an Anglican priest and that the liturgy of the Church of England be used daily.

Whitefield was already on record as saying that the college must be founded upon a "broad bottom." Still he attempted to counter the archbishop's points. As to the liturgy, he said, "I love to use it, I have fallen a martyr, in respect to bodily health, to the frequent reading it in Tottenham-Court chapel." Further, he said, it "has been constantly read twice every Sunday in the Orphan-House, from its first institution to this very day. . . . But I cannot enjoin it by charter." To

46. *Ibid.*, IX, 259–261.
47. *Ibid.*, 261, XVII, 145–146.
48. *Ga. Gaz.*, Feb. 21, 1765.

Secker's insistence that the president of the college be an Anglican minister, Whitefield replied he could not in conscience make it obligatory. "The first master will assuredly be a clergyman of the church of England—By far the majority of the intended wardens are, and always will be members of that communion; and consequently the choice of a master will always continue to run in that channel. . . . But lest this should not always be the case, I dare not, as persons of all denominations have been contributors, confine or fetter the future electors." Whitefield added that the greatest proportion of the donations already received had come from dissenters.[49]

It was soon clear that Whitefield would not get the charter. In 1768 word of his failure was reported in the *Georgia Gazette*, together with an announcement that the orphanage would add an academy rather than become a college. This new academy would educate the children of the wealthy in addition to orphan students.[50]

Bethesda continued as a bastion for dissenters until the end of colonial times, even though two Anglican priests, Ellington and the Reverend William Piercy, were its presidents. Ellington became president in 1770 but served only six months, leaving for South Carolina to assume a pastorate there in January 1771. Piercy took over after Ellington in late 1772 or early 1773. Whitefield had earlier announced his intention of severing all official connections with Bethesda but did not live to do so, for in September 1770 he died while on a preaching tour. By his will Bethesda passed to Selina, countess of Huntingdon, his friend and a patron of Methodists in England. Lady Huntingdon never came to Georgia, and in the few years that remained before the Revolution, she administered Bethesda poorly but as best she could from England, acting through Piercy. Bethesda's effectiveness was much impaired in 1773 by a fire that destroyed the principal building, the library, and the chapel.[51]

The public and private schools described here were, of course, set up to educate white students only. Yet, as we have seen, black children and adults were occasionally taught to read and write by instructors like Ottolenghe, Winter, and Rennie, or through arrangements made by sympathetic masters like Habersham. A few black children were

49. Whitefield, *Letter to Gov. Wright* (1768), 6–7, 8, 17.
50. *Ga. Gaz.*, June 29, 1768.
51. Ga. Hist. Soc., *Colls.*, VI, 228–229.

taken into the German schools in and near Ebenezer and educated there, but such occurrences were uncommon.

The history of education for white as well as black people was, in any event, more than a mere history of schools. From parents and from older persons, both white and black, children learned much that was practical about making do in the world. That, too, was education. And on a frontier where the practical was more useful than the theoretical, it was education of a necessary kind.

Epilogue: Some Observations on Colonial Georgia

In this review of the colonial past of Georgia, last founded of the thirteen American colonies, an interesting question arises: At what stage of development did Georgia enter the stream of the American experience? Did the province, in its forty-three-year history, repeat the entire process begun in the older colonies in the seventeenth century, or did its founding in 1733 immediately thrust it into the pattern of development then in progress in its sister colonies?

In two instances Georgia rather strikingly repeated stages already passed through elsewhere. Most important was the method of Georgia's founding. A large number of the older colonies had been established as proprietary ventures with feudalistic trappings. Georgia was not fashioned in imitation of any of them, but even after the earlier proprietary projects had failed, it constituted in 1733 yet another attempt at founding a colony based squarely upon a model of land control suffused with medievalism. The proprietors in London were so committed to this policy—which forbade possession of property in fee simple title, crippled the free exchange of land, and stifled female inheritance—that they forced Georgians to endure it for seventeen years before reality overtook them in 1750. (The policy was such a failure that it was being modified in practice well before that date.) Georgians had to work through this unhappy period before they took their place on the bottom rung of the ladder upon which the other colonies stood in the eighteenth century. That this latest, and final, proprietary venture was a failure like its predecessors was evident when the trustees surrendered their charter to the king before it expired.

The second significant example of Georgia's evolution by stages concerns the changes in its social structure. Many scholars believe that citizens in seventeenth-century colonial society were more nearly "equal" than they later became in the eighteenth. Although the Georgia proprietors never intended to found a colony devoid of social distinctions, the economics of Georgia's first two decades dictated that such distinctions would not be so obvious as they became in the twenty years preceding the Revolution. For although a handful of local trust officials enjoyed status based upon power and position, few of the early Georgians had money enough to insist upon differentiations based upon wealth. Many of them had come at the expense of others, and although some had not, poverty was widespread. Even five years after the trustee period was over, there were not ten men in Georgia worth £500 each.[1] Soon after, however, this condition began to change. A decade later (in 1767), there were 8,000 slaves in the colony, and Governor Wright and members of the council, about twelve persons in all, owned 954 of them—almost one in eight.[2] Social differentiation based upon wealth was advancing at that point.

But opportunity was never choked off, even for the poor. As the Revolution approached, Georgians were indeed "less equal" than they had been twenty or thirty years earlier, but opportunity for advancement, based largely upon the easy availability of land, was still open for all white men.

The most remarkable social advancement in Georgia was enjoyed by men of ability who had come early and worked hard—by a schoolmaster who became a rich merchant, planter, and president of the

1. *Col. Records of Ga.*, XXVIII, Pt. i a, 58. The observations contained in this short chapter have been influenced by Kenneth A. Lockridge's "Social Change and the Meaning of the American Revolution," *Journal of Social History*, VI (1973), 403–439, and by studies published in Stephen G. Kurtz and James H. Hutson, eds., *Essays on the American Revolution* (Chapel Hill, N.C., 1973), especially Bernard Bailyn's "The Central Themes of the American Revolution: An Interpretation," 3–31; Jack P. Greene's "An Uneasy Connection: An Analysis of the Preconditions of the American Revolution," 32–80; and Rowland Berthoff and John M. Murrin's "Feudalism, Communalism, and the Yeoman Freeholder: The American Revolution Considered as a Social Accident," 256–288.

2. *Col. Records of Ga.*, XXXVII, 182–183.

council; by a converted Jew who had once been jailed for debt in England; by a former servant and potter who became an assemblyman and a leader of the Revolution; by a few doctors of undistinguished medical preparation; by a former baker's apprentice; by an ambitious young Scot who in little more than twenty years worked his way up to the lieutenant governorship; and by numerous self-made planters, only a few of whom were really wealthy when they first set foot in Georgia. With the exception of the few officials who owed their power to their appointments, real influence rested with persons such as these. They had earned it. Even a surprising number of royal officials integrated themselves into the life of the province.

In the midst of this social mobility, class distinctions existed. Georgia artisans, part of the solid middle class, in 1750 organized the Union Society to advance and protect their interests. In the 1760s and 1770s artisans began to display aspirations through another channel—political office. They were satisfied to have "gentlemen" sit for them in the Commons House of Assembly, on church vestries, and as churchwardens, but they generated a lively interest in the minor governmental commission on the workhouse. At length the artisans won control and kept it. This incursion into power politics, although modest compared to what artisans did in other colonies, bespoke an underlying social tension and a realization of class self-interest.

Wherever they found themselves on the economic scale, Georgians tended to be adaptable. A contemporary noted that "even the most lowly peasant is an absolute freeholder in his house and on his land, and cannot complain in the least about any difficulty, oppression and violence."[3] Colonial Georgians were able to adjust to their environment. Local conditions put no premium upon vocational specialization, so people learned to do many things passably rather than one thing well. In Europe many men had been specialists following well-defined trades under rules laid down in the ancient guilds. In Georgia these same men might do a variety of things satisfactorily, if imperfectly, including carpentry, coopering, tailoring, blacksmithing, brickmaking, and farming. These adaptable people saw their colony become increasingly prosperous as the Revolution approached. True, it was a relative prosperity, remarkable only when one compares local conditions in the 1770s with the poverty-stricken days of the 1740s and

3. Loewald, Starika, and Taylor, trans. and eds., "Bolzius Answers a Questionnaire," Pt. i, *WMQ*, 3d Ser., XIV (1957), 226.

1750s. Still, it made some people wealthy and, as a result, helped make other Georgians "less equal" than they had been earlier.

What brought about the prosperity? It was largely a result of an increase in the population. An influx of new people multiplied the sheer number of productive persons within Georgia's boundaries. It has been suggested that in other colonies the white population doubled every two or three decades. The figures for Georgia bear comparison. In 1751 there were 1,900 white persons in the province; twenty-two years later, in 1773, there were 18,000, a ninefold increase. For the total population, white and black, the increase was even more striking. The number rose from 2,300 in 1751 to 33,000 in 1773, more than a fourteenfold increase.

Most of the new people came into Georgia because of the availability of land, which was virtually free. Relations with the Indians were peaceful enough (at least before 1773) for a man to till his land with only occasional twinges of anxiety. Good relations with the Indians were also essential to the official policy of land acquisition from the moment of Oglethorpe's early beguilement of Tomochichi, by whose help 1,152,000 acres were obtained. But it fell to Governor Wright to induce both the Indians and the British government to help him multiply those acreages. And multiply them he did: 3,407,200 acres were added in 1763; 20,000 in 1766; and 2,116,298 in 1773. In ten years Wright increased the original cession almost fivefold, acquiring rich and tillable tracts that drew settlers at a satisfying rate.

What were these Georgians like? It is not surprising that they were self-confident and self-reliant at best, aggressive bullies at worst. They took in bad spirit any real or imagined infringement upon their persons or what they regarded as their rights and privileges. A "becoming resentment is necessary to check unmerited abuse," wrote one of them, "otherwise a door will be kept open for continual insult."[4] Personal conflicts were "the fashion of that day."[5] Georgians had a high sense of themselves. Even if they realized it, it mattered to them scarcely at all that the taxes they paid were insufficient to support their government in Savannah and in the parishes, and that the British Parliament made up the difference mostly out of monies collected in Great Britain. It has been estimated that this policy cost the British government almost £200,000, plus large additional sums for bounties, over a forty-three-

4. Letter of "Be Angry And Sin Not," *Ga. Gaz.*, July 16, 1766.
5. Gibbes, *Documentary History of the Revolution*, II, 248.

year period.[6] Georgians did realize that the British army was their principal protection in time of war against the French and Spaniards and, especially after 1773, against the Indians. But it was only when the Spaniards actually threatened in the late 1730s and early 1740s, and when Indian campfires blazed too close for comfort in the 1770s, that they dwelt long and hard upon this fact. Usually they looked to themselves.

Although it might be difficult for an age steeped in the spirit of republicanism to appreciate, many of these Georgians were genuine monarchists. Nearly all the "better sort of people" were.[7] They apparently liked their king, and perhaps a few actually convinced themselves that they loved him. As long as they could, they insisted that their dispute was with Parliament and not with the person who occupied the throne. It is likely that if an election had been held before the spring of 1775 and the question at issue had dealt with loyalty to and affection for his majesty, George III would have won by a substantial majority. Although he was physically distant, as head of state, head of church, and symbolic father to his people, his picture and that of Queen Charlotte were proudly displayed in homes in the province. Georgia had been named for his grandfather, the town of Frederica for his father, and Augusta for his mother.

It has been stated that King George lost his hold on the allegiance of the American people on the day in April 1775 when shots were fired at Lexington and Concord.[8] There is documentary evidence after that date that shows that Georgians' attachment to the monarchy, and to George III himself, died hard. However, they soon after put aside both the concept and the person as casually as they might lay off a cloak and as cheerfully as they might abandon a bad habit.

But what did colonial Georgians think of their auspices for the future? While the trustees were in power, the most vocal persons in the province were loudly proclaiming what fools the proprietors were and how miserable was the settlers' plight. The most vigorous critics took horse or boat to other parts, but not before they had impressed others

6. Jones, *History of Ga.*, II, 170.
7. Gibbes, *Documentary History of the Revolution*, II, 248–249.
8. Allen D. Candler, comp., *The Revolutionary Records of the State of Georgia*, I (Atlanta, Ga., 1908), 326–328. This allegation was made by the Revolutionary legislature in 1778. The use of the Apr. date was symbolic rather than actual, for news of the battle of Lexington and Concord did not reach Savannah until May 10, 1775.

with their prediction that the colony had no happy future under trustee management. The coming of royal rule in 1754 changed the outlook, however. Spirits were raised, as an enthusiastic poet attested in 1757:

> The Planter now, his Hopes elate,
> Pursues the rural Healthy plan;
> Foretels our Georgia's prosp'rous State.
> The great Idea charms the man.[9]

Other poems and writings, especially after 1763, evoke the same spirit. During much of royal times Georgians were optimistic concerning their future, even though they lived in an age when belief in automatic progress was neither universally held nor easily defensible. Had other considerations not intervened, their optimism would probably have been fulfilled under the royal system. It was finally fulfilled under the system that replaced royal government.

These Georgians did not see themselves as a "people apart" from the other American colonists. Despite the variety of their geographical backgrounds, Georgians were, with some exceptions, connected to other Americans by language and cultural heritage. There was also a strong commercial tie between Georgia and its neighbors, especially South Carolina. The major Georgia merchants had business connections all along the Atlantic seaboard and in Great Britain. Wealthier Georgians traveled in other colonies and to the mother country, and they often sent their sons to schools outside the colony. This cross-fertilization of money, people, and especially of ideas (spread through the extensive reading Georgians did), kept them from being entirely insular. It caused a great many Georgians to think of themselves not only as transplanted Britons but also as Americans and, after grievances were added, to consider themselves Americans first. When in 1776 a Revolutionary government took over in name as well as in fact, its leaders, and probably the people they represented, considered the interests of Georgia and America as one. By that time the issues at hand were "not Provincial, but Continental."[10]

When Georgia was forty-three years old, its Revolutionary government joined with other Americans in severing ties with the mother country. Although many Georgians were reluctant to take that step,

---

9. "On Governour Reynolds Departure for England" (anonymous poem), Henry Ellis Papers, Univ. of Ga. Lib., Athens.

10. Peter Force, comp., *American Archives*, 4th Ser., VI (Washington, D.C., 1846), 1674–1675.

and although some opposed the decision and left Georgia, history has demonstrated that the step taken was not to be reversed. The story of Georgia from its founding up to the moment of its independence had, except for setbacks under the trustees, been a story of positive, progressive growth. What only a few years earlier had been a weak and disheartened colony was by 1776 not unlike a newly matured bird—young, unsure of itself but full of life, its plumage developed if untested. Tempting fate and brushing danger, the fledgling province committed itself to flight.

Bibliographical Essay

Most of the original source material relating to the colony of Georgia was preserved in Great Britain. During the years that Georgia was a proprietary and royal province, tens of thousands of reports, letters, and other documents went from Georgia to London, where they were read, then filed away in official and private archives. Many of these documents are now available in published form. Photographic copies of others are held in various American depositories. Much of the material about Georgia that survived in America has also been published, but some papers remain in manuscript and are held in scattered depositories.

Manuscripts

The Georgia Historical Society in Savannah houses a number of manuscript collections from the colonial period. The journal of the Reverend John Joachim Zubly from March 5, 1770, to April 9, 1781, is a notebook kept by one of the colony's most influential religious and political figures. The chronology is occasionally uncertain, but work done on it by Lilla M. Hawes, director of the society, has rendered it more usable. The James Habersham Collection contains about twenty letters written to or by Habersham. These items, some of them recently discovered, concern agriculture, government, and the education of two of Habersham's children. The Noble Wimberly Jones Papers contain a half-dozen letters written by Noble Jones to Noble Wimberly Jones in 1760 and 1761. They mostly concern Indian affairs, with some mention of family and governmental matters. In the George Noble Jones Collection is a poem written by Noble Jones and copies of parts of letters on religious subjects written in 1739 by

James Habersham. The letters were partially copied in 1846 by two of Habersham's granddaughters, who apparently were concerned only with religion, for they copied sections of the letters dealing with Habersham's religious life and little else. Other sources at the Georgia Historical Society include the Telfair Family Papers, Archibald Bulloch Papers, John Wand Papers, and Joseph Clay Papers.

The University of Georgia Library at Athens houses the Phillipps Collection of Egmont manuscripts. This mass of documents was acquired in Great Britain in 1947 and is the largest of all the privately held collections pertaining to the colonial era in Georgia. The papers doubtless belonged originally to the earl of Egmont, a trustee of the colony whose interests extended to every detail of the founding and early governing of the province. The University of Georgia has had the original documents transcribed, and scholars are urged to consult the typed copies rather than the originals. The Keith Read Collection at the University of Georgia includes the Caleb Davis journal and papers relating to the Lewis, Flerl, and Sheftall families. The Benjamin Sheftall Papers are essential to a study of Jews in the province. The DeRenne Manuscript Collection pertains mostly to the Jones family. There are also a very few items of business interest in the Telemon Cuyler Papers and a few examples of locally written poetry in the Henry Ellis Collection. Dr. Kenneth Coleman of the University of Georgia recently secured photographic copies of documents in the British Public Record Office in London that either were of particular interest or had eluded earlier publication. These copies may be consulted at the University of Georgia Library. They are from the papers of the Colonial Office, the Admiralty, and the Treasury.

The Georgia Department of Archives and History, Atlanta, has the Georgia Loyalist Claims on microfilm. The originals are in the British Public Record Office in London. These claims were filed, mostly in the 1780s, by Georgians who had been driven into exile and were seeking recompense for property lost in Georgia during and after the Revolution. The claims contain personal and family data going far beyond a mere enumeration of lost resources. The Georgia Department of Archives and History also has a collection of legal documents, many unavailable elsewhere. Among the most important are Inventory Book F (or D) (1754–1771), Inventory Book FF (1776–1777), and Inventory Book GG (1777–1778). These inventories of colonial estates reveal much about the personal property and chattels of more than three hundred persons who died between 1754 and 1778. The archives also has other collections containing hundreds of mortgages, bonds, bills of sale, deeds of gift, powers of attorney, conveyances, entries of claims, schedules of land grants, marks and brands, and proclamations. Official copies of some colonial wills also survive at the archives for the period from 1754 to 1777. The originals have disappeared. Original land grants and some colonial plats are in the possession of the Georgia Surveyor General Department, Office of the Secretary of State, Atlanta.

Two depositories in Columbia, South Carolina, hold Georgia documents. A few items are to be found in the South Caroliniana Library at the University of South Carolina, mainly in the Manigault Family Papers and Pierce Butler Papers. The South Carolina Department of Archives and History has much broader holdings, including a microfilm collection of early South Carolina records, transcripts of records in the British Public Record Office relating to South Carolina, and the judgment rolls of South Carolina. The latter contain legal records of a few cases involving Georgia litigants; the former have to do mainly with government and commerce.

Guilford College near Greensboro, North Carolina, possesses the surviving records of the Georgia Quaker community of Wrightsborough. The minutes of Quaker monthly meetings run from November 4, 1773, to January 5, 1793.

In the Southern Historical Collection of the University of North Carolina at Chapel Hill, the Josiah Smith, Jr., Lettercopy Book, 1771–1784, contains about a half-dozen important letters from Smith, a Charleston merchant, written to and about Georgians.

Several collections are in the William R. Perkins Library, Duke University, Durham, North Carolina. The papers of William Gibbons, Jr., Raymond Demere, George Walton, Noble Wimberly Jones, Edward Telfair, Levi and Mordecai Sheftall, John Reynolds, John Gibbons, James Oglethorpe, and the Habersham family are significant. The Duke holdings are rich in content and are among the most useful of the privately held papers.

The Library of Congress possesses transcripts or photographic copies of many essential records. Its photographic copies of the papers of the Society for the Propagation of the Gospel in Foreign Parts (S.P.G. Papers) partially document the Church of England's attempts to serve Georgia, while those of the manuscripts of Dr. Bray's Associates contain letters by Joseph Ottolenghe, on the education of slaves and other matters, that are pivotal to an understanding of Georgia in the 1750s and the early 1760s. Both the S.P.G. collection and the Bray manuscripts are substantial in size, and both are housed in England at the S.P.G. archives in Westminster. Citations to these sources in this work will enable a scholar to find the cited reference either in England or in the Library of Congress copies, which are widely available on microfilm. The citations will give the number of the appropriate Library of Congress microfilm reel and, where available, will give a page number (in some instances, a double page number) assigned artificially by the Library of Congress to facilitate easy reference. Also available at the Library of Congress are copies of materials from the Fulham Palace manuscripts (papers of the bishop of London), Sloane manuscripts, Royal Society letter books, and various departments of the British Public Record Office. The Georgia collections of the Library of Congress contain scattered items. The library also has important letters of James Habersham and significant George Whitefield correspondence.

The James Wright Papers in the New-York Historical Society, New York City, contain a few letters of the Georgia governor.

Important Georgia papers, mainly upon military and governmental subjects, are at the William L. Clements Library, University of Michigan, Ann Arbor. These include the papers of William Knox, Lord Shelburne, Sir Henry Clinton, and William Henry Lyttelton, as well as the Gage papers (American Series). The miscellaneous collection of the Clements Library has a rare letter from Wrightsborough, written on January 13, 1776, by Thomas Taylor to a friend in London, that describes the arrival of a new group of Quaker settlers just before the Revolution.

Printed Primary Sources

No study can go far without Allen D. Candler and Lucian Lamar Knight's twenty-five-volume compilation of *The Colonial Records of the State of Georgia* (Atlanta, Ga., 1904–1916). These volumes, numbered I through XIX and XXI through XXVI, reproduce documents held in official depositories in Great Britain. Each volume is in large type, and there is some indexing. The charter of the colony and the journal of the trustees from 1732 to 1752 comprise the first volume, while the second contains the minutes of the common council of the trustees from 1732 to 1752 and the third enumerates the monies and effects contributed from various sources for establishing the province. The contents of subsequent volumes are as follows: a part of the *Journal of William Stephens*, IV and supplement; *Journal of the Earl of Egmont* (1738–1744), V; *Proceedings of the President and Assistants*, VI; *Proceedings and Minutes of the Governor and Council* (1754–1782), VII–XII; *Journals of the Commons House of Assembly* (1755–1782), XIII–XV; and *Journals of the Upper House of Assembly* (1755–1774), XVI–XVII. The *Statutes* passed by the royal legislature and its immediate successors are in volumes XVIII and XIX, parts one and two. (Colonial laws may also be found in Horatio Marbury and William H. Crawford, comps., *Digest Of The Laws Of The State of Georgia, From Its Settlement As A British Province, in 1755, To The Session Of The General Assembly in 1800, Inclusive* . . . [Savannah, Ga., 1802]. Also, a few laws not found in other compendia are in Robert and George Watkins's *Digest of the Laws of the State of Georgia* . . . *to 1798* [Philadelphia, 1800]; (Charles C. Jones, Jr., and George Wymberley-Jones DeRenne, eds.), *Acts Passed by the General Assembly of the Colony of Georgia, 1755 to 1774* [Wormsloe, Ga., 1881]; and *Acts Passed by the General Assembly of Georgia, 1755–1789*, facsimile ed. [Washington, D.C., 1905–1906].) Correspondence and other documents comprise volumes XXI to XXVI of the *Colonial Records of the State of Georgia.*

When Candler and Knight's compilation of the colonial records was printed early in the twentieth century from copies of documents surviving in Great Britain, several additional volumes were prepared for publication but were not then printed. They have remained in typescript at the Georgia Department of Archives and History and elsewhere, numbered volume XX and volumes XXVII through XXXIX. Some of these volumes are now being prepared for publication by the University of Georgia Press, Athens, under the editorship of Kenneth Coleman and Milton Ready. Citations in this book are to the unprinted collection.

Between 1972 and 1974 the Office of the Georgia Surveyor General issued a series of informal, paperbound volumes covering English crown grants in the colony from 1755 to 1775. These volumes, nine in all, are not commercially available. Information concerning them may be secured through the Office of the Surveyor General, Atlanta. They were prepared under the direction of Deputy Surveyor General Pat Bryant.

Another diversified source in print is the *Collections* of the Georgia Historical Society, particularly volumes I, II, III, VI, VIII, X, and XIII. Volume I (1840) contains early tracts on the colony and includes the important *Voyage to Georgia, begun in the year 1735*, by Francis Moore; II (1842) makes available some of the argumentative tracts debating the condition of Georgia in the 1730s and early 1740s; and III (1873) offers letters from General Oglethorpe and Governor Wright, plus a report on the condition of the colony prepared by Governor Wright in 1773.

The sixth volume of the *Collections* (1904) is an indispensable item— *The Letters of Hon. James Habersham, 1756–1775.* Habersham was a significant man in Georgia from 1738 until his death in 1775, and his letters contain information about every subject of importance in Georgia for two decades—economics, business, religion, politics, personalities, and, finally, war. Items bearing on the period were also included in volume VIII (1913), entitled *Letters of Joseph Clay, Merchant of Savannah, 1776– 1793.* Lilla M. Hawes edited volume X in the series, *The Proceedings and Minutes of the Governor and Council of Georgia, October 4, 1774, through November 7, 1775, and September 6, 1779, through September 20, 1780* (Savannah, Ga., 1952). Mrs. Hawes also edited volume XIII, *The Letter Book of Thomas Rasberry, 1758–1761* (Savannah, Ga., 1959). Rasberry was a Savannah merchant and member of the lower house of assembly. This volume deals with his mercantile house.

Many of the tracts printed in the early volumes of the Georgia Historical Society *Collections*, plus additional materials, were also published in Peter Force's four-volume compilation of *Tracts and Other Papers, Relating Principally to the Origin, Settlement, and Progress of the Colonies in North America, from the Discovery of the Country to the Year 1776* (Washington, D.C., 1836–1846).

A valuable series of Wormsloe Foundation Publications from the University of Georgia Press has presented materials and commentary of both a primary and secondary nature. A lost portion of William Stephens's journal that was discovered in the Phillipps Collection at the University of Georgia has been edited by E. Merton Coulter as *The Journal of William Stephens, 1741–1745*, Wormsloe Foundation Publications, Nos. 2–3 (Athens, Ga., 1958–1959). Both sides of the Malcontent dispute are shown in Clarence L. Ver Steeg, ed., *A True and Historical Narrative of the Colony of Georgia by Pat. Tailfer and Others, with Comments by the Earl of Egmont* (Athens, Ga., 1960), No. 4 of this series. Other primary documents of the period have been published as Nos. 5 and 6: Robert G. McPherson, ed., *The Journal of the Earl of Egmont: Abstract of the Trustees Proceedings for Establishing the Colony of Georgia, 1732–1738* (Athens, Ga., 1962), and E. Merton Coulter, ed., *The Journal of Peter Gordon, 1732–1735* (Athens, Ga., 1963).

An account of British upper-class life during the reign of George II that includes important information on the founding and progress of Georgia available nowhere else is found in the three-volume *Manuscripts of the Earl of Egmont. Diary of Viscount Percival, Afterwards First Earl of Egmont, 1730–1747* (Historical Manuscripts Commission, *Sixteenth Report* [London, 1920–1923]).

The most significant document pertaining to the German migration to Georgia and the progress of the Germans once arrived is a three-volume account entitled *Der ausführlichen Nachrichten von der Königlich-Gross-Britannischen Colonie Saltzburgischer Emigranten in America* (Halle, 1735–1752). These volumes were edited in Germany by Samuel Urlsperger. Much of the material contained in them was written by the first two German pastors in Georgia, Johann Martin Bolzius and Israel Christian Gronau, and virtually everything in them pertains directly to the Georgia Germans. Only a part of this work is yet available in English. George Fenwick Jones has begun translation and publication of these records, assisted by Marie Hahn and relying in part upon an earlier bit of translation done by Hermann Lacher. Three volumes of this work have appeared as *Detailed Reports on the Salzburger Emigrants Who Settled In America... Edited by Samuel Urlsperger* (Athens, Ga., 1968, 1969, 1972), Nos. 9, 10, and 11 in the Wormsloe series. One additional section from the end of volume III of *Ausführliche Nachrichten* has been translated and published in English as Klaus G. Loewald, Beverly Starika, and Paul S. Taylor, trans. and eds., "John Martin Bolzius Answers a Questionnaire on Carolina and Georgia," *William and Mary Quarterly*, 3d Ser., XIV (1957), 218–261, and XV (1958), 228–252. In these excerpts may be found Pastor Bolzius's responses to questions concerning Georgia and South Carolina written in the early 1750s. *Ausführliche Nachrichten* makes it possible to follow the Georgia Germans closely for almost two decades; it then breaks off and is succeeded by another account that is valuable but less full and interesting. The second series is styled *Americanisches Ackerwerk Gottes; oder zuverlässige Nachrichten, den Zustand der americanisch englischen und von salzburgischen Emigranten erbauten Pflanzstadt Ebenezer in Georgien betreffend, aus dorther eingeschikten glaubwürdigen Diarien genommen, und mit Briefen der dasigen Herren Prediger noch weiter bestättiget* (Augsburg, 1754–1767). Additional information about the Georgia Germans, after *Americanisches Ackerwerk Gottes* ceases in the 1760s, may be found in volumes I and II of Theodore G. Tappert and John W. Doberstein, trans., *The Journals of Henry Melchoir Muhlenberg* (Philadelphia, 1942–1958). Volume II, which contains the diary of Pastor

Muhlenberg's visit to Georgia in 1774 and 1775, is of special interest. This Lutheran official went to Georgia to settle a religious dispute in and around Ebenezer and stayed several months. His diary affords insights not only into German culture in the colony but also into other phases of the social and political life of the province. Volume I of the *Journal* includes the diary of a short visit that Pastor Muhlenberg made to Georgia in the 1740s.

Original documents pertaining to the Germans are found in English throughout the *Colonial Records of the State of Georgia* and in several other published sources: George Fenwick Jones, ed., *Henry Newman's Salzburger Letterbooks*, Wormsloe Foundation Publications, No. 8 (Athens, Ga., 1966); George Fenwick Jones, ed., "The Secret Diary of Pastor Johann Martin Boltzius," *Georgia Historical Quarterly*, LIII (1969), 78–110; Georg Philipp Friedrich, Baron von Reck, and Johann Martin Bolzius, *An Extract of the Journals of Mr. Commissary Von Reck ... and of the Reverend Mr. Bolzius* (London, 1734); and C. A. Linn, ed., and A. G. Voigt, trans., *Ebenezer Record Book, Containing Early Records of Jerusalem Evangelical Lutheran Church, Effingham, Ga., More Commonly Known as Ebenezer Church* (Savannah, Ga., 1929). The manuscript of the Bolzius "secret" diary is part of the collections of the Georgia Historical Society.

Printed sources bearing mainly upon religion are plentiful. Lutheran sources have already been described. Statements of the Anglican position on religious matters in the 1730s and 1740s are to be found in the *Journals of William Stephens* mentioned above. (The Anglican position in the 1750s, 1760s, and 1770s is most easily found in the S.P.G. papers that are not published.) Gawin L. Corbin has made available materials on established Anglicanism in Savannah by editing "The First List of Pew Holders of Christ-Church, Savannah," *Georgia Historical Quarterly*, L (1966), 74–86. The manuscript of this list belongs to the Georgia Historical Society. The Anglican church was established in Georgia in 1758 in part through the exertions of a converted Jew named Joseph Ottolenghe. Some details of his early life and conversion may be gleaned from his pamphlet entitled *To Two Papers Lately publish'd by Gabriel Treves, a Jew of the City of Exeter ...* (London, probably 1735). Much can be learned about the state of Anglicanism in Georgia from men whose followers later became Methodists. John and Charles Wesley and George Whitefield all served as clergymen in the colony. Their writings disclose much about Anglicanism and what later became Methodism.

Nehemiah Curnock edited the standard version of *The Journal of the Rev. John Wesley, A.M.* (London, 1909). Of the eight volumes in this series, I (1909) relates to Wesley's ministry in Georgia. *The Journal of the Rev. Charles Wesley M.A. Sometime Student of Christ Church of Oxford. The Early Journal, 1736–1739* (London, 1909) covers Charles Wesley's brief stay in the colony. The seven-volume *Works of the Reverend John Wesley, A.M.* (New York, 1831) also contains useful information.

Published Whitefield documents include *George Whitefield's Journals (1737–1741) to Which Is Prefixed His "Short Account" (1746) and "Further Account" (1747).* This is a facsimile reproduction of a 1905 edition by William Wale with a new introduction by William V. Davis (Gainesville, Fla., 1969). These *Journals* are useful for a study of Georgia, but they should be used cautiously. They reflect little of the tension that surrounded Whitefield. In fact, the *Journals* were promotional, and they assisted Whitefield in raising money for his favorite charity, Bethesda orphanage. Another source on Whitefield is *The Works of the Reverend George Whitefield, M.A.,* 6 vols. (London, 1772).

Several pamphlets by Whitefield that pertain to his work in Georgia are *An Account of Money Received and Disbursed for the Orphan-House in Georgia. . . . To which is prefixed a Plan of the Building* (London, 1741); *A Continuation of the Account of the Orphan-House in Georgia, From January 1740/1 to June 1742 . . .* (Edinburgh, 1742); *A Continuation of the Account of the Orphan-House in Georgia, From January 1740/1 to January 1742/3. To which is prefixed The Preface to the former Account, And A Plan of the Building* (London, 1743); *A Further Account of God's Dealings With the Reverend Mr. George Whitefield, From The Time of his Ordination to his Embarking for Georgia. To which is Annex'd, A Brief Account of the Rise, Progress, and Present Situation of the Orphan-House in Georgia. In a Letter to a Friend* (London, 1747); *A Brief Account of the Rise, Progress, and present Situation, of the Orphan-House in Georgia. In a Letter to a Friend* (Edinburgh, 1748); and *A Letter to His Excellency Governor Wright, giving an Account of the Steps taken relative to the converting the Georgia Orphan-House into a College; together with the Literary Correspondence that passed upon that Subject between his Grace the Archbishop of Canterbury and the Reverend Mr. Whitefield. To which also is annexed the Plan and Elevation of the present and intended Buildings and Orphan-House Lands adjacent* (London, 1768). Some of Whitefield's ideas, particularly upon slavery, may be found in *Three Let-*

ters from the Reverend Mr. G. Whitefield (Philadelphia, 1740). A sermon that Whitefield delivered in Georgia is *The Eternity of Hell Torments. A Sermon preached at Savannah in Georgia* (London, 1738).

A report on religious life at Bethesda is available in James Harbersham's *Letter From Mr. Habersham, (Super-Intendent of Temporal Affairs at the Orphan-House in Georgia,) To the Reverend Mr. Whitefield: Containing A particular Account of the Spiritual and Temporal State thereof. Dated March 2, 1744, and sent with others, bearing Date June 7* (London, 1744).

Cornelius Winter, a catechist to the slaves of the Reverend Bartholomew Zouberbuhler, left a memoir of his Georgia experiences, published eventually in Volume III of *The Works of the Rev. William Jay, of Argyle Chapel, Bath . . .* (New York, 1844). Winter tells much about religion, slavery, and attitudes. His memoir includes a letter from Joseph Clay bewailing the quality of the Anglican clergy serving the colony in the years before the Revolution.

The Reverend Samuel Frink, rector of Christ Church Parish, was Clay's pastor for a number of years and was the kind of clergyman of whom Clay disapproved. In 1770 Frink very nearly brought the wrath of the Commons House of Assembly of Georgia to bear upon his church. Something of Frink's actions and attitudes and those of his chief antagonist in that dispute, the Reverend John J. Zubly, may be learned from Zubly's *Letter To The Reverend Samuel Frink, A.M., Rector of Christ's Church Parish in Georgia, Relating To Some Fees demanded of some of his Dissenting Parishioners* (Savannah, Ga.? 1770?). "The Will of Dr. John Joachim Zubly" was printed in the *Georgia Historical Quarterly*, XXII (1938), 384–390. Letters of Zubly may be found in Franklin Bowditch Dexter, ed., *Extracts from the Itineraries and Other Miscellanies of Ezra Stiles, D.D., LL.D., 1755–1794, with a Selection from His Correspondence* (New Haven, Conn., 1916), and in the *Proceedings* of the Massachusetts Historical Society for 1864–1865, IX (Boston, 1866).

Published documents relating to Jews in Georgia are in Malcolm H. Stern's edition of "The Sheftall Diaries: Vital Records of Savannah Jewry (1733–1808)," *American Jewish Historical Quarterly*, LIV (1965), 243–277, and in Jacob Rader Marcus's edition of *American Jewry: Documents, Eighteenth Century . . .* (Cincinnati, Ohio, 1959).

Information about Baptists is scant. One source is the Reverend Abraham Marshall's "Biography of the late Rev. Daniel Marshall," *Georgia Analytical Repository*, I (1802), 23–31. This article is the closest to a contemporary account of Marshall's ministry.

The records of the Congregational community in St. John Parish (Midway), edited by James Stacy, were presented as volume I of *The Published Records of Midway Church* (n.p., 1951). Also, John J. Zubly's funeral sermon for the Reverend John Osgood has been published as *The Faithful Minister's Course finished: A Funeral Sermon, Preached August the 4th, 1773, in the Meeting at Midway in Georgia, at the Internment of the Rev. John Osgood, A.M. Minister of that Congregation* (Savannah, Ga., 1773). The Georgia Historical Society at Savannah has a copy of this rare pamphlet. The religion of some of the slaves in Georgia may be studied in the *Journal of Negro History*, I (1916), 69–92, in "Letters Showing the Rise and Progress of the Early Negro Churches of Georgia and the West Indies." The letters were written by George Liele and Andrew Bryan and date from the 1790s.

Data concerning education are scattered, but Edgar W. Knight has assembled and edited some Georgia materials in volume I of *A Documentary History of Education in the South before 1860* (Chapel Hill, N.C., 1949).

Travel accounts may be found in "William Logan's Journal of a Journey to Georgia, 1745," *Pennsylvania Magazine of History and Biography*, XXXVI (1912), 1–16, 162–186; John Bartram's *Diary of a Journey Through the Carolinas, Georgia, and Florida from July 1, 1765, to April 10, 1766* (American Philosophical Society, *Transactions*, N.S., XXXIII, Pt. 1 [Philadelphia, 1942]); William Bartram's *Travels Through North and South Carolina, Georgia, East and West Florida . . .* (Philadelphia, 1791); and in a *Journal kept by Hugh Finlay, Surveyor of the Post Roads on the Continent of North America, during his Survey of the Post Offices between Falmouth and Casco Bay, in the Province of Massachusetts, and Savannah, in Georgia; begun the 13th Septr. 1773 and ended 26th June 1774* (Brooklyn, N.Y., 1867). Newton D. Mereness's edition of *Travels in the American Colonies* (New York, 1916) has scattered Georgia references.

Itinerant Observations in America (Savannah, Ga., 1878) is an interesting early travel account of the colony. This document, written anonymously by Edward Kimber, was first published in the *London Magazine* in 1745 and 1746.

John Gerar William DeBrahm, a surveyor who played an important role in the colony, wrote a *History of the Province of Georgia: With Maps of Original Surveys* (Wormsloe, Ga., 1849), which has great value in spite of its brevity. DeBrahm's *History* more recently has been edited and reissued by Louis De Vorsey, Jr., as *DeBrahm's Report of the General Sur-*

vey in the Southern District of North America (Columbia, S.C., 1971). De Vorsey prefaces DeBrahm's work with an essay on the life and contributions of DeBrahm himself. Bernard Romans, another contemporary writer, was interested chiefly in Florida but had some pertinent things to say about Georgia in *A Concise Natural History of East and West Florida* (1775), facsimile edition with an introduction by Rembert W. Patrick (Gainesville, Fla., 1962). Anthony Stokes, a chief justice of the province, made some interesting observations about it in *A View of the Constitution of the British Colonies in North America and the West Indies* (London, 1969 [orig. publ. London, 1783]). Stokes also wrote anonymously *A Narrative of the official conduct of Anthony Stokes, of the Inner Temple London* (London, 1784).

George White's *Historical Collections of Georgia: Containing the Most Interesting Facts, Traditions, Biographical Sketches, Anecdotes, Etc. . . .* (New York, 1854) is valuable, as is R. W. Gibbes's *Documentary History of the American Revolution: Consisting of Letters and Papers Relating to the Contest for Liberty, Chiefly in South Carolina, from Originals in the Possession of the Editor, and Other Sources, 1764–1782,* 3 vols. (Columbia, S.C., 1853; New York, 1855–1857).

An example of an almanac in use, and one of the earliest items printed in the colony, is John Tobler's *The South-Carolina and Georgia Almanack, For The Year of Our Lord 1764* (Savannah, Ga., 1763). This, as well as many other rare published items, is in the DeRenne Collection of the University of Georgia, Athens. A published catalog of the collection lists its contents.

Kenneth Coleman extracted from the University of Georgia's Phillipps Collection a contemporary description of agriculture in the colony and published it as "Agricultural Practices in Georgia's First Decade," *Agricultural History,* XXXIII (1959), 196–199.

In the 1730s a youth named Philip Thicknesse lived for a time in Savannah and later wrote his memoirs, which contain some recollections of Georgia. They may be found in *Memoirs and Anecdotes of Philip Thicknesse, late Lieutenant Governor of Land Guard Fort, and Unfortunately Father to George Touchet, Baron Audley* (Dublin, 1790). Thomas Stephens, son of William Stephens, wrote (but did not sign) *The Castle-Builders; or, the History of William Stephens, of the Isle of Wight, Esq., lately deceased* (London, 1759).

Three works that assist in identifying individual persons are *Abstracts of Colonial Wills of the State of Georgia, 1733–1777* (Atlanta, Ga.,

1962), published by the Atlanta Town Committee of the National Society, Colonial Dames of America, in the State of Georgia, for the Department of Archives and History in the Office of the Secretary of State; *Some Early Epitaphs in Georgia* (Durham, N.C., 1924), compiled by the Georgia Society of the Colonial Dames of America, with a foreword and sketches by Mrs. Peter W. Meldrim, and copyrighted by the society; and, a very important document, E. Merton Coulter and Albert B. Saye, eds., *A List of the Early Settlers of Georgia* (Athens, Ga., 1949).

Surviving records of an early Savannah organization are the *Minutes of the Union Society: Being an Abstract of Existing Records, from 1750 to 1858* ... (Savannah, Ga., 1860).

Ulrich B. Phillips edited "Some Letters of Joseph Habersham," *Georgia Historical Quarterly*, X (1926), 144–163, and Lilla M. Hawes edited "Letters to the Georgia Colonial Agent, July, 1762, to January, 1771," *Georgia Historical Quarterly*, XXXVI (1952), 250–286.

A memoir written in 1836 by a woman who was born near Savannah in 1764 and who spent her childhood in the province supplies glimpses of social life. Elizabeth Lichtenstein Johnston was the daughter of the master of the provincial scout boat and was to become the daughter-in-law of Councillor Lewis Johnston. Her memoir is *Recollections of a Georgia Loyalist* (New York and London, 1901). Mrs. Johnston fled Georgia at the end of the Revolution and lived subsequently in Scotland, Jamaica, and Nova Scotia. Her volume contains about forty family letters written during colonial and Revolutionary times.

Newspapers and Magazines

The *Georgia Gazette* is indispensable to a study of colonial Georgia. James Johnston began its publication in Savannah on April 7, 1763, and produced it weekly until at least February 7, 1776, with a gap of several months between November 21, 1765, and May 21, 1766, when he suspended publication during the Stamp Act crisis. Between 1763 and May 23, 1770, except for the gap, most issues survive. From May 1770 through the end of 1773, copies are lost, although it can be proved that the *Gazette* was published. Only a little less valuable are the newspapers of South Carolina. The *South-Carolina Gazette*, 1732–1775, the *South-Carolina Gazette; And Country Journal*, 1765–1775, and the *South-Carolina and American General Gazette*, 1764–1775, are available, and so are a few surviving copies of the *South-Carolina Weekly Gazette* (1750 and 1764). Two British periodicals printed Georgia materials frequently. One was the *London Magazine: Or, Gentleman's Monthly Intelligencer*; the other was the *Gentleman's Magazine: Or, Monthly Intelligencer.* (For a part of this period, the latter was called the *Gentleman's Magazine: And Historical Chronicle.*)

Dissertations, Articles, and Books

Hermann Winde's dissertation, "Die Frühgeschichte der Lutherischen Kirche in Georgia," written for Martin Luther University in Halle-Wittenberg, is based mainly on German records at the Francke Foundation in Halle and on holdings in the library of the University of Tübingen. The dissertation, submitted in 1960, is a study of the Lutheran church in Georgia from the earliest Salzburg immigrations to the end of colonial times and beyond. Milton L. Ready, in "An Economic History of Colonial Georgia, 1732–1754," has investigated economic life during the proprietary period. This work was his doctoral dissertation at the University of Georgia in 1970. At the University of Chicago in 1953, Robert L. McCaul, Jr., completed a dissertation entitled "A Documentary History of Education in Colonial Georgia."

Other significant dissertations are Billups Phinizy Spalding's "Georgia and South Carolina during the Oglethorpe Period, 1733–1743" (University of North Carolina at Chapel Hill, 1963); David T. Morgan, Jr.'s "The Great Awakening in the Carolinas and Georgia, 1740–1775" (University of North Carolina at Chapel Hill, 1967); William Martin Kelso's "Captain Jones' Wormslow: A Historical, Archaeological, and Architectural Study of an Eighteenth Century Plantation Site Near Savannah, Georgia" (Emory University, 1971); and Jack Wolf Broucek's "Eighteenth Century Music in Savannah, Georgia" (Florida State University, 1963).

The *Georgia Historical Quarterly* from the year of its first issue in 1917 has published numerous articles on early Georgia. This source is so significant that all back issues should be consulted. A few particularly valuable citations are Ulrich Bonnell Phillips's "New Light upon the Founding of Georgia," VII (1922), 277–284; Albert B. Saye's "Was Georgia a Debtor Colony?," XXIV (1940), 323–341; and E. Merton Coulter's "Was Georgia Settled by Debtors?," LIII (1969), 442–454. In 1970 an article by

Neil J. O'Connell appeared that may modify viewpoints concerning Bethesda—"George Whitefield and Bethesda Orphan-House," LIV (1970), 41–62.

Other articles in learned journals are Alex M. Hitz's "The Wrightsborough Quaker Town and Township in Georgia," *Bulletin of Friends Historical Association*, XLVI (1957), 10–22; E. R. R. Green's "Queensborough Township: Scotch-Irish Emigration and the Expansion of Georgia, 1763–1776," *William and Mary Quarterly*, 3d Ser., XVII (1960), 183–199; Malcolm H. Stern's "New Light on the Jewish Settlement of Savannah," *American Jewish Historical Quarterly*, LII (1963), 169–199; and Robert V. Williams's "George Whitefield's Bethesda: The Orphanage, the College and the Library," Florida State University Library History Seminar No. 3, *Proceedings* (Tallahassee, Fla., 1968), 47–72.

The oldest history of Georgia that has survived is Hugh McCall's *History of Georgia, Containing Brief Sketches of the Most Remarkable Events Up to the Present Day* (Atlanta, Ga., 1909 [orig. publ. 1784]). McCall's book is interesting principally as a curiosity. Two general works from the nineteenth century that still have value in their own right are William Bacon Stevens's two-volume *History of Georgia, from Its First Discovery by Europeans to the Adoption of the Present Constitution in MDCCXCVIII* (New York, 1847, 1859) and Charles C. Jones, Jr.'s two-volume *History of Georgia* (Boston, 1883). James Ross McCain wrote a basic work in *Georgia as a Proprietary Province: The Execution of a Trust* (Boston, 1917). Paul S. Taylor has treated the same period in a different way in his newer study, *Georgia Plan: 1732–1752* (Berkeley and Los Angeles, 1972). An interpretative look at the official policies of both the proprietary and royal governments can be found in Milton Sydney Heath's *Constructive Liberalism: The Role of the State in Economic Development in Georgia to 1860* (Cambridge, Mass., 1954). E. Merton Coulter's *A Short History of Georgia* (Chapel Hill, N.C., 1933) extends its scope beyond the colonial period, but it is good as a short survey. Albert B. Saye's *New Viewpoints in Georgia History* (Athens, Ga., 1943) is also a work of value. Verner W. Crane, in "The Promotion Literature of Georgia," has examined some of the material that helped to advance the movement toward the province's founding and support. Crane's essay is in *Bibliographical Essays: A Tribute to Wilberforce Eames* (Freeport, N.Y., 1967).

Margaret Davis Cate wrote *Early Days of Coastal Georgia* (St. Simons Island, Ga., 1955) to focus attention upon historic sites in the coastal region. She illustrates her work with photographs by Orrin S. Wightman. Amanda Johnson supplies a look at colonial Georgia in *Georgia as Colony and State, 1733–1937* (Atlanta, Ga., 1938).

Sarah B. Gober Temple and Kenneth Coleman trace some of the early settlers in an interestingly conceived book published in 1961. They describe social conditions in the colony in terms of people rather than of institutions. Their work is *Georgia Journeys: Being an Account of the Lives of Georgia's Original Settlers and Many Other Early Settlers from the Founding of the Colony in 1732 until the Institution of Royal Government in 1754* (Athens, Ga., 1961). Essays concerning three Georgians of the royal period are found in Horace Montgomery, ed., *Georgians in Profile: Historical Essays in Honor of Ellis Merton Coulter* (Athens, Ga., 1958). The essays concern Governor James Wright, written by Kenneth Coleman; Chief Justice Anthony Stokes, written by Alexander A. Lawrence; and Governor Henry Ellis, written by W. W. Abbot.

Georgia as seen through the administrations of its three royal governors is depicted by W. W. Abbot in *The Royal Governors of Georgia, 1754–1775* (Chapel Hill, N.C., 1959). Jack P. Greene examines attempts by the Georgia lower house of assembly to augment its powers and makes a comparison with similar movements in other southern colonies in *The Quest For Power: The Lower Houses of Assembly in the Southern Royal Colonies, 1689–1776* (Chapel Hill, N.C., 1963).

A comprehensive study of the province in one volume is Kenneth Coleman's *Colonial Georgia: A History* (New York, 1976).

Trevor Richard Reese in *Colonial Georgia: A Study in British Imperial Policy in the Eighteenth Century* (Athens, Ga., 1963) depicts Georgia as it figured in the British Empire. So, to a degree, does John Tate Lanning in *The Diplomatic History of Georgia* (Chapel Hill, N.C., 1936). Kenneth Coleman's book *The American Revolution in Georgia, 1763–1789* (Athens, Ga., 1958) treats not only the Revolution but the period preceding it, beginning in 1763. Indian relations are examined in John P. Corry's *Indian Affairs in Georgia, 1732–1756* (Philadelphia, 1936). Also see Louis De Vorsey, Jr.'s *The Indian Boundary in the Southern Colonies, 1763–1775* (Chapel Hill, N.C., 1966).

A number of colonial towns did not survive as permanent settlements. Charles C. Jones, Jr., has described them in *The Dead Towns of Georgia* (Savannah, Ga., 1878), also issued as volume IV of the Georgia Historical Society *Collections*. For other Georgia towns see Trevor Richard Reese's *Frederica: Colonial Fort and Town, Its Place in History* (St. Simons Island,

Ga., 1969); Pearl Baker's *The Story of Wrightsboro, 1768–1964* (Thomson, Ga., 1969); and Berry Fleming's *Autobiography of a Colony: The First Half-Century of Augusta, Georgia* (Athens, Ga., 1957). E. Merton Coulter's *Wormsloe: Two Centuries of a Georgia Family* (Athens, Ga., 1955) concerns the Jones family and its seat at Wormsloe near Savannah. This volume is the first of the Wormsloe Foundation Publications Series. Edith Duncan Johnston described the Houstoun family in *The Houstouns of Georgia* (Athens, Ga., 1950). Mary Granger edited a volume on plantations of the colonial era and afterward. Its contents were published in the *Georgia Historical Quarterly* beginning in 1938, and the series ran for five years. The published volume is *Savannah River Plantations*, Savannah Writer's Project (Savannah, Ga., 1947). Agriculture is treated in James C. Bonner's *A History of Georgia Agriculture, 1732–1860* (Athens, Ga., 1964).

The relation of church and state is the subject of Reba Carolyn Strickland's *Religion and the State in Georgia in the Eighteenth Century* (New York, 1939). Adelaide L. Fries in *The Moravians in Georgia, 1735–1740* (Raleigh, N.C., 1905) examines the Moravian settlement and its unhappy outcome. P. A. Strobel's *The Salzburgers and Their Descendants* (Athens, Ga., 1953 [orig. publ. Baltimore, 1855]) and Carl Mauelshagen's *Salzburg Lutheran Expulsion and Its Impact* (New York, 1962) deal with the Georgia Salzburger venture. James Stacy is not only the editor of the records of Midway Congregational Church but also the church's historian. In a 1951 edition a single volume contains both the records and the history. The spine of the volume lists the title as *History and Records of Midway Church* (n.p., 1951), and inside, the history and records sections each carry a separate title page and are each paginated separately. The records section was first published in 1894 as *The Published Records of Midway Church* (Newnan, Ga., 1894). *The History of Midway Congregational Church* was first published in Newnan, Ga., in 1899.

Lowry Axley has written *Holding Aloft the Torch: A History of the Independent Presbyterian Church of Savannah, Georgia* (Savannah, Ga., 1958), which has information and comment on Georgia Presbyterianism in colonial and Revolutionary times.

The opening two chapters of Henry T. Malone's *The Episcopal Church in Georgia, 1733–1957* (Atlanta, Ga., 1960) are enlightening concerning the colonial Anglican church. Insights into the Jewish community may be had from Abram V. Goodman's *American Overture: Jewish Rights in Colonial Times* (Philadelphia, 1947), and from Leon Huhner's *Jews in*

America in Colonial and Revolutionary Times (New York, 1959). Baptists were not active in an organized way until after 1770, and secondary works deal scantily with the Baptist effort. A significant item, which in some ways should be considered a primary source, is Charles D. Mallary's *Memoirs of Elder Edmund Botsford* (Charleston, S.C., 1832). Also important is Jesse Mercer's *A History of the Georgia Baptist Association* . . . (Washington, Ga., 1838).

Other information and comment were provided in J. H. Campbell's *Georgia Baptists: Historical and Biographical* (Macon, Ga., 1874). For helpful commentary on Negro Baptists, see James M. Simms's *The First Colored Baptist Church in North America. Constituted at Savannah, Georgia, January 20, A. D. 1788. With Biographical Sketches of the Pastors* (Philadelphia, 1888).

James Johnston has interested several writers. Alexander A. Lawrence wrote *James Johnston: Georgia's First Printer* (Savannah, Ga., 1956), and Louis T. Griffith and John E. Talmadge dealt with Johnston's *Georgia Gazette* in *Georgia Journalism, 1763–1950* (Athens, Ga., 1951). Also on this subject are *James Johnston: First Printer in the Royal Colony of Georgia* (London, 1929), and chapter 35 of *A History of Printing in the United States*, II (New York, 1936), both written by Douglas C. McMurtrie. The latter work was first published in the *Georgia Historical Quarterly*, XVI (1932), 77–113.

Education was studied by Elbert W. G. Boogher in *Secondary Education in Georgia, 1732–1858* (Philadelphia, 1933) and by Dorothy Orr in *A History of Education In Georgia* (Chapel Hill, N.C., 1950). Berry Fleming dealt with books in *199 Years of Augusta's Library—A Chronology* (Athens, Ga., 1949), and Robert Cumming Wilson surveyed medicine in *Drugs and Pharmacy in the Life of Georgia, 1733–1959* (Atlanta, Ga., 1959). Frederick Doveton Nichols, in *The Early Architecture of Georgia, with a Pictorial Survey by Frances Benjamin Johnston* (Chapel Hill, N.C., 1957), looked at building styles and materials. Slavery received the attention of Ralph Betts Flanders in *Plantation Slavery in Georgia* (Chapel Hill, N.C., 1933). Flanders's interpretation belongs to a school of scholarship that saw slavery as having some beneficial effects.

Index

A

Abercorn, village of, 14, 21, 47
Aberdeen, University of, 237
Academies, 180, 237, 249. *See also* Schools
Acadians, 19n
Accountant: trustees', 113
Account of several late Voyages and Discoveries to the South and North, An, 182
Act of establishment. *See* Establishment, act of
Acton, 21, 236
Adams, Samuel, 114n
Addison, Joseph, 186
Admiralty, British, 103n
Admiralty, judge of, 116, 166
Adultery, 160, 216
Advertisements, newspaper, 23–24, 36n, 39 and n, 40n, 42n, 43, 45n, 46 and n, 50n, 55n, 56n, 58n, 64n, 67 and n, 69n, 70 and n, 72, 73 and n, 77 and n, 82n, 87n, 88 and n, 91n, 92n, 93n, 96 and n, 99n, 102–119n *passim*, 130n, 131 and n, 132 and n, 133, 136 and n, 137n, 138 and n, 139, 140n, 151, 152 and n, 160 and n, 161n, 170n, 173n, 176 and n, 183n, 184n, 186 and n, 188, 189n, 190 and n, 191n, 192n, 196n, 204n, 213 and n, 229 and n, 237 and n, 242 and n, 243n
Advocate general: of court of vice admiralty, 156
Affleck, Thomas, 101
Africa, 55, 90, 106, 131 and n, 138, 139
Agave plant, 174
Agent, colonial: Franklin as, 108
Agriculture, 17, 31, 95, 97, 100, 103, 121–124, 145, 155–156, 158, 183, 184,

199. *See also* Farmers; Farms; Silk culture
Ague, 93
Alcohol, 75 and n, 93, 118, 128, 140
Ale, 75
Alehouse keepers. *See* Taverners
Alehouses, 60, 73. *See also* Taverns
Alexander, James, 192n
Alexander, Rev. John, 202, 228–229
Alexander Fyffe and Company, 113n, 186
Alligators, 61, 113 and n
Allotments: yearly, to charity settlers, 59
Almanacs, 186
Altamaha River, 20, 28, 29 and n, 51, 204, 212
Altherr, Johannes, 102 and n
Amatis, Paul, 149
American experience: Georgia in mainstream of, 3, 251, 256
American Revolution: as a time reference, 3, 22, 25, 26, 31 and n, 32, 40, 48, 64, 100, 108, 142, 144, 145, 173, 180, 192, 200, 203, 204n, 211, 212, 232, 233, 237, 239, 249, 252, 253; spirit of, 51; religion adversely affected by, 230; society more rigid at time of, 164
Amicable Club, 173 and n
Ammunition: assigned to whites on road work, 49
Anchor, 102
Anderson, Elizabeth, 101–102, 102n
Anderson, Capt. George, 54
Anderson, James, 101, 170
Andrew, Benjamin, 62, 174
Andrew, James, 163 and n
Anglican church. *See* Churches, Anglican
Angola, 131
Animals, 41, 66, 102; as pets, 65–66

[277]